Buenos Aires

"All you've got to do is decide to go and the hardest part is over.

So go!"

TONY WHEELER, COFOUNDER – LONELY PLANET

Isabel Albiston

Contents

Plan Your Trip 4

Explore Buenos Aires 52

Understand Buenos Aires 179

Survival Guide 203

Buenos Aires Maps 232

PHILIP LEE HARVEY/LONELY PLANET ©

ROCHARIBEIRO/SHUTTERSTOCK ©

(left) Decorative bottles at a market in San Telmo (p85)

(above) Meat cooking on a *parrilla* (grill)

(right) *Floralis Genérica* (p114) sculpture by Eduardo Catalano

GABRIEL MASLIAH/500PX ©

Welcome to Buenos Aires

Buenos Aires combines faded European grandeur with Latin passion. Sexy and alive, this beautiful city gets under your skin.

Steak, Wine & Ice Cream

BA's food scene is increasingly dynamic, but for many travelers it's the city's carnivorous pleasures that shine. Satisfying a craving for juicy steaks isn't hard to do in the land that has perfected grilling wonderfully flavorful sides of beef, washed down with a generous glass of malbec or bonarda. *Parrillas* (steakhouses) sit on practically every corner and will offer up myriad cuts, from *bife de chorizo* (sirloin) to *vacio* (flank steak) to *ojo de bife* (rib eye). But leave room for ice cream, if you can – a late-night cone of *dulce de leche* (caramel) *helado* can't be topped.

Art & Architecture

Look closely: this city is beautiful. Sure, it might look like a concrete jungle from certain angles, but stroll through the streets, paying attention to the magnificent architecture around you, and you'll soon be won over. Grand French- and Italian-style palaces grab the limelight, but you'll see interesting architectural details in the buildings of even low-key, local barrios. These days the beauty of these traditional neighborhoods is further enhanced by colorful murals painted by artists involved in the city's vibrant street-art scene. For these talented individuals, the city is their canvas.

Nightlife

Take a disco nap, down some coffee and be prepared to stay up all night – this city doesn't sleep. Restaurants get going at 9pm, bars at midnight and clubs at 2am at the earliest; serious clubbers don't show up until 4am. And it's not just the young folk who head out on the town in this city; BA's diverse range of bars, clubs and live-music venues offers something for everyone, from DJs spinning electronica to live jazz sets. Just remember you'll be doing it all very late.

Tango

BA's famous dance is possibly the city's greatest contribution to the outside world, a steamy strut that's been described as 'making love in the vertical position'. Folklore says it began in the bordellos of long-ago Buenos Aires, when men waiting for their 'ladies' passed time by dancing among themselves. Today, glamorized tango shows are supremely entertaining with their grand feats of athleticism. You'll also find endless venues for perfecting your moves, from *milongas* (dance salons) to dance schools. Be aware that some people become addicted – and can spend a lifetime perfecting this sensual dance.

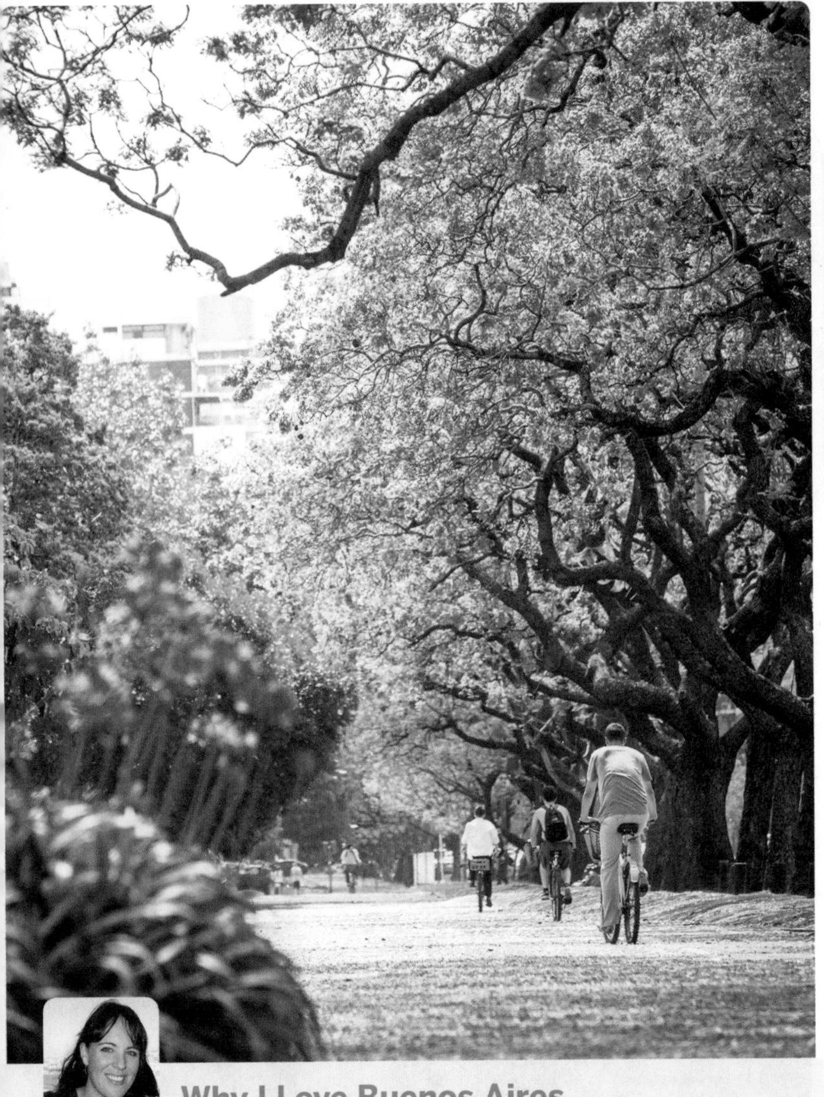

Why I Love Buenos Aires

By Isabel Albiston, Writer

When I first arrived in Buenos Aires in 2010, Argentina was celebrating 200 years of independence and the city was a carnival. I fell hard and fast for this crazy place with its dogs in soccer shirts and passionately held opinions on everything from politics to how to prepare *mate* (the yerba tea infusion). For the next four years, my days were spent cycling between parks and timeless neighborhood cafes; nights began with *asados* (barbecues) and ended at sunrise. In spring, when the blossom of the jacaranda trees turns the city purple, there's nowhere I'd rather be.

For more about our writer, see p256.

Top: Jacaranda trees in springtime

Buenos Aires' Top 10

1

Cementerio de la Recoleta *(p113)*

1 Meander through the maze of narrow lanes lined with elaborate mausoleums in what must be the world's most ostentatious necropolis. This 'city of the dead' was BA's first public cemetery, though it quickly became exclusive; some of Argentina's most illustrious historical figures are buried here, including Eva Perón ('Evita'). Myriad styles decorate the crumbling tombs, from art nouveau and art deco to neoclassical and neo-Gothic. There are also wonderfully flamboyant statues to discover, so pay your respects to Evita before getting lost among the marble angels.

Recoleta & Barrio Norte

Tangoing at a Milonga *(p44)*

2 Nothing captures the essence of Buenos Aires like the sensual and melancholy tango, and no visit to the city is complete without experiencing tango in some form. To experience it in its most authentic form, head to a *milonga* (dance event), held at dozens of venues. Tango classes are often held before *milongas*, so take part – or just watch, but don't look too long at that handsome stranger across the room; a stare is an invitation to dance, and you could be breaking some hearts!

Tango

FANDRADE / GETTY IMAGES ©

2

JUICE IMAGES LTD / SHUTTERSTOCK ©

Attending a Football Game *(p40)*

3 In Buenos Aires, *fútbol* isn't just a game. The national pastime inspires near-religious passion in *porteños* (residents of Buenos Aires), clearing the streets and sending spectators into fits of ecstasy and anguish as they huddle around TV screens or brave the explosive stadium crowds. The atmosphere is particularly boisterous (read: out of control) when River Plate and arch-rivals Boca Juniors face off during the much-anticipated *superclásico* games (p103). The tension is palpable, and for two hours on a Sunday afternoon here, nothing else really matters.

Sports & Activities

3

Savoring a Steak Dinner *(p24)*

4 Believe the hype: Argentine beef is some of the best in the world. Eat, drink and be merry at one of BA's hundreds of *parrillas* (steakhouses), where a leisurely meal begins with waiters pouring malbec and carving generous slabs of prime beef. *Parrillas* run the gamut from neighborhood joints to classic establishments to upscale restaurants, so there's a price for every pocket. There are even closed-doors restaurants offering *asado* (barbecue) experiences. One thing is certain: you can expect some of the best meat you've ever eaten.

Eating

Plaza de Mayo *(p58)*

5 Founded in 1580, Plaza de Mayo is the stage on which many of the dramatic events in Argentina's history were played out, from military bombings in 1955 to Evita's emotional speeches to massive union demonstrations (still going today). Most of the time, however, it's a peaceful place where families feed pigeons. It's where you'll find the Casa Rosada presidential palace, which you can visit for free on weekends. If you're here on a Thursday afternoon, you might witness Las Madres de la Plaza de Mayo: mothers peacefully marching for social-justice causes.

The Center

Strolling through San Telmo *(p85)*

6 The neighborhood of San Telmo is a beguiling mix of faded grandeur and bohemian spirit. The elegant belle-epoque architecture and crumbling villas are throwbacks to the district's 19th-century heyday, before yellow fever and cholera sent the aristocratic masses to higher ground. Today, you can wander along Defensa or Balcarce streets toward leafy Parque Lezama, taking in picturesque vistas of romantic facades and drooping balconies. The neighborhood continues to evolve, but much of the old-world atmosphere remains. Come on Sunday for the famous street fair.

San Telmo

Spotting Street Art *(p147)*

7 From the city's leafy northern suburbs to the abandoned warehouses of its gritty, southernmost edge, Buenos Aires has become a canvas for talented street artists from all over the world, who come here to paint in collaboration with Argentina's own graffiti superstars. Little pockets of the city are home to a particular concentration of murals – explore them on a guided tour with Graffitimundo. Keep your eyes open as you walk around Palermo, Colegiales and San Telmo; you might even see the city's next masterpiece being created.

Street Art

6

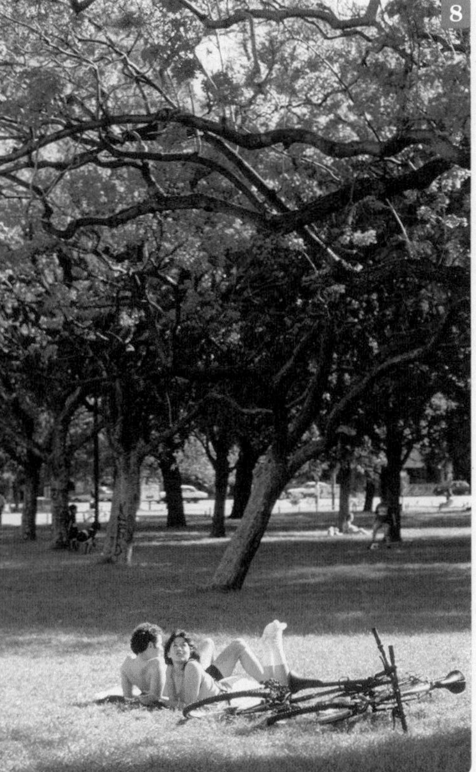

Cycling through Palermo's Parks

(p207)

8 It's official: Buenos Aires is bike friendly! With an extensive network of cycle lanes and a free city bike program, there is no better way to explore the city than on two wheels. But if the thought of taking on the traffic makes you nervous, fear not. A bike tour of Buenos Aires – especially around Palermo's green parks – is a great way to experience cycling in this vehicle-dominated city. Here, miles of safe bike lanes exist, and you can enjoy the green of grass instead of the gray of concrete.

Palermo

Taking a Nature Walk at the Reserva Ecológica Costanera Sur *(p72)*

9 In the shadow of Puerto Madero's shiny skyscrapers, an incredible nature reserve emerged from an area of abandoned, marshy wasteland. These days the remarkable park is home to hundreds of birds, colorful butterflies, turtles and iguanas. Take a walk along the paths that loop up past the coastline of the Río de la Plata. Amid the refreshing river breezes, peace and sense of space it's hard to believe you're just a 20-minute walk from the city center.

Puerto Madero

Feria de Mataderos *(p152)*

10 Folk music emanates from the outdoor stage, local couples take to the streets to perform the traditional *chacarera* and *chamamé* folk dances, and food stalls dish out hearty country dishes such as *locro* (a meaty stew), deep-fried *empanadas* and *humitas* (a kind of tamale). This is Feria de Mataderos, an authentic celebration of Argentine country traditions. You might also see gauchos demonstrating their horse-riding skills by playing *sortija*, a game where they stand in their saddles and ride at full speed to spear a tiny dangling ring. Catch it on Sundays.

South of Palermo

What's New

Craft Beer & Burgers

Buenos Aires (BA) has gone mad for craft beer, with new bars and microbreweries opening every week. Accompanying the beer trend is a hunger for juicy burgers. Big Sur is one of the most recent to appear on the scene. Look for the free BA Tap Map to help you plan your way around. (p133)

La Mar Cebicheria

The much anticipated opening of Peruvian restaurant La Mar Cebicheria has left BA's foodies swooning over the quality of the fresh ceviche and *leche de tigre* (citrus-based marinade) salsa. (p136)

Espacio Memoria y Derechos Humanos

More commonly known as the Ex ESMA, this former naval campus was a secret detention and torture center during the military dictatorship of 1976 to 1983. Now the building where the human-rights abuses took place has been converted into a memorial museum. (p124)

Barrancas de Belgrano

This elegant Belgrano park has been given a facelift and it's looking gorgeous. Come for the *milonga* La Glorieta, held at the park's bandstand in the evening. (p126)

Los Galgos

Formerly a run-down but historic cafe, Los Galgos has been completely transformed into a classy cocktail bar. (p83)

Centro Cultural Kirchner

The spectacular cultural center is now fully open, with a packed schedule of free concerts and events – get in quick if you want to score a ticket. (p59)

Coffee

The days of bad coffee in BA are over, thanks to a crop of new cafes dedicated to producing high-caliber brews using imported Colombian beans. (p138)

South of Scalabrini Ortiz

Threatening to knock Palermo Viejo off its foodie perch is the increasingly hip neighborhood located on the south side of Av Scalabrini Ortiz. It's where you'll find Proper (p136), Benaim (p139) and NoLa (p133), among other hot new bars and restaurants.

City Government Tourist Program

As well as opening a new tourist information kiosk in La Boca, the Buenos Aires city government has launched a series of free walking tours, plus rowing tours in Puerto Madero and even eco-car trips around the Reserva Ecológica and Parque 3 de Febrero. Be sure to check out the current program. (p217)

Underground Art

Some of BA's top street artists have brightened up Subte stations with wonderful murals. Check out recent works at Federico Lacroze on the Línea B.

For more recommendations and reviews, see **lonelyplanet.com/buenos-aires**

Need to Know

For more information, see Survival Guide (p203)

Currency
Peso (AR$)

Language
Spanish

Visas
Generally not required for US, Canadian, Australian, New Zealand and European citizens. Canadians and Australians must pay a reciprocity fee online before entering Argentina.

Money
Carrying cash and an ATM card is best; credit cards are also widely accepted.

Mobile Phones
It's best to bring your own factory unlocked tri- or quad-band GSM cell phone, then buy an inexpensive SIM chip (you'll get a local number) and credits (or *cargo virtual*) as needed.

Time
Argentina Time (GMT/UTC minus three hours)

Tourist Information
There are several tourist offices and kiosks in Buenos Aires. Staff speak English and can provide maps and information about free guided walks and other activities.

Daily Costs

Budget: Less than US$60

- Dorm bed: US$15
- Double room in budget hotel: US$80
- *Choripan* (sausage sandwich) from a roadside stall: US$5

Midrange: US$80–$150

- Three-star hotel room: US$100–175
- Average main dish: US$10–15
- Museum admission: US$1–8

Top End: More than US$150

- Five-star hotel room: US$200
- Fine main dish: US$15–20
- Taxi trip across town: US$10–15

Advance Planning

Two months before Book accommodation if traveling during busy times and your hotel is popular.

One month before Check the website to see what's on at the Teatro Colón and book tickets.

One week before Pack smart, comfortable clothing. *Porteños* are a well-dressed lot, and you'll stick out as a tourist in a loud shirt, shorts and flip-flops.

Useful Websites

- **Pick up the Fork** (www.pickupthefork.com) Restaurant and bar reviews, plus where to shop for ingredients.
- **The Bubble** (www.thebubble.com) Current affairs, culture and listings.
- **Buenos Aires Ciudad** (https://turismo.buenosaires.gob.ar/en) BA city government's English-language tourist site with up-to-date info, articles and advice.
- **My Beautiful Air** (http://mybeautifulair.com) Vivi Rathbone's arts and lifestyle guide to BA.
- **Lonely Planet** (www.lonelyplanet.com/argentina/buenos-aires) Destination information, hotel bookings, traveler forum and more.

WHEN TO GO

Spring (September to November) and fall (March to May) are the best temperature-wise; winter (June to August) is cold but not freezing.

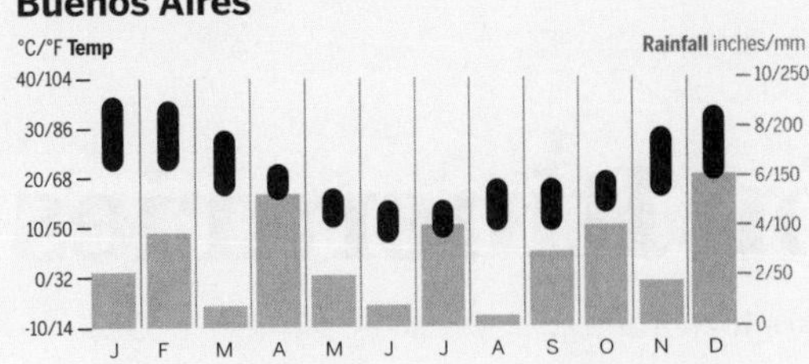

Arriving in Buenos Aires

Ezeiza airport (EZE; officially Aeropuerto Internacional Ministro Pistarini) Shuttle services are a good way to get downtown; the transport booth area is beyond customs and has a couple of companies with frequent shuttles. For taxis, go past the first transport booth area (taxis are overpriced here) to the reception area in arrivals, inside the terminal building. A few steps beyond the place where relatives wait to meet their loved ones, find the city's official taxi stand (a blue sign says 'Taxi Ezeiza'). Avoid taxi touts like the plague.

Aeroparque airport (officially Aeroparque Jorge Newbery) Close to downtown and easily accessible by local bus or taxi.

For much more on **arrival** see p204 

Getting Around

Despite Buenos Aires' heavy traffic, the city's public-transportation system is efficient and usually a better way to get around than driving. Use Como Llego (http://comollego.ba.gob.ar), the city government website, to plot your journey, or download the free app.

- **Bus** The city has hundreds of bus lines that can take you within a few blocks of any destination.
- **Subte** BA's underground, or subway, is not difficult to figure out and a quick way to get around – though it gets hot and very crowded during rush hour.
- **Taxi** Black-and-yellow street taxis are ubiquitous and generally fine.

For much more on **getting around** see p206 

Sleeping

Buenos Aires has a very wide range of accommodations, including hostels, guesthouses, B&Bs, homestays, apartments and hotels of all stripes and budgets. Services range widely; some hostels' private rooms are nicer than many budget hotels', and can cost more. Boutique hotels are a dime a dozen in Palermo, while five-star luxury is easily found in the Retiro and Recoleta neighborhoods. November through February are busy times, so book ahead if your hotel is a popular one.

Useful Websites

- **Oasis Collections** (https://oasiscollections.com/buenos-aires) Provides hotel booking and concierge services.
- **Stay in Buenos Aires** (www.stayinbuenosaires.com) Furnished apartments for temporary rent.
- **Spare Rooms BA** (www.spareroomsba.com) Rooms in shared apartments.
- **Lonely Planet** (www.lonelyplanet.com/hotels) Recommendations and bookings.

For much more on **sleeping** see p167 

Top Itineraries

Day One

San Telmo (p85)

Stroll through this colonial neighborhood's cobbled streets and window-shop for antiques. Come on a Sunday, when the famous **Feria de San Telmo** street market takes over the neighborhood. Book a tour to the stunning **El Zanjón de Granados** for a peek into the city's origins.

Lunch Snag a sidewalk table at Bar Plaza Dorrego (p93) for great people-watching.

La Boca (p98)

The colorful corrugated houses along **El Caminito** are indeed photogenic, though this area is a bit of a tourist trap. It's still fun, however; check out the souvenir shops and artists' paintings and perhaps catch a street-tango show. Art lovers shouldn't miss **Fundación Proa**, a cutting-edge gallery, while soccer fans can head to **La Bombonera Stadium** and visit the Boca team's **Museo de la Pasión Boquense**. But don't stray too far from the tourist hordes; La Boca is at times a sketchy neighborhood.

Dinner Reserve for Café San Juan (p92), serving exceptional international cuisine.

San Telmo (p85)

If it's Wednesday or Sunday, take a tango class then watch the dancing and the live tango orchestra at **Maldita Milonga**. Or go drinking at one of the many great watering holes in the area, such as **Doppelgänger**, an upscale cocktail bar.

Day Two

Palermo (p127)

Walk (or take a bike ride) along Palermo's **Parque 3 de Febrero**, where you can also visit a rose garden, botanical garden and Japanese garden. Bike paths are laced throughout.

Lunch Big Sur (p133) is great for a burger and a pint of craft beer.

Palermo (p127)

Visit **MALBA**, a beautiful art museum showcasing the collection of art patron Eduardo F Costantini. The **Museo Nacional de Arte Decorativo** is another must-see; it's a beaux-arts mansion that once belonged to a Chilean aristocrat, and is full of his posh belongings. Finally, Evita fans can't miss **Museo Evita**, which chronicles the life of Argentina's most internationally famous woman.

Dinner For an excellent steak, get a table at Don Julio (p134).

Palermo (p127)

Palermo is nightlife central. There are dozens of bars to check out, and people come from all over to dance at the famous clubs here. Begin with wine at **Pain et Vin**, a cocktail at **Verne** or craft beer at **Bluedog** or **On Tap**.

Puerto Madero

Day Three

The Center (p56)

From leafy **Plaza San Martín**, walk south on pedestrian Florida and experience masses of people shopping, busking, selling or just power-walking to their next destination. You'll eventually come within a block of **Plaza de Mayo**, the heart of Buenos Aires. This historic plaza is surrounded by **Casa Rosada**, **Catedral Metropolitana** and **Cabildo**.

Lunch For outside seating and fresh offerings, try i Central Market (p74).

Puerto Madero (p70)

Lined with renovated old brick warehouses, Puerto Madero is replete with fancy lofts and apartment towers, plus some of the city's most expensive (and some say overpriced) restaurants. It's a very scenic and pleasantly vehicle-free place to stroll the cobbled paths along the dikes. Art lovers shouldn't miss **Colección de Arte Amalia Lacroze de Fortabat**, highlighting the collection of Argentina's wealthiest woman. For a shot of nature, visit **Reserva Ecológica Costanera Sur**.

Dinner Casual but excellent Peruvian can be had at Chan Chan (p82).

Congreso & Tribunales (p76)

Take in an opera, ballet or classical-music show at **Teatro Colón**, Buenos Aires' premier theater. The traditional entertainment district of **Avenida Corrientes** still hops these days, showcasing many films, art events and plays.

Day Four

Recoleta & Barrio Norte (p111)

Explore Recoleta's famous **cemetery**; you can wander for hours among the crumbling sacrophagi and marble angels. It's a veritable city of the dead, fascinating and mysterious; to seek out Evita's tomb, just follow everyone else.

Lunch Have *empanadas* at El Sanjuanino (p117), one of the area's few cheap eateries.

Recoleta & Barrio Norte (p111)

Check out the **Museo Nacional de Bellas Artes**, Argentina's top classic-arts museum. Just north is **Floralis Genérica**, a giant metal flower whose petals open during the day and close at night (when the gears are working!). And if you've got the bucks, the city's most expensive boutiques are along **Avenida Alvear**, worth a stroll to eyeball some huge old mansions. Visit **Museo de Arte Hispanoamericano Isaac Fernández Blanco** and **Palacio Paz**, in nearby Retiro, if you like gorgeous palaces filled with antiques.

Dinner Looking for the locals? Then head to classic Rodi Bar (p117).

Retiro (p104)

Time to drink up: **Florería Atlántico** is a basement speakeasy located within a flower shop selling cocktails and house-brewed gin, while **BASA Basement Bar** is a fashionable restaurant-bar selling excellent (but pricey) Moscow mules.

If You Like...

Museums

Museo de Arte Latinoamericano de Buenos Aires (MALBA) Gorgeous, glassy art museum showcasing the private collection of art patron Eduardo F Costantini. (p129)

Museo Nacional de Bellas Artes From European impressionists to Latin American maestros, this national art museum covers them all. (p131)

Museo Nacional de Arte Decorativo Beautiful beaux-arts mansion strewn with the posh belongings of a Chilean aristocrat. (p131)

Colección de Arte Amalia Lacroze de Fortabat Impressive private art collection in an architectually interesting building. (p73)

Fundación Proa Cutting-edge gallery-museum with contemporary art exhibits, plus a rooftop cafe with a view of La Boca. (p101)

Museo de Arte Moderno de Buenos Aires Spacious, multistory museum in a former warehouse exhibiting the works of Argentine contemporary artists. (p88)

Museo Evita Learn about the life and legacy of Argentina's iconic first lady. (p131)

Museo Histórico y Numismático José Evaristo Uriburu The history of Argentina's national currency tells the story of the country's ups and downs. (p61)

Jardín Japonés (p132)

Historic Places

Plaza de Mayo Buenos Aires' original main square, dating to the 1580s and surrounded by significant buildings. (p58)

El Zanjón de Granados Beautifully renovated, underground architectural site of the city's first settlements. (p88)

Plaza San Martín Pleasant leafy park that was once home to Spanish governors, slave quarters, a bullring and a battlefield. (p107)

Manzana de las Luces Taking up a whole city block, this was BA's most important center of culture and learning during colonial times. (p62)

Plaza Dorrego BA's second-oldest square was once a pit stop for caravans bringing produce into the city. (p87)

Green Spaces

Reserva Ecológica Costanera Sur Low-lying, 350-hectare landfill site that's become a haven for wildlife and nature seekers. (p72)

Parque 3 de Febrero Laced with miles of bike trails, this large green park also has a rose garden, planetarium and small lakes. (p130)

Parque de la Memoria Landscaped park on the Costanera Norte that serves as a memorial to the victims of Argentina's military dictatorships. (p125)

Jardín Japonés Tidy green oasis of tranquility in Palermo, complete with sushi restaurant and cultural offerings. (p132)

Jardín Botánico Carlos Thays Surrounded by busy avenues, this modest botanical garden offers a peaceful break from the city. (p131)

Free Stuff

Cementerio de la Recoleta BA's most popular tourist attraction and a must-visit for its decorative tombs and statues. (p113)

Centro Cultural Kirchner Catch a concert at this magnificent venue housed in the former central post office. (p59)

La Glorieta Dance the tango at this romantic open-air *milonga* in a bandstand at the Barrancas de Belgrano. (p126)

Museo Nacional de Bellas Artes Spend an afternoon at this large and excellent national art museum. (p131)

Hipódromo Argentino Head to Palermo's horse-racing track and place some bets. (p141)

Feria de San Telmo See street performers among the stalls at this famous Sunday street market. (p88)

Reserva Ecológica Costanera Sur Marshy lands located in Puerto Madero near the city center, but miles away in atmosphere. (p72)

Cementerio de la Chacarita A larger, less flashy version of Recoleta's cemetery. (p115)

Free City Tour Locals who love their city offer free walking tours in English (tips appreciated). (p208)

Campo Argentino de Polo Qualifying matches for the Palermo Open (in September and October) are free to attend. (p141)

Unusual Tours

Tango Trips Tango your way around some of BA's best *milongas*. (p209)

For more top Buenos Aires spots, see the following:

- Eating (p24)
- Drinking & Nightlife (p30)
- Entertainment (p34)
- Shopping (p37)
- Sports & Activities (p40)

Biking Buenos Aires Pedal around Palermo's parks and on bike lanes; a fun and easy way to tour the city. (p207)

Graffitimundo See the city through its colorful and dynamic street-art scene. (p208)

Foto Ruta Unique self-guided tour via photographing clues around BA's neighborhoods. (p209)

Parrilla Tour Explore the city's off-the-beaten-track *parrillas* (steakhouses) and learn about Argentina's food and culture. (p28)

The Offbeat

Tierra Santa Visit this kitschy 'world's first religious theme park' and witness the resurrection every half-hour. (p125)

Museo del Agua y de la Historia Sanitaria Pretty tiles, ceramic pipes and old bidets and toilets are highlighted at this small, quirky museum. (p79)

Museo Nacional Ferroviario See assorted memorabilia and evocative photographs relating to Argentina's railways. (p108)

Museo de la Policía Federal Exhibits on cockfighting, drug paraphernalia and hacked-up murder victims – only at the Police Museum. (p61)

Month By Month

TOP EVENTS

Feria Masticar, May

Tango BA Festival y Mundial, August

Vinos y Bodegas, September

La Noche de los Museos, October

Campeonato Abierto Argentino de Polo, December

February

It's still summer, but vacationing *porteños* start to return home. There are plenty of tourists in the city, some passing through on their way to or from Patagonia.

Buenos Aires Fashion Week

Four days of clothing stalls and catwalk action (www.bafweek.com.ar) show off the city's latest threads and their makers. It takes place at Palermo's La Rural in February (fall/winter collections) and August (spring/summer collections). Expect plenty of beautiful people – including models, of course.

Carnaval

Usually occurring in late February, BA's Carnaval is a small affair compared to Rio's or Bahia's, but it's still lots of fun. Catch some *murga* groups (traditional Carnaval ensembles), with dancing and drumming in different neighborhoods around the city.

April

It's fall in BA, and one of the best times to visit – but always be prepared for a downpour. There are still plenty of activities as the city heads into low season.

Festival Internacional de Cine Independiente (Bafici)

This independent film festival (http://festivales.buenosaires.gob.ar) highlights national and international films, with awards given out in separate categories. Over 100 films are screened, with a main venue being the Abasto shopping mall.

May

Late autumn has hit and it's pleasantly cool as the rains die back a bit. Look for travel deals as low season starts in earnest.

Arte BA

Arte BA features exhibitions from hundreds of art galleries, dealers, institutions and organizations, with both national and international contemporary art on display. Conferences, presentations and discussions make the rounds, while young new artists get exposure.

Feria Masticar

Chefs from the city's top restaurants gather in Colegiales for this four-day food fair (p181). Small sampling plates are available, as well as cooking demonstrations and classes.

July

It's mid-winter, so bring warm layers and be prepared to use them. Locals who can afford it head to the ski slopes down south.

Exposiciòn de Ganaderìa, Agricultura e Industria Internacional (La Rural)

The mother of all livestock fairs, where prize cows, sheep, goats, horses and bulls, all strut their stuff. Gaucho shows provide entertainment. It takes place for two weeks in late July at Palermo's La Rural.

August

It's still cold, so keep those layers on, but it's also a great time to explore the city's theaters, museums and art galleries.

Tango BA Festival y Mundial

Taking place in mid-August, this two-week-long tango festival offers a great way to see some of the country's best tango dancers and musicians do their thing. Plenty of competitions, classes and workshops take place.

September

Spring has sprung and it's a lovely time to be in BA. Polo season begins and the tourists start returning.

Vinos y Bodegas

A can't-miss event for wine aficionados, with vintages from dozens of Argentine *bodegas* (wineries). Mix with thousands of sommeliers, restaurateurs, journalists and general wine lovers at Palermo's La Rural. Expect cooking demonstrations and live music, too.

October

The weather is getting warmer but it's not too hot – really, the best time to be in the city.

La Noche de los Museos

On one night in late October over a hundred museums, galleries and cultural spaces open their doors for free from 8pm to around 3am. There are guided tours, special shows, music festivities and even free buses that whisk visitors between the venues (www.lanochedelosmuseos.gob.ar).

November

It's pretty darn near perfect weather in BA, and the jacaranda trees are showing off their gorgeous purple blooms. High season has arrived, so reserve your accommodations ahead.

Marcha del Orgullo Gay

Each year on the first Saturday in November, thousands of BA's gays, lesbians, transgenders and more strut their way through the city's center at the city's gay pride march.

Día de la Tradición

The closest thing to authentic gaucho culture you'll probably ever witness, with traditional foods, feats of horsemanship, and folk music and dancing. It happens in San Antonio de Areco, a day trip from BA; call the Areco tourist office (p160) for exact dates, which vary yearly.

Gran Premio Nacional

In mid-November the country's biggest horse race takes place in Palermo's opulent and French-styled *hipódromo* (p141). First held in 1884, this is a fine event that not only attracts the well-to-do and celebrity-watchers, but regular families as well. Watch for the *granaderos* (presidential horseback guards) in their impressive outfits, marching around for the crowds.

Buenos Aires Jazz

This jazz festival (http://festivales.buenosaires.gob.ar/) takes place over five days in venues all over the city. Jazz musicians of all kinds are featured – emerging and established, avant-garde and traditional, national and international. Concerts and films also take place.

December

Summer in BA means hot and humid temperatures. There's still plenty going on in the city, however.

Campeonato Abierto Argentino de Polo

Argentina boasts the world's best polo, and the Abierto is the world's premier polo event. It takes place at Palermo's Campo Argentino de Polo. For exact dates and details, contact the Asociación Argentina de Polo (www.aapolo.com).

With Kids

For a megalopolis, BA is remarkably child-friendly. On sunny weekends Palermo's parks bustle with families taking walks and picnicking, while shopping malls fill with strollers. Museums and theme parks are also popular destinations – and don't forget those fun street fairs!

Parque de la Costa (p156)

Amusement Parks

Parque de la Costa

Head to Tigre, just north of the center, for a great day excursion. Hop on the fun Tren de la Costa to get to Parque de la Costa (p156), a typical amusement park with rides and activities.

Tierra Santa

Kids might enjoy this religious theme park (p125) unlike anywhere you've ever been.

Parque Norte

This large water park (p126) is perfect on a hot day.

Fun Museums

Museo Participativo de Ciencias

Be sure to visit this science museum (p114) in the Centro Cultural Recoleta, with interactive displays that focus on fun learning – signs say *'prohibido no tocar'* (not touching is forbidden).

Museo Argentino del Títere

In San Telmo, this small puppet museum (p90) has a fascinating collection of international and Argentine puppets, but it's the inexpensive shows that will amuse the kids. Call beforehand to get hours and show times, as they vary widely.

Museo Argentino de Ciencias Naturales

Outside the center in Caballito is the excellent natural history museum (p150), with myriad rooms containing giant dinosaur bones, dainty seashells, scary insects and amusing stuffed animals and birds.

Green Spaces

Buenos Aires has numerous plazas and public parks, many with playgrounds, and these are always popular gathering spots for families.

NICOBATISTA / SHUTTERSTOCK ©

hocolate and powdered sugar *alfajores*

Reserva Ecológica Costanera Sur

If you're downtown and need a nature break, try this large nature preserve (p72), with good birdwatching, pleasant dirt paths and no vehicular traffic.

Parque 3 de Febrero

Up north, the most attractive green spots are the wide open spaces of Palermo, especially Parque 3 de Febrero (p130). This huge park has a planetarium and a Japanese garden. Here you can rent bikes, boats and inline skates and range freely without worrying about cars!

NEED TO KNOW

- **Childcare** Get a babysitter or nanny at World Class Nannies (http://worldclassnannies.com).
- **Tango Shows** Nearly all offer 50% discount for children under 12.
- **Transport** Under fours travel free on the Subte, trains and buses.

Indoor Playgrounds

Many large modern shopping malls have indoor playgrounds (often on the top floor), along with video arcades, multiplexes and toy shops. On rainy days, these are great places to be with little ones.

Paseo Alcorta

This mall (p144) in Palermo has plenty of mechanical rides next to the large food court.

Mercado de Abasto

This beautiful shopping center (p150) boasts a full-blown 'Museo de los Niños' (more like a playground than a museum) where kids enter a miniature city complete with post office, hospital and even TV station. It also has a mini amusement park.

Eating & Sleeping

Many restaurants welcome kids, but if a place looks a bit too fancy, ask if they take children.

Most offer a wide selection of food suitable for kids (such as pizza, pasta, meats and vegetables); a few even have children's menus.

Waiters are accustomed to providing extra plates and cutlery for little ones, though you may not always find booster seats or high chairs.

Buenos Aires is a very late-night city; most restaurants don't open until 9pm, so you'll likely have to adjust your timetable during your travels here.

Don't forget to take the kids out for ice cream – it's a real Argentine treat. Other local sweets to try include *alfajores* (sandwich cookies usually covered in chocolate, available at corner stores) and *dulce de leche* (a milk caramel often used in desserts).

Small boutique hotels, hostels or guesthouses are sometimes not the best places for rambunctious kids, but most hotels accept them.

Some hotel rooms come with kitchenettes; apartment rentals are another good option.

Empanad

Eating

Argentines take barbecuing to heights you cannot imagine. Their best pizza and pastas vie with those of New York and Naples. They make fabulously tasty wines and impossibly delectable ice cream. And ethnic cuisine is rampant in Buenos Aires. In fact, you'll eat so well here that you'll need to power-walk between lunch and dinner to work off the excess calories.

ecuing meat on an open-pit *asado*

NEED TO KNOW

Price Ranges

The following price ranges refer to a main course.

$ less than AR$150

$$ AR$150–250

$$$ more than AR$250

Opening Hours

➡ Restaurants are generally open daily from noon to 3:30pm for lunch and 8pm to midnight or 1am for dinner.

➡ A sure bet for that morning *medialuna* (croissant) and *cortado* (espresso coffee with steamed milk) are the city's many cafes, which often stay open from morning to late at night without a break.

Reservations

Reserve at popular restaurants, especially on weekends. If you don't speak Spanish, ask a staff member at your hotel to make the call for you. Or check out www.restorando.com.ar.

Tipping

Tip 10% for standard service; make it 15% for exceptional service. Tips usually cannot be added to credit-card purchases. The word for tip in Spanish is *propina*.

Etiquette

➡ Most *porteños* (residents of Buenos Aires) eat no earlier than 9pm (later on weekends).

➡ Ask for your bill by saying, '*la cuenta, por favor*' ('the bill, please') or making the 'writing in air' gesture. Be aware that not all restaurants accept credit cards – always ask first.

➡ At upscale restaurants, a per-person *cubierto* (cover charge) is tacked on to the bill. This covers the use of utensils and bread – it does not relate in any way to the tip.

Local Specialties & Flavors

THE WORLD'S BEST STEAKS

Argentines have perfected the art of grilling beef on the *asado* (barbecue). This involves cooking with coals and using only salt to prepare the meat. On the grill itself, slanted runners funnel the excess fat to the sides, and an adjustable height system directs the perfect amount of heat to the meat. The *asado* is a family institution, often taking place on Sunday in the backyards of houses all over the country.

A traditional *parrillada* (mixed grill) is a common preparation at *parrillas* (steakhouses) and offers a little bit of everything. Expect *choripán* (a sausage appetizer), *pollo* (chicken), *costillas* (ribs) and *carne* (beef). It can also come with more exotic items such as *chinchulines* (small intestines), *mojellas* (sweetbreads) and *morcilla* (blood sausage).

Common steak cuts:

➡ **Bife de chorizo** Sirloin; a popular thick and juicy cut.

➡ **Bife de costilla** T-bone or Porterhouse steak.

➡ **Bife de lomo** Tenderloin; a tender, though less flavorful, piece.

➡ **Cuadril** Rump steak; often a thin cut.

➡ **Ojo de bife** Rib eye; a choice smaller morsel.

➡ **Tira de asado** Short ribs; thin, crispy strips of ribs.

➡ **Vacío** Flank steak; textured, chewy and flavorful.

If you don't specify how you want your steak cooked, it will come *a punto* (medium to well-done). Getting a steak medium-rare or rare is harder than you'd imagine. If you want some pink in the center, order it *jugoso;* if you like it truly rare, try *vuelta y vuelta*.

Don't miss *chimichurri,* a tasty sauce made with olive oil, garlic and parsley – it adds a tantalizing spiciness. Occasionally you can also get *salsa criolla,* a condiment made of diced tomatoes, onion and parsley.

Above: Woman eating *helado* (ice cream)
Left: *Mate*

ITALIAN

Thanks to Argentina's Italian heritage, the national cuisine has been highly influenced by Italian immigrants who entered the country during the late 19th century. Along with an animated set of speaking gestures, they brought their love of pasta, pizza, gelato and more.

Many restaurants make their own pasta – look for *pasta casera* (handmade pasta). Some of the varieties of pasta you'll encounter are ravioli, *sorrentinos* (large, round pasta parcels similar to ravioli), *ñoquis* (gnocchi) and *tallerines* (fettuccine). Standard sauces include *tuco* (tomato sauce, sometimes with meat), *estofado* (beef stew, popular with ravioli) and *salsa blanca* (béchamel). Occasionally, the sauce is not included in the price of the pasta – you choose and pay for it separately.

Pizza is sold at *pizzerías* throughout the country, though many regular restaurants offer it as well. It's generally very cheesy and excellent, so go ahead and order a slice or three! Other common Italian-based treats include *fugazzeta* (similar to focaccia) and *fainá* (garbanzo flatbread).

OTHER CUISINES

Spanish cooking is less popular than Italian but is a cornerstone of Argentine food. In BA's Spanish restaurants, many of them found in the Congreso neighborhood, you'll find *paella,* as well as other typically Spanish seafood dishes.

The Palermo Viejo neighborhood offers a selection of Armenian, Brazilian, Mexican, French, Indian, Japanese, Southeast Asian and Middle Eastern cuisines (among many others). If you're craving spicy food (anathema to most Argentines), this is the place to come.

DESSERTS

One of Argentina's most definitive treats is *dulce de leche,* a milk-caramel sauce that is dripped on everything from flan to cake to ice cream. *Alfajores* (round, cookie-type sandwiches) are also delicious – Argentina's version of the candy bar. The most upscale and popular brand is Havanna (also a coffee-shop chain), but kiosks carry many other kinds.

Because of Argentina's Italian heritage, Argentine *helado* is comparable to the best ice cream anywhere in the world. Amble into a *heladería* (ice-cream shop), order up a cone (usually you pay first) and the creamy concoction will be artistically swept up into a mountainous peak and handed over with a small plastic spoon tucked in the side. Important: *granizado* means with chocolate chips.

Some of the best *heladería* chains – with branches all over the city – are Persicco, Freddo and Una Altra Volta, but many smaller independent shops are excellent too.

COOKING COURSES

Taking a small-group cooking class or private class is probably the best option for short-term visitors who don't speak Spanish. At **Norma Soued** (p145) you can learn how to cook Argentine dishes such as *empanadas*, traditional stews and *alfajores* (traditional cookies).

If you have time, speak Spanish and are considering making cooking a profession, try the highly regarded **Instituto Argentino de Gastronomía** (IAG; ☎011-4816-1414; www.iag.com.ar; Montevideo 968; Ⓢ Línea D Callao) or **Mausi Sebess** (☎011-4791-4355; www.mausi.com; Av Maipú 594, Vicente López; Aristóbulo del Valle), located in BA's suburb of Vicente López.

Vegetarians & Vegans

Argentine cuisine is internationally famous for its succulent grilled meats, but this doesn't mean vegetarians – or even vegans – are out of luck.

Most restaurants, including *parrillas,* serve a few items acceptable to most vegetarians, such as green salads, omelets, mashed potatoes, pizza and pasta. Words to look out for include *carne* (beef), *pollo* (chicken), *cerdo* (pork) and *cordero* (lamb), though all meat cuts are described in different words. *Sin carne* means 'without meat', and the phrase *soy vegetariano/a* ('I'm a vegetarian') comes in handy. *Pescado* (fish) and *mariscos* (seafood) are sometimes available for pescatarians.

In the Center there's the popular cafeteria Granix (p64) and Vita (p64); Broccolino (p65) also has good vegetarian options. In San Telmo, head to Hierbabuena (p92). Palermo has plenty of options, including Artemisia (p135), Bio (p135) and Buenos Aires Verde (p135).

Eat Like a Local

WHEN TO EAT

Argentines eat little for breakfast – usually just coffee with *medialunas*, either *de manteca* (sweet) or *de grasa* (plain). *Tostadas* (toast) with *manteca* (butter) or *mermelada* (jam) is an alternative, as are *facturas* (pastries). Most hotels offer this basic breakfast, but some higher-end hotels have breakfast buffets.

Argentines make up for breakfast at lunch and dinner, and they love to dine out. Every neighborhood has basic restaurants serving the staples of *empanadas* (a pastry turnover filled with a variety of savoury ingredients and baked or fried), pasta, pizza and steak (though for the best meats, head to a *parrilla*).

WHERE TO EAT

Cafes (which serve snacks, light meals and sometimes more) and *confiterías* (restaurant-cafes) are open all day and into the night. Bars or pubs usually have a more limited range of snacks and meals, though some offer full meals. A *tenedor libre* (literally, 'free fork') is an all-you-can-eat restaurant; quality is usually decent, but drinks are often mandatory and cost extra.

Large, modern, chain supermarkets are common, and they'll have whatever you need for self-catering, including (usually) a takeout counter with a decent range of offerings. Smaller, local grocery stores – usually family-run – are also ubiquitous, though they won't have takeout.

TEA FOR TWO

Following in the grand tradition of Londoners and society ladies, *porteños* have taken to the ritual of afternoon tea. Which isn't to say that *mate* is on its way out, mind you – taking a break for chamomile and crumpets is just another excuse for these highly social souls to get together and dish the latest gossip.

At these grand tea institutions, you won't just be sipping Earl Grey – with an array of crustless sandwiches, sweets and pastries, the experience is more like a full meal. The grandmother of the tea scene is the lavish L'Orangerie (p117) at the Alvear Palace Hotel, where white-gloved service and impossibly elegant little cakes await guests fond of old-fashioned pleasantries. For something more casual but endlessly charming, go for a cuppa at El Gato Negro (p83).

Eating by Neighborhood

- **The Center** (p63) Many restaurants here cater to the business crowd, with quick takeout and power lunches.
- **Puerto Madero** (p74) Upscale – and some say overpriced – restaurants here offer great dockside atmosphere and more traditional cuisine.
- **Congreso & Tribunales** (p80) BA's political center, this neighborhood has Spanish cuisine, along with the odd Korean or Peruvian gem.
- **San Telmo** (p91) Traditionally has supported many *parrillas*, though gentrification over the years translates to wider horizons.
- **Recoleta & Barrio Norte** (p114) BA's most exclusive neighborhood means expensive restaurants; those near the cemetery cater to tourists.
- **Palermo** (p133) Ground zero for the city's most creative and ethnically diverse dining scene.

STEAK OUTSIDE THE BOX

Going to a *parrilla* is probably on every BA visitor's to-do list, but if you want to eat meat in a different way, try these options:

Argentine Experience (p145) Learn the meaning of local hand gestures, the story of Argentina's beef and how to make *empanadas* and *alfajores*. Plus you'll eat a supremely tender steak.

Steaks by Luis (p138) An upscale *asado* experience where you'll nibble on cheese and sip boutique wine while watching large hunks of meat being grilled.

Parrilla Tour (☎15-4048-5964; www.parrillatour.com; per person US$79; ⏲Palermo tour noon & 7:30pm Tue, noon Fri & Sat, San Telmo tour noon Mon & Wed) Meet your knowledgeable guide at a restaurant for a *choripan* (traditional sausage sandwich), then an *empanada*. You'll finish at a local *parrilla*.

Lonely Planet's Top Choices

Café San Juan (p92) Tattooed celebrity chef serves up fabulously tasty dishes.

Proper (p136) Innovative dishes cooked in a wood-fired oven.

La Carnicería (p136) BA's first boutique *parrilla.*

Chila (p74) Fine-dining dishes prepared by chef Soledad Nardelli.

Best by Budget

$

Chan Chan (p82) Colorful, casual Peruvian eatery with great ceviche (seafood cured in citrus).

Chori (p133) New gourmet *choripan* joint lifting the humble sausage to new heights.

NoLa (p133) Cajun cuisine in a casual gastro-pub setting.

$$

Gran Dabbang (p134) Creative fusion dishes with truly global inflections.

Las Pizarras (p134) Delicious, very creative dishes that change daily.

El Refuerzo Bar Almacen (p91) Popular San Telmo eatery serving bistro-style meals.

$$$

Aramburu (p83) Molecular gastronomy – not for everyone, but for some it's a peak experience.

Proper (p136) Flavorsome plates cooked in a wood-fired oven.

Elena (p117) One of the best meals you'll have in BA.

Best Steak

Don Julio (p134) Great traditional steakhouse with classy service.

La Carnicería (p136) Quality meat in a butcher-themed dining room.

La Cabrera (p136) Overly popular and touristy – but worth the wait.

Parrilla Peña (p82) No-nonsense, well-priced, excellent meats.

El Desnivel (p91) Long-running, touristy and still reasonably priced.

Best Seafood

La Mar Cebicheria (p136) Quality ceviche that's making waves on the BA food scene.

Casal de Catalunya (p92) Spanish restaurant with an old-time atmosphere.

Chan Chan (p82) Great-value Peruvian eatery in Congreso.

Best Closed-Door Restaurants

i Latina (p152) Colombian cuisine in Villa Crespo.

Casa Coupage (p136) Tasting menus with expertly paired wines.

Casa Felix (p152) Creative dishes made utilising home-grown herbs and vegetables.

Casa Saltshaker (p117) Shared meals at Chef Dan Perlman's home.

Best Burgers

Burger Joint (p133) The original and the best, located in Palermo.

Big Sur (p133) Juicy burgers and a range of street-food-style alternatives.

180 Burger Bar (p64) Downtown burger joint that's busy at lunch.

Best Italian

Siamo nel Forno (p134) Awesome Naples-style, thin-crust pizza.

Il Matterello (p101) Famous for its exceptional pastas and sauces.

Filo (p109) Trendy restaurant with a variety of Italian specialties.

Best Vegetarian

Artemisia (p135) Airy corner restaurant serving a variety of vegetarian meals.

Hierbabuena (p92) Popular San Telmo eatery on beautiful Av Caseros.

Bio (p135) Sophisticated and very tasty vegetarian dishes.

Granix (p64) Modern cafeteria catering to meat-weary office workers.

Best Asian

Sunae Asian Cantina (p136) Dishes from all over Asia prepared by chef Christina Sunae.

Sudestada (p138) Consistently good, Asian-fusion cuisine that can be spicy.

Green Bamboo (p138) Vietnamese-style foods in BA-trendy dining room.

Furaibo (p65) Japanese ramen and other delicacies in authentic surroundings.

Comedor Nikkai (p93) A good place for sushi, tempura and teriyaki.

Drinking & Nightlife

Buenos Aires' nightlife is legendary. What else could you expect from a country where dinner rarely starts before 10pm? In some neighborhoods, finding a good sports bar, classy cocktail lounge, atmospheric old cafe or upscale wine bar is as easy as walking down the street. And dancers will be in heaven, as BA boasts spectacular nightclubs showcasing top-drawer DJs.

The Local Scene

Porteños (residents of Buenos Aires) rarely imbibe to the point of drunkenness – it's just not cool – but they do like to go out drinking, especially in groups, and always stay up late. Walk into any corner bar or cafe in the city and you'll see groups of friends or families sitting around a table, sipping tiny white cups of espresso or splitting a bottle of Quilmes (a popular local beer). More fashionable bars, pubs and breweries draw more of a mixed crowd of party-going tourists, with style-conscious men trying to impress their dates or girlfriends celebrating a special occasion.

How to handle the late-night scene like a *porteño*? If you're going out clubbing (some clubs open at 2am), take a nap after dinner and go easy on the booze – it will help you avoid conking out too early.

What to Drink

WINE

By now you've probably heard: Argentine wines are world-class. Most famous is malbec, that dark, robust plum-flavored wine that has solidly stomped the region of Mendoza on every oenophile's map (the Mendoza region produces 60% of the country's wine). But Argentina has other fine varietals that are very worthy of a sip or three – fresh *torrontés*, fruity bonarda and earthy pinot noir.

So which to try? They say there's a perfect Argentine wine for every occasion and a good *vinoteca* (wine boutique) will help you find it. In Palermo, try Lo de Joaquín Alberdi (p142); in San Telmo there's Vinotango (p95). Aldo's Restoran & Vinoteca (p65) is a restaurant that sells wines at retail prices – even when you eat there.

Supermarket selections are usually adequate, though you miss out on the tailored advice. Among the mainstay brands are Norton, Trapiche, Zuccardi and Santa Julia, with different lines that cater to every price range. Spend a bit more to try the elegant Rutini (from Bodega La Rural) or Luigi Bosca.

For informal wine tastings, inquire at Pain et Vin (p145), a casual wine and bread shop. Bar du Marché (p145) is a low-key bistro offering 50 wines by the glass, while Gran Bar Danzón (p118) is an upscale lounge-restaurant that also has a good selection of wines by the glass.

Many *puertas cerradas* (closed-door) restaurants offer fine wines with their meals; Casa Coupage (p136), run by an Argentine sommelier couple, is especially wine-oriented.

MATE

Mate (mah-teh) is Argentina's unofficial national beverage. More than a simple drink such as tea or coffee, *mate* is more like an elaborate ritual shared among family and friends.

There's an informal etiquette to preparing and drinking *mate*. The *cebador* (server) fills the gourd with *yerba,* then pours in very hot water. Each participant drinks the gourd dry, then the *cebador* refills it and hands it to the next person. Germaphobes beware: the *bombilla* (a silvery straw with built-in filter), used to sip the *mate,* is shared by everyone.

An invitation to drink *mate* is a cultural treat you shouldn't turn down, though it's definitely an acquired taste. The tea is grassy, bitter and very hot; adding sugar can help. Saying '*gracias*' is a sign you want to stop drinking. And remember not to hold the *mate* too long before passing it on – it's not a microphone.

Because it is such a personal ritual, not many restaurants offer *mate* on the menu – but a few do, so try it if you can.

BEER, COFFEE & WATER

If Argentina has a national beer, it's Quilmes. Order a *porrón* and you'll get a half-liter bottle, or a *chopp* and you'll get a frosty mug of draft.

Argentines love their *café con leche* (coffee with milk). An espresso with a drop of milk is a *café cortado*. Black and herbal teas are also commonly available.

In Buenos Aires, the *agua de la canilla* (tap water) is drinkable. In restaurants, however, most people order bottled mineral water – ask for *agua con gas* (with bubbles) or *agua sin gas* (without). In older, more traditional restaurants, carbonated water in a spritzer bottle (*un sifón de soda*) is great for drinking, though Argentines often mix it with cheap wine.

Where to Drink

CAFES

Cafes are an integral part of *porteño* life, and you shouldn't miss popping into one of these beloved hangouts for an afternoon break. Many cafes are old classics that have been around for more than a hundred years, and undoubtedly will take you back in time. Others are contemporary or bohemian joints with sidewalk tables – perfect spots to take a load off while sightseeing or to delve into Borges' short stories at a corner table.

Most cafes serve all meals and everything in between (including a late-night snack).

BARS

Bars abound in every neighborhood of Buenos Aires, and they come in all shapes, sizes and styles. You can choose from sports bars, cocktail lounges, Irish pubs, microbreweries, local holes-in-the-wall and more. Many of the city's upscale restaurants and hotels also have lively bars worth a visit.

NEED TO KNOW

Opening Hours

Bars Vary widely depending on location and clientele, but most are usually open from the evening into the early-morning hours.

Cafes Usually from around 6am or 7am to 2am or 3am.

Clubs From 2am to dawn.

Door Policies

All clubs have bouncers. Dress well – smart casual is good enough at most clubs. You can also sign up in advance via online reservation forms that some clubs keep; this sometimes gets you in more easily and/or offers discounts.

Resources

Many newspapers have entertainment supplements published on Friday. Also check www.vuenosairez.com (in Spanish) and www.thebubble.com (in English) for current happenings.

Most bars serve beer, hard alcohol and wine, plus coffee and juice. Some make cocktails, and many offer a fair range of finger foods or even main dishes. Microbreweries and beer bars have taken off in the last few years, and you'll be spoilt for choice when it comes to the hoppy stuff.

Younger travelers and backpackers looking to barhop in a group should check out **Buenos Aires Pub Crawl** (☎011-3678-0170, 011-5257-0897; www.pubcrawlba.com; AR$150).

CLUBBING

Buenos Aires is famous for its *boliches* (nightclubs). Every weekend – and even on some weeknights – the city's clubs come alive with beautiful people moving to electronic and house music. Some of the most impressive nightlife hot spots are located in grandiose restored theaters, warehouses or factories – or perched on the banks of the Río de la Plata where party-goers can watch the sun rise over the water as the festivities wind down. Clubs are spread out over the city, with main clusters in Palermo and on the Costanera Norte.

Drinking & Nightlife by Neighborhood

- **The Center** (p65) Irish pub knock offs cater to the business crowd, though there are several good cafes and clubs.
- **Congreso & Tribunales** (p83) This neighborhood, the political center of BA, has a few interesting bars and cafes.
- **San Telmo** (p93) Gentrified San Telmo is home to many classy modern spots mixing it up with a few old classics.
- **Retiro** (p109) A wide choice of drinking holes attracts business people during the day and into the evening, and the traveler/expat crowd at night.
- **Recoleta** (p117) Across from the cemetery is a two-block strip of restaurants, cafes and bars with great patios.
- **Palermo** (p138) BA's hippest nightlife is located here. Las Cañitas, a sub-neighborhood, is also very lively.
- **South of Palermo** (p152) As Palermo becomes more expensive, these neighborhoods are attracting their own attention.

Las Violetas (p152), South of Palermo

GAY & LESBIAN BUENOS AIRES

Despite the fact that Argentina is a Catholic country, Buenos Aires is one of the world's top gay destinations, with dedicated hostels and guesthouses, bars and nightclubs. In 2002 BA became the first Latin American city to legalize same-sex civil unions, and in July 2010 Argentina became the first Latin American country to legalize same-sex marriage. Today, the city is home to South America's largest **gay pride parade** (p21), as well as a dedicated tango festival.

An especially gay-friendly accommodations is **Lugar Gay** (p173), a casual guesthouse that also acts as an information center.

Check out the gay bars **Sitges** (p140), **Flux** (p110) and **Pride Cafe** (p93). The best nightclubs are **Glam** (p139), Rheo at **Crobar** (p140) and **Amerika** (p153). A long-running lesbian bar is **Bach Bar** (p140).

Casa Brandon (p150) is an art gallery/cultural center. And for a fun night of guided drinking and partying, there's **Out & About Pub Crawl** (☎011-5257-0897; www.outandaboutpubcrawl.com/buenosaires/; AR$200; ⏲10pm Sat).

Finally, gay tango classes and *milongas* (events) are given at La Marshall at **El Beso** (p84) and **Tango Queer** (p94).

Good general websites are www.thegayguide.com.ar and www.nighttours.com/buenosaires.

Lonely Planet's Top Choices

Florería Atlántico (p109) Look for this cocktail bar in the basement of a flower shop.

LAB (p138) Turning coffee-making into an art form.

On Tap (p138) Some of the best local breweries on tap.

Los Galgos (p83) Old-school neighborhood bar transformed in chic cocktail joint.

Benaim (p139) Fabulous beer garden and craft beers.

Best Cocktail Bars

Florería Atlántico (p109) 'Secret' basement bar located inside a flower shop.

Verne (p138) Fancy drinking hole with awesome cocktails and smoking patio.

Frank's (p139) Elegant speak-easy with classic cocktails; enter via the telephone booth.

Los Galgos (p83) Stop by for an expertly mixed vermouth cocktail.

Milión (p117) Glamorous setting in a lovely mansion with an elegant garden.

Best Craft Beer

On Tap (p138) Successful craft-beer bar with five branches in BA.

Bluedog (p139) Palermo bar selling beers brewed by some of BA's best local breweries.

Benaim (p139) Craft ales served from a caravan in the beer garden.

Antares (p140) Argentina's original artisan brewery, from Mar del Plata.

Buller Brewing Company (p118) Recoleta microbrewery with six kinds of beer.

Cossab (p152) Dedicated beer bar that boasts over 50 beers.

Best Cafes

Las Violetas (p152) BA's most beautiful cafe, with stained-glass awnings and afternoon tea.

LAB (p138) Serious coffee shop serving expertly prepared brews.

El Gato Negro (p83) Aromatic tea shop with a gorgeous wooden interior.

Bar Británico (p93) Classic San Telmo cafe overlooking Parque Lezama.

Café Tortoni (p65) Very historic, very scenic and very touristy – but a classic that can't be ignored.

Best Gay Hot Spots

Glam (p139) Casual yet very sexy club in an old mansion.

Crobar (p140) Saturday night's Rheo is the place to be.

Amerika (p153) Rough and tumble, with all-you-can-drink nights.

Pride Cafe (p93) Casual San Telmo coffee shop.

Best Clubs

Niceto Club (p138) Best for its raucous Thursday-night, over-the-top burlesque show.

Club Museum (p94) Party in a building designed by Eiffel.

Crobar (p140) Electronica, Latin beats and more at this perennially popular Palermo club.

Kika (p140) Draws Tuesday-night crowds with its well-known 'Hype' party.

Best Museum Cafes

Museo Evita Restaurante (p135) Excellent patio cafe-restaurant with sophisticated cuisine.

Fundación Proa (p101) Fancy cafe with awesome rooftop terrace offering La Boca views.

MALBA (p129) Not cheap, but a nice atmosphere and good people-watching.

Entertainment

The entertainment scene in Buenos Aires has always been lively, but there was an outburst of creative energy in the decade following the economic crisis of 2001. Filmmakers began producing quality works on shoestring budgets, troupes performed in new avant-garde theaters and live-music groups played in more mainstream venues. Today nearly every neighborhood offers great entertainment options.

Live Music

There are some fine venues that only feature live music, but many theaters, cultural centers, bars and cafes also put on shows. Centro Cultural Torquato Tasso (p94) is an especially good choice for tango-music performances.

CLASSICAL

Several venues offer classical-music concerts. Teatro Colón (p78) is the grandest and most famous; everyone who's anyone has played, acted, sung or danced here. It often features guest conductors from throughout Latin America. Two new venues – both renovated old buildings with excellent acoustics – are the Centro Cultural Kirchner (p59) and the Usina del Arte (p102); be sure to check what's on. The classical-music scene takes a break from December to February, and is best from June to August.

ROCK, BLUES & JAZZ

Buenos Aires boasts a thriving rock-music scene. Smaller venues, like La Trastienda (p94), showcase mostly local groups; when huge international stars come to town they tend to play soccer stadiums or Luna Park (p67).

Blues and jazz aren't as popular as rock but still have their own loyal following. Thelonious Bar (p141) and Notorious (p118) are top-notch venues for jazz concerts.

FOLK

Música folklórica definitely has its place in Buenos Aires. There are several *peñas* (traditional music clubs) in the city, including Los Cardones (p141) and La Peña del Colorado (p141), but other venues – such as Clásica y Moderna (p118) – occasionally host folk performances.

Cinema

BA's traditional cinema districts are along pedestrian Lavalle (west of Florida) and on Av Corrientes. Newer cinemas are in shopping malls throughout the city. Most cinemas offer big discounts for matinees, midweek shows or first screenings of the day. There is usually a *trasnoche* (midnight or later showing) scheduled for Friday and Saturday night.

Except for children's films and cartoon features, which are dubbed, foreign films almost always appear in their original language with Spanish subtitles.

Cosmos-UBA (p84) often shows retrospectives, documentaries, foreign film cycles and art-house movies. Espacio INCAA Gaumont (p84) screens Ibero-American films only (essentially from Spanish- or Portuguese-speaking countries).

Some cultural centers have their own small cinemas, while places such as Alianza Francesa (p214) and the British Arts Centre (p214) showcase movies in their respective languages.

Theater

Theater is big in Buenos Aires. The city's venues number more than 100, and annual attendance is in the hundreds of thousands. While productions range from classic plays to multimedia performances to lavish cabarets, the acting tends to be of a professional level across the board. Note that, unsurprisingly, performances tend to be in Spanish.

Traditionally, the center for theater has been Av Corrientes between Avs 9 de Julio and Callao, but there are now dozens of venues all over the city.

Many alternative (or 'off-Corrientes') theater companies and independent troupes receive relatively little attention from the mainstream media, but they're worth seeking out if you're looking for something different. If you read Spanish, www.alternativateatral.com is a good source for current non-mainstream performances.

Tickets are generally affordable, but check *carteleras* (discount ticket offices) for bargain seats. The season is liveliest in winter (June through August), when upwards of 100 events may take place, but you can find a good variety of shows any time. Many of the most popular shows move to the provincial beach resort of Mar del Plata for the summer.

Circo Moderno

A popular movement in Argentina that found international fame through the Broadway performance of the De la Guarda troupe is *circo moderno* (contemporary circus). This combination of traditional circus and contemporary dance and theater features a lot of aerial action, acrobatics and no words – great for those who don't speak Spanish. Cirque du Soleil is a well-known example of this modern gymnastic theater.

In 2005, Diqui James, one of the creators of De la Guarda, launched his solo act **Fuerzabruta** (http://fuerzabrutaglobal.com/). It's a jaw-dropping, mind-blowing show of lights, electronic music, aerial dancing and water – and often the performance is above you. If you go to a show, you could get wet. The troupe is often on tour around the world, so check its website for listings.

Discount Tickets & Booking

Major entertainment venues often require booking through **Ticketek** (☎011-5237-7200; www.ticketek.com.ar; Av Santa Fe 4389; ⏲1-8pm Mon-Sat; Ⓢ Línea D Plaza Italia). The service charge is about 10% of the ticket price.

Carteleras sell a limited number of discounted tickets for many events, such as movies, theater and tango shows, with savings of 20% to 50%. Try **Cartelera Baires** (☎011-4372-5058; Av Corrientes 1382, Galería Apolo; ⏲10am-6pm Mon, 1-8pm Tue-Thu, 1-9pm Fri, 2-9pm Sat; Ⓢ Línea B Uruguay), **Cartelera Vea Más** (☎011-6320-5319; www.veamasdigital.com.ar; Av Corrientes 1660, Local 2; ⏲10am-8pm Mon, to 9:30pm Tue-Wed & Sun, to 10:30pm Thu, to 11pm Fri & Sat; Ⓢ Línea B Callao) or **Cartelera Espectáculos** (☎011-4322-1559; www.123info.com.ar; Lavalle 742; ⏲noon-9pm Mon-Sat, to 8pm Sun; Ⓢ Línea C Lavalle). Buy tickets as far in advance as possible.

NEED TO KNOW

Opening Hours

Show times can vary widely, but this is a city that stays up all night, so expect to be out late. Restaurants usually open around 9pm – and 10pm is a more common dinner time – so many shows start around midnight.

Resources

Check www.vuenosairez.com (in Spanish) and www.thebubble.com (in English).

Entertainment by Neighborhood

- **The Center** (p66) Has a little of everything – theater, live music, cinemas and tango shows.
- **Congreso & Tribunales** (p83) Home to Av Corrientes, BA's traditional theater district; also has several cinemas and flamenco venues.
- **San Telmo** (p94) Some live music and tango spots.
- **La Boca** (p102) Home to Boca Juniors soccer club's ground La Bombonera.
- **Palermo** (p141) A few tango *milongas* (dance halls) and live-music venues, as well as the Hipódromo Argentino racing track.
- **South of Palermo** (p153) Ground zero for BA's avant-garde theater.

Lonely Planet's Top Choices

Centro Cultural Kirchner (p59) World-class acoustics in the beautiful former Central Post Office building.

Teatro Colón (p78) Landmark, seven-story theater seating 2500 and boasting renowned acoustics.

Usina del Arte (p102) Old electricity factory remodeled into a premier symphony hall.

Centro Cultural Borges (p66) One of BA's top cultural centers, with countless offerings.

Best Cultural Centers

Centro Cultural Kirchner (p59) The biggest and the best cultural center in BA – and possibly the continent.

Centro Cultural Borges (p66) Quality art galleries, cinema, workshops, music and shows.

Centro Cultural Recoleta (p114) Many free or inexpensive events, plus a science museum for kids.

Centro Cultural San Martín (p80) Large cultural center with galleries, concerts, exhibitions and shows.

Best Theaters

Teatro Colón (p78) Buenos Aires' grandest entertainment concert hall and a gorgeous building.

El Camarín de las Musas (p153) Innovative contemporary dance and theater in Almagro.

Teatro San Martín (p84) Large venue that's great for classic theater and much more.

Teatro Nacional Cervantes (p80) Traditional old venue showing contemporary productions.

Best Live Music

Usina del Arte (p102) Amazing and beautiful new performance venue in La Boca seating 1200.

Ciudad Cultural Konex (p194) Famous for its one-of-a-kind, Monday-night percussion parties.

Centro Cultural Torquato Tasso (p94) Excellent venue for concerts, including tango music.

Thelonious Bar (p141) BA's best jazz bar.

Best Alternative Theater

El Camarín de las Musas (p153) Contemporary dance and theater.

El Cubo (p153) Hosts gutsy theater pieces and offbeat performances.

Espacio Callejón (p153) Showcases edgy new theater, music and dance.

Shopping

Buenos Aires is laced with shopping streets lined with clothing and shoe stores, leather shops and nearly everything else you can think of. Large shopping malls are modern and family-friendly, offering designer goods, food courts and even children's play areas. But perhaps the city's best shopping is in Palermo Viejo, where you'll find upscale boutiques. San Telmo is where antiques aficionados flock.

Specialties & Souvenirs

Wine is one of the more obvious gifts, though it's hard to carry. Some stores will ship outside Argentina; expect to pay a premium for this service. Food items that make nice gifts are *dulce de leche* (a delicious milk caramel that Argentines have perfected) and *alfajores,* cookie sandwiches usually bathed in chocolate (Havanna is a popular brand and available at Ezeiza Airport). *Mate* gourds are also good, and they're small and light.

Argentina is known for its leather goods. There are leather stores all over the city, but for the best prices head to Calle Murillo. Silverwork is also high quality, and many items are gaucho-inspired. Looking for a gift for that aristocratic friend? There are a few polo stores with items that might fit the bill – whether or not he or she plays polo.

Ferias (street markets) are full of craftspeople selling their homemade wares. These markets happen every weekend all over the city. Finally, soccer memorabilia always make popular souvenirs – especially from Boca, the most well-known team.

Street Markets

Wandering through a weekend *feria* is a quintessential BA experience. Artisans display their wares while buskers, mimes and tango dancers entertain. Often there are nearby restaurants with sidewalk tables for people-watching. At some of the more touristed markets, especially Feria de San Telmo, watch for pickpockets.

Check out Feria Artesenal Plaza Francia (p119) in Recoleta, Feria de Mataderos (p152) in Mataderos, San Telmo's Feria de San Telmo (p88) and Palermo's Feria Plaza Serrano (p144).

Antique Markets

A couple of antique markets might be worth your time. Try Mercado de las Pulgas (p142) or Mercado de San Telmo (p88). Don't expect dirt-cheap bargains, though you might find a cool glass soda bottle or vintage lamp. The Feria de San Telmo (p88) is a fun place to look for old coins and jewelry, though there's a lot of kitsch as well. The San Telmo neighborhood has some pricey antique stores, too.

Shopping Malls

Many of the bigger shopping malls in BA are slick and modern; some cater to families with children by offering special play areas and video arcades. Paseo Alcorta (Alcorta Shopping; p144) has an especially large kids' playground on the 3rd floor, while Mercado de Abasto (p150) sports an excellent children's museum and small amusement park complete with rides. Almost all of these malls also have multiplex cinemas and large food courts complete with fast-food outlets and ice-cream parlors. Expect all the popular chain stores; some even offer health clubs, beauty shops and internet cafes.

NEED TO KNOW

Opening Hours

Store hours generally run from 9am or 10am to 8pm or 9pm weekdays, with many open for a few hours on Saturday. Most stores close on Sunday.

Bargaining

Bargaining is not acceptable in stores, except possibly for high-price items like jewelry and leather jackets (in some places). Some shops will give a *descuento* (discount) for cash payments. At street markets you can try negotiating, but keep in mind you may be talking to the artists themselves.

Be clear about whether the vendor is quoting in pesos or dollars. Always check your change before walking away.

Fashion

Interested in clothing design? Then make a beeline for Palermo Soho, where the boutiques of avant-garde fashion designers grace the pretty tree-shaded streets. After the 2001 economic crash, dozens of young designers emerged from the woodwork to set up shop in this then-affordable neighborhood (rents have gone way up since then, driving some out). Some made it big, maturing into fully fledged designers with luxury sportswear lines and outposts in the US, Europe and Asia. Names you may come across include Maria Cher (known for deconstructed garments with an urban twist), Jazmín Chebar (with playful, feminine designs) and Martín Churba (known for recycling fabrics). Cora Groppo and Jessica Trosman are other big names with chain stores in Buenos Aires malls and elsewhere.

If you're looking for leather bargains, avoid Calle Florida and head to the shops on Calle Murillo's 600 block, in the neighborhood of Villa Crespo. This is the best place in town to snag a relatively cheap but high-quality leather jacket and accessories.

For outlet shopping there's the 800 block of Calle Aguirre, with deals on shoes and clothes. Ladies, check out the Prüne outlet for stylish leather bags. There are also lots of other outlets on nearby Av Córdoba.

The largest concentration of jewelry shops is on Libertad south of Av Corrientes.

Shopping by Neighborhood

- **The Center** (p67) The area on and around Calle Florida offers modern shops selling pretty much everything.
- **Congreso & Tribunales** (p84) Not known for its shopping, though there are discount bookstores along Av Corrientes.
- **San Telmo** (p94) *The* place for antique stores, with clothing and other boutiques here and there.
- **Retiro** (p110) Bustling Av Santa Fe starts here and heads through Palermo, lined the whole way with shops of every kind.
- **Recoleta & Barrio Norte** (p119) Upscale stores selling the city's most expensive threads and leather products live on Av Alvear.
- **Palermo** (p142) Best known for its locally designed clothing stores, with plenty of housewares shops and boutiques.
- **South of Palermo** (p154) Av Pueyrredón near Once train station has cheap goods, many of them imported from China.

Lonely Planet's Top Choices

El Ateneo Grand Splendid (p119) Spectacular bookstore housed in a former theater.

Elementos Argentinos (p142) Fair-trade, hand-woven rugs and blankets.

Lo de Joaquín Alberdi (p142) A wine lover's paradise; offers tastings too.

Gil Antiguedades (p95) Gorgeous vintage clothes are the star here, though there are *objets* too.

Autoría (p110) Ingenious, edgy, high-quality art and accessories, with an emphasis on Argentine designers' work.

Best for Clothes

Rapsodia (p144) At times exotic clothing utilizing various genres and different textiles.

Juana de Arco (p142) Frilly, silky, cute, sexy and very feminine items for the girl inside every woman.

Hermanos Estebecorena (p143) Cutting-edge, creative and stylish clothes for men.

Bolivia (p144) Metrosexual designs for men who aren't afraid of patterns and pastels.

Punto Sur (p95) Dozens of designers stock the racks here with awesome, creative clothing.

Best for Souvenirs

Feria de San Telmo (p88) Everything goes, multi-block street fair selling anything you can think of.

Arte y Esperanza (p67) Fair-trade Argentine souvenirs handmade by Argentina's indigenous peoples.

Harapos Patagonia (p144) Woolen goods, alpaca jewelry, wood and ceramics from Patagonia.

Best for Gifts

Materia Urbana (p95) Funky things such as leather animal desk accessories and wood jewelry.

Autoría (p110) Creative, high-quality and well-priced contemporary items made by local designers.

L'Ago (p94) Kitschy home decor including colorful metal *mate* sets, paper lamps and vintage-look pillows.

Calma Chicha (p144) Cow- and sheepskin rugs, fun tablecloths, leather bags and more.

Best for Books

El Ateneo Gran Splendid (p119) One of the world's most impressive bookstores is housed in a former theater.

Walrus Books (p95) A terrific range of new and used books, plus Argentine classics translated into English.

Libros del Pasaje (p143) Arty books and a cafe, too.

Sports & Activities

When it comes to spectator sports, only one thing really matters to most porteños – fútbol (soccer). If you go to a game – or even watch one on TV – you'll witness human passion to the core. But other spectator sports also exist in Buenos Aires. And for those who'd rather play than watch, you'll have opportunities to run, bike, swim and even rock climb – though some activities will be harder to seek out than others.

Spectator Sports

FÚTBOL

Fútbol is a national obsession, and witnessing a live game is an integral part of the BA experience. This is no amateur league – Argentina's national team won the World Cup in both 1978 and 1986 (one of only eight nations to have ever won the cup). The men's team also walked away with gold at the 2004 and 2008 summer Olympics. And Lionel Messi, currently Argentina's most famous player, has won FIFA's World Player of the Year (or Ballon d'Or) award five times – from 2009 to 2012 and again in 2015.

Argentines are avid fans of the sport, and on game day (and there are many) you'll see TVs everywhere tuned to the soccer channels. Cheers erupt when goals are scored and after a big win cars sporting team flags go honking by – especially around the Obelisco.

For more information on Argentine *fútbol*, see www.futbolargentino.com and www.afa.org.ar.

GOING TO A GAME

In a land where Maradona is God, going to see a *fútbol* game can be a religious experience. The *superclásico* match between the Boca Juniors and River Plate has been called the number-one sporting event to see before you die, but even the less-celebrated games will give you an insight into Argentina's national passion.

Attending a regular match isn't too difficult. Keep an eye on the clubs' websites, which inform when and where tickets will be sold; often they're sold at the stadium before the game. You'll get a choice between *populares* (bleachers) and *plateas* (seats). Avoid the *populares*, as these can get far too rowdy and sometimes dangerous.

If you want to see a *clásico* – a match between two major teams – getting a ticket will be much harder. Plus Boca doesn't even put tickets for its key matches on sale; all tickets go to *socios* (members). Instead, you're better off going with an agency such as **Tangol** (☎011-4363-6000; www.tangol.com; Florida 971, Suite 31; ⏰9am-6pm Mon-Fri; Ⓢ Línea C San Martín) or via organizations like www.landingpad.com. It won't be cheap, but it's much easier (and safer) getting a ticket this way; fake tickets do exist.

If you want to chance getting your own *clásico* or *superclásico* ticket, however, you can always look online at www.buenosaires.craigslist.org or www.mercadolibre.com.ar. And if you're confident in your bargaining skills, scalpers will always exist.

Dress down, and try to look inconspicuous when you go. Take only minimum cash and keep your camera close. You probably won't get in with water bottles, and food and drink in the stadium is meager and expensive. Arrive early to get a good seat and enjoy the insane build-up to the game. And most importantly: don't wear the opposing team's colors.

The following are some of the clubs based in Buenos Aires:

- Boca Juniors (p103)
- River Plate (p126)
- San Lorenzo (p154)
- **Argentinos Juniors** (☎011-4551-6887; www.argentinosjuniors.com.ar; Gavilán 2151; 63, 113, 110)
- **Vélez** (☎011-4641-5663; www.velezsarsfield.com.ar; Juan B Justo 9200; 166, 8)
- **Huracán** (☎011-4911-0757; www.clubahuracan.com.ar; Av Amancio Alcorta 2570; S Línea H Parque Patricios)
- **Club Ferro Carril Oeste** (Map p254; ☎011-4431-8282; www.ferrocarriloeste.org.ar; Federico G Lorca 350; S Línea A Primera Junta)

BASKETBALL

The basketball scene in Buenos Aires has been picking up significantly since 2002, when Argentina's men's team played in the World Basketball Championship in Indianapolis. They only won silver but made history by beating the US 'Dream Team' in international competition. Then, with a similar roster, they defeated the US squad again (along with Italy in the finals) to win gold in the 2004 summer Olympics – their first Olympic medal in basketball ever. No team had beaten the Americans in the Olympics since 1992, when pro basketball players were allowed to play. They also won the FIBA Americas Championship in 2011.

Today, BA has several major squads, the most popular being Boca Juniors. You can watch them play in La Boca at Estadio Luis Conde (p103). Other popular basketball teams include Obras Sanitarias and Ferro Carril Oeste.

RUGBY

Rugby is becoming more popular by the year in Argentina, in part because the country's national team – Los Pumas – has done well in past years. After placing third at the Rugby World Cup in 2007 (no mean feat), Los Pumas was rated the best rugby team in the Americas. And at the 2011 Rugby World Cup it put in a pretty decent showing.

In Buenos Aires, the long-running **Club Atlético de San Isidro** (www.casi.org.ar; Roque Sáenz Peña 499; San Isidro) is the capital's best rugby team; in 1935 it gave birth to its own biggest rival, the **San Isidro Club** (☎011-4766-2030; www.sanisidroclub.com.ar; Av Blanco Encalada 404; 60).

NEED TO KNOW

- In October, Buenos Aires' marathon (www.maratondebuenosaires.org) attracts more than 10,000 runners. The 42km route begins in Palermo and passes some of BA's most iconic sights, including the Obelisco, Plaza de Mayo, La Boca and Puerto Madero.
- Buenos Aires Fútbol Amigos (p145) arranges friendly five-aside soccer games for men and women at pitches in Palermo and Villa Crespo.
- Yoga bunnies should look up Buena Onda Yoga (p145), which runs a range of English-language classes at studios in Palermo, San Telmo and Villa Crespo.
- Bike rentals (p207) are available at Palermo's Parque 3 de Febrero (where you can also rent inline skates and pedal boats) and via bike-tour companies.
- For water sports including windsurfing, kitesurfing and stand-up paddle, head to Perú Beach (p159) north of Buenos Aires near San Isidro.
- Tigre is the jumping-off point for kayaking tours deep inside the delta. Try El Dorado Kayak (p157).

Rugby season runs from April to October; contact the **Unión de Rugby de Buenos Aires** (Map p244; ☎011-4805-5858; www.urba.org.ar; Pacheco de Melo 2120; 1-9pm Mon & Wed, 10am-6pm Tue & Thu-Fri; S Línea H Las Heras) for current happenings.

HORSE RACING

Races in BA are held at the Hipódromo Argentino (p141), a grand building designed by French architect Louis Fauré-Dujarric that dates from 1908 and holds up to 100,000 spectators. Race times vary, so check the schedule for exact details. The most important races take place in November, both here and at San Isidro's famous grass racetrack.

POLO

Add Argentina's history of gauchos and horses to its past British influence, and you'll understand why the best polo in the world is played right here. The country has dominated the sport for over 70 years, boasting most of polo's top players. Forget those British princes: the world's best player is considered to be the handsome Adolfo Cambiaso.

Matches take place in Buenos Aires from September to mid-November. They culminate in the annual Campeonato Argentino Abierto de Polo (Argentine Open Polo Championship) – the world's most prestigious polo tournament – in Palermo's Campo Argentino de Polo (p141). For current information, contact the **Asociación Argentina de Polo** (www.aapolo.com), which keeps a schedule of polo-related activities throughout the country. To spend a day learning to play polo yourself (outside BA), check out **Puesto Viejo** (https://puestoviejoestancia.com.ar/).

PATO

Of gaucho origins, the polo-like game of *pato* (literally 'duck') takes its name from the original game ball – a live duck encased in a leather bag. The unfortunate fowl has since been replaced by a ball with leather handles, and players no longer face serious injury in what was once a very violent sport.

For information on *pato* matches and tournaments (which usually take place 30km outside the city in the Campo Argentino de Pato) contact the **Federación Argentina de Pato** (Map p234; ☎011-4342-5271; www.pato.org.ar; Av Rivadavia 717, 7th fl; Ⓢ Línea A Piedras). The national championships occur in December, and are more centrally located in Palermo's polo grounds.

Activities

Extensive greenery in Palermo provides good areas for recreation, especially on weekends when the ring road around the rose garden is closed to motor vehicles. Recoleta also has grassy parks, but not as extensive. Best of all is the Reserva Ecológica Costanera Sur, an ecological paradise just east of Puerto Madero that might just make you forget you're in a big city.

CYCLING

The city's bike lanes make cycling in the city a safer proposition. Bike paths run along many roads in Parque 3 de Febrero (p130), or head to the Reserva Ecológica Costanera Sur (p209), on the eastern side of Puerto Madero along the coast. This green and tranquil space has some flat dirt paths that are great to bike on. Pick up one of the free **city bikes** (EcoBici; ☎0800-333-2424; www.buenosaires.gob.ar/ecobici/sistema-ecobici/turistas; ⏲24hr) FREE or hire one from

A game of *pato*

BA CITY GOVERNMENT TOURS

The **BA city government** (https://turismo.buenosaires.gob.ar) offers a number of free neighborhood guided walking tours in English and Spanish, as well as low-cost cycling tours, new rowing excursions in Puerto Madero (free but often booked out months in advance) and even 5km, 8km and 18km 'urban trekking' tours – see the website for the full list of current offerings; most tours require advance booking.

a tour company such as Biking Buenos Aires (p207) or Urban Biking (p207).

SWIMMING

Some upscale hotels have decent-size pools, but they charge hefty prices for nonguests (so hefty you might as well stay there). The fee generally includes gym use, at least. Try the **Panamericano Hotel** (www.panamericano.us), whose pool has the best view in BA.

A more economical option is to find a health club with an indoor pool; **Megatlon** (www.megatlon.com) is a popular gym with many branches. For a more casual environment, especially with kids, head to Parque Norte (p126).

TENNIS

A few places in BA offer courts, such as **Parque Manuel Belgrano** (Map p250; ☎011-4807-7879; Salguero 3450; park entry AR$10, court hire per hr AR$60, after 7pm per hr AR$130; ⏲8am-11pm Mon-Fri, till 7pm Sat & Sun; 🚌130, 33), in Palermo. Bring your own racket from home if you're serious about getting in touch with the Nalbandian or del Potro inside you.

GOLF

BA's most convenient course is the 18-hole **Campo Municipal de Golf** (☎011-4772-7261; www.golfpalermo.com; Tornquist 6397; 9/18 holes Tue-Fri AR$40/70, Sat & Sun AR$50/100; ⏲7:30am-5pm Tue-Sun; 🚌130, 160, 34); be sure to reserve your spot in advance. Practice your long shots at the **Costa Salguero Driving Range** (☎011 4805-4732; http://costasalguerogolf.com; Av Rafael Obligado 1221; 50 balls AR$45; ⏲noon-10pm Mon, 8am-10pm Tue-Fri, to 9pm Sat & Sun; 🚌160, 33, 45), which also has a golf store, a cafe and a nine-hole, family-friendly course.

HORSEBACK RIDING

If you want to get out of town for a few hours and hop on a horse, forget those touristy *estancias* (ranches) and check out **Caballos a la Par** (www.caballos-alapar.com). Guided, private rides are given in a provincial park about an hour's drive from central Buenos Aires, and it's not just one of those 'follow-the-horse-in-front' deals. They'll take you around woodsy lanes and fields, and you'll have fun learning how to ride and even gallop on the fine horses.

Sports & Activities by Neighborhood

- **Puerto Madero** Reserva Ecológica Costanera Sur is great for running, bicycling or walking. These activities are also possible along the dikes.
- **Palermo** Provides most of BA's green spaces, along with tennis and golf courses, running paths and bicycling lanes.
- **Belgrano, Nuñez & the Costanera Norte** Head here for the family-friendly swimming complex Parque Norte.

Best Spectator Sports

La Bombonera Stadium (p103) Boca Juniors' home ground.

Hipódromo Argentino (p141) Glamorous horse-racing track in Palermo.

Campo Argentino de Polo (p141) Hosts some of the most important events in the polo calendar.

Best Activities

Buenos Aires Fútbol Amigos (p145) Join locals in friendly five-aside soccer games for men and women.

Biking Buenos Aires (p207) American and Argentine guides lead themed bike tours throughout the city.

Parque Norte (p126) Water park with huge shallow pools and a waterslide.

Buena Onda Yoga (p145) Yoga classes taught in English.

Professional tango danc

Tango

Once a furtive dance relegated to the red-light brothels of early-1900s Buenos Aires, tango has experienced great highs and lows throughout its lifespan. These days, however, the sensual dance is back with a vengeance. Everyone from Seattle to Shanghai is slinking their way down the parquet floor, trying to master those elusive dance steps and the rhythm that make it so damn hard to perfect.

ing a bandoneón

NEED TO KNOW

➡ For discount tickets, show and venue descriptions, and some reviews, check out www.tangotix.com.

➡ *Milongas* either start in the afternoon and run until 11pm or start at around midnight and run until the early-morning light (arrive late for the best action). They're affordable, and classes are often offered beforehand.

➡ For a unique outdoor experience, head to the bandstand at the Barrancas de Belgrano, where the casual *milonga* La Glorieta (p126) takes place on Saturday and Sunday evenings around 7pm (and possibly other evenings). Tango classes are also given.

➡ Tango Trips (p209) offers *milonga* tours where you can see locals dance – and have a go yourself.

Origins

In the words of its poet laureate Discépolo, the 'tango is a sad thought you can dance to'. Though the exact origins can't be pinpointed, the dance is believed to have started in Buenos Aires in the 1880s. Legions of European immigrants, mostly lower-class men, arrived here to seek their fortune. They settled on the capital's fringes, such as La Boca and Barracas, but missing their motherlands and the women they left behind, sought out cafes and bordellos to ease the loneliness. Here (so the myth goes), these immigrant men danced with each other while they waited for their paramours to become available – women were scarce back then!

The perceived vulgarity of the dance that mainly belonged to the poor southern barrios was deeply frowned upon by the reigning *porteño* (residents of Buenos Aires) elites of the plush northern suburbs, but it did manage to influence some brash young members of the upper classes. These rebel jet setters, known as *niños bien*, took the novelty to Paris and created a craze – a dance that became an acceptable outlet for human desires, expressed on the dance floors of elegant cabarets. The trend spread around Europe and even to the USA, and 1913 was considered by some as 'the year of the tango'. When the evolved dance, now refined and famous, returned to Buenos Aires, it finally earned the respectability it deserved. And so the golden years of tango began.

In 1955, however, Argentina became a military state intolerant of artistic or 'nationalistic' activities – including the tango, which had been highly popular with the people. Some tango songs were banned, and the dance was forced underground due to curfews and a limit on group meetings. The dance didn't resurface until 1983, when the junta fell – and once it was back in the open again, it underwent a renaissance. After being constrained by the rigors of military rule, Argentines suddenly wanted to experience new life, be creative and move. The tango became popular once again – and remains so to this day.

Tango for Export: the Shows

If there's one thing Buenos Aires isn't short of it's tango shows. The best known are the expensive, tourist-oriented spectacles that are very entertaining and awe-inspiring, and showcase amazing feats of grace and athleticism. However, they are highly glamorized and not what purists consider 'authentic' tango.

The theatrical shows usually include various tango couples, an orchestra, a couple of singers and possibly some folkloric musicians. They last about 1½ hours and come with a dinner option – the food is usually good. VIP options mean a much higher price tag for better views, meal choices and refreshments. Nearly all of them require reservations; some offer modest online discounts and pick-up from your hotel. (Many hotels will book shows for you – which is fine, since

MICHAEL TAYLOR / GETTY IMAGES ©

Above: People dancing tango in a plaza

Left: A street performer singing tango music

CLASSES

Tango classes are available just about everywhere, from youth hostels to general dance academies to cultural centers to nearly all *milongas* (dance halls). Even a few cafes and tango shows offer them.

There are also several tango schools in town, including DNI Tango (p154).

Private teachers are also ubiquitous; there are so many good ones that it's best to ask someone you trust for a recommendation.

sometimes the price is similar to what you'd pay at the venue anyway.)

More modest shows cost far less; some are even free but require you to order a meal or drink at the restaurant. If you don't mind eating there this is a decent deal. For free (or rather, donation) tango, head to San Telmo on a Sunday afternoon – or sometimes other days. Dancers do their thing in the middle of Plaza Dorrego, though you have to stake out a spot early to snag a good view. Another sure bet is weekends on El Caminito in La Boca; some restaurants have couple dancing for customers. Many *milongas* (dance halls) also have good, affordable shows.

One thing to note: nearly all tango shows are touristy by nature. They've been sensationalized to make them more exciting for observers. 'Authentic' tango (which happens at *milongas*) is a very subtle art, primarily done for the pleasure of the dancers. It's not something to be observed so much as experienced, and not particularly interesting for casual spectators. Going to a *milonga* just to watch isn't all that cool, either: folks are there to dance. So feel free to see a more flashy tango show and enjoy those spectacular high kicks – be wowed like the rest of the crowd.

If you like listening to live tango music, head to Centro Cultural Torquato Tasso (p94). It's one of BA's best live-music venues, so don't expect any dancing.

The Real Tango: Milongas

Tango's popularity is booming at both amateur and professional levels, and among all ages and classes. And *milongas* are the dance events where people strut their stuff. The atmosphere at these venues can be modern or historical, casual or traditional. Most have tango DJs that determine musical selections, but a few utilize live orchestras. The dance floor is surrounded by many tables and chairs, and there's often a bar to the side where you can keep hydrated.

At a proper, established *milonga,* choosing an adequate partner involves many levels of hidden codes, rules and signals that dancers must follow. After all, no serious *bailarina* (female dancer; the male equivalent is a *bailarín*) wants to be caught out dancing with someone stepping on her toes (and expensive tango heels). In fact, some men considering asking an unknown woman to dance will do so only after the second song, to avoid being stuck for the three to five songs that make a session. These sessions (known as *tandas*) alternate between tango, *vals* (the Argentine version of the waltz) and *milonga*; they're followed by a *cortina* (a short break when non-tango music is played). It's considered polite to dance an entire *tanda* with any partner, so if you are given a curt *gracias* after just one song, consider that partner unavailable for the rest of the night.

Not easy to describe, tango needs to be seen and experienced for its full effect. The upper bodies are traditionally held upright and close, with faces almost touching. The man's hand is pressed against the woman's back, guiding her, with his other hand and one of hers held together and out. The lower body does most of the work. The woman swivels her hips, her legs alternating in short or wide sweeps and quick kicks, sometimes

RESOURCES

➡ **Hoy Milonga** (www.hoy-milonga.com) is a useful webite listing the day's *milonga* schedule.

➡ For a very practical book on tango in BA, check out Sally Blake's *Happy Tango: Sallycat's Guide to Dancing in Buenos Aires* (2nd edition). It has great information on *milongas* – how to dress for them and act in them and whom you can expect to see – plus much more.

➡ There are, of course, many tango clothing and shoe stores in BA – the best shoe shop is Comme Il Faut (p119).

➡ Finally, if you're in town in mid- to late August, don't miss the tango festival (p21).

between the man's legs. The man guides, a complicated job since he must flow with the music, direct the woman, meld with her steps and avoid other dancers, all at once. He'll add his own fancy pivoting moves, and together the couple flows in communion with the music. Pauses and abrupt directional changes punctuate the dance. It's a serious business that takes a good amount of concentration, so while dancing the pair often wear hard expressions. Smiling and chatting are reserved for the breaks between songs.

Your position in the area surrounding the dance floor can be critical. At some of the older *milongas*, the more established dancers have reserved tables. Ideally, you want to sit where you have easy access to the floor and to other dancers' line of sight. You may notice couples sitting further back (they often dance just with each other), while singles sit right at the front. If a man comes into the room with a woman at his side, she is considered 'his' for the night. For couples to dance with others, they either enter the room separately, or the man signals his intent by asking another woman to the floor. Then 'his' woman becomes open for asking.

The signal to dance, known as *cabeceo,* involves a quick tilt of the head, eye contact and uplifted eyebrows. This can happen from way across the room. The woman to whom the *cabeceo* is directed either nods yes and smiles or pretends not to have noticed (a rejection). If she says yes the man gets up and escorts her to the floor. A hint: if you're at a *milonga* and don't want to dance with anyone, don't look around too much – you could be breaking some hearts.

So why is it that tango becomes so addictive for some, like an insidious drug? Experienced dancers will tell you this: the adrenaline rush you get from an excellent performance is like a successful conquest. Some days it lifts you up to exhilarating heights and other days it can bring you crashing down. You fall for the passion and beauty of the tango's movements, trying to attain a physical perfection that can never be fully realized. The best you can do is to make the journey as graceful and passionate as possible.

Tango Music

Small musical ensembles that accompanied early tango dances were influenced by polka, habanera, Spanish and Italian melodies, plus African *candombe* drums. The *bandoneón,* a type of small accordion, was

Couples taking tango lessons

brought into these sessions and has since become tango's signature instrument. The tango song was permeated with nostalgia for a disappearing way of life; it summarized the new urban experience for the immigrants. Themes ranged from profound feelings about changing neighborhoods to the figure of the mother, male friendship and betrayal by women. The lyrics, sometimes raunchy and sometimes sad, were sung in the street argot known as *lunfardo*.

No other musician has influenced tango like Carlos Gardel (see box, p150), the legendary singer who epitomized the soul of the genre. He achieved stardom during tango's golden age, then became a cultural icon when his life was cut short by a plane crash at the height of his popularity. Over the years, other figures including Osvaldo Pugliese, Susana Rinaldi and Eladia Blázquez have also given life to the tango song. It was Ástor Piazzolla, however, who completely revolutionized the music with his *nuevo tango*, which introduced jazz and classical-music currents into traditional songs – and ruffled some feathers along the way.

Today, a clutch of new arrivals is keeping tango music alive and well, and in the spotlight. The most popular is the 12-musician cooperative **Orquesta Típica Fernández Fierro** (www.fernandezfierro.com), with its charismatic singer Walter Chino Laborde and several fantastic albums boasting new arrangements of traditional tangos. An award-winning documentary was made about them by Argentine-born, Brooklyn-based director Nicolas Entel.

Two other young orchestras to watch out for are Orquesta Típica Imperial, which sometimes plays at *milongas* around town (check its Facebook page), and El Afronte, which plays at Maldita Milonga (p94) in San Telmo.

Neo Tango

Like the rest of the music scene in Buenos Aires, a newer tango has evolved that's a hybrid of sounds and styles – making tango cool again with a younger audience. Musicians have been sampling and remixing classic tango songs, adding dance beats, breaks, scratches and synth lines, and committing other delightful heresies. This edgy genre has been called by many names: fusion tango, electrotango, tango electronica or neo-tango.

JUPITERIMAGES / GETTY IMAGES ©

SOLANGE ZANGIACOMO / GETTY IMAGES ©

Top: A couple dancing tango

Middle: Souvenirs displaying tango dancers and El Caminito

Bottom: A tango show

VBMC327 / BUDGET TRAVEL ©

ÁSTOR PIAZZOLLA

Gardel may have brought tango to the world, but it was El Gran Ástor (the Great Ástor), as Argentines like to call Ástor Piazzolla (1921–92), who pushed its limits. The great Argentine composer and *bandoneón* (small accordian) virtuoso, who played in the leading Aníbal Troilo orchestra in the late 1930s and early 1940s, was the greatest innovator of tango. He revolutionized traditional tango by infusing it with elements of jazz and classical music such as counterpoints, fugues and various harmonies.

This new style, known as *nuevo tango*, became an international hit in Europe (Piazzolla lived on and off in Italy and France) and North America (he spent his early years and a couple of later stints in New York). In his native land, however, it encountered considerable resistance; a saying even stated 'in Argentina everything may change – except the tango'. It took years for Piazzolla's controversial new style to be accepted, and he even received death threats for his break with tradition.

Piazzolla was an incredibly prolific composer; it's estimated that his output includes some 1000 pieces. These include soundtracks for about 40 films; an opera that he wrote with poet Horacio Ferrer, *María de Buenos Aires*; and compositions based on texts and poems by Jorge Luis Borges.

Piazzolla's legacy lives on. Some of the greatest contemporary musicians, such as Yo-Yo Ma, have recorded albums dedicated to El Gran Ástor (such as the 1999 *Soul of the Tango – The Music of Ástor Piazzolla*). The new wave of electronic tango often samples his music and the 2003 album *Astor Piazzolla Remixed* features his songs remixed with dance beats and added vocals, all done by an international cast of DJs and producers.

Paris-based Gotan Project (a Franco-Suizo-Argentine trio) was the first to popularize this style, with its debut album *La Revancha del Tango,* which throws into the mix samples from speeches by Che Guevara and Eva Perón and remixes by the likes of Austrian beatmeister Peter Kruder. Its follow-up albums don't break the mold like the first but are still great if you like the Gotan sound.

The best of the genre's albums so far is likely *Bajofondo Tango Club,* by the Grammy-winning collective Bajofondo. It's spearheaded by Argentine producer Gustavo Santaolalla, who won two best-original-score Oscars for *Brokeback Mountain* and *Babel;* he also scored the films *Amores Perros* and *21 Grams,* and has produced albums by such prominent artists as Café Tacuba and Kronos Quartet. Praised as more Argentine than Gotan Project (whose trio is composed of only one Argentine), its first album has subtle performances by a variety of *bandoneónistas* within a hypnotic framework of lounge, house and trip-hop. Its third album, *Mar Dulce,* is a catchy creation that throws more folk and rock into the mix and has a strong international cast of singers, such as Spanish hip-hop star Mala Rodríguez and the Canadian-Portuguese Nelly Furtado.

Another neo-tango collective to make an international name for itself is Tanghetto, with two Latin Grammy nominations. This six-member group mixes elements of rock, jazz, flamenco and *candombe* (a drum-based musical style of Uruguay).

Lonely Planet's Top Choices

Maldita Milonga (p94) Tango classes, dancing demonstrations and live orchestras at this friendly *milonga*.

Café de los Angelitos (p83) Well-constructed, imaginative show with great visual appeal.

Feria de San Telmo (p88) Best for its casual ambience and price – a few coins!

Salon Canning (p141) Traditional, very popular and well-located *milonga*.

Best Fancy Shows

Café de los Angelitos (p83) Well choreographed, with impressive costumes and props.

Rojo Tango (p75) Very intimate, cabaret-style show that's supremely sexy.

El Viejo Almacén (p94) Great athleticism, small venue and great folkloric segment.

La Ventana (p94) Good overall show with comedic gaucho swinging *boleadoras* (hunting weights).

Best Less-Fancy Shows

Centro Cultural Borges (p66) Good-value tango shows in the city center.

Feria de San Telmo (p88) It's street tango at San Telmo's Sunday market – hustle for a good view!

Café Tortoni (p65) Decent basement show in BA's oldest, most traditional cafe.

Best Milongas

Maldita Milonga (p94) The tango orchestra El Alfronte plays at this friendly *milonga*.

Salon Canning (p141) Famous, popular and stylish *milonga* in Palermo, with good music.

La Catedral (p153) Casual, bohemian warehouse space that attracts hip young dancers.

La Glorieta (p126) Open-air *milonga* held in a park bandstand.

La Marshall (p84) Gay-friendly *milonga* where everyone is welcome – and where role reversals are OK.

Explore Buenos Aires

BUENOS AIRES' TOP SIGHTS

Neighborhoods at a Glance

❶ The Center p56

Buenos Aires' Center (geographically on the edge of the city and not in the middle) is where endless lines of business suits move hastily along the narrow streets in the shadow of skyscrapers and old European buildings. Stretching from Retiro to San Telmo, this downtown area is the heart and brains of the city, and is made up of the sub-neighborhoods of the Microcentro and Montserrat.

❷ Puerto Madero p70

BA's newest and shiniest barrio is Puerto Madero, home to lofty skyscrapers and regenerated brick warehouses that have been converted into some of the city's most exclusive lofts, offices, hotels and restaurants. Cobbled waterside promenades make walking a pleasure for pedestrians, the open green spaces provide room to breathe and there are plenty of upscale restaurants and cafes to check out.

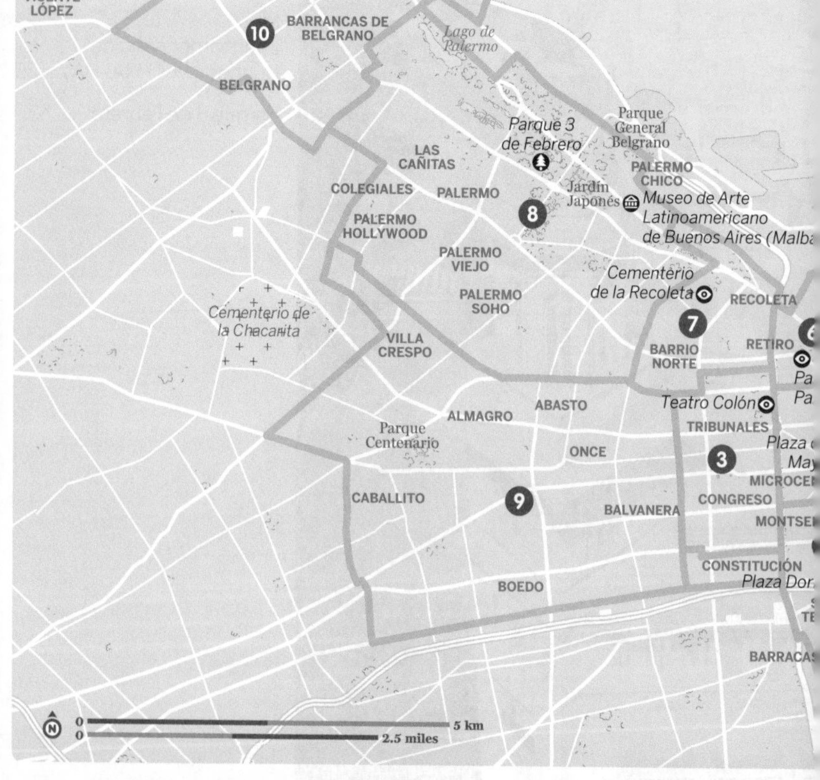

❸ Congreso & Tribunales p76

Congreso is an interesting mix of old-time cinemas, theaters and bustling commerce. It's the city's top entertainment district, home to the Teatro Colón and the bright lights of Av Corrientes, BA's Broadway. On Av de Mayo the buildings still hold a European aura, but this area has more faded-glory atmosphere and grittiness than in the Center.

❹ San Telmo p85

San Telmo is one of BA's most attractive neighborhoods, with narrow cobbled streets and low-story colonial houses. This is where some of the first homes were built in the early years of the colony and where tango music was born. Take a walk around; history oozes from every corner of this barrio.

❺ La Boca p98

Blue-collar and raffish to the core, La Boca is very much a locals' neighborhood. Its colorful shanties are often portrayed as a symbol of Buenos Aires, while El Caminito is the barrio's most famous street, full of art vendors, buskers and tango dancers.

❻ Retiro p104

Sandwiched between the Center and Recoleta, Retiro was once the most exclusive neighborhood in Buenos Aires. Vast mansions dating from BA's early-20th-century heyday along with art-deco apartments and other landmark buildings characterize this area.

❼ Recoleta & Barrio Norte p111

Recoleta is where the rich live in luxury apartments and mansions while spending their free time sipping coffee at elegant cafes and shopping in expensive boutiques. Full of lush parks, grand monuments, art galleries, French architecture and wide avenues, Recoleta is also famous for its cemetery.

❽ Palermo p127

Palermo's large, grassy parks are popular destinations on weekends, when families fill the shady lanes, cycle the bike paths and paddle on the peaceful lakes. The subneighborhood of Palermo Viejo (itself subdivided into Soho and Hollywood) is home to dozens of restaurants, bars, nightclubs and shops and boutique hotels.

❾ South of Palermo p148

The neighborhoods south of Palermo are part of the 'real' Buenos Aires. Villa Crespo is increasingly hip, benefiting from its proximity to Palermo; Almagro is full of alternative theaters, music venues and local restaurants and bars; Abasto and Once are cultural melting pots and busy commercial districts; and Boedo has bohemian flavor and some very traditional cafes.

❿ Belgrano, Nuñez & the Costanera Norte p122

Belgrano and Nuñez are home to a number of worthwhile museums, parks and plazas, as well as a pleasant weekend market. The Costanera Norte on the river's edge provides open spaces where you can walk next to the water as well as a number of attractions – including a kitschy religious theme park and a water park – that may appeal to families.

The Center

MICROCENTRO | MONTSERRAT

Neighborhood Top Five

❶ **Plaza de Mayo** (p58) Hanging out at BA's historic heart surrounded by some of the city's most important buildings, including the cathedral, the Cabildo, the Museo Casa Rosada and – last but not least – Casa Rosada, where Argentina's president's office is located.

❷ **Centro Cultural Kirchner** (p59) Catching a concert at this magnificent new cultural center housed in the city's former central post office.

❸ **Manzana de las Luces** (p62) Taking a tour of this historic center of culture and higher learning during the day and returning on Friday night to dance tango at the atmospheric *milonga*.

❹ **Galerías Pacífico** (p61) Shopping at a beautiful shopping mall with a gorgeous painted ceiling.

❺ **Centro Cultural Borges** (p66) Watching a tango show (that won't break the bank) and seeing the latest exhibitions.

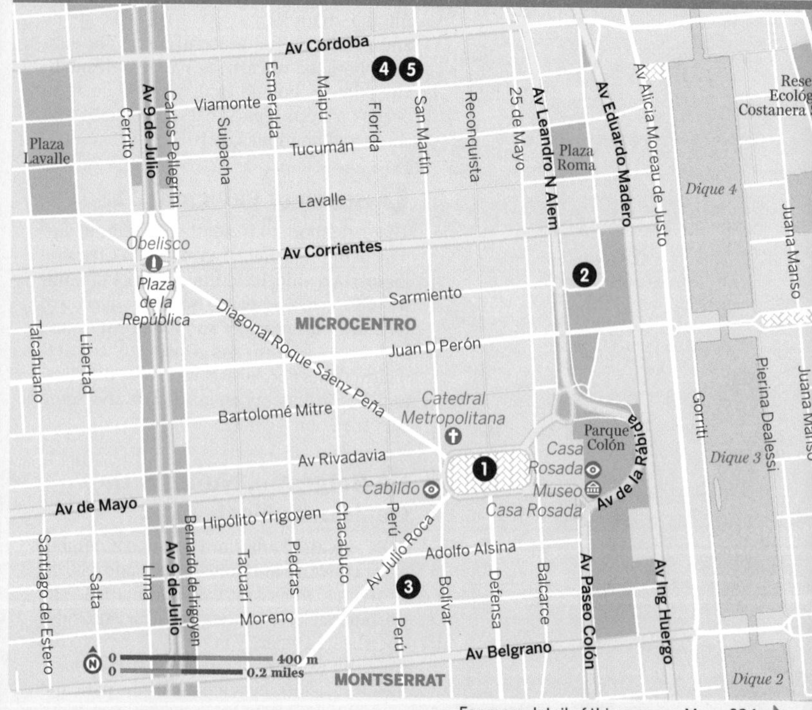

For more detail of this area see Map p234

Explore: The Center

During the day, the Center is a heaving mass of humanity moving hastily along narrow streets. The 2015 pedestrianization of 80 blocks of the neighborhood has helped, though a substantial amount of 'local traffic' continues to use the roads here, so watch out behind you. Come evening, the neighborhood can feel deserted.

Stretching from Retiro to San Telmo (and flanked by Congreso and Puerto Madero), this area is the heart and brain of the city. It's made up of the Microcentro and Montserrat sub-neighborhoods.

Plaza de Mayo is a good place to start. Here you'll see the Casa Rosada presidential palace, with the Museo Casa Rosada right behind it. The Catedral Metropolitana is nearby – stop by for a Pope Francis souvenir – and the Cabildo offers great vie ws of the square. If you want to see the Madres de la Plaza de Mayo, time your visit for Thursday afternoon.

From here you can head south just one block, crossing over into Montserrat, and visit the Manzana de las Luces, a city block full of historic buildings. There are also a couple of small but interesting museums to visit around here. Further south a few more blocks is San Telmo.

If you're going north, walk along Calle San Martín, where there are a number of interesting little museums. Head east via Calle Sarmiento to reach the Centro Cultural Kirchner. Ideally you'll have secured tickets to a concert here, but even if you haven't, be sure to take a look inside this impressive cultural center.

Local Life

➡ **Hangouts** Join office workers for lunch on the hoof at 180 Burger Bar (p64) or Latino Sandwich (p63).

➡ **The Square** Enjoy Plaza de Mayo as the locals do by sitting on a bench and chatting to the people around you. Topics of conversation might include tutting at the traffic chaos caused by the latest roadblock or complaining about the price of meat.

➡ **Shopping** Mingle among the throngs of street vendors, business people, buskers and hustlers on Calle Florida.

Getting There & Away

➡ **Bus** Take bus 29 from San Telmo; 29, 64 and 152 from La Boca; 59 from Recoleta; 29, 59, 64 and 152 from Palermo's Plaza Italia.

➡ **Subte** Líneas A (Plaza de Mayo station), D (Catedral station) and E (Bolívar station) all terminate at Plaza de Mayo. Línea C stops Lavalle and Diaganol Norte are also in this neighborhood.

Lonely Planet's Top Tip

As there are so many businesspeople in the Center, many restaurants offer *menús ejecutivos* – or lunch specials – to attract this valuable clientele. These set lunches are offered weekdays and usually consist of a main course with dessert and a drink, all for a reasonable fixed price. It's a good way to try out otherwise pricey restaurants.

Best Museums

➡ Museo Casa Rosada (p59)

➡ Cabildo (p61)

➡ Museo Histórico y Numismático José Evaristo Uriburu (p61)

➡ Museo Etnográfico Juan B Ambrosetti (p62)

For reviews, see p59. ➡

Best Places to Drink

➡ La Puerto Rico (p65)

➡ La Cigale (p66)

➡ Café Tortoni (p65)

For reviews, see p65. ➡

Best Places to Shop

➡ Galerías Pacífico (p61)

➡ Arte y Esperanza (p67)

➡ El Coleccionista (p67)

For reviews, see p67. ➡

TOP SIGHT
PLAZA DE MAYO

Plaza de Mayo is the political, social and symbolic center of Buenos Aires. Surrounded by the Casa Rosada, the Cabildo and the city's main cathedral, the elegant, grassy plaza has borne witness to many of the key events of Argentina's turbulent recent history. It's where Argentines continue to gather for political rallies, peaceful and violent protests, and jubilant celebrations.

The City's Historic Heart

When Juan de Garay refounded Buenos Aires in 1580, he laid out the large Plaza del Fuerte (Fortress Plaza) in accordance with Spanish law. Later called the Plaza del Mercado (Market Plaza), then the Plaza de la Victoria (after victories over British invaders in 1806 and 1807), the plaza acquired its present name of Plaza de Mayo after the date Buenos Aires declared independence from Spain: May 25, 1810.

At the center of the plaza is the **Pirámide de Mayo**, a white obelisk built to mark the first anniversary of independence from Spain. Looming on the plaza's northern side is the headquarters of Banco de la Nación (Map p234; 1939), the work of famed architect Alejandro Bustillo. Most other public buildings in this area belong to the late 19th century, when the Av de Mayo first connected the Casa Rosada (p63) with the **Plaza del Congreso**, obliterating much of the historic and dignified Cabildo (p61) in the process.

Plaza de Mayo has long been the preferred site of many civil protests; note the unsightly barricades separating the plaza in two, meant to discourage large numbers of *piqueteros* (picketers) from congregating. But these barricades haven't prevented the **Madres de la Plaza de Mayo** – the mothers of the 'disappeared', those abducted by the state during the military dictatorship of 1976 and 1983 – from gathering in the plaza every Thursday afternoon at 3:30pm since 1977, and circling the pyramid holding photographs of their missing children. To this day they march on as a reminder of the past – and for other social justice causes.

DON'T MISS

- Pirámide de Mayo
- Statue of General Belgrano
- Fountains

PRACTICALITIES

- Map p234, D5
- cnr Av de Mayo & San Martín
- S Línea A Plaza de Mayo

SIGHTS

Since the Center is the very place where Buenos Aires was founded by Juan de Garay and his men in 1580, this is where you'll find the city's most important historical sights. Plaza de Mayo has been at the center of political life since those early days, when a fort sat where Casa Rosada is today; the Cabildo and cathedral were also established on the same spots as they are now. As well as historical buildings, there are some excellent museums and cultural centers to visit in this part of the city.

Microcentro

PLAZA DE MAYO — PLAZA

See p58.

CASA ROSADA — NOTABLE BUILDING

See p63.

★CENTRO CULTURAL KIRCHNER — CULTURAL CENTER

Map p234 (☎0800-333-9300; www.culturalkirchner.gob.ar; Sarmiento 151; ⌚noon-8pm Tue-Sun; Ⓢ Línea B Alem) FREE It was Néstor Kirchner who, in 2005, first proposed turning the abandoned former central post office into a cultural center. He died in 2010 before the project was completed, but the breathtaking cultural center was named in his honor. Within the vast beaux-arts structure – that stands eight stories tall and takes up an entire city block – are multiple art galleries, events spaces and auditoriums. The highlight, however, is the Ballena Azul, a concert hall with world-class acoustics that seats 1800.

The original building, which was modeled on New York City's main post office, took nearly 30 years to complete (in 1928). Restoration for the cultural center began in 2009 and it opened in May 2015. The architects used glass and stainless steel to maintain and add to the beauty of the original structure.

The result is one of BA's grandest buildings, and it's well worth a visit. It's free to enter and there may be exhibitions to see that don't require tickets, but there are a host of activities (such as yoga and dance classes as well as concerts) that are free but ticketed – check the website to see what's on and act quickly if you want to book. Free guided tours of the center are given at 2pm and 3:30pm at weekends with advance online bookings.

MUSEO CASA ROSADA — MUSEUM

Map p234 (☎011-4344-3802; www.casarosada.gob.ar/la-casa-rosada/museo; cnr Av Paseo Colón & Hipólito Yrigoyen; ⌚10am-6pm Wed-Sun; Ⓢ Línea A Plaza de Mayo) FREE Behind the Casa Rosada you'll notice a glass wedge that's the roof of this bright and airy museum, housed within the brick vaults of the old *aduana* (customs house). Head down into the open space, which has over a dozen side rooms, each dedicated to a different era of Argentina's tumultuous political history. There are videos (in Spanish) and a few artifacts to see, along with an impressive restored mural by Mexican artist David Alfaro Siqueiros.

MINISTERIO DE ECONOMÍA — NOTABLE BUILDING

Map p234 (Balcarce 186; Ⓢ Línea A Plaza de Mayo) In June 1955 Argentine naval aircraft strafed Plaza de Mayo in the first step of a military coup, killing more than 300 civilians who were gathered in support of Juan Domingo Perón and forcing the president to flee into exile in Spain. On the northern side of the Ministerio de Economía, an inconspicuous plaque commemorates the attacks (look for the bullet holes to the left of the doors).

CATEDRAL METROPOLITANA — CATHEDRAL

Map p234 (⌚7:30am-6:30pm Mon-Fri, 9am-7pm Sat & Sun, museum 10am-1:30pm Mon-Fri; Ⓢ Línea D Catedral) FREE This cathedral was built on the site of the original colonial church and not finished until 1827. It's a significant religious and architectural landmark, and carved above its triangular facade and neoclassical columns are bas-reliefs of Jacob and Joseph. The spacious interior is equally impressive, with baroque details and an elegant rococo altar. There's a small museum (admission AR$50) dedicated to the cathedral's history inside. For Pope Francis souvenirs, visit the small gift shop near the entrance.

The cathedral is also a national historical site that contains the mausoleum of **General José de San Martín**, Argentina's most revered hero, who led the country to independence in 1816. In the chaos that followed, San Martín chose exile in France, never again returning to Argentina; his remains were

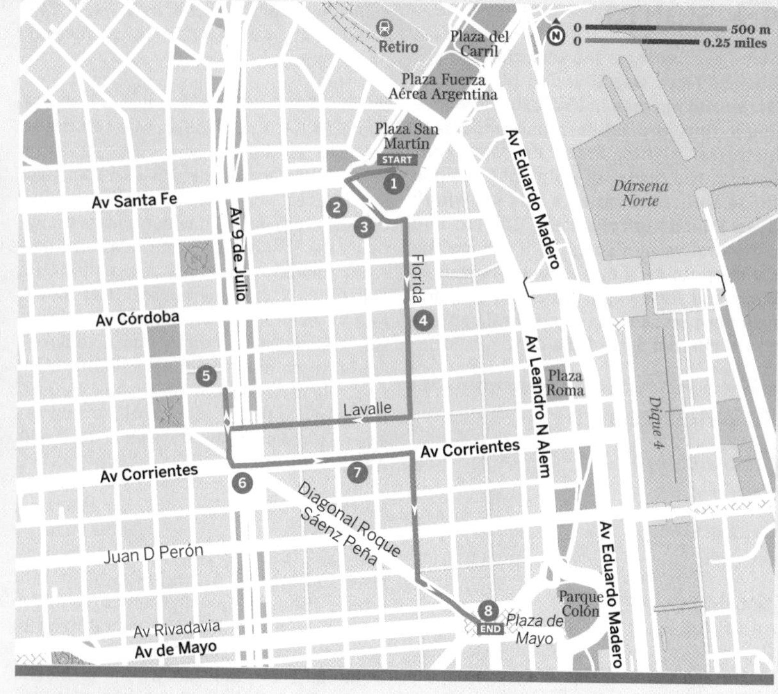

Neighborhood Walk
Through the Heart of the City

START PLAZA SAN MARTÍN
END PLAZA DE MAYO
LENGTH 3KM; THREE HOURS

Start at leafy 1 **Plaza San Martín** (p107), the green heart of Retiro and a haven for loungers on a sunny day. It was designed by French landscape architect Carlos Thays; notice the statue of a proud José de San Martín astride his horse at the western tip of the plaza.

Cross Av Santa Fe to the striking 2 **Palacio Paz** (p106) mansion. Time it right so you can catch an English-speaking tour (otherwise they're in Spanish), and take in the grandeur of a long-ago era.

On the same block is the 3 **Museo de Armas** (p108), an astounding collection of guns, swords and cannon. Weapons buffs will definitely want to spend some time here.

Find your way down to pedestrian Calle Florida and walk south to the elegant 4 **Galerías Pacífico** (p61) shopping mall, one of the capital's most beautiful. Even if you don't like to shop, you should take a peek inside at the ceiling murals.

Now head west a few blocks on pedestrian Lavalle and cross Av 9 de Julio, claimed by many to be the world's widest street. Your destination is the impressive 5 **Teatro Colón** (p78), BA's opera house and a major source of pride for *porteños*.

The 67m 6 **Obelisco** (p79) monument is one of the city's most reconginzable landmarks. Erected in 1936 on the 400th anniversary of the first Spanish settlement on the Río de la Plata, it's the place to honk your car's horn when the Argentinian national soccer team wins a major victory.

Back in the day 7 **Avenida Corrientes** was the main theater district in BA, and even today some of the city's largest theaters are still located here. It's also known for its many bookstores (though the books sold here are mostly in Spanish).

Hit Florida again and make your way south to Diagonal Roque Sáenz Peña. You'll end up at historic 8 **Plaza de Mayo** (p58), where you'll want to linger and take in the atmosphere.

brought to Buenos Aires in 1880, 30 years after his death. Outside the cathedral you'll see a flame keeping his spirit alive.

CABILDO MUSEUM

Map p234 (☎011-4342-6729; https://cabildonacional.cultura.gob.ar; Bolívar 65; AR$15, Tue free; ⏲10:30am-5pm Tue, Wed & Fri, to 8pm Thu, to 6pm Sat & Sun; Ⓢ Línea A Perú) This mid-18th-century town hall building is now an interesting museum largely dedicated to the revolution of May 1810, when Argentina declared independence. Exhibits cover the history of the Cabildo during colonial times (when it was also a prison) through to the British invasions of 1806 and 1807 and independence three years later. Guided tours in English are given on Saturday and Sunday at 11:30am from October to March.

There are good views of Plaza de Mayo from the 2nd-floor balcony.

GALERÍAS PACÍFICO NOTABLE BUILDING

Map p234 (☎011-5555-5110; www.galeriaspacifico.com.ar; cnr Florida & Av Córdoba; ⏲10am-9pm, food court to 10pm, tours 11am daily & 4:30pm Wed-Sun; Ⓢ Línea B Florída) Covering an entire city block, this beautiful building inspired by Le Bon Marché in Paris has fulfilled the commercial purpose that its designers envisioned when they constructed it in 1889. Galerías Pacífico is now a shopping center – dotted with lovely fairy lights at night – and boasts upscale stores along with a large food court. Free tours are given in English and Spanish; inquire at the information kiosk. The excellent Centro Cultural Borges (p66) takes up the top floor.

When you step inside, check out the ceiling. In 1945 the completion of a central cupola made space for a dozen paintings by muralists Antonio Berni, Juan Carlos Castagnino, Manuel Colmeiro, Lino Enea Spilimbergo and Demetrio Urruchúa. All were adherents of the *nuevo realismo* (new realism) school, heirs of an earlier social-activist tendency in Argentine art. For many years the building was semi-abandoned, but a joint Argentine-Mexican team repaired and restored the murals in 1992.

MUSEO HISTÓRICO Y NUMISMÁTICO JOSÉ EVARISTO URIBURU MUSEUM

Map p234 (Central Bank Museum; ☎011-4348-3882; www.bcra.gov.ar; San Martín 216; ⏲10am-3pm Mon-Fri; Ⓢ Línea D Catedral) Housed in the former Buenos Aires Stock Exchange (1862), this interesting little museum tells the story of Argentina through its money. Starting with examples of Pre-Columbian currency (cocoa seeds and leaves), there are examples of colonial coins, replicas of the first coins of the independent republic and other historic notes, including an AR$1,000,000 bill issued during the hyperinflation of 1981, the provincial bonds issued after the 2001 crisis and the appearance of Eva Perón on the AR$100 in 2012.

IGLESIA SANTA CATALINA CHURCH

Map p234 (☎011-5238-6040; www.santacatalina.org.ar; San Martín 705; ⏲8am-8pm Mon-Fri, guided tours 3pm Mon; Ⓢ Línea B Florida) FREE Santa Catalina was founded in 1745, when it became Buenos Aires' first convent. In 1807 British troops invaded the city for the second time and took shelter in the convent for two days; despite damaging the property they didn't hurt the nuns. Today, Santa Catalina is a church, and a peek inside reveals beautiful gilded works and a baroque altarpiece created by Isidro Lorea, a Spanish carver.

MUSEO MUNDIAL DEL TANGO MUSEUM

Map p234 (☎011-4345-6967; Av de Mayo 833, 1st fl; AR$20; ⏲2:30-7:30pm Mon-Fri; Ⓢ Línea A Piedras) Located below the Academia Nacional del Tango is this small museum. Just a couple of large rooms are filled with tango memorabilia, from old records and photos to historical literature and posters. Tango shoes are also featured, but the highlight has to be one of Carlos Gardel's famous fedora hats. Another entrance is at Rivadavia 830.

MUSEO MITRE MUSEUM

Map p234 (☎011-4394-8240; www.museomitre.gob.ar; San Martín 336; AR$20; ⏲1-5:30pm Mon-Fri; Ⓢ Línea B Florida) This museum is located in the colonial house where Bartolomé Mitre – Argentina's first legitimate president elected under the constitution of 1853 – resided with his family from 1859 to 1906. Mitre's term ran from 1862 to 1868, and he spent much of it leading the country's armies against Paraguay. Two courtyards, salons, an office, a billiards room and Mitre's old bedroom are part of this complex. Since part of the museum is open air, it sometimes closes when it rains.

MUSEO DE LA POLICÍA FEDERAL MUSEUM

Map p234 (☎011-4394-6857; San Martín 353, 7th fl; ⏲2-7pm Tue-Fri; Ⓢ Línea B Florida) FREE This quirky and extensive police museum displays a whole slew of uniforms and medals, along with 'illegal activities' exhibits (cockfighting and gambling), drug paraphernalia (including an anal smuggling tube and a rubber arm stuck with a needle) and even a stuffed police dog. The fake Stradivarius violin and counterfeit bills are also entertaining. Look for it in an incongruous high-rise building marked Circulo Policía Federal; there's no sign for the museum.

Montserrat

★MANZANA DE LAS LUCES NOTABLE BUILDING

Map p234 (Block of Enlightenment; ☎011-4342-6973; www.manazadelasluces.org; Perú 222; ⏱10am-8pm Mon-Fri, 2-8pm Sat & Sun; Ⓢ Línea E Bolívar) FREE In colonial times, the Manzana de las Luces was Buenos Aires' most important center of culture and learning and today the block still symbolizes education and enlightenment. Two of the five original buildings remain; Jesuit defensive tunnels were discovered in 1912. Tours (in Spanish; AR$50) are given at 3pm daily and also at 4:30pm and 6pm at weekends, but you can go inside and see the main patio area for free.

The first people to occupy the Manzana de las Luces were the Jesuits, who built several structures including the Procuraduría (1730; administrative headquarters), part of which still survives today. (Unfortunately for the Jesuits, they were later expelled from the premises – and Argentina – in 1767 by the King of Spain.) Along with housing offices, these buildings hosted converted indigenous people from the provinces. Later, during the 19th century, they were home to various museums, legislative offices, schools and universities.

Today, a cultural center on the premises offers workshops and music, film and theater events and a wonderfully atmospheric *milonga* (p66) takes place in here on Friday nights.

MUSEO ETNOGRÁFICO JUAN B AMBROSETTI MUSEUM

Map p234 (☎011-5287-3050; www.museoetnografico.filo.uba.ar; Moreno 350; AR$20; ⏱1-7pm Tue-Fri, 3-7pm Sat & Sun; Ⓢ Línea A Plaza de Mayo) This small but worthwhile anthropological museum was created by Juan B Ambrosetti not only as an institute for research and university training but also as an educational center for the public. On display are archaeological and anthropological collections from the Andean Northwest and Patagonia. Beautiful indigenous costumes are also featured, while an African and Asian room showcases some priceless pieces.

POPE FRANCIS

After Cardinal Jorge Mario Bergoglio, the archbishop of Buenos Aires, was named successor to Pope Benedict XVI in March 2013, he took the name Francis I. Not only was he the first pontiff to bear that moniker (adopted to honor St Francis of Assisi), he was also the first to hail from the Americas and the first to belong to the Jesuit order, which incidentally was expelled from most of South America for 47 years (1767–1814).

It's a fair bet that he's also the first pope to have grown up drinking *mate*, tangoing at *milongas* and ardently supporting the San Lorenzo *fútbol* club.

Bergoglio was a humble man who had eschewed the archbishop's palace in Olivos, remaining in his modest apartment and getting around Buenos Aires by bus and the Subte rather than with a car and driver. As Francis I he has continued these habits, emulating his namesake and personal hero, the saint from Assisi who once renounced all worldly possessions including his clothing. This humility, coupled with the very personable humanity Pope Francis displays, has made him an extremely popular pontiff.

Over the past few years, however, some of Pope Francis' declarations have been controversial. He has criticized capitalism, practically supported evolution and highlighted the need to protect the natural environment. He's also noted the importance of women's roles in the church, and while he opposes same-sex marriage, he does believe that gay people should be treated with love and respect. Many Catholics speak of feeling understood by him, and his popularity extends beyond the faithful.

TOP SIGHT
CASA ROSADA

On the eastern side of Plaza de Mayo stands the Casa Rosada (Pink House), named for its distinctive color. It was from the balcony here that Eva Perón famously addressed the throngs of impassioned supporters packed into Plaza de Mayo. The building houses the Argentine President's offices; the presidential residence is in the suburb of Olivos, north of the center.

One theory goes that the Casa Rosada's pink hue represented President Sarmiento's attempts to make peace during his 1868–74 term (by blending the red of the Federalists with the white of the Unitarians), but the more likely explanation is that it was caused by mixing white paint with bovine blood, a common practice in the late 19th century.

The side of the palace that faces Plaza de Mayo is actually the back of the building. It was from these balconies that Juan and Eva Perón preached to throngs of impassioned Argentines, and a triumphant Diego Maradona hoisted the 1986 World Cup. On December 20, 2001, President Fernando de la Rúa fled the Casa Rosada's roof by helicopter as the economy collapsed. Free hour-long guided tours are given at weekends and must be booked online in advance; bring ID.

DON'T MISS

- The Evita balcony
- The busts of former presidents (including Néstor Kirchner)
- Eva Perón's former desk
- The 1910 presidential elevator

PRACTICALITIES

- Map p234, E5
- ☎011-4344-3804
- https://visitas.casarosada.gob.ar
- Plaza de Mayo
- admission free
- ⏲tours in Spanish 10am-6pm Sat & Sun, in English 2:30pm Sat & Sun
- S Línea A Plaza de Mayo

FARMACIA DE LA ESTRELLA NOTABLE BUILDING

Map p234 (☎011-4343-4040; http://farmaciadelaestrella.com/; Defensa 201; ⏲8am-8pm Mon-Fri, to 1pm Sat; S Línea E Bolívar) The Farmacia de la Estrella (1835) is a functioning homeopathic pharmacy with gorgeous woodwork and elaborate late-19th-century ceiling murals depicting health-oriented themes.

LA LIBRERÍA DE AVILA NOTABLE BUILDING

Map p234 (http://libreriaavila.mercadoshops.com.ar/; Adolfo Alsina 500; ⏲8:30am-8pm Mon-Fri, 10am-3pm Sat; S Línea E Bolívar) The city's oldest bookstore – there has been a bookshop on this historic corner site since 1785 – has a number of rare and antique texts as well as recent publications. Look for the picture near the entrance depicting the store as it looked in colonial times.

IGLESIA SAN IGNACIO DE LOYOLA CHURCH

Map p234 (www.sanignaciodeloyola.org.ar; Bolívar 225; ⏲8am-8pm Mon-Wed & Fri, to 8:30pm Thu, 9am-1pm & 4-8pm Sat & Sun; S Línea E Bolívar)  The city's oldest church, the Iglesia San Ignacio de Loyola (1734), was originally built in adobe in 1661 and has been rebuilt or remodeled several times since.

EATING

You won't find Buenos Aires' best cuisine in the Center, as most restaurants here cater to business power-lunches or quick takeout. Some eateries don't even open for dinner since the working masses beeline home after the day is done; even bars tend to open and close relatively early here. All this doesn't mean you won't find a decent bite to eat, however, and vegetarians especially might find some good choices.

LATINO SANDWICH SANDWICHES $

Map p234 (☎011-4331-0859; www.latinosandwich.com; Tacuari 185; sandwiches AR$65-75; ⏲8am-5pm Mon-Fri; S Línea A Piedras) Some

TAKING IT TO THE STREETS

Along with soccer, tango and meat, Buenos Aires is famous for the propensity of its citizens to take to the streets in protest. Whether the city is booming or in the midst of a depression, unless there's martial law, someone is out on the street demonstrating against something. Plaza de Mayo has long been the focal point of direct action.

The best-known voices of dissent are the Madres de la Plaza de Mayo (the Mothers of Plaza de Mayo). On April 30, 1977, 14 mothers whose children had disappeared under the military dictatorship gathered in the Plaza de Mayo and demanded to know what had happened to their missing children. The military government dismissed them, claiming that their children had simply moved abroad, but the women continued to march in their iconic white handkerchiefs every Thursday. They played an essential, historical role as the first group to openly oppose the military junta and opened the doors for later protests.

Even in 1996, when the economy was booming and the country was a democracy, a number of protests broke out against corruption and the reform of pensions. Senior citizens hurled eggs at government buildings and were chased by trucks mounted with water cannon. The protests after the economic collapse in 2001 were particularly large and vociferous. Thousands of people – in the poorer areas as well as middle-class neighborhoods – spontaneously gathered in public parks in Buenos Aires. To the shouts of '*¡Que se vayan todos!*' (Get rid of them all!), they banged pots and pans – an act known as a *cacerolazo*. Both the economic minister and the president eventually stepped down, and some of the politicians who hadn't fled the country were beaten in the streets.

There are still occasional grievances on Plaza de Mayo, whether it's a protest against the price of beef and tomatoes, or against the closure of a hospital. You can always count on protests being loud, but these days they're usually peaceful.

of the best eateries in BA are holes-in-the-wall – and here's a case in point. This is the downtown place to grab sandwiches such as Argentine *milanesa* (but with rocket and guacamole!), barbecue pork with cheddar cheese, or grilled zucchini and eggplant. There's only one communal table, as they cater to a mostly to-go business clientele.

180 BURGER BAR BURGERS $

Map p234 (☎011-4328-7189; www.facebook.com/180burgerbar/; Suipacha 749; burgers AR$90; ⏰noon-4pm Mon-Fri; Ⓢ Línea C Lavalle) Hankering for a hamburger? Then join the young crowd that will likely be lined up at this small diner. Choose a 'salsa' (mayochimi, tzatziki, barbacoa) and add the cheese option if you wish. Chow down within the confines of concrete walls, clunky furniture and blasting music.

VITA HEALTH FOOD $

Map p234 (☎011-4600-8164; www.vitamarket.com.ar; Hipólito Yrigoyen 583; mains AR$70-95; ⏰8am-8pm Mon-Wed, to 1am Thu & Fri, 10:30am-1am Sat, 11am-7pm Sun; 🌿; Ⓢ Línea E Bolívar) Here's a casual and health-oriented eatery offering tasty vegetarian dishes such as organic seitan pizzas, lentil burgers and vegetable calzones. Various freshly mixed juices are available (with the option of adding a wheatgrass shot) and there are plenty of gourmet salads. Organic coffee is also served. Another branch is in Palermo.

GRANIX VEGETARIAN $

Map p234 (☎011-4343-7546; Florida 165, 1st fl, Galería Güemes; per kilo AR$210; ⏰11am-3:30pm Mon-Fri; 🌿; Ⓢ Línea D Catedral) Stepping into this large, modern vegetarian eatery will make you wonder if *porteños* (residents of Buenos Aires) have had enough steak already. Pick from the many hot appetizers and mains; there's also a great salad bar and plenty of desserts. It's only open for weekday lunches, and located in a shopping mall.

D'ORO ITALIAN $$

Map p234 (☎011-4342-6959; Perú 159; mains AR$190-300; ⏰noon-4pm Mon-Fri; Ⓢ Línea E Bolívar) This popular lunch spot is a serious Italian wine bar and restaurant to rival others in more gastronomically famous neighborhoods. Come for thin, crispy, oven-baked pizzas, mushroom risotto, fettuccine with shellfish and garlic-topped focaccia.

BROCCOLINO
ITALIAN $$

Map p234 (☎011-4322-7754; www.broccolino.com; Esmeralda 776; mains AR$120-280; ⏰noon-11:30pm; ☑; Ⓢ Línea C Lavalle) Pick from over 20 sauces (including squid ink!) for your pasta, with a choice of rigatoni, fusilli, pappardelle and all sorts of stuffed varieties. If you can't decide on your topper, try the delicious Sicilian sauce (spicy red peppers, tomato and garlic) or the pesto with mushrooms and garlic. Portions are large and the bread homemade.

TOMO 1
ARGENTINE $$$

Map p234 (☎011-4326-6695; www.tomo1.com.ar; Carlos Pellegrini 521, Hotel Panamericano; 3-course lunch AR$900, dinner AR$1050, 9-course tasting menu AR$1700; ⏰noon-3pm & 5:30pm-midnight Mon-Fri, 5:30pm-midnight Sat; Ⓢ Línea C Lavalle) At renowned Tomo 1, European-influenced chef Federico Fialayre promotes a blend of Italian and Spanish cooking methods in dishes featuring seasonal produce, homemade pasta and fresh fish. Sample his famed cuisine with a three-course menu; it comes with wine, mineral water, coffee and petits fours.

ALDO'S RESTORAN & VINOTECA
ARGENTINE $$$

Map p234 (☎011-4334-2380; www.aldosvinoteca.com; Moreno 372; mains AR$245-370; ⏰noon-midnight Sun-Thu, to 1am Fri, 7pm-1am Sat; Ⓢ Línea A Plaza de Mayo) This restaurant and wine shop is an upscale eatery serving a small but tasty menu of meat, seafood and pasta dishes, all amid walls lined with wine. What makes this place unique, however, is that the wine is sold at retail prices – thus making it easier to sample (and buy) the nearly 600 labels available.

FURAIBO
JAPANESE $$$

Map p234 (☎011-4334-3440; www.furaiboba.com.ar; Adolfo Alsina 429; mains AR$205-355; ⏰noon-11pm; Ⓢ Línea A Plaza de Mayo) Walk up the staircase of this old building into a calm space meant to resemble a Buddhist temple; on weekend evenings, live instrumentalists set the mood with ambient ceremonial music. The house specialty is homemade ramen noodles with pork. The menu also includes excellent sushi and *katsu* (a type of cutlet), plus unusual sweet treats such as ginger ice cream.

DRINKING & NIGHTLIFE

Many watering holes in the Center are Irish-pub knockoffs that cater to the business crowd on weekdays. Because of this, some might close a bit earlier than in other neighborhoods, but the most popular ones stay packed all night long. The Center also has some of the oldest cafes in town, delightfully atmospheric venues that offer a welcome break while you're wandering around.

LA PUERTO RICO
CAFE

Map p234 (☎011-4331-2215; www.lapuertoriccafe.com.ar; Adolfo Alsina 416; ⏰7am-8pm Mon-Fri, 8am-7pm Sat, noon-7pm Sun; Ⓢ Línea E Bolívar) One of the city's most historic cafes, La Puerto Rico has been going strong since 1887. Located a block south of Plaza de Mayo, the place serves coffee and great pastries, the latter baked on the premises. Pope Francis used to come here for his morning *café con leche* (coffee with milk) and *medialunas* (croissants) when he was Archbishop of Buenos Aires.

CAFÉ TORTONI
CAFE

Map p234 (☎011-4342-4328; www.cafetortoni.com.ar; Av de Mayo 829; Ⓢ Línea A Piedras) BA's oldest and most famous cafe, Tortoni has become so popular with foreigners that the bus loads of tourists detract from its charm. Still, it's practically an obligatory stop for any visitor to town: order a couple of *churros* (fried pastry dough) with your hot chocolate and forget about the inflated prices. There are also nightly tango shows – reserve ahead.

NEW BRIGHTON
BAR

Map p234 (☎011-4322-1515; Sarmiento 645; ⏰8am-close Mon-Sat; Ⓢ Línea C Diagonal Norte) This beautifully restored historical bar feels like the well-kept secret of refined local gentlemen who gather here after work. A doorman welcomes guests while bartenders stir and shake drinks behind a polished-wood bar; during mealtimes, a pianist entertains on the baby grand. Order a classic cocktail and enjoy the tray of elegant finger food that comes with it.

KEEPING YOUR PEÑAS & MAYOS STRAIGHT

Some first-time (or maybe second-time) visitors may get confused with certain similar-sounding street and attraction names. Keep them straight:

25 de Mayo Street that goes north–south from Retiro to Plaza de Mayo (Mayo is Spanish for the month of May).

Avenida de Mayo Large avenue that goes east–west from Plaza del Congreso to Plaza de Mayo.

Plaza de Mayo BA's most important plaza.

Diagonal Roque Sáenz Peña Diagonal street that stretches from Plaza de Mayo to the Obelisco.

Luis Sáenz Peña Street that goes from Plaza del Congreso through Constitución.

Rodríguez Peña Street that goes from Recoleta to Plaza del Congreso.

BAHREIN CLUB

Map p234 (☎011-6225-2731; www.bahreinba.com; Lavalle 345; ⏰Fri & Sat; Ⓢ Línea B Alem) Attracting a good share of BA's tattooed youth, Bahrein is a hugely popular downtown club housed in an old bank (check out the 'vault' in the basement). On the ground floor is the lounge-like Funky Room where resident DJs spin house music and electronica. Downstairs is the Xss discotheque, an impressive sound system and a dance floor for hundreds.

LA CIGALE BAR

Map p234 (☎011-4893-2332; www.facebook.com/lacigalebar; 25 de Mayo 597; ⏰noon-4pm & 6pm-close; Ⓢ Línea B Alem) This upstairs bar-restaurant is popular with office workers during the week, and fusion foods are served for both lunch and dinner. Come on the second Monday of the month for the Buenos Aires Pub Quiz (www.buenosairespubquiz.com). Happy hour is from 6pm to 10pm.

COCOLICHE CLUB

Map p234 (☎011-4342-9485; www.facebook.com/cocolicheclub/; Av Rivadavia 878; ⏰Tue-Sat; Ⓢ Línea A Piedras) An effortlessly cool club, this electronic-music paradise is based in a slightly run-down old mansion. It's the downstairs basement, gritty and nearly always packed, that holds the main stage, a fantastic sound system and a state-of-the-art light show. Breakbeat, drum and bass, reggaeton and electronic cumbia entertain; when you need a break, head to the 2nd-floor chill-out room.

LONDON CITY CAFE

Map p234 (☎011-4342-9057; Av de Mayo 599; ⏰6am-2am; Ⓢ Línea A Perú) This classy cafe has been serving java enthusiasts for over 50 years, and claims to have been the spot where Julio Cortázar wrote his first novel. Your hardest work here, however, will most likely be choosing which pastry to try with your cup of coffee.

☆ ENTERTAINMENT

★CENTRO CULTURAL BORGES TANGO

Map p234 (☎011-5555-5359; www.ccborges.org.ar; cnr Viamonte & San Martín; shows US$20-25; Ⓢ Línea C Lavalle) This excellent cultural center has many quality offerings, including recommended, reasonably priced tango shows several times per week. Bien de Tango, on Friday and Saturday nights at 8pm, is especially good and comparable to other tango shows that are triple the cost. Check the cultural center's website or stop in beforehand to see what's on and get an advance ticket.

PATIO DE TANGO TANGO

Map p234 (Milonga de la Manzana de las Luces; ☎011-4343-3260; www.facebook.com/PatioDeTangoManzana/; Perú 222; donation recommended; ⏰class 7:30-9pm, milonga 9pm-midnight Fri; Ⓢ Línea E Bolívar) FREE This wonderfully atmospheric *milonga* takes place in the outdoor patio and surrounding salons of the historic Manzana de las Luces (p62), one of the city's oldest buildings. There's no entrance fee but you may wish to contribute a little money 'to the hat', which goes to the teachers and musicians.

PIAZZOLLA TANGO TANGO

Map p234 (☎011-4344-8200; www.piazzollatango.com; Florida 165, Galaría Güemes; show from US$60, show & dinner from US$107; Ⓢ Línea D Catedral) This beautiful art-nouveau theater, just off pedestrian Calle Florida, used to be a red-light cabaret venue. The show here is based on the music of Ástor Piazzolla, a *bandoneón* (small accordian) player and composer who revolutionized tango music by fusing in elements from jazz and classical music. Be aware most tables are communal. Free tango class before the show.

LUNA PARK STADIUM

Map p234 (☎011-5279-5279; www.lunapark.com.ar; cnr Bouchard & Av Corrientes; Ⓢ Línea B Alem) Originally a boxing stadium, this huge venue has a capacity of 15,000 and is the fateful location where Juan Perón met Eva Duarte (aka Evita), and where Maradona got married.

EL QUERANDÍ TANGO

Map p234 (☎011-5199-1770; www.querandi.com.ar; Perú 322; show from US$45, dinner & show from US$110; Ⓢ Línea E Belgrano) This large corner venue is also an upscale restaurant. The show follows tango's evolution from its bordello origins to cabaret influences to *milongas* and modernism. There's more low-key dancing than at other shows – and also more singing and musical interludes – so don't expect overly athletic moves. One minus: columns can block some views.

ACADEMIA NACIONAL DEL TANGO TANGO

Map p234 (☎011-4345-6967; www.facebook.com/academianacionaldeltango/; Av de Mayo 833; Ⓢ Línea A Piedras) Hosts occasional *milongas* and free concerts; check the Facebook page for details.

SHOPPING

The main shopping street in the Center is Florida. Most travelers to Buenos Aires take the obligatory stroll down this heaving pedestrian street lined with shops and vendors selling clothes, shoes, jewelry, housewares and cheesy souvenirs. Touts zero in on tourists, offering currency exchange and leather jackets. We'll tell you now: you won't find the cheapest prices on leather jackets here (try Calle Murillo or Calle Aguirre in the Villa Crespo neighborhood instead) and you should definitely avoid changing money on the streets – fake bills and other scams are an occasional problem here.

ARTE Y ESPERANZA ARTS & CRAFTS

Map p234 (☎011-4343-1455; www.arteyesperanza.com.ar; Balcarce 234; ⏰10am-6pm Mon-Fri; Ⓢ Línea A Plaza de Mayo) This store sells fair-trade, handmade products that include many made by Argentina's indigenous craftspeople. Shop for silver jewelry, pottery, ceramics, textiles, *mate* gourds, baskets, woven bags, wood utensils and animal masks.

EL COLECCIONISTA MUSIC

Map p234 (☎011-4322-0359; www.facebook.com/el.coleccionista.7/; Esmeralda 562; ⏰noon-7:30pm Mon-Fri; Ⓢ Línea C Lavalle) This music store has an eclectic selection of jazz, blues, salsa, Celtic and symphonic rock CDs. It will buy used musical instruments, so trade in that guitar or drum you're tired of lugging around for a cool *bandoneón*. Staff members are knowledgeable.

EL ATENEO BOOKS, MUSIC

Map p234 (☎011-4325-6801; Florida 340; ⏰9am-8pm Mon-Fri, to 5pm Sat; Ⓢ Línea B Florida) Branch of Buenos Aires' landmark bookseller, which stocks a limited number of books in English.

1

2

LONELY PLANET IMAGES / GETTY IMAGES ©

'ederal (p109), Retiro **2.** Café Tortoni (p65), The Center
'é *con leche* (coffee with milk)

Cafes of Buenos Aires

Thanks to its European heritage, Buenos Aires has a serious cafe culture. *Porteños* will spend hours dawdling over a single *café cortado* (espresso coffee with steamed milk) and a couple of *medialunas* (croissants), discussing the economy, politics and the latest soccer results. Indeed, everything from marriage proposals to revolutions have started at the local corner cafe.

Some of BA's cafes have been around for over 100 years, and many retain much of their original furniture, architectural details and rich atmosphere. They've always been the haunts of Argentina's politicians, activists, intellectuals, artists and literary greats, including Jorge Luis Borges and Julio Cortázar.

Most cafes have adapted to modern times by serving alcohol as well as coffee, and many offer a surprisingly wide range of food and snacks; you can often order a steak as easily as a *cortado*. A few even double as bookstores or host live music, poetry readings and other cultural events. Serious coffee drinkers might be disappointed by the quality of the brew at BA's most historic cafes (go there for the atmosphere, not the quality java). Luckily there are new coffee shops opening all the time serving flat whites to please even the most discerning; try **LAB** (p138), **Lattente** (p139) or **Coffee Town** (p93).

Cafes have long hours and are usually open from early morning to late at night, making them easy places to visit. And visit you should; sipping coffee and hanging out at an atmospheric cafe, perhaps on some lazy afternoon, is part of the Buenos Aires experience. At the very least, they're great for a late tea or a welcome break from all that walking you'll be doing.

Puerto Madero

For more detail of this area see Map p236

Neighborhood Top Five

❶ **Reserva Ecológica Costanera Sur** (p72) Escaping the city's hustle and bustle with a walk or bike ride through these wild wetlands where you can spot birds or perhaps a nutria or iguana.

❷ **Colección de Arte Amalia Lacroze de Fortabat** (p73) Viewing the impressive private art collection at this contemporary museum.

❸ **Puente de la Mujer** (p73) Seeing the bridge lit up at night and strolling around the cobbled lanes next to Puerto Madero's dikes.

❹ **Chila** (p74) Eating lunch or dinner at an upscale restaurant with water views – it'll be pricey but good.

❺ **Faena Hotel + Universe** (p171) Splashing out on a night at this unique hotel; see if there's a current exhibition at the Faena Arts Center and catch a performance of Rojo Tango.

Explore: Puerto Madero

Put on your most comfortable walking shoes, because you'll be on your feet all day here. You can start walking pretty much anywhere and make a big loop around the dikes. There are a few interesting museums to see here, including the Colección de Arte Amalia Lacroze de Fortabat (p73; also called Museo Fortabat). This shiny, glassy museum is in a cutting-edge building and art lovers shouldn't miss it. Another quirky place is the Museo Fragata Sarmiento (p73). Walk the plank, pay your ticket and explore all the fascinating holds of this naval vessel. The Corbeta Uruguay (p73), a couple of blocks away, is another similar 'ship' museum. In between these two is the Puente de la Mujer (p73) – a pedestrian bridge that you'll be tempted to cross.

When you get toward the south, cut east on R Vera Peñaloza and look for the elegant fountain called Fuente de las Nereidas (p74). Just beyond is the southern entrance to the marshy Reserva Ecológica Costanera Sur (p72), which offers the only real nature walk (or bike ride) in central BA. It's a peaceful place full of reedy lagoons, wildlife and dirt paths, and you can get a close-up look at the muddy waters of the Río de la Plata. The reserve is a sharp contrast to the upscale lofts, restaurants and hotels nearby, and thankfully it's available to everyone for no cost at all – just be sure you're not there on a Monday, when it's closed.

Local Life

- **Food stands** The road running parallel to the Reserva Ecológica Costanera Sur is lined with mobile food truck *parrillas* (steakhouses). Mingle with office workers on their lunch break, taxi drivers at 3am or post-clubbing revelers at day break as you eat your cheap *choripán* (sausage sandwiches) or *bondiola* (pork) sandwiches.
- **Jogging** Join locals for a run around the Reserva Ecológica – or a stroll, if that's more your thing.
- **Picture perfect** In Parque Mujeres Argentinas (the green landscaped space between the docks and the Costanera) you'll no doubt see dressed-up, heavily styled teenage girls starring in their own professional photo shoots. These are 15-year-olds celebrating their *quinceañera*.

Getting There & Away

- **Bus** Buses 64, 126 and 152 run along LN Alem/Paseo Colón, which gets you within three blocks of Puerto Madero.
- **Subte** The closest Subte stops are LN Alem (Línea B) and the end-of-line stations of Líneas A, D and E, which terminate at Plaza de Mayo.

Lonely Planet's Top Tip

If you want to explore every corner of Puerto Madero and the Reserva Ecológica Costanera Sur, it's much easier on a bike. Hire one from a bike-tour company such as Biking Buenos Aires (p207) or Urban Biking (p207), or pick up one of the free yellow city bikes.

Best Museums

- Colección de Arte Amalia Lacroze de Fortabat (p73)
- Fragata Sarmiento (p73)
- Corbeta Uruguay (p73)

For reviews, see p73.

Best Places to Eat

- Chila (p74)
- i Central Market (p74)
- Le Grill (p75)

For reviews, see p74.

TOP SIGHT
RESERVA ECOLÓGICA COSTANERA SUR

The beautiful marshy land of this nature preserve makes it a popular site for sunny weekend outings, when picnickers, cyclists and families come for fresh air and spectacular river views. If you're lucky, you may spot a river turtle, iguana or nutria (semi-aquatic rodent); birdwatchers will adore the 300-plus bird species that pause to rest here.

Murky Past

During the military dictatorship of 1976 to 1983, access to the Buenos Aires waterfront was limited, as the area was diked and filled with sediments dredged from the Río de la Plata. While plans for a new satellite city across from the port stalled, trees, grasses, birds and rodents took advantage and colonized this low-lying, 350-hectare area that mimics the ecology of the Delta del Paraná.

Nature Lovers' Paradise

In 1986 the area was declared an ecological reserve. Mysterious arson fires, thought to have been started by those with financial interests in the prime real estate, have occasionally been set. But permanent scars haven't remained – this beautifully lush marshy land survives hardily, and the reserve has become a popular site for outings and walks. Bring binoculars if you're a birder – ducks, swans, woodpeckers, parakeets, hawks, flycatchers and cardinals are just a few of the some 300 species of feathered critters that can be spotted here. Further in at the eastern shoreline of the reserve you can get a close-up view of the Río de la Plata's muddy waters – a rare sight in Buenos Aires.

DON'T MISS

- Walking the trails
- Birdwatching
- Bike riding
- Views of the Río de la Plata

PRACTICALITIES

- Map p236, D2
- ☎011-4893-1588
- visitasguiadas_recs@buenosaires.gob.ar
- Av Tristán Achaval Rodríguez 1550
- admission free
- 8am-7pm Tue-Sun Nov-Mar, to 6pm Apr-Oct
- 🚌2

SIGHTS

Puerto Madero's impressive art galleries, exhibition spaces and quirky museums are all within walking distance of each other around the picturesque waterfront. The striking Puente de la Mujer bridge is difficult to miss, and is even more beautiful when it's lit up at night. Allow plenty of time to explore the neighborhood's best sight, the vast Resérva Ecologica Costanera Sur.

RESERVA ECOLÓGICA COSTANERA SUR — NATURE RESERVE

See p72.

COLECCIÓN DE ARTE AMALIA LACROZE DE FORTABAT — MUSEUM

Map p236 (Museo Fortabat; ☎011-4310-6600; www.coleccionfortabat.org.ar; Olga Cossettini 141; adult/child AR$80/40; ⏲noon-8pm Tue-Sun, tours in Spanish 3pm & 5pm; Ⓢ Línea B Alem) Prominently located at the northern end of Puerto Madero is this stunning art museum showcasing the private collection of the late billionaire, philanthropist and socialite Amalia Lacroze de Fortabat. There are works by Antonio Berni and Raúl Soldi, as well as pieces by international artists including Dalí, Klimt, Rodin and Chagall; look for Warhol's colorful take on Fortabat herself in the family portrait gallery.

The building was designed by renowned Uruguayan architect Rafael Viñoly, and is constructed from steel, glass and concrete – the last a most appropriate material considering its patron (Fortabat was the major stockholder of Argentina's largest cement company).

FAENA ARTS CENTER — ARTS CENTER

Map p236 (☎011-4010-9233; www.faena.com/faena-art-center; Aime Paine 1169; admission varies; ⏲vary depending on exhibition; Ⓢ Línea A Plaza de Mayo) This very large, airy art space – in a beautifully renovated flour mill – highlights the contemporary dreams of local and international artists and designers. If your visit coincides with a show, you should expect cutting-edge exhibits that utilize these spaces to the maximum – think rope nets hanging from the ceiling or light pyramids reaching for the sky. Check the website for upcoming shows; when there is no exhibition the center is closed.

ℹ VISITING THE RESERVA ECOLÓGICA COSTANERA SUR

- Tours are given on the last Friday of the month at 10am.
- Monthly Friday night full-moon tours are also available (call for latest schedule).
- There are water fountains near the entrances to the reserve but nowhere to buy food and drinks; bring your own.
- To learn more about the nature around you, book a tour with Seriema Nature Tours (p209).

FRAGATA SARMIENTO — MUSEUM

Map p236 (☎011-4334-9386; Dique 3; AR$10; ⏲10am-7pm; Ⓢ Línea A Plaza de Mayo) Over 23,000 Argentine naval cadets and officers have trained aboard this 85m sailing vessel, which traveled around the world 37 times between 1899 and 1938. On board are detailed records of its lengthy voyages, a gallery of its commanding officers, plenty of nautical items including old uniforms, and even the stuffed remains of Lampazo (the ship's pet dog). Peek into the ship's holds, galley and engine room and note the hooks where sleeping hammocks were strung up.

Built in Birkenhead, England, in 1897 at a cost of £125,000, this impeccably maintained ship never participated in combat.

CORBETA URUGUAY — MUSEUM

Map p236 (☎011-4314-1090; Dique 4; AR$10; ⏲10am-7pm; Ⓢ Línea B Alem) This 46m-long military ship conducted surveys along Argentina's coast and supplied bases in Antarctica until it was decommissioned in 1926, after 52 years of service. Displayed below the main deck are interesting relics from Antarctica expeditions, such as crampons and snowshoes, along with historical photos and nautical items. Check out the tiny kitchen, complete with *mate* (tea-like beverage) supplies (of course).

PUENTE DE LA MUJER — BRIDGE

Map p236 (Women's Bridge; Dique 3; Ⓢ Línea A Plaza de Mayo) The striking Puente de la Mujer is Puerto Madero's signature monument. Unveiled in 2001, this gleaming-white structure spans Dique 3 and resembles a sharp fishhook or even a harp – it's supposed to represent a couple dancing the tango. Designed by acclaimed Spanish architect Santiago Calatrava and mostly built in Spain, this 160m-long pedestrian bridge cost US$6 million and rotates 90 degrees to allow water traffic to pass.

FUENTE DE LAS NEREIDAS FOUNTAIN

Map p236 (Av Tristán Achaval Rodríguez 1600; 2) This marble fountain dating from 1903 by the controversial Argentine sculptor Lola Mora was originally intended for Plaza de Mayo, but was considered distasteful and placed instead in a less prominent location, on the corner of Av Alem and Perón. It was later moved to its current location in Puerto Madero.

EATING

Most of Puerto Madero's restaurants are upscale and expensive, and many sport covered outdoor terraces with views of the nearby *diques* (dikes). You won't get the best bang for your buck in this elegant strip and the cuisine is more traditional than inspired, but it's the location here that counts.

I CENTRAL MARKET ARGENTINE $

Map p236 (011-5775-0330; www.icentralmarket.com.ar; Av Macacha Güemes 302; mains AR$90-160; 8am-10pm; ; Línea B Alem) Especially pleasant on sunny days is this modern restaurant on the waterfront – the tables on the promenade are great for people-watching. Order espresso and scones for breakfast, and panini (Italian-style sandwiches) or contemporary Argentine dishes for lunch. There's also more casual seating at the gourmet deli, plus a kitchenwares shop to poke around.

I FRESH MARKET ARGENTINE $

Map p236 (011-5775-0335; www.icentralmarket.com.ar; Olga Cossettini 1175; mains AR$90-160; 8am-10pm; Línea A Plaza de Mayo) It's not on the water, but a sidewalk table does just fine at this upscale cafe-restaurant. Choose a gourmet sandwich or salad, and be sure to peek at the luscious dessert case. Its sister restaurant, i Central Market, is a few blocks away.

★CHILA MODERN ARGENTINE $$$

Map p236 (011-4343-6067; www.chilaweb.com.ar; Alicia Moreau de Justo 1160; 3-course menu AR$1300, 7-course menu AR$1800, not incl

View of Dique 3 and Puerto Madero's cityscape

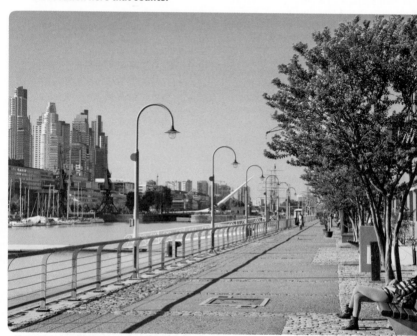

A FAILED PORT

Buenos Aires' waterfront was the subject of controversy in the mid-19th century, when competing commercial interests began to fight over the location of a modernized port for Argentina's burgeoning international commerce. Two ideas came to light. One was to widen and deepen the channel of the Riachuelo to port facilities at La Boca, which indeed happened as planned. The other was proposed by Eduardo Madero, a wealthy exporter with strong political ties and solid financial backing. Madero proposed transforming the city's mudflats into a series of modern basins and harbors consistent with the aspirations and ambitions of a cosmopolitan elite. This also occurred, but not quite as he had planned.

By the time of its completion in 1898 (four years after Madero's death), Puerto Madero had exceeded its budget and Madero himself had come under scrutiny. Suspicions arose from Madero's attempts to buy up all the landfill in the area and from his links to politicians who had acquired nearby lands likely to increase in value. And the practical side of the scheme didn't go so well either. By 1910 the amount of cargo was already too great for the new port, and poor access to the rail terminus at Plaza Once made things even worse. New facilities in a rejuvenated La Boca partly assuaged these problems, but congressional actions failed to solve the major issues – until the 1926 completion of Retiro's Puerto Nuevo.

drinks; 8pm-midnight Tue-Sun; S Línea A Plaza de Mayo) Some of Buenos Aires' best and most original cuisine is created by award-winning chef Soledad Nardelli. Her three- and seven-course, haute-cuisine dishes utilize only the best seasonal ingredients, and the restaurant also works closely with quality producers. Expect beautifully presented food, a professional staff and – if you're lucky – a table with a romantic view of the docks.

LE GRILL PARRILLA **$$$**

Map p236 (011-4331-0454; www.legrill.com.ar; Alicia Moreau de Justo 876; mains AR$260-490; 12:30-3pm & 7pm-midnight Mon-Fri, 7pm-1am Sat, 12:30-3.30pm Sun; S Línea A Plaza de Mayo) No surprise – grilled meat is the specialty at this sophisticated *parrilla*. Go for the rack of lamb, suckling pig or Kobe beef. There are a few seafood and pasta dishes for noncarnivores. Try to reserve a table in the atrium, with a full view of Puente de la Mujer.

LA PAROLACCIA TRATTORIA ITALIAN **$$$**

Map p236 (011-4343-1679; www.laparolaccia.com; Av Alicia Moreau de Justo 1052; set lunch AR$255-297, mains AR$200-350; noon-1am; S Línea A Plaza de Mayo) This Italian eatery specializes in homemade pastas. Reserve one of the few tables with a water view, then enjoy sweet-potato gnocchi, gorgonzola ravioli or *cappelletti* (a small stuffed pasta) in four cheeses.

A nearby branch, **La Parolaccia del Mare** (Map p236; 011-4343-0063; www.laparolaccia.com.ar; Av Alicia Moreau de Justo 1170; noon-4pm & 8pm-1am Mon-Sat, noon-1am Sun; S Línea A Plaza de Mayo), specializes in seafood.

ENTERTAINMENT

ROJO TANGO TANGO

Map p236 (011-4952-4111; www.rojotango.com; Faena Hotel + Universe, Martha Salotti 445; show US$220, show & dinner US$290; 111, 43, 143) This sexy performance is the tango show to top all others, though it comes with a hefty price tag. Offering only 100 seats, the Faena's cabaret room is swathed in blood-red curtains and gilded furniture. The show itself loosely follows the history of the tango, starting from its cabaret roots to the modern fusions of Ástor Piazzolla.

Congreso & Tribunales

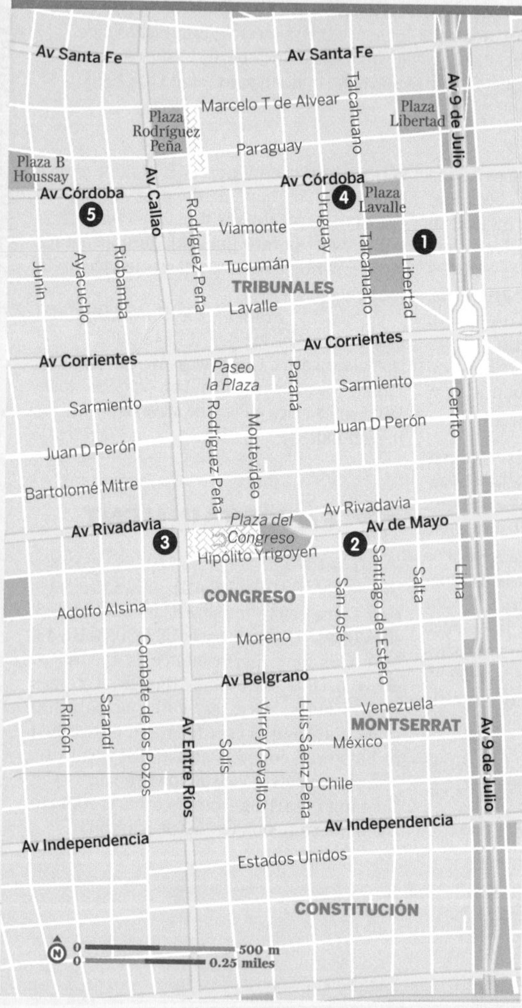

For more detail of this area see Map p238

Neighborhood Top Five

1 Teatro Colón (p78) Peeking behind the scenes on a backstage tour or catching a performance at this historical venue.

2 Palacio Barolo (p79) Learning about the symbolic architecture of this unique Dante-inspired building and taking in the views from the rooftop lighthouse.

3 Palacio del Congreso (p79) Exploring the building that houses Argentina's legislative branch on a guided Senate tour.

4 Pizzería Güerrín (p80) Stopping for a late-night slice of thick doughy pizza and *fainá*, eaten standing at the counter.

5 Palacio de las Aguas Corrientes (p79) Admiring the stunning tiled exterior of the building that once housed the city's water tanks before viewing the range of toilets and bidets displayed in the bizarre little museum on the 1st floor.

Explore: Congreso & Tribunales

Plaza del Congreso is at the heart of this neighborhood and an easy walk from Plaza de Mayo (in the Center) along the important thoroughfare Av de Mayo. This avenue connects the city's executive and legislative houses and is itself lined with beautiful buildings, so be sure to take a stroll along it.

To do this, however, you'll have to experience crossing Av 9 de Julio, which is 16 lanes at its widest; the parallel streets Cerrito and Carlos Pellegrini make it look even broader. Fortunately, traffic islands provide raised breaks for the thousands of pedestrians who cross it every day, but it's still an intimidating barrier (and can't be done in one green light without breaking into a run – trust us).

Once you've explored the Plaza de Congreso area, head along Callao to Av Corrientes – it's the city's traditional theater district, and there's still plenty going on. Further north is Plaza Lavalle, home to its own important cluster of buildings, including one of the city's most important sights, the Teatro Colón. Just a couple blocks from here is the Obelisco, Buenos Aires' key landmark, with a small plaza near the base.

Local Life

➡**Parklife** Join office workers on their lunch break and buy a takeaway sandwich or *empanada* (a pastry turnover filled with a variety of savoury ingredients and baked or fried) to eat in Plaza Lavalle (p79).

➡**Hangouts** Break for afternoon tea at local favorite El Gato Negro (p83) or grab a slice of pizza at Pizzería Güerrín (p80).

➡**Cinema** Catch an Argentinian film (and practice your Spanish listening skills) at the Espacio INCAA Gaumont (p84).

Getting There & Away

➡**Bus** Take bus 29 from Palermo or San Telmo and bus 64 (among others) from the Microcentro.

➡**Subte** Línea A runs along Av de Mayo and Rivadavia, linking Congreso with the Microcentro. Línea B runs along Av Corrientes to the Microcentro and Línea D links Tribunales (at Plaza Lavalle) with Palermo and the Microcentro.

Lonely Planet's Top Tip

The big theaters, including Teatro San Martín and Teatro Colón, occasionally put on inexpensive or even free events, while cultural centers (such as Centro Cultural San Martín) are also good sources of free or affordable entertainment.

Best Places to Eat

➡ Chan Chan (p82)

➡ Pizzería Güerrín (p80)

➡ Parrilla Peña (p82)

➡ Cadore (p82)

For reviews, see p80.

Best Places to Drink

➡ Los Galgos (p83)

➡ El Gato Negro (p83)

➡ Los 36 Billares (p83)

For reviews, see p83.

Best Entertainment

➡ Teatro Colón (p78)

➡ El Beso (p84)

➡ Café de los Angelitos (p83)

For reviews, see p83.

TOP SIGHT
TEATRO COLÓN

Sinking into a red velvet seat for a performance at Teatro Colón is a magical experience. This is one of the world's greatest opera houses, and you can discover it for yourself by attending a performance here or taking a behind-the-scenes tour.

A Grand Opening

The impressive seven-story building is one of Buenos Aires' landmarks (and greatest sources of pride). The theater's opening night in 1908 was a presentation of Verdi's *Aïda*, and visitors have continued to be wowed ever since. After all, the acoustics are considered among the top five of the world's concert venues.

Architecture

Occupying an entire city block, the Teatro Colón can seat 2500 spectators and provide standing room for another 500 – it was the southern hemisphere's largest theater until the Sydney Opera House was built in 1973. Italian Francesco Tamburini was the main architect, but after his death in 1891 his partner Vittorio Meano – who designed the Palacio del Congreso – was put in charge. After Meano was murdered (possibly due to a love triangle!), Belgian Jules Dormal took over and added some French elements to the theater.

DON'T MISS

- Backstage tour
- Grand marble foyer
- Salón Dorado
- Mozart (in the busts room)
- Magnificent painted *cúpula*

PRACTICALITIES

- Map p238, F2
- 011-4378-7100
- www.teatrocolon.org.ar
- cnr Tucumán & Cerrito tours AR$250
- tours 9am-5pm
- S Línea D Tribunales

SIGHTS

TEATRO COLÓN THEATER

See p78.

★PALACIO BAROLO NOTABLE BUILDING

Map p238 (☎011-4381-1885; www.palaciobarolotours.com; Av de Mayo 1370; tour AR$200; ⊙tours 10am-7pm Wed-Sun; S Línea A Sáenz Peña) One of Buenos Aires' most beautiful buildings is this 22-story office block, whose unique design was inspired by Dante's *Divine Comedy*; its height (100m) is a reference to each canto (or song), the number of floors (22) to verses per song, and its divided structure to hell, purgatory and heaven. To see Palacio Barolo you'll need to book a guided tour, during which you'll get to ride in the 1920s elevator and admire the panoramic views from the rooftop lighthouse.

Completed in 1923, Palacio Barolo was BA's tallest skyscraper until the construction of Edificio Kavanagh in 1935. In Montevideo, Uruguay is Palacio Barolo's 'twin,' the Palacio Salvo, a similar building that was also designed by the architect Mario Palanti.

★MUSEO BOTICA DEL ÁNGEL MUSEUM

Map p238 (☎011-4384-9396; http://boticadelangel.usal.edu.ar/; Luis Sáenz Peña 543; guided tour AR$120, admission to ground fl only free; ⊙3-6pm Tue-Fri, guided tours 7pm dates vary; S Línea E Independencia) For an overview of the world of Argentinian showbiz, join a tour of the wonderfully kitsch Botica del Ángel and view the former home of the late Eduardo Bergara Leumann, the flamboyant TV presenter and actor who was Argentina's answer to Liberace. Tours are in Spanish; see website for dates.

PALACIO DEL CONGRESO NOTABLE BUILDING

Map p238 (Congress Building; ☎011-2822-3000; www.senado.gov.ar/ComoLlegar; Hipólito Yrigoyen 1849; ⊙senate tours 12:30pm & 5pm Mon, Tue, Thu & Fri; S Línea A Congreso) FREE The green-domed Palacio del Congreso was modeled on the Capitol Building in Washington, DC and was completed in 1906. Worthwhile free tours of the Senate chamber, the Chamber of Deputies and the gorgeous, walnut-paneled Congress library are given in English and Spanish. The tour also includes the pink room where until 1951 women met to discuss policies; their notes were then passed to a male deputy. Go to the entrance on Hipólito Yrigoyen and bring photo ID.

Separate tours in Spanish only are run by the Chambers of Deputies, accessed via the entrance on Av Rivadavia.

Note the stone statues on either side of the steps at the front of the palace, facing the square; these were sculpted by the controversial artist Lola Mora and caused a scandal when they were erected in 1907. Conservatives insisted that they be removed; in 2014 President Cristina Kirchner returned replicas of the sculptures to their original location.

Across the way, the **Monumento a los Dos Congresos** (Map p238; Plaza del Congreso, cnr Avs Rivadavia & Entre Rios; S Línea A Congreso) honors the assembly of 1813 and the 1816 Congress in Tucumán, when independence was declared.

PALACIO DE LAS AGUAS CORRIENTES NOTABLE BUILDING

Map p238 (☎011-6319-1104; www.aysa.com.ar; Riobamba 750; ⊙museum 9am-1pm Mon-Fri; S Línea D Callao) FREE Completed in 1894 when Buenos Aires was booming, this gorgeous, palace-like waterworks building has an elaborate exterior intended to convey the importance of the purified water it housed in huge tanks. On the 1st floor is the small and quirky **Museo del Agua y de la Historia Sanitaria** FREE, where the collection of ornate tiles, faucets, ceramic pipe joints, and old toilets and bidets is well displayed. Guided visits offer a backstage glimpse of the building's inner workings.

OBELISCO MONUMENT

Map p238 (cnr Avs 9 de Julio & Corrientes; S Línea B Carlos Pellegrini) One of the city's most iconic monuments is the needle-like Obelisco, which soars 67m above the oval Plaza de la República and was erected in 1936 on the 400th anniversary of the first Spanish settlement on the Río de la Plata. To celebrate major soccer victories, boisterous fans gather at the Obelisco to sing, jump in unison and honk horns.

PLAZA LAVALLE PLAZA

Map p238 (Libertad, btwn Córdoba & Lavalle; S Línea D Tribunales) Just northwest of the Obelisco is Plaza Lavalle, three blocks of parks (popular with office workers on their lunch break) surrounded by some important buildings. The most worthwhile sights here are the Teatro Colón and the Teatro Nacional Cervantes (p80), but there's also the neoclassical **Escuela Presidente Roca**

SCORING TICKETS FOR THE TEATRO COLÓN

- The theater offers occasional free concerts – check the website and click on 'Intérpretes Argentinos.'
- Buy tickets online in advance as soon as you know your travel dates.
- The cheapest tickets are standing spaces at the highest tier – look for 'Paraiso de Pie.'
- If a performance appears sold out online, try asking at the ticket office – sometimes there are seats available that don't show up on the website.
- If all else fails, hotel concierges have been known to get hold of last-minute tickets for 'sold-out' concerts.

(Map p238; Libertad 581; S Línea D Tribunales), an educational facility that's often mistaken for Teatro Colón, and across from it, the French-style Palacio de Justicia (1904) housing the Supreme Court.

TEATRO NACIONAL CERVANTES NOTABLE BUILDING

Map p238 (011-4815-8883; www.teatrocervantes.gov.ar; Libertad 815; tours AR$35; M Línea D Tribunales) From the grand tiled lobby to the red-and-gold-hued main theater, you can smell the long history of the ornately decorated Cervantes. Though it's definitely showing its age, there is an undeniable faded elegance to the place. Take it in on a weekend tour (call for current schedules), or catch a play, musical show or dance performance.

MUSEO JUDÍO DE BUENOS AIRES MUSEUM

Map p238 (011-4123-0832; www.museojudio.org.ar; Libertad 769; AR$140; 11am-5:30pm Tue-Thu, to 4:30pm Fri; S Línea D Tribunales) Jewish symbols adorn the facade of the **Templo Libertad** (www.templolibertad.org.ar), Argentina's oldest and largest synagogue, located at the northeastern end of Plaza Lavalle. Attached to the synagogue is a small museum that traces the history of Jewish immigration to Argentina and displays items relating to Jewish culture and religious practices. Don't miss taking a look inside the synagogue itself (accessed via the museum). Bring photo ID for admission.

PALACIO DE JUSTICIA NOTABLE BUILDING

Map p238 (https://turismo.buenosaires.gob.ar/es/atractivo/palacio-de-justicia-tribunales; Talcahuano 550; tours in Spanish 2:30pm Fri; S Línea D Tribunales) FREE Occupying an entire city block overlooking leafy Plaza Lavalle, this beautiful beaux-arts structure is home to the Supreme Court, and was built in stages between 1904 and 1949. Ninety-minute guided tours of the courts are given in Spanish on Fridays at 2:30pm. Reserve in advance via https://ba.tours/ and bring photographic ID.

CENTRO CULTURAL SAN MARTÍN CULTURAL CENTRE

Map p238 (011-4374-1251; www.elculturalsanmartin.org; Sarmiento 1551; S Línea B Uruguay) FREE One of Buenos Aires' best cultural resources, this large arts center has free or inexpensive galleries, music, films, lectures, art exhibitions, classes and workshops. See the website for the current program of events and tickets.

EATING

The Congreso area caters mostly for a business clientele with cheap *parrillas* (steakhouses) and quick takeout joints. Dotted between the theaters and cinemas of Av Corrientes and Av Rivadavia are a number of pizzerias serving *empanadas* and traditional stodgy Argentinian-style pizza by the slice. In the blocks around Av de Mayo and Salta you'll find a few good Spanish and Basque eateries serving traditional food.

★PIZZERÍA GÜERRÍN PIZZA $

Map p238 (011-4371-8141; www.facebook.com/pizzeriaguerrin/; Av Corrientes 1368; pizza slices AR$19-27; 11am-1am Sun-Thu, to 2am Fri & Sat; S Línea B Uruguay) This much-loved pizza joint on Av Corrientes has been feeding the masses since 1932. For a quick pit stop (and the cheapest prices), order a slice of thick, doughy *muzzarella* at the counter and eat standing up at the benches with the rest of the crowd. Add a portion of *fainá* (chickpea-based flatbread) and wash it down with Moscato and soda.

There are also tables with waiter service where you can choose a freshly baked pizza from a more extensive menu. *Empanadas* and plenty of desserts are also available.

Neighborhood Walk
Congreso to Plaza de Mayo

START PALACIO DEL CONGRESO
END PLAZA DE MAYO
LENGTH 2.5KM; TWO HOURS

Begin your walk at the 1 **Palacio del Congreso** (p79). Wander east through Plaza del Congreso and look for the sculpture of Rodin's *The Thinker* (one of three sculptures cast from the original mold).

Head east along Av de Mayo, stopping at the incredible, Dante-inspired 2 **Palacio Barolo** (p79); if you time things right, hop on a tour. You'll get a grand vista of Buenos Aires from the cupola on the 22nd floor.

Continue along Av de Mayo, noting the French-style architecture of this grand avenue as you go, then turn right on Perú. Soon you'll come to what was once BA's center of learning, the 3 **Manzana de las Luces** ('Block of Enlightenment'; p62). Built in 1730 it is one of the city's oldest building clusters.

Head up Moreno and turn left on Calle Defensa, pausing to peek inside the 4 **Farmacia de la Estrella** (p63), which has been a functioning pharmacy since 1835. Note the elaborate late-19th-century ceiling murals depicting health-oriented themes. Take a break at 5 **La Puerto Rico** (p65), one of BA's most historic cafes.

Steeped in history, 6 **Plaza de Mayo** (p58) is the city's most important plaza and the main location where throngs of citizens gather on occasion to air their many grievances.

The plaza's main attraction, the 7 **Casa Rosada** (p63), houses the president's office. You can take tours inside at weekends; a modern museum lies off to the south side and holds ruins of the old customs building in its basement.

Also on the plaza is the 8 **Catedral Metropolitana** (p59), where Cardinal Bergoglio gave masses before he became Pope Francis in 2013. Pop inside for a look around. The tomb of General José de San Martín is located here, and a flame burns outside to keep his spirit alive.

Across from the cathedral is the 9 **Cabildo** (p61); it's BA's old town council. There are great views of the plaza from the 2nd-floor balcony.

★CHAN CHAN PERUVIAN $

Map p238 (☎011-4382-8492; Hipólito Yrigoyen 1390; mains AR$70-135; ⏲noon-4pm & 8pm-12:30am Tue-Sat, to 11:30pm Sun; Ⓢ Línea A Sáenz Peña) Thanks to fair prices and quick service, this colorful Peruvian eatery is usually packed with office workers devouring plates of ceviche (seafood cured in citrus) and *ajiaco de conejo* (rabbit and potato stew). There are also *arroz chaufa* (Peruvian-style fried rice) dishes, easily washed down with a tangy pisco sour or a pitcher of *chicha morada* (a sweet fruity drink).

★CADORE ICE CREAM $

Map p238 (☎011-4374-3688; http://heladeriacadore.com.ar/; Av Corrientes 1695; 250g ice cream AR$80; ⏲11am-midnight Mon-Thu, to 2am Fri-Sun; Ⓢ Línea B Callao) This, one of BA's classic *heladerías* (ice-cream parlors), was founded by the Italian Olivotti family in 1957 and gets busy with the post-theater crowds late into the night. Try the *dulce de leche*, made using a process which involves boiling *dulce leche* (sweetened milk) for 14 to 16 hours.

EL CUARTITO PIZZA $

Map p238 (☎011-4816-1758; Talcahuano 937; slices AR$25-31, pizzas AR$135-200; ⏲12:30pm-1am Sun & Tue-Thu, to 2am Fri & Sat; Ⓢ Línea D Tribunales) In a hurry? Order your slice of pizza and eat it at the counter (*el mostrador*) standing up. Not only is it cheaper and quicker this way, but you get a good view of the old sports posters and soccer shirts on the walls of this traditional, local restaurant. The *empanadas* are great here, too – try the *atún* (tuna).

ARAMBURU BIS MODERN ARGENTINE $$

Map p238 (☎011-4304-5697; www.aramburubis.com.ar; Humberto Primero 1207; mains AR$195-210, tasting menu AR$650; ⏲12:30-3pm & 8:30-11:30pm Mon-Sat; Ⓢ Línea E San José) Just around the corner from Aramburu is this casual bistro (or Bis), serving a delectable menu of steaks, fish, risotto, lamb and the like, all exquisitely executed. The *pulpería* (country store) style interior is nice, too. Afterwards head downstairs to Aramburu Ünder for a cocktail.

PARRILLA PEÑA PARRILLA $$

Map p238 (☎011-4371-5643; www.parrillapenia.url.ph; Rodríguez Peña 682; mains AR$150-370; ⏲noon-4pm & 8pm-midnight Mon-Sat; Ⓢ Línea D Callao) This simple, traditional, long-running *parrilla* is well-known for its excellent quality meats and generous portions. The service is fast and efficient and it's great value. Also on offer are homemade pastas, salads and *milanesas* (breaded cutlets), along with several tasty desserts and a good wine list.

CHIQUÍN PARRILLA $$

Map p238 (☎011-4373-5163; www.chiquin.com.ar; Sarmiento 1599; mains AR$142-245; ⏲noon-3am; Ⓢ Línea B Callao) A local mainstay for 90 years, Chiquín is an excellent place to safely take, say, your parents. It's a large, comfortable restaurant with a cozy and classic atmosphere (including hanging hams). Dressed-up staff are efficient, which is great because this place can bustle – even at 1am on a Saturday night. The best choices here are steak and pasta.

BUENOS AIRES' CARTONEROS

You'll see them mostly at night, hunched over at the curb, picking through the garbage and pushing loaded-down carts. These are some of Buenos Aires' poorest citizens, the *cartoneros* (cardboard collectors).

It's estimated that around 20,000 *cartoneros* rummage through Buenos Aires' trash heaps; some are even accredited by the city and wear uniforms. They sort through the city's 5000 daily tonnes of waste, collecting cardboard, paper, metal, plastic, glass – anything they can sell by the kilo to the *depositos* (recycling companies). They stake out their territory, perhaps about 15 city blocks, and are occasionally forced to pay police bribes.

While most *cartoneros* work independently, some work for neighborhood cooperatives that pay them a regular wage and organize vaccinations. Some cooperatives even provide child care for parents who go off on their nightly rounds. In the poorest families, however, even the young children have to work, and some *cartoneros* are in their 50s and 60s.

PLAZA ASTURIAS SPANISH $$

Map p238 (011-4382-7334; Av de Mayo 1199; mains AR$120-350; 11:30am-5pm & 7pm-1am Sun & Tue-Thu, to 2:30am Fri & Sat; S Línea A Lima) This old-fashioned Spanish restaurant draws in a regular midday crowd with its set lunch (AR$195), which includes a main dish, coffee and a glass of wine. Otherwise, the regular menu features staples such as chorizo, ham and potato casserole, and pasta, as well as more adventurous dishes like *cazuela de mariscos,* a seafood stew rich with mussels, garlic and herbs.

★ARAMBURU MODERN ARGENTINE $$$

Map p238 (011-4305-0439; www.aramburu's resto.com.ar; Salta 1050; 18-course menu AR$1800; 8:30-11pm Tue-Sat; S Línea E San Jose) Chef Gonzalo Aramburu's 18-course 'molecular' meal is astounding; each artistically created plate is just a few bites of gastronomic delight. Expect enlightening tastes, textures and smells, plus unique presentations – all will translate into a highly memorable dining experience. Located in the edgy but up-and-coming neighborhood of Montserrat.

DRINKING & NIGHTLIFE

This neighborhood is not known for its drinking holes, but there are a few atmospheric spots where you can toast the town while the politicos scurry past on the sidewalks.

★LOS GALGOS BAR

Map p238 (011-4371-3561; www.facebook.com/LosGalgosBarNotable/; Av Callao 501; mains AR$170-250; 7am-7pm Mon, to 1am Tue-Sat; S Línea B Callao) This classic neighborhood bar – formerly frequented by the neighborhood's elderly *señores* – has been immaculately restored and transformed into a sophisticated bar and restaurant serving modern Argentine food. It's open all day, for breakfast, lunch, *merienda* (afternoon tea) and dinner. Come from 6pm for an expertly mixed cocktail in the candlelight accompanied by a *picada* (shared appetizer plate) of meats, olives and cheeses.

EL GATO NEGRO TEAHOUSE

Map p238 (011-4374-1730; Av Corrientes 1669; 9am-10pm Mon, to 11pm Tue, to midnight Wed & Thu, to 2am Fri & Sat, 3-11pm Sun; S Línea B Callao) Tea-lined wooden cabinets and a spicy aroma welcome you to this pleasant little sipping paradise. Enjoy imported cups of coffee or tea, along with breakfast and dainty *sandwiches de miga* (thin, crustless sandwiches, traditionally eaten at tea time). Imported teas and coffees are sold in bulk, and a range of exotic herbs and spices are also on offer.

LOS 36 BILLARES BAR

Map p238 (011-4122-1500; www.los36billares.com.ar; Av de Mayo 1271; portion pizza AR$18-32, empanadas AR$23-28; 7am-2am Mon-Thu, to 3am Fri, to 4am Sat, to 1am Sun; S Línea A Lima) Dating from 1894, this is one of the city's most historic cafe-bars and serves a good selection of pizzas and *empanadas*. As its name implies, it's big on billiard tables (check out the basement). Also hosts tango shows (both music-only concerts and dance performances) in the 60-seat back theater.

ENTERTAINMENT

CAFÉ DE LOS ANGELITOS TANGO

Map p238 (011-4952-2320; www.cafedelosangelitos.com; Av Rivadavia 2100; show from US$90, show & dinner from US$130; cafe 8am-midnight; S Línea A Congreso) Originally called Bar Rivadavia, this cafe was once the haunt of poets, musicians and even criminals, which is why a police commissioner jokingly called it *los angelitos* (the angels) in the early 1900s. As well as being an elegant hangout for a coffee or tea, come evening time Los Angelitos puts on one of the best tango shows in Buenos Aires.

The performers dress in top-notch costumes and use interesting props, such as drapes and moving walls. They also dance to modern tunes, including those by local band Bajofondo, and despite a nightclub feel at times – especially due to the lighting – it's all tastefully and creatively done. The stage is well set up (the musicians are on a different level, out of the way but well in sight) and everyone gets a good view.

EL BESO TANGO

Map p238 (☎011-4953-2794; http://elbeso.com.ar/; Riobamba 416, 1st fl; Ⓢ Línea B Callao) This small, intimate dance salon hosts various different *milongas* (tango events); the most popular is **Milonga Cachirulo** on Tuesdays from 9pm to 3am. The Cachirulo attracts some very good dancers – you should be confident of your skills if you plan to take to the floor. On Friday nights, El Beso hosts **La Marshall Milonga Gay** (https://lamarshallmilonga.com.ar) from 10:30pm to 4am.

CENTRO CULTURAL RICARDO ROJAS ARTS CENTER

Map p238 (☎011-4954-5521; www.rojas.uba.ar; Av Corrientes 2038; Ⓢ Línea B Callao) Part of the Universidad de Buenos Aires (UBA), this exceptionally good cultural center has a wide range of affordable classes (in Spanish), including in dance, music, photography, theater and film, as well as language courses and a program of concerts, theater and dance performances.

TEATRO SAN MARTÍN THEATER

Map p238 (☎011-4375-5018; www.complejoteatral.gob.ar; Av Corrientes 1530; Ⓢ Línea B Uruguay) This major venue has several auditoriums (the largest seats over 1000 people) and showcases international cinema, theater, dance and classical music, covering conventional and more unusual events. Recent renovations saw the theater close in 2016; check the website for updates on the progress of the works and future performance schedules.

TANGO PORTEÑO TANGO

Map p238 (☎011-4124-9400; www.tangoporteno.com.ar; Cerrito 570; show from US$28, show & dinner from US$120; Ⓢ Línea D Tribunales) Staged in a renovated art-deco theater, this tango show features snippets of old footage interspersed with plenty of athletic (and at times sensual) dancing. There's an interesting blindfold number and the orchestra is excellent. There's a complimentary tango class before the show.

TEATRO PASEO LA PLAZA THEATER

Map p238 (☎011-6320-5300; www.paseolaplaza.com.ar; Av Corrientes 1660; Ⓢ Línea B Callao) Located in a small and pleasant outdoor shopping mall, this complex features several theater halls that run both classic and contemporary productions, including tango, theater and comedy.

TEATRO AVENIDA CLASSICAL MUSIC

Map p238 (☎011-4812-6369; www.balirica.org.ar; Av de Mayo 1222; Ⓢ Línea A Lima) This historic theater dating from 1908 originally staged mostly Spanish plays, including Federico Garcia Lorca's *Bodas de Sangre* in 1933. Today, the Avenida's biggest strength is opera, particularly productions by the Buenos Aires Lirica.

ESPACIO INCAA GAUMONT CINEMA

Map p238 (☎011-4371-3050; www.facebook.com/EspacioIncaa/; Av Rivadavia 1635; tickets AR$30; Ⓢ Línea A Congreso) Screens mostly Argentinian and other South American films.

COSMOS-UBA CINEMA

Map p238 (☎011-4953-5405; www.cosmos.uba.ar; Av Corrientes 2046; Ⓢ Línea B Pasteur) Often shows retrospectives, documentaries, foreign film cycles and art-house movies.

SHOPPING

Av Corrientes has a number of discount bookstores and although most of the publications are in Spanish, it's fun to wander around and sift through the bargain bins. You'll also find a few well-stocked record stores on Av Corrientes, so if you're keen to take home a tango CD this is the place to look.

ZIVALS MUSIC

Map p238 (www.facebook.com/Zivals/; Av Callao 395; ⏰9:30am-9:30pm Mon-Sat; Ⓢ Línea B Callao) This is one of the better music stores in town, especially when it comes to tango, folk, jazz and classical music. Listening stations are a big plus, and there are also books for sale.

San Telmo

For more detail of this area see Map p240

Neighborhood Top Five

❶ **Feria de San Telmo** (p88) Jostling with fellow shoppers at the Sunday fair, where vendors sell all manner of goods, and buskers and tango dancers compete for your spare change.

❷ **Plaza Dorrego** (p87) Taking a break at this atmospheric and historic square – when it's not Sunday.

❸ **El Zanjón de Granados** (p88) Exploring the reconstructed tunnels at this unique site.

❹ **Museo Histórico Nacional** (p88) Getting up to speed on the history of Argentina's fight for independence at this museum in Parque Lezama.

❺ **Pasaje de la Defensa** (p90) Strolling cobbled streets and taking in the old-time atmosphere at places such as this former *conventillo* (tenement house).

Lonely Planet's Top Tip

On Sundays the *feria* (street market) is full-on, which means tonnes of people are visiting and you'll need to watch for pickpockets. On the other hand, it's the liveliest time to be in the neighborhood and the museums and most stores are all open. For more peace, visit San Telmo from Tuesday to Saturday (many places close on Monday), especially to sit at one of Plaza Dorrego's outdoor tables.

Best Museums

- Museo de Arte Moderno de Buenos Aires (p88)
- Museo Histórico Nacional (p88)
- Museo de Arte Contemporáneo (p88)

For reviews, see p88.

Best Places to Eat

- Café San Juan (p92)
- El Refuerzo Bar Almacen (p91)
- Cafe Rivas (p92)
- Hierbabuena (p92)

For reviews, see p91.

Best Places to Drink

- Bar Plaza Dorrego (p93)
- Doppelgänger (p93)
- Bar Británico (p93)

For reviews, see p93.

Explore: San Telmo

Everyone is drawn to Plaza Dorrego, the heart and soul of San Telmo. It's a nice leafy place to snag an outdoor table under an umbrella and have a coffee or full meal (though on Sundays the *feria* takes over and tables disappear). Sometimes tango dancers provide entertainment for a few pesos. Keep a good hold of your bag, just in case.

Generally everything of interest is reachable by walking in this neighborhood; keep a look out for street art as you go. From Plaza Dorrego you can stroll up or down the main drag of Defensa, window-shopping for pricey antiques or trendy new trinkets along the way. Several museums are also on or just off this street. If you head south, you'll hit Parque Lezama, a local park where families hang out at the playground and lovers smooch on benches. Be sure to take a stroll down elegant Av Caseros to admire the architecture of the buildings lining the block between Defensa and Bolívar; you could stop here for a meal or a drink.

Heading north, you can be in the Plaza de Mayo area in 15 minutes, or take a bus south down busy Av Almirante Brown to La Boca.

Local Life

- **Markets** Explore the Mercado de San Telmo (p88) to get a dose of history and a feel for how the locals buy their meats and vegetables.
- **Hangouts** Classic cafes such as Bar Plaza Dorrego (p93), Bar El Federal (p91) and La Poesia (p91) drip with traditional atmosphere and old-time locals taking in their morning *medialunas* (croissants) or afternoon coffee breaks.
- **Games** Like chess? Then head to Parque Lezama (p90) and find the cluster of chess tables there – and, if you dare, make a challenge.

Getting There & Away

- **Bus** Take bus 59 from Recoleta and Palermo; bus 29 from La Boca, Plaza de Mayo and Palermo.
- **Subte** Línea C connects the western edge of San Telmo with the Center, Congreso and Retiro.

TOP SIGHT
PLAZA DORREGO

At the heart of San Telmo is Plaza Dorrego, normally a peaceful little plaza strewn with locals and tourists sitting at tables under their umbrellas. A few hippie street vendors hawk their wares on the sidewalks while tango dancers occasionally perform for a few pesos.

Feria de San Telmo

Come Sundays the plaza and Calle Defensa become packed with stalls at the weekly Feria de San Telmo (p88). It's a bit of a crazy scene, but worth experiencing nonetheless.

Originally started in 1970 as an antiques fair, the *feria* is now a craft market offering all manner of items – jewelry, souvenirs, quality artwork, vintage clothing, old collectibles, handmade crafts, leather items and much more. Defensa is closed to traffic from Plaza de Mayo to Av San Juan and lined with hundreds of stalls. Street performers, from metallic human statues to *candombe* drumming groups to professional tango dancers, entertain the crowds, while sidewalk tables provide welcome breaks.

The *feria* is a tight and crowded scene, so be prepared to bump into people – and watch your bag carefully. Haggling isn't essential and most vendors won't budge much on price, but you can try your luck and attempt some friendly negotiation if you're buying several items.

Historic Plaza

Plaza Dorrego is the city's second-oldest plaza and was originally a pit stop for caravans bringing supplies into the city from around Argentina. At the turn of the 19th century it became a public square, surrounded by colonial buildings that survive to this day.

DON'T MISS

- Feria de San Telmo
- Bar Plaza Dorrego
- Street performers
- Colonial buildings

PRACTICALITIES

- Map p240, C4
- 🚌24, 29, 111

SIGHTS

The central thoroughfares of this neighborhood are Balcarce and Defensa; they're where you'll find most of the sights. As well as visiting the museums, take some time to wander around the neighborhoods streets, parks and squares.

PLAZA DORREGO — PLAZA

See p87.

★FERIA DE SAN TELMO — MARKET

Map p240 (Defensa; 10am-6pm Sun; 10, 22, 29, 45, 86) On Sundays, San Telmo's main drag is closed to traffic and the street is a sea of both locals and tourists browsing craft stalls, waiting at vendors' carts for freshly squeezed orange juice, poking through the antique glass ornaments on display on Plaza Dorrego, and listening to street performances by myriad music groups. Runs from Av San Juan to Plaza de Mayo. It's a tight and crowded scene, so be prepared to bump into people and watch your bag carefully.

★MERCADO DE SAN TELMO — MARKET

Map p240 (btwn Defensa & Bolívar, Carlos Calvo & Estados Unidos block; 8:30am-8pm; S Línea C Independencia) This market was built in 1897 by Juan Antonio Buschiazzo, the same Italian-born Argentine architect who designed Cementerio de la Recoleta. It occupies the inside of an entire city block, though you wouldn't be able to tell just by looking at the modest sidewalk entrances. The wrought-iron interior (note the beautiful original ceiling) makes it one of BA's most atmospheric markets; locals shop here for fresh produce and meat. Peripheral antique stalls offer old treasures.

EL ZANJÓN DE GRANADOS — ARCHAEOLOGICAL SITE

Map p240 (011-4361-3002; www.elzanjon.com.ar; Defensa 755; 1hr tour Mon-Fri AR$200, 40min Sun AR$160; tours noon, 2pm & 3pm Mon-Fri, every 30min 11am-6pm Sun; S Línea C Independencia) One of the more unique places in BA is this amazing urban architectural site. A series of old tunnels, sewers and cisterns (built from 1730 onwards) were constructed above a river tributary and provided the base for one of BA's oldest settlements, which later became a family mansion and then tenement housing and some shops.

The Zanjón is the realized dream of Jorge Eckstein, who found these ruins in 1986 after purchasing land for a business project and then spent years renovating them into what you see today. It offers a fascinating glimpse into the city's history; meticulously reconstructed brick by brick and very attractively lit, this site also contains several courtyards and even a watchtower. There are a few relics on display in the various halls and rooms, but the highlights are the spaces themselves.

MUSEO DE ARTE CONTEMPORÁNEO BUENOS AIRES — MUSEUM

Map p240 (MACBA; 011-5263-9988; www.macba.com.ar; Av San Juan 328; AR$60, Wed AR$40; noon-7pm Mon & Wed-Fri, 11am-7:30pm Sat & Sun; 24, 29, 111) Art lovers shouldn't miss this fine museum, which specializes in geometric abstraction drawn from the technology-driven world that surrounds us today (think architecture, maps and computers). So rather than traditional paintings, you'll see large, colorful and minimalist pieces meant to inspire reflection.

MUSEO HISTÓRICO NACIONAL — MUSEUM

Map p240 (011-4300-7540; www.cultura.gob.ar/museos/museo-historico-nacional/; Defensa 1600; AR$20; 11am-6pm Wed-Sun, tours in English noon Wed, Thu & Fri; 29) Located in Parque Lezama (p90) is the city's national historical museum. It's dedicated to Argentina's revolution of May 25, 1810, though there is some coverage of precolonial times too. There are several portraits of presidents and other major figures of the time, along with a beautifully lit generals' room. Peek into the re-created version of José de San Martín's bedroom – military hero and liberator of Argentina (along with other South American countries).

Exhibit highlights include an Argentine flag taken by General Belgrano to Alto Perú (now Bolivia) in 1812 and, best of all, a sword belonging to San Martín himself, now guarded by grenadiers; you'll need to walk through a tunnel displaying other revolutionary heroes' swords, lit up like a nightclub with piped-in music, to reach it.

MUSEO DE ARTE MODERNO DE BUENOS AIRES — MUSEUM

Map p240 (MAMBA; 011-4361-6919; www.museodeartemoderno.buenosaires.gob.ar; Av San Juan 350; AR$20, Tue free; 11am-7pm Tue-Fri, to 8pm Sat & Sun; 29, 24, 111) Housed in a

Neighborhood Walk
Historical Saunter

START EL ZANJÓN DE GRANADOS
END BAR BRITÁNICO
LENGTH 1.5KM; 2½ HOURS

Time your walk to tour the amazing series of tunnels and brick archways of 1 **El Zanjón de Granados** (p88), which formed the foundations of BA's oldest homes.

The decaying white-stucco-and-brick 2 **Casa Mínima** at San Lorenzo 380 is a good example of the style known as *casa chorizo* (sausage house). Barely 2m wide, the lot was reportedly an emancipation gift from slave owners to their former bondsmen.

Head south on Defensa and stop at the lively 3 **El Desnivel** (p91) for a classic Argentinian steak feast. And don't miss strolling through the covered 4 **Mercado de San Telmo** (p88), which has been running since 1897.

Back on Defensa you'll soon reach the heart of the barrio, 5 **Plaza Dorrego** (p87). From Monday to Saturday it's a relatively peaceful place, but come Sunday the lively 6 **Feria de San Telmo** (p88) sets up in the plaza and surrounding streets.

Stop to have a look at the patios and rooms of 7 **Pasaje de la Defensa** (p90), a microcosm of San Telmo's history.

A block south, the 8 **Museo de Arte Moderno de Buenos Aires** (p88) offers cutting-edge exhibitions, along with works by Argentine artists. Next door is the 9 **Museo de Arte Contemporáneo Buenos Aires** (p88), great for abstract art.

The freeway location of the 10 **Club Atlético Memorial** is simply awful – but so is its history. This is one of the secret detention centers where thousands of 'disappeared' people were tortured and killed during the military dictatorship of 1976 to 1983.

Amid San Telmo's European-style buildings, it's something of a surprise to see the 11 **Iglesia Ortodoxa Rusa** (p90) – a reminder of the importance of European immigration in the neighborhood's history.

Stroll through the large 12 **Parque Lezama** (p90) to the 13 **Museo Histórico Nacional** (p88) for an insight into Argentina's history. And finally, rest your tired feet at the atmospheric corner 14 **Bar Británico** (p93). Snag a prized window seat and order a drink – you deserve it.

SAN TELMO: A BRIEF HISTORY

San Telmo is known for the violent street fighting that took place when British troops, at war with Spain, invaded the city in 1806. They occupied it until the following year, when covert *porteño* resistance became open counter-attack. British forces advanced up narrow Defensa, but the impromptu militia drove the British back to their ships. Victory gave *porteños* confidence in their ability to stand apart from Spain, even though the city's independence had to wait another three years.

After this San Telmo became a fashionable, classy neighborhood, but in the late 19th century a yellow-fever epidemic hit and drove the rich onto higher ground, west and north of the present-day Microcentro. As European immigrants began to pour into the city, many older mansions in San Telmo became *conventillos* (tenements) to house poor families. It was in the shared patios of these *conventillos* that tango music first emerged, a blend of the musical traditions of the immigrant neighborhood.

former tobacco warehouse, this spacious, multistory museum shows off the works of (mostly) Argentine contemporary artists. Expect exhibitions showcasing everything from photography to industrial design, and from figurative to conceptual art. There's also an auditorium and gift shop.

BASÍLICA DE NUESTRA SEÑORA DEL ROSARIO — CHURCH

Map p240 (Santo Domingo; Defensa 422; ⌚7am-6:30pm Mon-Fri, 6am-7:30pm Sat, 10am-1pm & 3-6pm Sun; Ⓢ Línea E Bolívar) FREE Marking the approach into San Telmo, this 18th-century Dominican church and monastery has a long and colorful history. On the left tower you'll see replicas of cannons launched against British troops holed up here during the invasion of 1807; the basilica displays flags that were captured from the British. In front of the church is the mausoleum of General Belgrano, the independence hero best known as the creator of the Argentinian flag.

PASAJE DE LA DEFENSA — NOTABLE BUILDING

Map p240 (Defensa 1179; ⌚10am-6pm Tue-Fri, to 8pm Sun; 🚌29, 24, 111) Originally built for the Ezeiza family in around 1880, this building later became a *conventillo* (tenement house) that was home to 32 families. These days, it's a charmingly worn building with antique shops clustered around atmospheric leafy patios.

PARQUE LEZAMA — PARK

Map p240 (cnr Defensa & Av Brasil; 🚌29, 24, 111) Scruffy Parque Lezama was once thought to be the site of Buenos Aires' founding in 1536, but archaeological teams have refuted the hypothesis. Today's green park hosts old chess-playing gentlemen, bookworms toting *mate* (traditional Argentine tea) gourds and teenagers kissing on park benches.

IGLESIA ORTODOXA RUSA — CHURCH

Map p240 (www.iglesiarusa.org.ar; Av Brasil 315; guided tours AR$30; 🚌29) The striking late-19th-century Iglesia Ortodoxa Rusa (Russian Orthodox Church) on the north side of Parque Lezama is the work of architect Alejandro Christophersen and was built from materials shipped over from St Petersburg. Stop by to admire the church from outside; the doors are closed to the public except for once a month (usually the second Sunday) when guided tours are given at 3:30pm – call ahead.

MUSEO NACIONAL DE LA HISTORIA DEL TRAJE — MUSEUM

Map p240 (☎011-4343-8427; https://museodeltraje.cultura.gob.ar/; Chile 832; ⌚3-7pm Tue-Sun; Ⓢ Línea C Independencia) FREE This small clothing museum is always changing its wardrobe. You can hit upon wedding outfits from the late 1800s, popular fashions from the early 1900s or even clothing worn by travelers on the Silk Road. If you're lucky, accessories such as elaborate hair combs, top hats, antique eyeglasses and elegant canes might be on display.

MUSEO ARGENTINO DEL TÍTERE — MUSEUM

Map p240 (☎011-4307-6917; www.facebook.com/museoargentinodeltitere/; Estados Unidos 802; ⌚vary widely, call ahead; 👪; Ⓢ Línea C Independencia) FREE This puppet museum has inexpensive weekend shows that will amuse the little ones.

FACULTAD DE INGENIERÍA NOTABLE BUILDING

Map p240 (Av Paseo Colón 850; 29, 24, 111) This neoclassical building is the engineering school for the Universidad de Buenos Aires. It was originally built for the Fundación Eva Perón and is an oddball landmark once described by Gerald Durrell as 'a cross between the Parthenon and the Reichstag.' In front of the building and in the middle of Av Paseo Colón is **Plazoleta Olazábal**, a tiny park which features Rogelio Yrurtia's masterful sculpture *Canto al Trabajo*.

EATING

San Telmo has a wide range of eateries to choose from. Get a good-value meat fix at an old-school *parrilla* (steakhouse), soak in the atmosphere at a traditional neighborhood bar or splash out at one of the barrio's fine-dining spots.

LO DE FREDDY PARRILLA $

Map p240 (Carlos Calvo 471; choripan AR$35, vaciopan AR$80; 1:30-5:30pm & 8-11:30pm Mon-Fri, 2pm-midnight Sat & Sun; 29) Near the entrance to San Telmo market is this hole-in-the-wall *parrilla* serving some of the best-value *choripanes* (sausage sandwiches) and *vaciopanes* (beef sandwiches) in town. It's a rustic joint with just one bench and a few sidewalk stools (which are likely to be occupied by the regulars), but for a filling feed it can't be beat.

EL BANCO ROJO INTERNATIONAL $

Map p240 (011-4040-2411; https://elbancorojo.wordpress.com/; Bolívar 866; mains AR$70-85; noon-12:30am Tue-Sat, to 11:30pm Sun; Línea C Independencia) A San Telmo youth magnet, this trendy joint serves up sandwiches, falafels, burgers and tacos, as well as a range of beers and spirits. Try the *empanada de cordero* (lamb turnover) if they have it. This place, Banco Rojo's new digs (one block over from the old one), has more space to eat-in but the same grungy vibe.

LA POESIA ARGENTINE $

Map p240 (011-4300-7340; Chile 502; mains AR$57-200; 8am-2am Sun-Thu, to 4am Fri & Sat; Línea C Independencia) Step back in time at this traditional cafe. Originally a gathering place for artists and poets, this small corner spot still retains its bohemian atmosphere with live music recitals on Thursday and Friday. Snack on a turkey sandwich or *milanesa* (beef cutlet) and relive the past.

BAR EL FEDERAL ARGENTINE $

Map p240 (011-4361-7328; Carlos Calvo 599; mains AR$57-200; 8am-2am Sun-Thu, to 4am Fri & Sat; ; Línea C Independencia) Dating from 1864, this historical bar is a classic, with original wooden features, black-and-white floor tiles, and an eye-catching antique bar and cash register. The specialties here are sandwiches (especially turkey) and *picadas* (shared appetizer plates), but there are also lots of pastas, salads, desserts and tall mugs of icy beer.

ABUELA PAN VEGETARIAN $

Map p240 (011-4361-4936; http://abuelapan.com/; Chile 518; mains AR$100; 8am-7pm Mon-Fri, 9am-4pm Sun; ; Línea C Independencia) Tiny but atmospheric spot with just a handful of tables serving vegetarian and vegan food. The specials change daily – expect things like aubergine *milanesas*, stuffed cannelloni, tacos and lentils.

★**EL REFUERZO BAR ALMACEN** ARGENTINE $$

Map p240 (011-4361-3013; www.facebook.com/elrefuerzobaralmacen/; Chacabuco 872; mains AR$150-200; 10am-2am Tue-Sun; Línea C Independencia) The small dining room fills up quickly at this *almacén*-style restaurant. There's an excellent wine list to match the menu of top-notch dishes written on blackboards on the walls – think cured meats, cheeses, homemade pastas and bistro-style casseroles. It's a casual, friendly place that's popular with locals.

If you can't get in for dinner, try **El Refuerzo Provisiones** (Map p240; 011-4300-0023; www.facebook.com/RefuerzoProvisiones/; Estados Unidos 758; mains AR$150-200; 6pm-2am Mon-Sat; Línea C Independencia) around the corner, which serves the same menu.

EL DESNIVEL PARRILLA $$

Map p240 (011-4300-9081; Defensa 855; mains AR$120-280; noon-midnight Tue-Sun, 7pm-midnight Mon; Línea C Independencia) This long-running, low-key *parrilla* joint packs in both locals and tourists, serving them treats such as chorizo sandwiches and *bife de lomo* (tenderloin steak). The delicious smells from the sizzling grill out front are torturous as you wait for a table – get here early, especially on weekends.

PULPERÍA QUILAPÁN ARGENTINE $$

Map p240 (011-4307-6288; pulperiaquilapan.com; Defensa 1344; set menu AR$120-220, mains AR$140-230; 9am-1am Tue-Sat, to 8pm Sun; ; 29) Get a taste of life in the rural pampas without leaving the city at Pulpería Quilapán, a former colonial-era house that has been transformed into the kind of bar that's traditionally frequented by gauchos. Traditional Argentine meats, pastas and stews are served; at AR$120 for a main course, drink and dessert, the *menú ejecutivo* is a good deal.

There's also a great little *almacén* (grocery store) selling cheeses, jams, wines from small vineyards, *mates* and *pingüinos* (penguin-shaped wine jugs).

CASAL DE CATALUNYA CATALAN $$

Map p240 (011-4361-0191; www.casal.org.ar; Chacabuco 863; mains AR$180-320; noon-4pm & 8pm-midnight Tue-Thu, till 1am Fri & Sat, noon-4pm Sun; S Línea C Independencia) Located in BA's Catalan cultural center is this excellent Catalan restaurant. Big on seafood, its specialties run from garlic shrimp to fresh mussels and clams in tomato sauce to fish of the day with aioli. Other typical dishes include *jamón serrano* (prosciutto-like ham), seafood paella and suckling pig.

GRAN PARRILLA DEL PLATA PARRILLA $$

Map p240 (011-4300-8858; www.parrilladelplata.com; Chile 594; mains AR$170-230; noon-4pm & 8pm-1am Mon-Sat, noon-1am Sun; S Línea C Independencia) There's nothing too fancy at this traditional corner *parrilla* (one of the best in San Telmo) – just old-time atmosphere and generous portions of tasty grilled meats at decent prices. There are also pastas for that unfortunate vegetarian who might get dragged along.

ORIGEN CAFÉ INTERNATIONAL $$

Map p240 (011-4362-7979; Humberto Primo 599; mains AR$160-270; 8am-10pm Tue-Fri & Sun, to 9:30pm Mon & Sat; ; 29) Modern but unpretentious, this stylish corner bistro spills out onto the wide sidewalks; snag an outdoor table on a sunny afternoon. The creative menu features health-conscious dishes from stir-fries and whole-wheat pizzas to homemade soups and green salads. There's an emphasis on vegetarian food, and the cappuccinos are served in delightfully oversized mugs.

★CAFÉ SAN JUAN INTERNATIONAL $$$

Map p240 (011-4300-1112; www.facebook.com/CafeSanJuanrestaurant/; Av San Juan 450; mains AR$280-380; 12:30-4pm & 8pm-midnight Sun & Tue-Thu, to 1am Fri & Sat; S Línea C San Juan) Having studied in Milan, Paris and Barcelona, TV-chef Leandro Cristóbal now runs the kitchen at this renowned San Telmo bistro. Start with fabulous tapas, then delve into the grilled Spanish octopus (AR$780), *molleja* (sweetbreads) cannelloni and amazing pork *bondiola* (deliciously tender after nine hours' roasting). Reserve ahead for lunch and dinner.

★HIERBABUENA VEGETARIAN $$$

Map p240 (011-4362-2542; www.hierbabuena.com.ar; Av Caseros 454; mains AR$195-260; 9am-midnight Tue-Sun, to 5pm Mon; ; 29, 33, 159, 130) Offering a wide selection of healthy vegetarian dishes, smoothies and juices, Hierbabuena is a good option for those looking for a satisfying, non-meat-based meal. It's in a pretty spot, too, looking out onto Av Caseros. Brunch is served on weekends from 11am to 3pm.

CAFE RIVAS ARGENTINE $$$

Map p240 (011-4361-5539; www.facebook.com/caferivas/; Estados Unidos 302; mains AR$220-275; 9:30am-1:30am Tue-Fri, 10am-1:30am Sat, 11am-8pm Sun; ; 29) On a picturesque San Telmo corner looking out onto cobblestone streets is this fabulous restaurant with an immaculate wooden interior that oozes timeless charm. Open all day, it serves breakfast, lunch and dinner with a *merienda* (afternoon tea) menu of sandwiches and pastries in between. The menu focuses on Argentine classics such as pork *milanesas* (fried breaded cutlets), fish stews and beef steaks.

Equally good care is taken with the drinks menu; an excellent selection of teas and coffees, wines and cocktails are served.

CANTINA SAN JUAN ARGENTINE $$$

Map p240 (011-4300-9344; www.facebook.com/CafeSanJuanrestaurant/; Chile 474; mains AR$280-370; 12:30-6pm & 8pm-midnight Tue-Sun; S Línea C Independencia) At this casual joint, chef Leandro Cristóbal sticks with simple dishes such as antipasto, mini pizzas, fresh pastas and a few meat and fish mains – but it's all excellent. Afterwards, try the in-house vermouth from the '*vermutería*' bar.

COMEDOR NIKKAI JAPANESE $$$

Map p240 (☎011-4300-5848; Av Independencia 732; mains AR$170-300; ⏰noon-3pm & 7:30-11pm Mon-Thu, noon-3pm & 8pm-midnight Fri, 8pm-midnight Sat; Ⓢ Línea C Independencia) Housed in the Asociación Japonesa building, this restaurant has some of BA's most authentic Japanese food, and the locals know it – come early if you don't want to wait. All your favorites are here, including tempura, teriyaki, ramen or udon noodles and – of course – lots of sushi and sashimi choices. Sake is available too.

DRINKING & NIGHTLIFE

New bars continue to pop up with regularity in San Telmo, where cocktail bars and craft-beer pubs sit side by side with historic cafes that have hardly changed over the years. Here older gentlemen still show up for their morning coffee and *medialunas*, but there's space for everyone.

★**BAR PLAZA DORREGO** CAFE

Map p240 (☎011-4361-0141; Defensa 1098; ⏰8am-midnight Sun-Thu, to 3:30am Fri & Sat; 🚌29, 24, 33) You can't beat the atmosphere at this traditional joint; sip your *submarino* (hot milk with chocolate) by a picturesque window and watch the world pass by, or grab an outdoor table next to the busy plaza. Meanwhile, traditionally suited waiters, piped-in tango music, antique bottles and scribbled graffiti on walls and counters might take you back in time.

DOPPELGÄNGER COCKTAIL BAR

Map p240 (☎011-4300-0201; www.doppelganger.com.ar; Av Juan de Garay 500; ⏰7pm-2am Tue-Thu, to 4am Fri, 8pm-4am Sat; 🚌29, 24) At this cool, emerald-hued corner bar you can count on being served a perfectly mixed martini. That's because Doppelgänger specializes in vermouth cocktails. The lengthy menu is full of creative concoctions: start with the journalist, a martini with a bitter orange twist, or channel Don Draper and go for the bar's best seller – an Old Fashioned.

ON TAP CRAFT BEER

Map p240 (www.ontap.com.ar; Av Caseros 482; ⏰5pm-midnight Sun, Tue & Wed, to 1am Thu-Sat; 🚌29) Sample some of the 20 locally brewed craft beers at the San Telmo branch of On Tap, located on elegant Av Caseros.

COFFEE TOWN COFFEE

Map p240 (☎011-4361-0019; http://coffeetowncompany.com; Bolívar 976, inside Mercado de San Telmo; ⏰8am-8pm; Ⓢ Línea C Independencia) For some of BA's best coffee, drop by this casual kiosk or larger coffee shop inside the Mercado de San Telmo (p88; enter via Carlos Calvo). Experienced baristas serve up organic, fair-trade coffee derived from beans from all over the world – Colombia, Kenya, Sumatra and Yemen. A few pastries help the java go down.

BAR BRITÁNICO CAFE

Map p240 (☎011-4361-2107; Av Brasil 399; ⏰24hr Tue-Sun, 8am-midnight Mon; 🚌29, 24, 33) A classic corner cafe on the edge of Parque Lezama, Bar Británico has an evocative old wooden interior and big glass windows that open to the street. Drop in for a *café cortado* (small espresso with milk) in the morning or a beer on a sunny afternoon.

PRIDE CAFE CAFE

Map p240 (☎011-4300-6435; Balcarce 869; ⏰8am-8pm Mon-Fri, 11am-8pm Sat, 9am-8pm Sun; 📶; 🚌29, 24, 33) This small, gay-friendly cafe is especially busy on Sunday during San Telmo's antiques fair, when crowds descend on the homemade pastries (the chocolate brownie has a following), healthy snacks and flavored coffees. It's the kind of place where you'll get chatting to the other customers and lose track of time.

GIBRALTAR PUB

Map p240 (☎011-4362-5310; www.thegibraltarbar.com; Perú 895; ⏰noon-4am; 🚌29, 24, 33) One of BA's classic pubs, the Gibraltar has a cozy atmosphere and good bar counter for those traveling alone. For a little friendly competition, head to the pool table in the back. There are sports on TV, and happy hour runs from noon to 8pm every day.

BAR SEDDÓN BAR

Map p240 (☎011-4342-3700; Defensa 695; ⏰8am-4am; 🚌29, 24, 33) This long-running corner bar-restaurant, outfitted with black-and-white tiles and rustic wood tables, is housed in an old restored pharmacy. Drop in for an icy *chopp* (mug of draft beer) or a late-night glass of red – there are also sandwiches, pizzas and daily specials if you're hungry.

CLUB MUSEUM CLUB

Map p240 (☎011-4781-7061; www.museumclub.com.ar; Perú 535; ⏰1am-5am Fri & Sat; 🚌29, 24) This cavernous disco is housed in a beautiful old factory designed by Eiffel – the same man behind the famous Parisian landmark. It's a huge space with multiple balconies and a great sound system pumping out '80s and '90s pop music and Latin tunes. Note that Club Museum has a reputation for being a bit of a meat market.

ENTERTAINMENT

★MALDITA MILONGA TANGO

Map p240 (☎011-15-2189-7747; www.elafronte.com.ar; Perú 571, Buenos Ayres Club; AR$140; ⏰class 9pm, milonga 10:30pm Wed & Sun; Ⓢ Línea E Belgrano) Maldita Milonga, held on Wednesdays and Sundays at Buenos Ayres Club, is a well-run and popular event, and one of the best places to see tango being danced by real couples. The highlight of the night is when the dynamic orchestra El Afronte plays at 11pm; at midnight there's a professional dance demonstration.

TANGO QUEER TANGO

Map p240 (☎011-15-3252-6894; www.tangoqueer.com; Perú 571, Buenos Ayres Club; AR$100; ⏰class 8:30pm, milonga 10pm-2am Tue; Ⓢ Línea E Belgrano) On Tuesday nights anyone can dance with anyone, leading or following as they choose, at this excellent gay tango class and *milonga*.

CENTRO CULTURAL TORQUATO TASSO LIVE MUSIC

Map p240 (☎011-4307-6506; www.torquatotasso.com.ar; Defensa 1575; 🚌29, 168, 24) One of BA's best-loved live-music venues, with top-name tango music performances – keep an eye out for Rodolfo Mederos Trio and La Chicana. Attracts bands that mix genres, such as fusing tango or *folklórico* (folk music) with rock.

LA VENTANA TANGO

Map p240 (☎011-4334-1314; www.laventanaweb.com; Balcarce 431; show from US$70, show & dinner from US$120; Ⓢ Línea E Belgrano) This long-running basement venue is located in an old converted building with rustic brick walls in San Telmo. The tango show includes a folkloric segment with Andean musicians and a display of *boleadores* (gaucho hunting weapons). There's also a patriotic tribute to Evita, and the dinner offers a wide variety of tasty main dishes – unusual for tango shows.

EL VIEJO ALMACÉN TANGO

Map p240 (☎011-4307-7388; www.viejoalmacen.com; Balcarce 799; show from US$90, show & dinner from US$140; 🚌29, 24, 111) One of BA's longest-running shows (since 1969), this venue is a charming old building from the 1800s. Dinner is served at a multistory restaurant in the main building, then everyone heads across the street to the small theater with an intimate stage. The show starts with a quick movie about the tango show's history, then moves on to the highly athletic dancers with plenty of glitz.

LA SCALA DE SAN TELMO CLASSICAL MUSIC

Map p240 (☎011-4362-1187; www.lascala.org.ar; Pasaje Guiffra 371; 🚌29) This small San Telmo venue, located in a refurbished colonial building, puts on classical and contemporary concerts that highlight piano, tango, musical comedies and other musical-related shows and workshops. Affordable or free admission.

LA TRASTIENDA LIVE MUSIC

Map p240 (☎011-5254-9100; www.latrastienda.com; Balcarce 460; Ⓢ Línea E Belgrano) This large, atmospheric theater in San Telmo welcomes over 700, features a well-stocked bar, and showcases national and international live-music acts almost nightly. Check the website for the latest line-up.

SHOPPING

San Telmo has traditionally been Buenos Aires' antiques neighborhood. In recent years, however, the neighborhood has attracted other kinds of stores. Fashion boutiques and housewares shops have appeared, changing the general feel on the streets. Locals fear that their beloved neighborhood might become another Palermo, but even with rising real-estate prices, San Telmo is not likely to lose its gritty authenticity or charm.

L'AGO HOMEWARES

Map p240 (☎011-4362-4702; www.lagosantelmo.com; Defensa 970; ⏰11am-8pm; 🚌29) Kitschy-cool home decor – from fluorescent-hued *mate* sets and fun pillows to Frida Kahlo kitchen magnets, eclectic lighting, recycled Elvis wallets and Marilyn Monroe handbags – can be found at cute-as-a-button L'Ago.

PUNTO SUR CLOTHING

Map p240 (011-4300-9320; www.feriapuntosur.com.ar; Defensa 1135; 11am-7pm; 29) This is a great clothing store highlighting the works of nearly 70 Argentine designers. Creativity is rampant and it's a fun walk-through for one-of-a-kind threads including interesting knitwear, colorful skirts, printed T-shirts, jewelry and accessories, cool handbags and even kids' stuff.

SIGNOS JEWELRY

Map p240 (011-15-5949-9193; www.signosac.blogspot.com.ar; Carlos Calvo 428; 11am-7pm Mon-Fri, to 5pm Sun; 29) This is the tiny silversmithing shop of Alberto Codiani and Laura Romero, both artists who create beautiful jewelry. Amber, ammonites and precious stones are incorporated into unique pieces that are sure to attract attention. Custom work available.

WALRUS BOOKS BOOKS

Map p240 (011-4300-7135; www.walrus-books.com.ar; Estados Unidos 617; noon-8pm Tue-Sun; S Línea C Independencia) Run by an American photographer, this tiny shop is probably the best English-language bookstore in BA. Thousands of new and used literature and nonfiction books line the shelves here, and there's a selection of Latin American classics translated into English. Bring your quality books to trade; literary workshops offered too.

IMHOTEP ANTIQUES

Map p240 (011-4862-9298; Defensa 916; 11am-6pm Sun-Fri; 29) Come find old knickknacks at this eccentric shop. Small oddities such as Indian statuettes, Chinese snuff boxes, precious stone figurines and gargoyles make up some of the bizarre trinkets here. Also look for fantastical and mythological creatures; there are also plenty of skulls.

MOEBIUS CLOTHING

Map p240 (011-4361-2893; Defensa 1356; 11am-8pm Tue-Fri, noon-8pm Sat & Sun; 29) This little shop's racks are crowded with owner-designer Lilliana Zauberman's kaleidoscopic products: 1970s-style jersey dresses, whimsical ruffled bikinis, skirts printed with koi fish and frog patterns, cherry-red trench coats and handbags made from recycled materials. Around 60 designers sell their work here, so there's always something different, fun and new to keep an eye out for.

PUNTOS EN EL ESPACIO FASHION & ACCESSORIES

Map p240 (011-4307-7906; www.puntosenelespacio.com.ar; Carlos Calvo 450; 11am-8pm) With over 40 designers represented, this store is a good place to check out edgy women's collections by rising stars in the local fashion world. There are also kids' and men's clothes, handbags, jewelry and a few shoes.

MATERIA URBANA ART, HOMEWARES

Map p240 (011-4361-5265; www.materiaurbana.com; Defensa 702; 11am-7pm Sun & Wed-Fri, 2-7pm Sat; 29) This innovative design shop shows the work of over 100 local artists; cool finds include leather animal organizers, retro tote bags, plastic *mates* and jewelry made from metal, wood and leather.

GIL ANTIGUEDADES ANTIQUES

Map p240 (011-4361-5019; gilantiguedades.com.ar; Humberto Primo 412; 11am-1pm & 3-7pm Tue-Sat, 11am-7pm Sun; 29) Going on 45 years, this cluttered antique shop sells everything you can imagine – china tea sets, leather hatboxes, old toys, mirrors, vintage suitcases, lace tablecloths and crystal glassware. Its annex (by appointment only) has wedding dresses and accessories.

VINOTANGO FOOD & DRINKS

Map p240 (011-4361-1101; www.vinotango.com.ar; Estados Unidos 488; 10:30am-9pm; 29) A decent wine shop in San Telmo.

SPORTS & ACTIVITIES

★BIKING BUENOS AIRES CYCLING

Map p240 (011-4300-5373; www.bikingbuenosaires.com; Perú 988; 9am-6pm; S Línea C Independencia) Friendly American and Argentine guides take you on various tours of Buenos Aires; tour themes include graffiti and architecture. Recommended.

PATAGONIALANDSCAPES / SHUTTERSTOCK ©

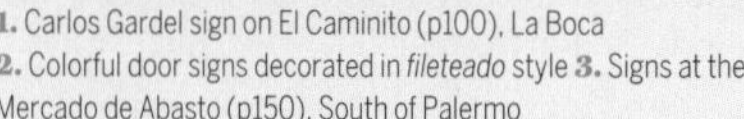

1. Carlos Gardel sign on El Caminito (p100), La Boca
2. Colorful door signs decorated in *fileteado* style **3.** Signs at the Mercado de Abasto (p150), South of Palermo

ALEXANDR VOROBEV / SHUTTERSTOCK ©

MARCELO CANTÓ / 500PX ©

Fileteado Porteño

Walk around Buenos Aires enough and you can't help noticing the colorful painted swirls of *fileteado* (also known as *filete*) decorating some public signs and buildings. Thought to have been inspired by intricate Italian metal designs, this beautiful stylistic artwork originally appeared on early-20th-century horse carts.

As time progressed, *fileteado* migrated to trucks and buses, softening these hulking vehicles with gaudy colors and symbols such as flowers, vines, birds, dragons and – of course – the Argentine flag. Today, *fileteado* on plaques serves to communicate proverbs and poetry.

Interestingly, this art form was once in danger of extinction. During the military dictatorship of 1976 to 1983 *fileteado* was banned from public-transportation systems. *Fileteadores* (*fileteado* artists) had to think of other creative places for their works. They started decorating signs, posters, newsstands and buildings, eventually evolving their labors from simple decorative touches into independent works of art. *Fileteado* has since become an integral part of Buenos Aires' artistic culture.

You can buy plaques at *ferias* (street fairs), especially in San Telmo, where Carlos Gardel is a popular subject. At the **Mercado de las Pulgas** (p142) you'll find *fileteadores* selling hand-painted signs, some of them from their workshops. To see buildings covered in *fileteado*, keep your eyes peeled in San Telmo, La Boca and Abasto (especially near **Museo Casa Carlos Gardel**; p150). You can also visit the **Bar de Filete** (at Defensa 217), a restaurant with an informal filete museum next door.

And to create this lovely artwork yourself, check out the classes given by **Alfredo Genovese** (www.fileteado.com.ar) or **Lucero Maturano** (www.fileteadoslucerom.com.ar).

La Boca

Neighborhood Top Five

❶ **El Caminito** (p100) Strolling the cobblestones and admiring the colorful houses of this little street, where art vendors and buskers vie for your spare change.

❷ **La Bombonera** (p103) Watching Argentina's most famous *fútbol* (soccer) club, Boca Juniors, play in front of an exuberant crowd.

❸ **Usina del Arte** (p102) Catching a concert at the spectacular former power station turned arts center.

❹ **Fundación Proa** (p101) Checking out the latest contemporary art exhibition at the neighborhood's cutting-edge gallery.

❺ **Museo Benito Quinquela Martín** (p101) Viewing the powerful artwork of Quinquela Martín on display in his former home and taking in the views of the Riachuelo from the roof terrace.

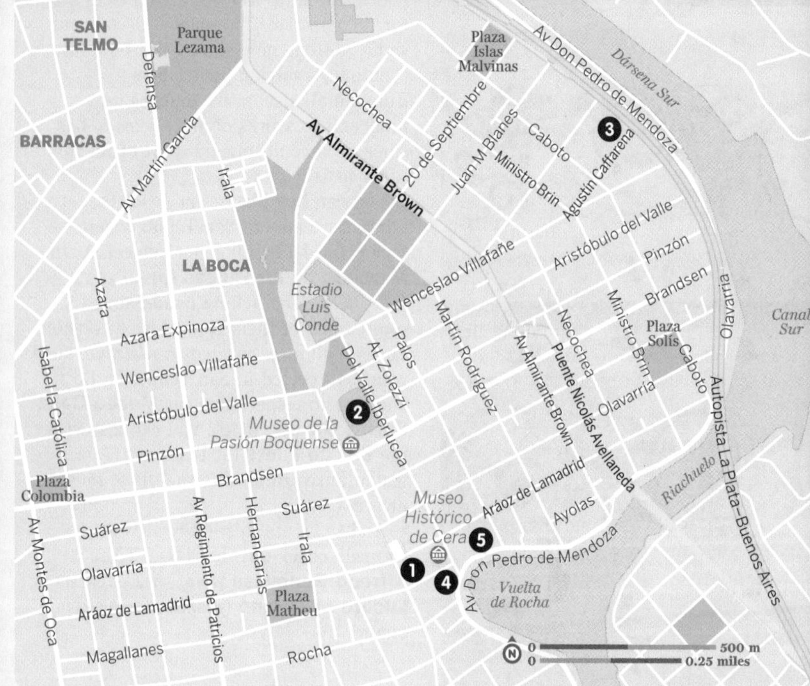

For more detail of this area see Map p242

Explore: La Boca

Since some areas of La Boca can be a little sketchy, it's best to visit the neighborhood during the day and take a bus or taxi to the sights. Don't stray too far from the riverside walk, El Caminito and La Bombonera Stadium, especially with expensive cameras. Be discreet, stick close to the busier streets and you should be fine. On your way in, note the **Casa Amarilla** (Map p242; Av Almirante Brown 401; 29, 168, 33) on Av Almirante Brown. This is a replica of the country house belonging to Irish-born admiral and founder of Argentina's navy William (Guillermo) Brown, after whom the avenue is named. Three blocks further on (look to your left at the kink in the road), you'll notice the curious Gothic structure called **Torre Fantasma** (Ghost Tower; Map p242; Av Almirante Brown 800; 29, 33, 64) local legend has it that the place is haunted.

When you reach the river, take a look at the Puente Nicolás Avellaneda which spans the Riachuelo, linking La Boca to the industrial suburb of Avellaneda; before the bridge's completion in 1940, floods had washed away several others. From here, the road follows the river's edge to El Caminito (p100).

The neighborhood's great pride and joy is Boca Juniors soccer team, whose stadium and excellent museum (p101) is four blocks north of El Caminito.

Local Life

- **Soccer** There's no better way to experience the spirit of La Boca than watching the neighborhood's beloved soccer team Boca Juniors play at La Bombonera (p103).
- **Live Music** *Porteños* (residents of Buenos Aires) love to take advantage of the city's packed program of free concerts and other cultural offerings. Join them for a performance at the fantastic Usina del Arte (p102) arts center.
- **Hangouts** Just a couple of streets away from the tourist restaurants of El Caminito is the atmospheric neighborhood joint Café Bar Roma (p102), where the local *señoras* have been meeting for a *café con leche* (coffee with milk) and a gossip since 1905.

Getting There & Away

- **Bus** Take buses 33, 64 and 29 from Palermo and the Center; they all end up at El Caminito.

Lonely Planet's Top Tip

The new tourist information booth (p217) runs a free walking tour in English on Wednesdays at 11am (reserve online).

Best Museums

- Fundación Proa (p101)
- Museo Benito Quinquela Martín (p101)

For reviews, see 101.

Best Places to Eat & Drink

- Il Matterello (p101)
- El Obrero (p101)
- Proa Cafe (p102)
- Café Bar Roma (p102)

For reviews, see p101.

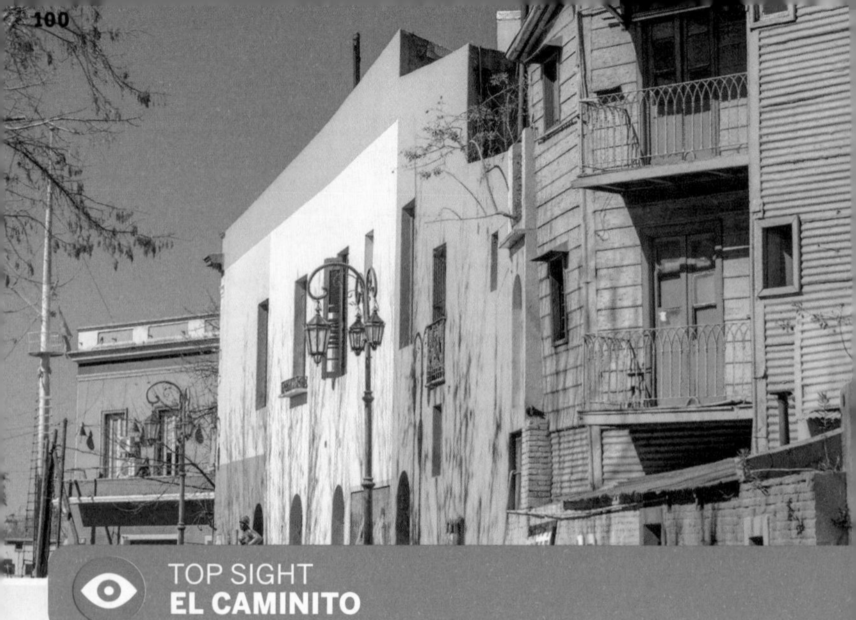

TOP SIGHT
EL CAMINITO

The colorful houses of La Boca's most famous street are a magnet for visitors, who come to snap photos of tango dancers and buy souvenirs. It's certainly geared toward tourists, but don't be put off; this block-long cobbled walk does have its charms, including the various bas-reliefs, tiled artworks and fun sculptures dotted around the self-styled 'open air' museum.

A Neighborhood of Genoese Dock Workers

The great wave of European immigration to Argentina from 1876 to 1925 brought workers from the docks of Genoa in Italy to the port of La Boca, where they found work at the shipyards. Here they constructed tenement shacks using corrugated zinc and other materials found discarded at the shipyards and brushed the makeshift houses with leftover paint from the ships. It was in the shared patios of these brightly colored *conventillos* (tenements) in La Boca that tango music first emerged.

DON'T MISS

- Tiled reliefs
- *Conventillos* (tenements)
- Sculptures of famous Argentines
- Tango dancers

PRACTICALITIES

- Map p242, B5
- Av Don Pedro de Mendoza, near Del Valle Iberlucea
- admission free
- 33, 64, 29, 168, 53

Enter Benito Quinquela Martín

By the 1950s, much of the colorful tenement housing was being replaced with drab housing blocks. Local artist Benito Quinquela Martín, who had made his name with his dramatic paintings of the port and its workers, wanted to preserve the essence of the neighborhood to which he owed so much. He joined forces with a group of friends and neighbors to rescue some of La Boca's historic tenements and reconstruct them to create an open-air museum in 1959. The name Caminito (or 'little path') comes from a 1926 tango song by Juan de Dios Filiberto (look for the lyrics on a wall plaque), which tells of a love lost.

Quinquela Martín's house and studio have been turned into an excellent museum (p101), but you can get an idea of his style on Caminito. Look for a small tiled reproduction of his *Día de Trabajo* (Day of Work) on a green wall and a much bigger one of his *Regreso de la Pesca* (Return from Fishing) at the end of the street, both by Ricardo Sánchez.

SIGHTS

EL CAMINITO
STREET

See p100.

★FUNDACIÓN PROA
GALLERY

Map p242 (011-4104-1000; www.proa.org; Av Don Pedro de Mendoza 1929; AR$50; 11am-7pm Tue-Sun; 33, 64, 29) Only the most cutting-edge national and international artists are invited to show at this contemporary art center, with its high ceilings, white walls and large display halls. The innovative installations utilize a wide variety of media and themes, while the rooftop terrace cafe (p102) is the most stylish place in La Boca for pausing for a drink or snack as you take in the spectacular views of the Riachuelo.

★MUSEO BENITO QUINQUELA MARTÍN
MUSEUM

Map p242 (011-4301-1080; www.buenosaires.gob.ar/museoquinquelamartin; Av Don Pedro de Mendoza 1835; AR$30; 10am-6pm Tue-Fri, 11:15am-6pm Sat & Sun; 33, 64, 29) Once the home and studio of painter Benito Quinquela Martín (1890–1977), this fine-arts museum exhibits his works and those of other Argentine artists. Quinquela Martín used silhouettes of laboring men, smokestacks and water reflections as recurring themes, and painted with broad, rough brushstrokes and dark colors. Don't miss the colorful tiles of his former kitchen and bathroom, his hand-painted piano and the sculptures on the rooftop terraces; the top tier has awesome views of the port.

MUSEO DE LA PASIÓN BOQUENSE
MUSEUM

Map p242 (011-4362-1100; www.museoboquense.com; Brandsen 805; museum only AR$160, museum & guided tour AR$180; 10am-6pm, guided tours hourly 11am-5pm; 29, 53, 152) This high-tech *fútbol* (soccer) museum chronicles the history of the boisterous neighborhood of La Boca and its famous soccer team Boca Juniors with displays on the club's idols, championships and trophies and, of course, the gooooals. There's a 360-degree theater in a giant soccer-ball auditorium and a good gift shop. It's worth paying the few extra pesos for the stadium tour, which includes the chance to step onto the pitch. Located at La Bombonera Stadium, three blocks north of El Caminito.

> **CIUDAD EMERGENTE**
>
> If you're in town in September, don't miss the **Ciudad Emergente** (http://festivales.buenosaires.gob.ar/2016/ciudademergente/; Sep). Held at the Usina del Arte, this six-day festival highlights the best of BA's up-and-coming musicians, artists, film-makers and designers with a program of free events, concerts and shows.

MUSEO DEL CINE
MUSEUM

Map p242 (Cinema Museum; www.buenosaires.gob.ar/museodelcine; Agustín R Caffarena 51; AR$5; 11am-6pm Mon & Wed-Fri, 10am-7pm Sat & Sun; 130, 86, 8) This small museum is housed in the former accommodations block of the electricity plant that is now the Usina del Arte (p102). It contains the original posters (painted by hand) for some of the first films to be screened in Argentina back in 1917, as well as props, cameras and the model tram used in the 1953 film *Dock Sud*.

EATING

★IL MATTERELLO
ITALIAN **$$**

Map p242 (011-4307-0529; Martín Rodríguez 517; mains AR$200-260; 12:30-3pm & 8:30pm-midnight Tue-Sat, 12:30-3pm Sun; 29, 53, 152) This Genovese trattoria serves up some of the best pasta in town, including perfectly al dente *tagliatelle alla rúcola* (tagliatelle with arugula), and *tortelli bianchi con burro foso al aglio* (pasta pillows stuffed with chard and Parmesan in a burned garlic sauce). For dessert there's a great tiramisu. Take a taxi here at night. Also in **Palermo** (Map p250; 011-4831-8493; Thames 1490; mains AR$230-290; noon-4pm & 8pm-1am Tue-Sun; 140, 39).

EL OBRERO
PARRILLA **$$**

Map p242 (011-4362-9912; Agustín R Caffarena 64; mains AR$175-360; noon-4pm & 8pm-midnight Mon-Sat; 130, 168, 29) The same family has been running El Obrero since 1954, and a number of famous people have passed through over the years, including Bono and Robert Duvall (check out the photos on the walls). You'll also see old Boca Juniors jerseys, antique furniture, old tile floors and chalkboards showing the day's specials and standard *parrilla* fare.

PROA CAFE CAFE $$

Map p242 (☎011-4104-1003; www.proa.org/eng/cafe.php; Av Don Pedro de Mendoza 1929; mains AR$92-170; ⏰cafe 11am-7pm, kitchen noon-4pm Tue-Sun; 🚌33, 64, 29) Chef Lucas Angelillo presides over this eatery, located on the top floor of Fundación Proa (p101; free access). Stop in briefly for a fresh juice and gourmet sandwich, or stay longer and order a meat, seafood or pasta dish. Don't miss the rooftop terrace on a sunny day – you'll get good views of the Riachuelo, hopefully without its corresponding scents.

DRINKING & NIGHTLIFE

The sidewalk tables at El Caminito's restaurants are a pleasant place to sink a cold beer on a sunny day (if you don't mind sharing the space with tango dancers and camera-toting tourists). Come sundown, it's best to move on; La Boca is not the kind of neighborhood to head to for a night out on the town.

CAFÉ BAR ROMA CAFE

Map p242 (☎011-4302-1354; Olavarría 409; mains AR$70-110; ⏰7am-9pm Mon-Fri, 8am-9pm Sat, 9am-8pm Sun; 🚌33, 64, 152) Join the locals for a *merienda* (afternoon snack) at this wonderfully atmospheric bar with exposed brick walls. It's been a neighborhood favorite since 1905 and the tango singer Carlos Gardel once performed here. Order a *café con leche* (coffee with milk) and *medialunas* (croissants) and pay at a cash register that looks as old as the bar itself.

ENTERTAINMENT

★USINA DEL ARTE CONCERT VENUE

Map p242 (www.usinadelarte.org; Agustín R Caffarena 1; 🚌130, 86, 8) FREE This former power station has been transformed into

MARADONA & MESSI

Born in 1960 in abject poverty in a Buenos Aires shantytown, Diego Armando Maradona played his first professional game before his 16th birthday. Transferring to his beloved Boca Juniors, he continued to prosper. After a good showing at the 1982 World Cup, he moved to Europe. Here, his genius inspired unfashionable Napoli to two league titles, and in 1986 he single-handedly won the World Cup for a very average Argentina side. In the quarter-final against England, he scored a goal first with his hand – later saying the goal was scored partly by the hand of God – and then a second one with his feet, after a mesmerizing run through the flummoxed defense that led to its being named the Goal of the Century by FIFA.

But the big time also ruined Maradona. Earning huge sums of money, he became addicted to cocaine and the high life. A succession of drug-related bans, lawsuits and weight issues meant that by his retirement in 1997 he had been a shadow of his former self for some years.

Since his retirement, overdoses, heart attacks, detoxes, his own TV program and offbeat friendships have all been par for the course in the Maradona circus. Most unbelievably of all, he was chosen to manage the national team: the highlight in a colorful spell was – after qualifying for the 2010 World Cup in South Africa – his triumphant suggestion that his critics could pleasure him orally. Nevertheless, those numerous touches of magic in the number 10 shirt have sealed his immortality. To many Argentines, the hand of God and the hand of Maradona are one and the same.

Every talented Argentine since has been dogged with the label 'the new Maradona,' but these days there's one who's the real deal. Rosario-bred Lionel Messi, a little genius who runs at defenses with the ball seemingly glued to his feet, has been captivating the world with his prodigious talents and record-breaking goal-scoring feats for Barcelona and, increasingly, for the national team. Many shrewd judges consider him better even than the great Diego, and his humble off-field demeanor is certainly an improvement. If he manages to inspire the *albiceleste* to win the World Cup again, it will truly be the Second Coming.

Andy Symington

LA BOCA & THE RIACHUELO

From the 1880s onwards, La Boca became home to poor Spanish and Italian immigrants who settled along the Riachuelo – the sinuous river that divides the city from the surrounding province of Buenos Aires. Most of them worked at the docks or in the numerous meat-packing plants and warehouses here, processing and shipping out Argentinian beef. After sprucing up the barges, the port dwellers splashed leftover paint on the corrugated-metal sidings of their houses, unwittingly giving the neighborhood what would become one of its main claims to fame.

However, La Boca's other leftover industrial materials have also found their way into the river. Decades of untreated sewage, garbage dumping and industrial wastes have taken their toll, and today the abandoned port's waters are trapped under a thick layer of smelly rainbow sludge. In recent years rusting boat hulks have been removed and other efforts to clean the river have taken place, but progress has been slow and the waterway remains one of the most polluted rivers in the world.

a spectacular concert venue in an effort to regenerate a somewhat sketchy area of La Boca. It's a gorgeous red-brick building complete with scenic clock tower and the two concert halls have top-notch acoustics. Nearly all the art exhibitions, concerts and dance performances here are free; check the website for upcoming events.

★LA BOMBONERA STADIUM STADIUM

Map p242 (☎011-5777-1200; www.bocajuniors.com.ar; Brandsen 805; 🚌29, 53, 152) Seeing Boca Juniors play at La Bombonera is one of the world's top spectator sports experiences, especially if the game happens to be the *superclásico* derby match against River. Tickets are hard to come by – it's best to go via an agent like LandingPadBA (http://landingpadba.com). You can see the stadium during a visit to the Museo de la Pasión Boquense.

On match days the streets around La Bombonera are a sea of yellow and blue (the colors of Boca's strip, inspired by the flag of a Swedish ship back in 1905). Across the neighborhood, the impassioned voices of match commentators drift out from TVs and radios, above the sound of the fans singing and cheering at the ground; when Boca scores you'll be sure to know about it.

ESTADIO LUIS CONDE BASKETBALL

Map p242 (La Bombonerita; www.bocajuniors.com.ar/deportes/noticias-deportes-basquet; Arzobispo Espinosa 600; tickets AR$100; 🚌29, 168, 33) Basketball is popular in Argentina and – like in the soccer league – one of the top teams is Boca Juniors. You can see them play at the Bombonerita; check the website for upcoming games.

TEATRO DE LA RIBERA THEATER

Map p242 (☎011-4302-9042; http://complejoteatral.gob.ar; Av Don Pedro de Mendoza 1821; 🚌33, 64, 29) This small, colorful theater, funded by the late painter and La Boca resident Benito Quinquela Martín, was built in 1971 and is now used mostly for tango performances and concerts. Even if you're not attending a show, pop into the lobby to see artworks by Quinquela Martín and an upright piano painted by the artist.

SHOPPING

On El Caminito street vendors sell sketches, paintings and prints of tango dancers and iconic city scenes, while from Thursday to Sunday further stalls are set up selling arts and crafts as well as souvenirs – don't expect top quality or bargain prices. At La Bombonera stadium, fans of Boca Juniors soccer club can buy all the team shirts and branded paraphernalia they could ever want; you can enter the shop without a ticket to the attached museum.

FERIA DE ARTESANOS CAMINITO MARKET

Map p242 (cnr Caminito & Mendoza; ⏱noon-6pm Thu-Sun; 🚌33, 64, 29) In addition to the stalls selling drawings and paintings every day along Caminito (p100), from Thursday to Sunday homemade crafts and tango-themed goods (as well as souvenirs and tat) are also sold at this small and lively crafts fair. Meanwhile, tango dancers and buskers compete for your attention.

Retiro

Neighborhood Top Five

❶ **Plaza San Martín** (p107) Wandering around this grand square and getting an eyeful of the impressive surrounding buildings.

❷ **Palacio Paz** (p106) Touring this opulent mansion, once Argentina's largest private residence at 12,000 sq meters.

❸ **Museo de Arte Hispanoamericano Isaac Fernández Blanco** (p107) Checking out the amazing silverwork at this under-the-radar museum.

❹ **Museo Nacional Ferroviario** (p108) Viewing the train memorabilia at Argentina's national railway museum.

❺ **Florería Atlántico** (p109) Ending the day with a cocktail at this speakeasy bar.

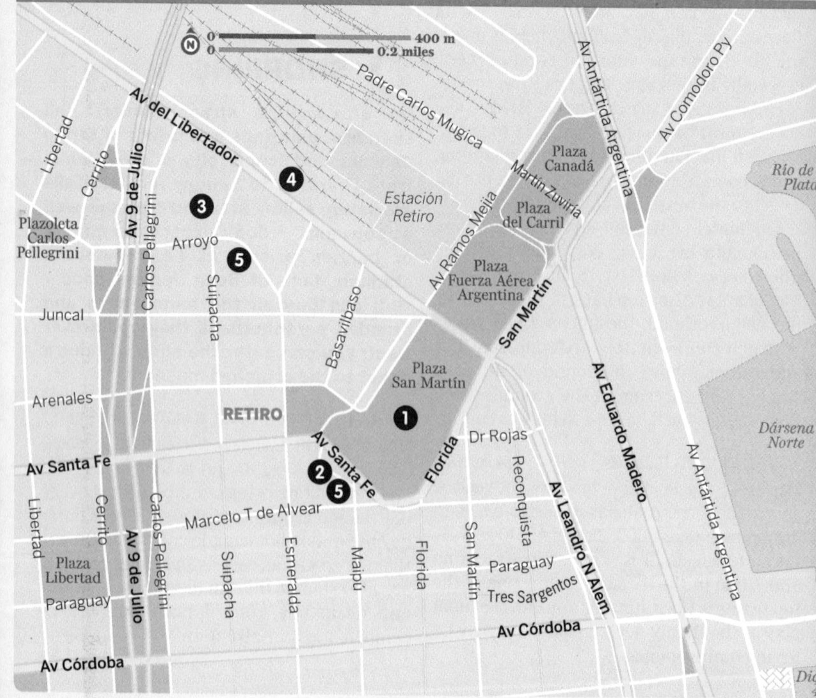

For more detail of this area see Map p246

Explore: Retiro

Retiro is a small, compact neighborhood most easily seen on foot. Wander around the Plaza San Martín area, perhaps touring a mansion or two – just double-check the visiting times as they're very limited. The museums around here also tend to be open just in the afternoon and closed on Mondays, so plan ahead if you want to visit them. Join the crowds on pedestrian Calle Florida and follow it down into the Center; Reconquista is another pedestrian street that isn't quite as crowded and is better for taking a lunch or coffee break, as there are many restaurants with sidewalk tables there.

From here you can head over to the pretty street of Arroyo. The Museo de Arte Hispanoamericano Isaac Fernández Blanco is not far from here and has a leafy garden if you need a green break. Continue west, crossing Av 9 de Julio into Recoleta; you're now on upscale Av Alvear. As you follow this route you'll see plenty of gorgeous art-deco buildings built by European immigrants decades ago.

Local Life

➡ **Hangouts** Sip a coffee or down a drink at one of the neighborhood's many cafes or bars catering to thirsty businesspeople.

➡ **Picnic** On a sunny day, grab a to-go lunch and head to Plaza San Martín's grassy lawns to join the locals out for some fresh air.

➡ **Shopping** Feel the bustle (and hustle!) of *porteño* crowds on Calle Florida, which starts near Plaza San Martín and heads south.

Getting There & Away

➡ **Bus** Take bus 59 from Recoleta and Palermo; buses 22, 45 and 126 from San Telmo; bus 150 from Congreso.

➡ **Subte** Línea C connects Retiro with the Center and the western edge of San Telmo.

Lonely Planet's Top Tip

If you're in Retiro at lunchtime, look out for the good-value *menú ejecutivo* option offered by many of the neighborhood's restaurants. Aimed at the local business crowd, the fixed-price menu usually includes a main course, drink and coffee or dessert.

Best Buildings

- Palacio Paz (p106)
- Edificio Kavanagh (p107)
- Palacio San Martín (p107)

For reviews, see p107.

Best Places to Eat

- El Federal (p109)
- Dadá (p109)
- Le Sud (p109)

For reviews, see p108.

Best Places to Drink

- Florería Atlántico (p109)
- BASA Basement Bar (p109)
- Café Porteño (p109)

For reviews, see p109.

TOP SIGHT
PALACIO PAZ

Once a private residence, this opulent, French-style palace is the grandest in BA. Inside its 12,000 sq meters are three wings, four floors and 140 rooms decorated with marble columns and gilded accents, while halls have beautiful wood-carved details and velvet-covered walls, giving visitors a glimpse of the wealth once found in Argentina.

Design & Construction

José Camilo Paz, founder of the newspaper *La Prensa* who had also served as Argentina's ambassador to France, originally commissioned French architect Louis-Marie Henri Sortais to design and build his personal mansion in 1902. Construction took 12 years and finished in 1914; unfortunately, Paz didn't see the mansion completed as he died two years earlier (check out his family's elaborate tomb in Recoleta cemetery). He also didn't realize his aspiration to become Argentina's president and make Palacio Paz his presidential residence.

Nearly all of the palace's materials – including the marble – were shipped from France. There's a definite resemblance to the Palace of Versailles, especially in the ballroom, but other rooms show more of a Louis XVI, Renaissance or Tudor style. With seven elevators and 40 bathrooms, it remains Argentina's largest single-family home ever built.

The labyrinth-like weapons museum, the Museo de Armas (p108), is located in the mansion's basement.

DON'T MISS

- The mosaic floors, marble details and the cupola of the Hall of Honor
- The presidential room
- The ballroom

PRACTICALITIES

- Map p246, C5
- ext 147, 011-4311-1071
- www.palaciopaz.com.ar
- Av Santa Fe 750
- tours AR$150
- tours English 3:30pm Thu, Spanish 3pm Tue, 11am & 3pm Wed-Fri
- S Línea C San Martín

SIGHTS

Retiro's sights are all located in and around Plaza San Martín, watched over by a statue of the great Libertador after whom the park is named.

PALACIO PAZ
NOTABLE BUILDING

See p106.

PLAZA SAN MARTÍN
PLAZA

Map p246 (S Línea C San Martín) French landscape architect Carlos Thays designed the leafy Plaza San Martín, which is surrounded by some of Buenos Aires' most impressive public buildings. The park's most prominent monument is an equestrian **statue of José de San Martín**; visiting dignitaries often come to honor the country's liberator by leaving wreaths at its base. On the downhill side of the park you'll see the Monumento a los Caídos de Malvinas, a memorial to the young men who died in the Falklands War.

Retiro was the site of a monastery during the 17th century, and later became the country *retiro* (retreat) of Agustín de Robles, a Spanish governor. Since then, Plaza San Martín – which sits on a bluff – has played host to a slave market, a military fort and even a bullring.

At the southern end of the plaza is Estación Retiro (Retiro train station), which was built in 1915 by the British.

PALACIO SAN MARTÍN
NOTABLE BUILDING

Map p246 (☎ext 7297, 011-4819-7000; Esmeralda 1231; ⏱guided tours 3pm Tue & Thu; S Línea C San Martín) This impressive art-nouveau mansion (1912) is actually three independent buildings around a courtyard. It was designed by Alejandro Christophersen for the powerful Anchorena family and later became the headquarters of the Foreign Ministry; today it's used mostly for official purposes. The only way to see inside is on a free guided tour, which are given in English and Spanish at 3pm on Tuesdays and Thursdays (bring ID), but are canceled without notice if there's an event on.

There is also a small museum on-site displaying pre-Columbian artifacts from the northwest, which can be visited with a guide by appointment only.

TORRE MONUMENTAL
LANDMARK

Map p246 (☎011-4311-0186; Plaza Fuerza Aérea Argentina; ⏱10am-6pm Mon-Fri, to 6:30pm Sat & Sun; S Línea C Retiro) FREE Standing prominently across from Plaza San Martín, this 76m-high clock tower was a donation from the city's British community in 1916 and built with materials shipped over from England. You can enter inside the base of the tower, where there are a few historical photos, but folks aren't allowed up the elevator.

MONUMENTO A LOS CAÍDOS DE MALVINAS
MONUMENT

Map p246 (S Línea C Retiro) On the downhill side of Plaza San Martín you'll see the Monumento a los Caídos de Malvinas, a memorial to the 649 soldiers who died in the Falklands War (1982). The monument faces the Torre Monumental, which until the war was called Torre de los Ingleses (Tower of the English); in 1982 it was renamed.

EDIFICIO KAVANAGH
NOTABLE BUILDING

Map p246 (Florida 1035; S Línea C San Martín) A feisty Irishwoman funded the construction of this handsome 120m art-deco apartment building, which was the tallest skyscraper in Latin America at the time of its construction in 1936.

A local rumor claims that the heiress, vengeful toward another aristocratic family for scorning her daughter, built the structure that high to block light from entering the basilica where her rivals attended Mass every Sunday.

MUSEO DE ARTE HISPANOAMERICANO ISAAC FERNÁNDEZ BLANCO
MUSEUM

Map p246 (Palacio Noel; ☎011-4327-0228; www.museofernandezblanco.buenosaires.gob.ar; Suipacha 1422; AR$10, Wed free; ⏱1-7pm Tue-Fri, 11am-7pm Sat & Sun; S Línea C San Martín) Dating from 1921, this museum is in an old mansion of the neocolonial Peruvian style that developed as a reaction against French influences in turn-of-the-19th-century Argentine architecture. Its exceptional collection of colonial art includes silverwork from Alto Perú (present-day Bolivia), religious paintings and baroque instruments (including a Guarneri violin). The curved ceiling in the main salon is beautifully painted, and there's also a peaceful garden. Signage is in Spanish.

Also known as the Palacio Noel, after the designing architect, the museum building and its collections suffered damage (since repaired) from the 1992 bombing of the Israeli embassy, which at the time was located at Arroyo and Suipacha. The space

AVENIDA 9 DE JULIO

It's one Buenos Aires landmark that all visitors to the city will have to cross, in one way or another – Avenida 9 de Julio, hailed as the world's widest avenue and named after Argentina's independence day. It's only 1km long but 16 lanes wide (140m) – and takes a walking pedestrian at least two traffic-light cycles to cross, via raised islands. *If* they don't dillydally.

When the widening construction started in 1935, the avenue was considered a patriotic symbol of the city's modern aspirations. Designers modeled it on Paris' Champs-Élysées, but made it twice as wide as a way to one-up its predecessor. For the construction, dozens of blocks of traditionally styled European buildings had to be demolished through the city's center, and thousands of residents displaced. It was an epic destruction of glorious architecture – all in the name of progress. But one significant building refused to be touched; the original French Embassy. It still stands today, as the lanes of 9 de Julio forcefully curve around it.

It took until 1980 to fully complete the widening of Av 9 de Julio. Today, several landmark buildings and monuments dot the thoroughfare. At its southern end lies Plaza de la Constitución, home to a beaux-arts train station (but not a safe place to hang out, day or night). At Av de Mayo is a statue of Don Quixote astride his horse. A bit further north, the 67m-high white Obelisco punctuates the sky, while nearby is the beautiful neoclassical facade of the Teatro Colón opera house. And finally, at the northern end of the avenue, you'll find the French Embassy – which stuck to its guns and won the right to remain.

where the embassy was located has since become a small memorial park; you can still see the outline of the building on a neighboring wall.

MUSEO NACIONAL FERROVIARIO — MUSEUM

Map p246 (011-4318-3343; Av del Libertador 405; 10am-6pm; S Línea C Retiro) FREE Trainspotters won't want to miss this museum dedicated to the history of Argentina's railway network. The ramshackle exhibits include porcelain from the presidential train, a collection of ornate train toilets and sinks dating from the 1870s, model trains, evocative old photographs and even the table where President Perón signed the decree that nationalized the railways in 1948.

The museum is located in a warehouse once used to store wool brought in by rail from the provinces before it was shipped overseas.

MUSEO DE ARMAS — MUSEUM

Map p246 (Weapons Museum; ext 179, 011-4311-1071; http://museodearmas.com.ar; Av Santa Fe 702; AR$70; 1-7pm Mon-Fri; S Línea C San Martín) This maze-like museum exhibits a frighteningly large collection of over 3500 bazookas, grenade launchers, cannons, machine guns, muskets, pistols, armor, lances and swords; even the gas mask for a combat horse is on display. The evolution of rifles and handguns is thoroughly documented, and there's a small but impressive Japanese weapons room. Those with an interest in such things won't want to miss it.

BASÍLICA DE SANTÍSIMO SACRAMENTO — CHURCH

Map p246 (San Martín 1039; 8am-7:30pm Mon-Thu, noon-7:30pm Fri, 8am-8:30pm Sun; S Línea C San Martín) FREE In the shadow of the Kavanagh building is this French-style church built by the Anchorena family in 1916. Inside, check out the original tiled floor, stained-glass windows, stone columns and wedding-cake-like altar.

EATING

Restaurants in Retiro tend to cater to the business crowds, offering good-value midday specials and food to go – so all you have to do is find yourself a nice, grassy spot or shady bench in nearby Plaza San Martín where you can enjoy your impromptu picnic. Don't ignore the area's bars and cafes, which also serve meals and are sometimes more casual and interesting than traditional restaurants.

DADÁ INTERNATIONAL **$$**

Map p246 (011-4314-4787; San Martín 941; mains AR$142-228; noon-2am Mon-Thu, to 5am Fri & Sat; Línea C San Martín) Tiny bohemian Dadá, with walls painted red and a bar cluttered with wine bottles, feels like an unassuming neighborhood bar in Paris. Order something savory, such as a stir-fry, off the bistro menu during the day; at night you can dine on grilled salmon and down an expertly mixed cocktail.

EL FEDERAL ARGENTINE **$$$**

Map p246 (011-4313-1324; www.elfederal restaurante.com; San Martín 1015; mains AR$200-320; 11am-midnight; ; Línea C San Martín) This traditional corner eatery is something of a neighborhood institution. You'll find Argentinian comfort food – simple pastas, steaks and *empanadas* – as well as higher-end specialties including Patagonian lamb, *ñandu milanesas* (cutlets of the emu-like, flightless *ñandu*) and northern river fish served here. Elaborate desserts top things off, and a rustic wooden bar adds charm.

LE SUD FRENCH **$$$**

Map p246 (011-4131-0131; Hotel Sofitel, Arroyo 841; set lunch AR$250, dinner mains AR$340-570; 12:30-3pm & 7:30pm-midnight Mon-Sat, 12:30-3pm Sun; Línea C San Martín) For a taste of Europe, dress up and head on over to Le Sud, perhaps the city's finest French restaurant, elegantly ensconced in a posh hotel. Chef Olivier Falchi whips out simple yet authentic French-Argentine fusion dishes such as brie and squash ravioli, seafood paella with smoked paprika, and grilled lamb chops with goat's cheese.

FILO ITALIAN **$$$**

Map p246 (011-4311-0312; www.filo-ristorante.com; San Martín 975; mains AR$195-345; noon-1am; ; Línea C San Martín) Popular with the business lunch crowd, this large, pop art–style Italian pizzeria tosses 30 kinds of thin-crust pies with fresh toppings – try a pie piled high with prosciutto and arugula. Other tasty choices include panini, gourmet salads, dozens of pastas and a whirlwind of drinks and desserts. The menu is extensive – there's something to please just about everyone here.

DRINKING & NIGHTLIFE

Retiro has a good number of bars and cafes catering to businesspeople during the day and into the evening; at night they attract a more foreign crowd.

★FLORERÍA ATLÁNTICO COCKTAIL BAR

Map p246 (011-4313-6093; http://floreria atlantico.com.ar; Arroyo 872; 7pm-2am Mon-Wed, to 2:30am Thu, to 4am Fri, 8pm-4am Sat, 8pm-2am Sun) This basement speakeasy is located within a flower shop, which adds an air of mystery and is likely a key reason for its success. Hipsters, artists, chefs, businesspeople and foreigners all flock here for the excellent cocktails, both classic and creative, and the lack of gas lines means the delicious tapas and main dishes are cooked on the *parrilla* (grill).

If you're a gin lover, note that the owner, Renato Giovannonni, produces and sells his own brand – called Príncipe de los Apóstoles – aromatically infused with mint, grapefruit, eucalyptus and *yerba mate*. Reserve ahead for dinner.

BASA BASEMENT BAR BAR

Map p246 (011-4893-9444; www.basabar.com.ar; Basavilbaso 1328; noon-3pm & 7pm-close Mon-Fri, 8pm-close Sat; Línea C San Martín) This fashionable and classy spot sets the mood with open spaces, dim lighting and sofas. Check out its cocktail list – the refreshing Moscow mule is a pleasant surprise, especially on warm days. BASA isn't cheap, so consider dropping by during happy hour (7pm to 9pm on weekdays and 8pm to 10pm on weekends) for drink specials.

DJs provide the sounds on weekends.

CAFÉ PORTEÑO CAFE

Map p246 (011-4516-0902; Retiro Station, Av Ramos Meija 1358; 7am-9pm Mon-Fri, 8am-7pm Sat; Línea C Retiro) Catching a train from Retiro? Allow an extra half hour for coffee at this grand cafe with soaring ceilings and a polished wood and bronze interior. One of the original fixtures of the station, built in 1915, the cafe has undergone a thorough restoration – the chandeliers twinkle beautifully at night. Look for it nearly opposite Torre Monumental.

BULLER PUB DOWNTOWN BAR

Map p246 (☎011-4313-0287; www.bullerpub.com; Paraguay 428; ⏰5pm-2am Mon-Fri; S Línea C San Martín) The downtown branch of Buller Brewing Company is a popular spot for after-office beers (the main pub is in Recoleta; p118). There are usually six beers on tap – if you can't make up your mind, order the five-beer sampler.

FLUX BAR

Map p246 (☎011-5252-0258; www.facebook.com/FluxBarBsAs/; Marcelo T de Alvear 980; ⏰7pm-2am Sun-Wed, to 3am Thu-Sat; S Línea C San Martín) Run by a friendly Englishman and his Russian partner, this gay bar is hetero-friendly – so everyone's welcome to come on down. The basement space has a slightly artsy feel. Feeling adventurous? Try the Buenos Aires iced tea (made with Fernet, that popular spirit that's something of an acquired taste). Thursday's Pop Hereje party is the biggest night here.

FLORIDA GARDEN CAFE

Map p246 (☎011-4312-7902; www.floridagarden.com.ar; Florida 899; ⏰6am-11pm; S Línea C San Martín) Usually full of businesspeople drinking coffee, this two-story cafe – now sporting modern touches such as glass walls and copper-covered columns – was historically popular with politicians, artists and writers. In fact, Jorge Luis Borges and Pérez Célis (a famous Argentine painter) used to hang out here before the era of skinny lattes. An excellent spot for people-watching.

SHOPPING

Retiro is home to a number of the city's upscale leather shops and art galleries, but it also serves the downtown business and tourism sector, with a mix of bookstores, outdoor clothing stores, and souvenir and wine shops.

★AUTORÍA ARTS & CRAFTS

Map p246 (☎011-5252-2474; www.autoriabsas.com.ar; Suipacha 1025; ⏰9:30am-8pm Mon-Fri, 10am-6pm Sat; S Línea C San Martín) This gallery-like store, stocked with edgy art books, fashion, accessories, whimsical leather desk sculptures, original artworks and unique handmade jewelry, strives to promote Argentinian designers. Especially interesting are the recycled materials – check out the bags made of Tyvek, inner tubes, fire hoses or even old sails. Products are of high quality and prices are accessible.

LA MARTINA SPORTS & OUTDOORS

Map p246 (☎011-4576-7998; www.lamartina.com; Paraguay 661; ⏰10am-8pm Mon-Fri, 10am-2pm Sat; S Línea C San Martín) Polo is a high-class sport in Buenos Aires, an unmistakable symbol of wealth and refinement. Even if you've never mounted a horse, it's interesting to look around at the gorgeous leather riding boots, helmets and saddles at Argentina's premier polo shop. Street wear clothes are also available.

CASA LÓPEZ CLOTHING

Map p246 (☎011-4311-3045; www.casalopez.com.ar; Marcelo T de Alvear 640; ⏰9am-8pm Mon-Fri, 10am-6:30pm Sat & Sun; S Línea C San Martín) Start up the limousine and make sure there's enough room for some of BA's finest selection of quality leather jackets, luggage, bags and accessories. The look is conservative, not hip; service is almost too attentive, so be prepared to chat.

SPORTS & ACTIVITIES

URBAN BIKING CYCLING

Map p246 (☎011-4314-2325; www.urbanbiking.com; Esmeralda 1084; ⏰9am-6pm Mon-Fri, noon-6pm Sat & Sun; S Línea C San Martín) One- and two-day cycling tours, along with bike and kayak excursions to Tigre. Also rents out bamboo bikes.

Recoleta & Barrio Norte

Neighborhood Top Five

❶ **Cementerio de la Recoleta** (p113) Wandering among the tombs in an astonishing necropolis where, in death as in life, generations of the Argentine elite rest in ornate splendor.

❷ **Centro Cultural Recoleta** (p114) Catching a concert, film or theatrical performance or seeing an exhibition at this excellent cultural center.

❸ **L'Orangerie** (p117) Indulging in afternoon tea at the Alvear Palace Hotel's beautiful, flower-filled Orangerie.

❹ **El Ateneo Grand Splendid** (p119) Browsing the books in one of the world's most spectacular bookstores, housed in a former theater.

❺ **Feria Artesenal Plaza Francia** (p119) Finding that perfect handmade souvenir in one of the dozens of stalls at the weekend artisan market.

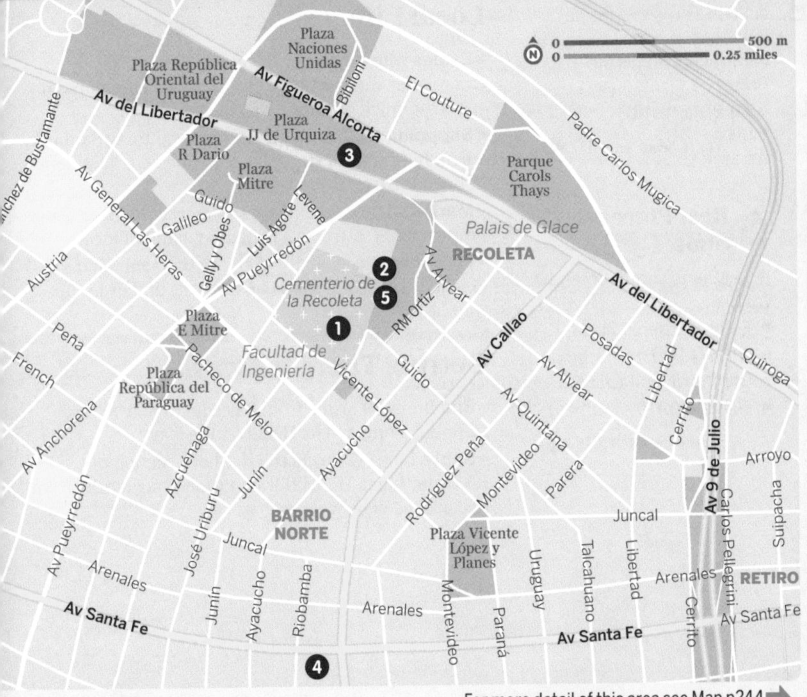

For more detail of this area see Map p244

Lonely Planet's Top Tip

Recoleta is an expensive neighborhood. For a cheap lunch, get takeout somewhere –such as *empanadas* from El Sanjuanino (p117) – and find a nice park bench, perhaps in Plaza Intendente Alvear, where you can hang out, eat and watch the world go by.

Best Places to Eat

- L'Orangerie (p117)
- Elena (p117)
- Rodi Bar (p117)
- El Sanjuanino (p117)

For reviews, see p114.

Best Places to Drink

- Milión (p117)
- Gran Bar Danzón (p118)
- Clásica y Moderna (p118)
- La Biela (p118)

For reviews, see p117.

Best Places to Shop

- El Ateneo Grand Splendid (p119)
- Feria Artesenal Plaza Francia (p119)
- Comme Il Faut (p119)
- Fueguia (p119)

For reviews, see p119.

Explore: Recoleta & Barrio Norte

Recoleta's main attractions are concentrated around the cemetery. This neighborhood was, interestingly enough, first constructed as a result of sickness; many upper-class *porteños* in the 1870s originally lived in southerly San Telmo, but during the yellow-fever epidemic they relocated as far away as they could, which meant clear across town to more rural Recoleta and Barrio Norte. Today, you can best see much of the wealth of this sumptuous quarter on Av Alvear, where many of the old mansions (and newer boutiques) are located.

Behind the cemetery is the impressive Museo Nacional de Bellas Artes and just beyond the museum is the landmark flower sculpture *Floralis Genérica*. From here you can walk to Palermo's fancy MALBA museum and green parks in about 15 to 20 minutes.

Barrio Norte is not an official neighborhood as such but rather a largely residential southern extension of Recoleta. Some people consider it a sub-neighborhood of Recoleta (and parts of it are sometimes lumped in with Retiro or Palermo, too) – it really depends on who you talk to. However, Barrio Norte does have a more accessible feel than its ritzier sibling, especially around busy Av Santa Fe. Here you'll find stores vying for shoppers' attention, all conveniently located on bus and Subte lines.

Local Life

- **Ladies who lunch** For Recoleta's upper class *señoras,* classy cafes such as Como en Casa (p117) are popular spots for lunch or afternoon coffee.
- **Shopping** Grab your wallet and head to Av Santa Fe, where hundreds of stores cater to *porteños'* (residents of Buenos Aires) every whim.
- **Markets** The weekend artisan market at Plaza Francia (p119) attracts a bohemian band of locals.
- **Ice Cream** Recoleta has more than its fair share of excellent ice-cream shops, so find one and order up.

Getting There & Away

- **Bus** Buses 59 heads from Palermo to San Telmo, stopping along Av Las Heras on the way.
- **Subte** Línea D covers the southern section of Recoleta; Línea H Las Heras station is six blocks from Recoleta cemetery.

TOP SIGHT
CEMENTERIO DE LA RECOLETA

Recoleta cemetery should be at the top of any visitor to BA's list. You can wander for hours in this city of the dead, where countless 'streets' are lined with impressive statues and marble sarcophagi. Peek into the crypts, check out the dusty coffins, and try to decipher the history of its inhabitants.

Illustrious Inhabitants

Originally the vegetable garden of the monastery next door, Recoleta cemetery was created in 1822. It covers four city blocks and contains about 4800 mausoleums decorated in many architectural styles, including art nouveau, art deco, classical, Greek, baroque and neo-Gothic. Popular motifs include crosses of all kinds, marble angels, stone wreaths, skulls and crossbones, draped urns, winged hourglasses and the occasional gargoyle. All decorate the final resting places of past presidents, military heroes, influential politicians, famous writers and other very noteworthy personages.

The most impressive tomb is not Evita's, though it's certainly the most visited. Get a good map and look for other sarcophagi; interesting stories, odd facts and myths abound. Also note the cemetery's rough edges – the cobwebs and detritus inside many of the tombs, the vegetation growing out of cracks, the feral cats prowling the premises. All add to the charm.

DON'T MISS

- Evita's grave
- Paz family tomb
- Rufina Cambacérès' tomb
- Boxer Luis Ángel Firpo's grave
- Almirante Guillermo Brown's tomb

PRACTICALITIES

- Map p244, D4
- 0800-444-2363
- Junín 1760
- admission free
- 7am-5:30pm
- S Línea H Las Heras

SIGHTS

CEMENTERIO DE LA RECOLETA — CEMETERY

See p113.

★CENTRO CULTURAL RECOLETA — CULTURAL CENTER

Map p244 (☎011-4803-1040; www.centroculturalrecoleta.org; Junín 1930; Línea H Las Heras) FREE Part of the original Franciscan convent and alongside its namesake church and cemetery, this excellent cultural center houses a variety of facilities, including art galleries, exhibition halls and a cinema. Events, courses and workshops are also offered – check the website for current offerings. Exhibitions are usually free, while tickets to films and shows are reasonably priced.

MUSEO PARTICIPATIVO DE CIENCIAS — MUSEUM

Map p244 (☎011-4806-3456; www.mpc.org.ar; Centro Cultural Recoleta, Junín 1930; AR$100; 10am-5pm Tue-Fri, 3:30-7:30pm Sat & Sun; ; Línea H Las Heras) This hands-on science museum designed with children in mind has interactive displays with plenty of levers to pull and buttons to press. A great place for kids to release their pent-up energy and produce electricity by cycling on a fixed bike to power a light bulb, for example.

With a total of nine rooms, there's enough here to keep the little ones occupied for a good few hours on a rainy or blisteringly hot day. Can be busy with school groups during the week.

BASÍLICA DE NUESTRA SEÑORA DEL PILAR — CHURCH

Map p244 (☎011-4806-2209; www.basilicadelpilar.org.ar; Junín 1904; museum adult/child AR$20/free; museum 10:30am-6:10pm Mon-Sat, 2:30-6:10pm Sun; Línea H Las Heras) The centerpiece of this gleaming white colonial church, built by Franciscans in 1732, is a Peruvian altar adorned with silver from Argentina's northwest. Inside, head to the left to visit the small but historic cloisters museum; it's home to religious vestments, paintings, writings and interesting artifacts, and there are good views of Recoleta cemetery.

On the left-hand side of the courtyard as you enter the church, look for a ceramic tiled artwork depicting Buenos Aires as it was in 1794, back when the church stood in open countryside outside the town.

VISITING RECOLETA CEMETERY

- Free tours are offered in Spanish at 11am from Tuesday to Friday (weather permitting). Tours in English are supposed to be at 11am on Tuesday and Thursday, but were suspended when we visited so call ahead.
- For a good map and detailed information, order Robert Wright's PDF guide (www.recoletacemetery.com).
- Touts also sell maps at the entrance.
- To get a good photograph of the cemetery from above, head to the cloisters museum at the Basílica de Nuestra Señora del Pilar.
- Remember to behave respectfully; people may be here to visit the graves of relatives and funerals sometimes take place.

PALAIS DE GLACE — GALLERY

Map p244 (☎011-4804-1163; www.palaisdeglace.gob.ar; Posadas 1725; noon-8pm Tue-Fri, 10am-8pm Sat & Sun; 130, 93, 62) FREE Housed in an unusual circular building that was once an ice-skating rink and a tango hall (happily not at once, however), the spacious Palais de Glace now offers a variety of rotating artistic and photographic exhibitions. Be sure to check out the 2nd floor, worth a peep for its interesting ceiling and other architectural details.

FLORALIS GENÉRICA — MONUMENT

Map p244 (cnr Av Figueroa Alcorta & Bibiloni; 130, 62, 93) This gargantuan flower sculpture, located smack in the center of Plaza Naciones Unidas, is the inspired creation of architect Eduardo Catalano, who designed and funded the project in 2002. The giant aluminum and steel petals are 20m high and used to close like a real flower, from dusk until dawn – until the gears broke, that is.

EATING

Recoleta is a playground for the wealthy elite. As you can imagine, the restaurants here aren't cheap, but if you want to rub shoulders with the upper classes, this is the place to be.

Practically everyone visits Recoleta's cemetery, so the two-block strip of touristy restaurants, bars and cafes lining RM Ortiz is very convenient. Food here tends toward the overpriced, but many restaurants have outdoor terraces that are choice hangout spots on warm days. The people-watching here is excellent, especially on weekends when the nearby craft market is in full swing.

CUMANÁ ARGENTINE $

Map p244 (☎011-4813-9207; Rodríguez Peña 1149; mains AR$82-145; ⏰noon-4pm & 8pm-1am; Ⓢ Línea D Callao) To sample Argentina's regional cuisine, check out this colorful, budget-friendly eatery with huge picture windows and an old-fashioned adobe oven. Cumaná specializes in delicious *cazuelas*, stick-to-your-ribs stews filled with squash, corn, eggplant, potatoes and meat. Also popular are the *empanadas*, *locro* (corn and meat stew) and *humita* (corn, cheese and onion tamales). Come early to avoid a wait.

UN ALTRA VOLTA ICE CREAM $

Map p244 (☎011-4805-1818; www.unaltravolta.com.ar; Av Quintana 502; 250g AR$80; ⏰11am-midnight Sun-Thu, to 1am Fri & Sat; 🚌124) Sample Argentina's fabulous Italian-style *gelato* at this upmarket ice-cream parlor. The *sambayón* (made with egg yolks, milk, cream, sugar and Marsala wine) is particularly good here.

PERSICCO ICE CREAM $

Map p244 (http://persicco.com/; Av Quintana 595; 250g AR$90; ⏰10am-midnight Mon-Thu, 10am-1am Fri, 9am-2am Sat, 9am-midnight Sun; 🚌124) With 11 branches around the city, Persicco is many *porteños'* ice-cream vendor of choice. The selection of flavors will leave you spoilt for choice – take our advice and order the *dulce de leche* (caramel).

GLORIOUS DEATH IN RECOLETA

Only in Buenos Aires can the wealthy and powerful elite keep their status after death. When decades of dining on rich food and drink have taken their toll, Buenos Aires' finest move ceremoniously across the street to the Cementerio de la Recoleta (p113), joining their ancestors in a place they have religiously visited all their lives.

Argentines tend to celebrate their most honored national figures not on the date of their birth, but on the date of their death (after all, they're nobody when they're born). Nowhere is this obsession with mortality more evident than at Recoleta, where generations of the elite repose in the grandeur of ostentatious mausoleums. Real estate here is among Buenos Aires' priciest: there's a saying that goes, 'It is cheaper to live extravagantly all your life than to be buried in Recoleta.'

It's not just being rich that gets you a prime resting spot here: your name matters. Those lucky few with surnames like Alvear, Anchorena, Mitre or Sarmiento are pretty much guaranteed to be laid down. Evita's remains are here (in the Duarte family tomb), but her lack of aristocracy and the fact that she dedicated her life to Argentina's poor infuriated the bigwigs.

A larger and much less touristy graveyard is **Cementerio de la Chacarita** (Map p254; ☎0800-444-2363; Guzmán 680; ⏰7:30am-5pm; Ⓢ Línea B Federico Lacroze), located in the neighborhood of Chacarita. The cemetery opened in the 1870s to accommodate the yellow-fever victims of San Telmo and La Boca. Although much more democratic and modest, Chacarita's most elaborate tombs match Recoleta's finest. One of the most visited belongs to Carlos Gardel, the famous tango singer. Plaques from around the world cover the base of his life-size statue, many thanking him for favors granted. Gardel's statue often has a lit cigarette resting between its fingers, left there by the city's taxi drivers who come here on their breaks to listen to one of the crooner's songs and share a cigarette with him. The anniversaries of Gardel's birth and death days see packs of pilgrims jamming the cemetery's streets.

Other famous Argentines buried in Chacarita include the poet Alfonsina Storni, the artist Benito Quinquela Martín and the composer Osvaldo Pugliese. To visit Chacarita, take Línea B of the Subte to the end of the line at Federico Lacroze and cross the street.

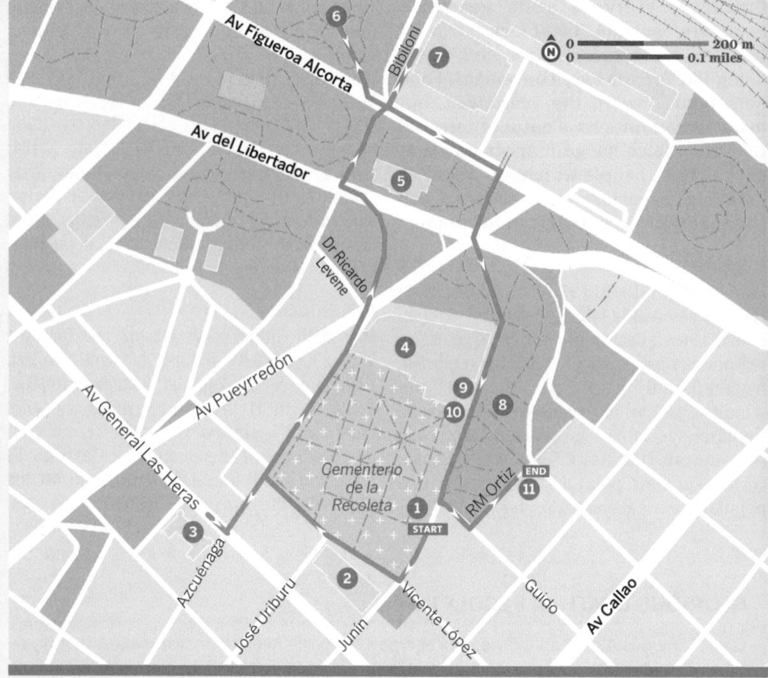

Neighborhood Walk
Death, Art & Shopping

START CEMENTERIO DE LA RECOLETA
END LA BIELA CAFE
LENGTH 2–3KM; THREE HOURS

Start with a bang and visit BA's top tourist destination: 1 **Cementerio de la Recoleta** (p113). You can easily spend hours in here examining the hundreds of elaborate tombs. Don't miss the grave of Eva Perón – to find her, go to the first major intersection and turn left at the statue; continue until a mausoleum blocks your way. Go around it and turn right at the wide 'street.' After three blocks, Evita's tomb is on the left. Leave the cemetery, turn right and swing past the upscale 2 **Recoleta Mall**.

Head to the neo-Gothic 3 **Facultad de Ingeniería** (p91), designed by Uruguayan architect Arturo Prins and never quite completed. Make your way up Azcuénaga and stop in at the large 4 **Buenos Aires Design mall** (p119), worth a look for the cutting-edge furniture and lifestyle products. Now cut across Plaza Francia and head to the excellent 5 **Museo Nacional de Bellas Artes** (p131), containing classical art from all over the world. Everything is well displayed and lit and, best of all, it's free.

Cross Av Figueroa Alcorta to reach the giant metal flower sculpture, 6 **Floralis Genérica** (p114); look for your reflection in the petals. Head back down Alcorta – passing the mammoth 7 **Facultad de Derecho** (School of Law) building along the way; it's considered bad luck for students to enter the building through the central door until they've graduated. Cross the footbridge and make your way up Plaza Intendente Alvear. If it's a weekend, browse through the craft stalls at 8 **Feria Artesenal Plaza Francia** (p119).

Stop by the 9 **Centro Cultural Recoleta** (p114) to explore the galleries. If you have small kids, the Museo Participativo de Ciencias will grab their attention. Right next to the cultural center is the pretty 10 **Basílica de Nuestra Señora del Pilar** (p114).

Amble down to restaurant-filled RM Ortiz and end your walk at the fine 11 **La Biela** (p118) cafe. If it's sunny, grab a table on the front patio – it's worth the extra pesos.

RODI BAR ARGENTINE $$

Map p244 (011-4801-5230; Vicente López 1900; mains AR$120-350; 7am-1am Mon-Sat; ; Línea H Las Heras) A great option for well-priced, unpretentious food in upscale Recoleta. This traditional neighborhood restaurant with a fine old-world atmosphere and extensive menu offers something for everyone, from inexpensive combo plates to relatively unusual dishes such as marinated beef tongue.

EL SANJUANINO ARGENTINE $$

Map p244 (011-4805-2683; www.elsanjuanino.com.ar; Posadas 1515; empanadas AR$24, mains AR$165-305; noon-4pm & 7pm-1am; 130, 93, 124) This long-running, cozy little joint has some of the cheapest food in Recoleta, attracting both penny-pinching locals and thrifty tourists. Order spicy *empanadas*, tamales or *locro* (corn and meat stew). The curved brick ceiling adds to the atmosphere, but many take their food to go – Recoleta's lovely parks are just a couple of blocks away.

COMO EN CASA ARGENTINE $$

Map p244 (011-4816-5507; www.tortascomoencasa.com; Riobamba 1239; mains AR$155-230; 8am-midnight Tue-Sat, to 9pm Sun & Mon; ; Línea D Callao) This gorgeous, upscale cafe-restaurant has a very elegant atmosphere and attracts Recoleta's wealthiest. Its best feature is the shady patio, complete with large fountain and surrounded by grand buildings, great on a warm day. For lunch there are sandwiches, salads, vegetable tarts and gourmet pizzas, while dinner options include goulash and homemade pastas. Plenty of luscious cakes and desserts, too.

★**L'ORANGERIE** FRENCH $$$

Map p244 (011-4808-2949; Alvear Palace Hotel, Av Alvear 1891; full tea Mon-Fri AR$450, Sat & Sun $490; afternoon tea 4:30-7pm Mon-Sat, 5-7pm Sun; 130, 92, 63) Afternoon tea at the Alvear Palace Hotel's beautiful, flower-filled Orangerie is a classic Recoleta experience for a special occasion. The formal tea, served from 4:30pm (from 5pm on Sunday), offers an endless array of exquisite cakes, sandwiches and pastries as well as a selection of loose-leaf teas and background piano music.

ELENA ARGENTINE $$$

Map p244 (011-4321-1728; www.elenaponyline.com; Four Seasons, Posadas 1086; mains AR$240-495; 7-11am, 12:30-3:30pm & 7:30pm-12:30am; 130, 62, 93) If you're looking to splurge on a night out, Elena should be your destination. Located at the Four Seasons Hotel, this highly rated restaurant uses the best-quality ingredients to create exquisite dishes. Order its specialty – the dry-aged meats – for something really special. The cocktails, desserts and service are five-star.

EL BURLADERO SPANISH $$$

Map p244 (011-4806-9247; www.elburladero.com.ar; José Uriburu 1488; mains AR$210-305; noon-4pm & 8pm-midnight; Línea H Las Heras) Treat yourself to an upscale meal in Recoleta at this excellent Spanish restaurant. The menu changes seasonally, but will usually include a paella dish and perhaps marinated rabbit, black hake fish or lamb with mushrooms.

CASA SALTSHAKER INTERNATIONAL $$$

(www.casasaltshaker.com; set menu incl wine pairings US$80; 8:45pm Tue-Sat) Ex–New Yorker Dan Perlman is the chef behind this respected place, which is a *puerta cerrada* (closed-door restaurant) in his own home. You'll need to book ahead, arrive at an appointed hour and sit at a communal table, which can be a lot of fun – especially for solo diners. Address and phone number given upon reservation.

Expect a five-course set menu focusing on creative Mediterranean- or Andean-inspired dishes.

DRINKING & NIGHTLIFE

From your breakfast coffee with *medialunas* to a late-night cocktail, there's no shortage of elegant cafes and swanky bars at which to wet your whistle.

MILIÓN COCKTAIL BAR

Map p244 (011-4815-9925; www.milion.com.ar; Paraná 1048; noon-2am Mon-Wed, to 3am Thu, to 4am Fri & Sat, 8pm-2am Sun; Línea D Callao) One of BA's most elegant bars, this sexy spot takes up three floors of a renovated old mansion. The garden out back is a leafy paradise, overlooked by a solid balcony that holds the best seats in the house. Nearby marble steps are also an appealing place to lounge with a frozen mojito or basil daiquiri.

GRAN BAR DANZÓN
BAR

Map p244 (011-4811-1108; www.granbardanzon.com.ar; Libertad 1161; 7pm-2am Mon-Fri, 8pm-2am Sat & Sun; Línea D Tribunales) Upscale restaurant-wine bar with a good selection of wines by the glass as well as fresh fruit cocktails, exotic martinis and Euro- and Asian-inspired dinner selections. It's very popular, so come early for happy hour and snag a good seat on a sofa.

PONY LINE BAR
BAR

Map p244 (011-4321-1200; www.elenaponyline.com; Four Seasons Hotel, Posadas 1086; 11am-1:30am Mon-Fri, 7pm-2:30am Sat, 5pm-12:30am Sun; 130, 62, 93) This sophisticated, upscale and polo-inspired bar is located in the five-star Four Seasons Hotel and attracts a well-heeled clientele. Drinks are top quality, from the craft beers to the exotic cocktails and fine international liquors; the food is good as well. Dress well, bring a fat wallet and come early if you'd like to avoid the crowds; otherwise reserve ahead.

DJs play on Friday and Saturday nights, so it can get loud at times.

LA BIELA
CAFE

Map p244 (011-4804-0449; www.labiela.com; Av Quintana 600; 7am-2am Sun-Thu, to 3am Fri & Sat; 130, 62, 93) A Recoleta institution, this classic cafe has been serving the *porteño* elite since the 1950s – when race-car champions used to frequent the place. The outdoor front terrace is unbeatable for a coffee or beer on a sunny afternoon. Just know that this privilege of seating here will cost 20% more.

The huge *gomero* (rubber tree) opposite across from La Biela was planted by a Franciscan monk in around 1800.

CLÁSICA Y MODERNA
CAFE

Map p244 (011-4812-8707; www.clasicaymoderna.com; Av Callao 892; 8am-midnight Mon-Sat, 6pm-midnight Sun; Línea D Callao) Catering to the literary set since 1938, this cozy and intimate bookstore-restaurant-cafe oozes history from its atmospheric brick walls. It's nicely lit, serves fine, simple meals and offers nightly live performances of folk music, jazz, bossa nova and tango (after 9pm). The late Mercedes Sosa, tango singer Susana Rinaldi and Liza Minnelli have all performed here.

BULLER BREWING COMPANY
MICROBREWERY

Map p244 (011-4808-9061; www.bullerpub.com; Junín 1747; noon-1am Mon-Wed, to 2am Thu & Sun, to 4am Fri & Sat; ; Línea H Las Heras) Six kinds of beer are brewed on the premises at this industrial-style microbrewery incongruously located opposite Recoleta Cemetery. If you can't choose between the stout, IPA, Hefe Weizen, rubia, honey beer or amber, order a sampler of all six. There's a great outdoor patio in front and an extensive menu of snacks and sandwiches. Also in Retiro (p110).

SHAMROCK
CLUB

Map p244 (011-4812-3584; www.theshamrock.com.ar; Rodríguez Peña 1220; bar 6pm-3am Tue-Fri, 10pm-6:30am Sat, club midnight-5:30am Thu, 1am-6:45am Fri & Sat; Línea D Callao) The Shamrock Basement is an unpretentious subterranean club known for its first-rate DJ line-ups, pounding house music and diverse young crowd. Thanks to the ever-popular Irish pub upstairs, the place sees plenty of traffic throughout the night. Come at 3am to see the club in full swing, or just descend the stairs after enjoying a few pints at ground level.

Women beware: this is a serious pick-up joint.

☆ ENTERTAINMENT

NOTORIOUS
JAZZ

Map p244 (011-4813-6888; www.notorious.com.ar; Av Callao 966; 10pm-midnight Mon-Thu, 10pm-1:30am Fri, 5pm-1:30am Sat, 5pm-12:30am Sun; Línea D Callao) This stylish, intimate joint is one of Buenos Aires' premier jazz venues, with a restaurant-cafe (overlooking a verdant garden) hosting live shows nearly every night at 9:30pm. Check the website for schedules; most performances are jazz, but there's also blues and Brazilian music.

TEATRO COLISEO
LIVE MUSIC

Map p244 (011-4814-3056; www.teatrocoliseo.org.ar; Marcelo T de Alvear 1125; Línea D Tribunales) Classical music, jazz, ballet, opera and symphony orchestras entertain at this theater most of the year, but a few surprises – such as Argentine-American rock star Kevin Johansen – occasionally show up.

SHOPPING

Exclusivity is the key word here. If you have the bucks and are willing to pay top dollar for the best-quality goods, then you'll want to shop in these neighborhoods. The city's best leather shops are based here, along with a few top fashion boutiques. Av Santa Fe is a catch-all for fashion, housewares and everything in between.

★EL ATENEO GRAND SPLENDID — BOOKS

Map p244 (011-4813-6052; www.yenny-elateneo.com/local/grand-splendid; Av Santa Fe 1860; 9am-10pm Mon-Thu, to midnight Fri & Sat, noon-10pm Sun; S Línea D Callao) This glorious bookstore in a converted theater continues to flourish in the age of the Kindle. The Grand Splendid theater opened in 1919 and was converted into a bookstore in 2000. Most of the seating was replaced with bookshelves, but the original features have been preserved, including the beautiful painted cupola and balconies.

Browse through potential purchases in one of the theater boxes or have a cup of coffee at the on-stage cafe.

COMME IL FAUT — SHOES

Map p244 (011-4815-5690; www.commeilfaut.com.ar; Arenales 1239, door 3, apt M; 11am-7pm Mon-Fri, to 3pm Sat; 111) If you're looking for quality tango shoes, this is the place to come. Not only are these shoes designed to withstand hours of dancing at the *milonga,* they're also beautiful to look at.

Visiting the boutique is like entering a bygone age: allow plenty of time to try on shoe after shoe until – just like Cinderella – the perfect pair is found.

FERIA ARTESENAL PLAZA FRANCIA — MARKET

Map p244 (www.feriaplazafrancia.com; Plaza Intendente de Alvear; 11am-7pm Sat & Sun; S Línea H Las Heras) Recoleta's popular artisan fair has dozens of booths and a range of creative, homemade goods. Hippies, mimes and tourists mingle. It's at its biggest on weekends, though there are usually a few stalls open during the week. Despite its name, the market is located just outside the Cementerio de la Recoleta in Plaza Intendente de Alvear.

FUEGUIA — PERFUME

Map p244 (011-4311-5360; www.fueguia.com; Av Alvear 1680; 11am-8pm; 130, 62, 93) On Recoleta's most *cheto* (posh) avenue you'll find this suitably upmarket perfumery selling a large selection of in-house scents and candles. Pop in to smell the latest creations.

MEMORABILIA — ARTS & CRAFTS

Map p244 (011-4811-7698; www.memorabiliabazar.com; Arenales 1170; 11am-7:30pm Mon-Fri, to 1:30pm Sat; 111) For unique, fun and handmade Argentine items, explore the corners of this tiny boutique. The stock is ever-changing, but can include such things as ceramic bowls and painted mugs, colorful jewelry in super-creative shapes and artsy notebooks. A good place to find small items easily packed into a suitcase for the flight back home.

GALERÍA BOND STREET — MALL

Map p244 (http://galeriabondstreet.com/; Av Santa Fe 1670; 11am-8pm Mon-Sat; S Línea D Callao) For the edgiest tattoos and piercings in town, you can't beat this grungy mall. BA's skateboarder-wannabes, along with their punk-rock counterparts, also come here to shop for the latest styles, sounds and bongs. Expect everything from Hello Kitty to heavy metal.

PATIO BULLRICH — MALL

Map p244 (011-4814-7500; www.shoppingbullrich.com.ar; Av del Libertador 750; 10am-9pm; 130, 62, 93) Buenos Aires' most exclusive shopping center once hosted livestock auctions, but these days it tends toward sales of Persian rugs, double-breasted tweed suits and Dior's latest designs. Three floors hold fine boutiques such as Lacoste, Salvatore Ferragamo and Christian Lacroix, along with fancy coffee shops, a cinema complex and a food court.

BUENOS AIRES DESIGN — MALL

Map p244 (011-5777-6000; www.designrecoleta.com.ar; Av Pueyrredón 2501; 10am-9pm Mon-Sat, noon-9pm Sun; S Línea H Las Heras) Fashionable home furnishing, appliances and housewares can be found under one roof here. This is the ideal place to look for that snazzy light fixture, streamlined toilet or reproduction Asian chair, as well as cute decor and art objects.

MEUNIERD / SHUTTERSTOCK ©

1. "Eva" by sculptor Alejandro Marmo and painter Daniel Santoro 2. Eva Perón's tomb in Cementerio de la Recoleta (p113)

The Immortal Evita

From her humble origins in the pampas to her rise to power beside President Juan Perón, María Eva Duarte de Perón is one of Argentina's most revered political figures. Known affectionately as Evita, she is Argentina's beloved First Lady.

At the age of 15 Eva Duarte left her hometown of Junín for Buenos Aires, looking for work as an actor and eventually landing a job in radio. Her big chance came in 1944, when she attended a benefit at Buenos Aires' Luna Park. Here Duarte met Colonel Juan Perón, who fell in love with her; they were married in 1945.

Shortly after Perón won the presidency in 1946, Evita went to work in the office of the Department of Labor and Welfare. During Perón's two terms, Evita empowered her husband both through her charisma and by reaching out to the nation's poor, who came to love her dearly. She created the Fundación Eva Perón, which built housing for the poor, created programs for children, extended subsidies and distributed clothing and food to needy families. She fervently campaigned for the aged, urging her husband to add elderly rights to the constitution and successfully pushing through a law granting pensions to elderly people in need. She successfully advocated for a law extending suffrage to women.

Perón won his second term in 1952, but that same year Evita – aged just 33 and at the height of her popularity – died of cancer. It was a blow to Argentina and to her husband's presidency.

Although Evita is remembered for extending social justice to those she called

the country's *descamisados* (shirtless ones), her rule with Perón was hardly free from controversy. Together they ruled the country with an iron fist, jailing opposition leaders and closing opposition newspapers. When *Time* magazine referred to her as an 'illegitimate child', she banned the publication, and when she traveled to Europe in 1947 she was refused entrance to Buckingham Palace. However, there is no denying the extent to which she empowered women at all levels of Argentine society and helped the country's poor.

When Evita said, 'I will come again, and I will be millions' in a speech shortly before her death, she probably had no idea of her words' prophetic truth. Today, she enjoys near-saint status and her image adorns the AR$100 bill (she is the first woman to appear on Argentine currency).

Get to know her better at **Museo Evita** (p131) or visit her tomb in the **Cementerio de la Recoleta** (p113). You can also read her autobiography *La razón de mi vida* (My Mission in Life; 1951).

Belgrano, Nuñez & the Costanera Norte

BELGRANO | NUÑEZ | COSTANERA NORTE

Neighborhood Top Five

❶ **Espacio Memoria y Derechos Humanos** (p124) Visiting the sobering Sitio de Memoria ESMA, now a memorial museum dedicated to the victims of the military dictatorship of 1976 to 1983.

❷ **La Glorieta** (p126) Dancing the tango – or watching it – at the most romantic *milonga* in BA.

❸ **Parque de la Memoria** (p125) Taking a stroll next to the river at this park on the Costanera Norte.

❹ **Parque Norte** (p126) Cooling off in the complex of swimming pools.

❺ **Museo Larreta** (p124) Eyeballing classic Spanish art at the elegant former mansion of Hispanophile novelist Enrique Larreta.

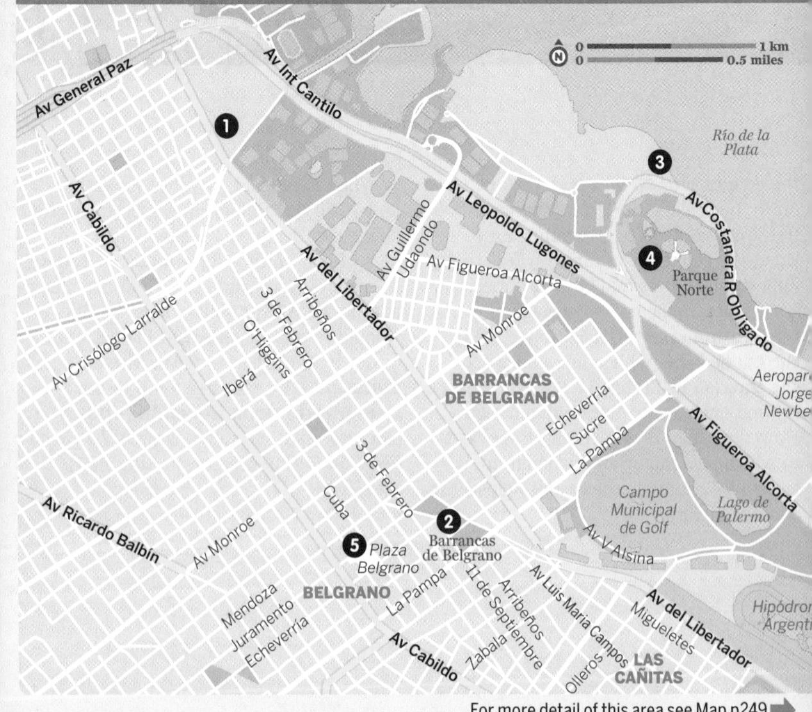

For more detail of this area see Map p249

Explore: Belgrano, Nuñez & the Costanera Norte

Bustling Av Cabildo, the racing heartbeat of Belgrano, is an overwhelming jumble of noise and neon. It's a two-way street of clothing, shoe and housewares shops. For a bit more peace and quiet, head to the blocks on either side of the avenue, where Belgrano becomes a leafy barrio of museums, plazas and good local eateries.

A block east of Av Cabildo, the barrio's plaza is the site of the modest but fun Feria Plaza Belgrano (p126). Just a few steps from the plaza is the Museo Histórico Sarmiento (p124), which honors one of the most forward-thinking Argentines in history. Also close by is the Museo Larreta (p124), a mansion with gorgeous art pieces and gardens. About five blocks north is yet another museum, the Museo Casa de Yrurtia (p124), honoring the well-known Argentine sculptor.

Four blocks northeast of Plaza Belgrano, French landscape architect Carlos Thays took advantage of the contours of Barrancas de Belgrano to create an attractive, green public space on one of the few natural hillocks in the city. The bandstand here hosts the popular outdoor *milonga* (tango event) La Glorieta (p126).

Across Juramento from Barrancas, BA's Chinatown fills three blocks on Arribeños. Don't come on Mondays, however, as many places are shut; do come on Chinese New Year, when festivities abound.

From the Barrancas de Belgrano, take a bus or train into Nuñez to visit the museums of the Espacio Memoria y Derechos Humanos (p124) memorial site.

Over on the Costanera Norte (take a bus here), Parque Norte (p126), Parque de la Memoria (p125) and Tierra Santa (p125) are all located close to one another.

Local Life

➡ **Parklife** Grab a picnic and head to the recently spruced-up Barrancas de Belgrano park, where retirees spend afternoons at the chess tables beneath the ombú tree, and on Saturday and Sunday evenings the bandstand hosts the romantic outdoor *milonga* (dance hall) La Glorieta.

➡ **Make a splash** When temperatures rise, *porteños* (residents of Buenos Aires) head to Parque Norte to cool off in the pools.

➡ **Markets** On weekends, local artisans flog their wares at the Feria Plaza Belgrano, a popular spot for shoppers and families with strollers.

Getting There & Away

➡ **Subte** Take Línea D Juramento.

➡ **Bus** Take the 29 or 55 from Palermo and the 29 from the Center.

Lonely Planet's Top Tip

Along Av Costanera Rafael Obligado on the Costanera Norte you'll find 24-hour food trucks selling cheap and tasty *choripanes* (sausage sandwiches) and *bondiola* (pork sandwiches). Take in the river views and the drone of planes (the food stands are opposite an airport runway) alongside fishermen and families picnicking on deckchairs by their cars.

Best Museums

➡ Sitio de Memoria ESMA (p124)

➡ Museo Larreta (p124)

➡ Museo Casa de Yrurtia (p124)

For reviews, see p124.

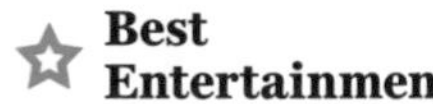

Best Entertainment

➡ La Glorieta (p126)

➡ River Plate (p126)

For reviews, see p126.

SIGHTS

Belgrano is home to a cluster of interesting little museums, the Barrancas de Belgrano park and a compact Chinatown, all within easy walking distance of Juramento Subte station. Head to the Costanera Norte for a number of family-friendly sights including a water park.

Located right on the city's northern boundary in Nuñez, the Espacio Memoria y Derechos Humanos is a sombre but fascinating complex of museums well worth visiting if you are interested in Argentina's recent history and the ground-breaking work of the country's human rights organizations.

Belgrano

MUSEO LARRETA — MUSEUM

Map p249 (☎011-4784-4040; www.buenosaires.gob.ar/museolarreta; Juramento 2291; admission AR$10, Thu free; ⏰noon-7pm Tue-Fri, 10am-8pm Sat & Sun; Ⓢ Línea D Juramento) Hispanophile novelist Enrique Larreta (1875–1961) resided in this elegant colonial-style house opposite Plaza Belgrano, which now displays his private art collection. It's a grand and spacious old building containing classic Spanish art, period furniture, wood-carved religious items, and shields and armor. The tiled floors are beautiful and the art is well-lit. Be sure to stroll the lovely gardens out back.

Tours in Spanish are given at 3pm and 5pm on Saturday and Sunday and in English at 3pm on the last Friday of the month.

MUSEO CASA DE YRURTIA — MUSEUM

Map p249 (☎011-4781-0385; https://museoyrurtia.cultura.gob.ar/; O'Higgins 2390; AR$10, Wed free; ⏰11:30am-6pm Wed-Fri, 3-7pm Sat & Sun; Ⓢ Línea D Juramento) Reclusive Rogelio Yrurtia (1879–1950), best known for his sculpture *Canto al Trabajo* (p91) on Plazoleta Olazábal in San Telmo, designed this neocolonial residence. The home is full of Yrurtia's work – which focuses on human torsos – and works by his wife, painter Lía Correa Morales. Some pieces are so huge they're almost oppressive in the small rooms housing them. There are also pieces by Yrurtia's teacher and father-in-law, Lucio Correa Morales. The museum is currently closed for renovations.

MUSEO HISTÓRICO SARMIENTO — MUSEUM

Map p249 (☎011-4782-2354; https://museosarmiento.cultura.gob.ar; Juramento 2180; ⏰1-6pm Mon-Fri, 2-7pm Sat & Sun; Ⓢ Línea D Juramento) FREE This museum at Plaza Belgrano contains memorabilia relating to Domingo F Sarmiento, one of Argentina's most celebrated presidents, diplomats and educators. Despite his provincial origins, Sarmiento was an eloquent writer who analyzed 19th-century Argentina from a cosmopolitan, clearly Eurocentric point of view, most notably in his masterful polemic *Facundo* (subtitled 'Civilization and Barbarism'). Text accompanying the exhibits is in Spanish.

Nuñez

ESPACIO MEMORIA Y DERECHOS HUMANOS — MUSEUM

Map p249 (Ex ESMA; ☎011-4702-9920; www.espaciomemoria.ar; Av del Libertador 8151, Nuñez; ⏰noon-5pm Fri-Sun; 🚌15, 29, 130) FREE Human rights groups estimate that during the military dictatorship of 1976 to 1983 up to 30,000 people were 'disappeared' by the state: kidnapped and taken to secret detention centers where they were tortured and killed. One such detention center was at the former naval campus known as the ESMA, where some 5000 men and women were held. Today, the complex serves as a memorial to the victims and houses museums, cultural centers and the offices of several human rights organizations.

SITIO DE MEMORIA ESMA — MUSEUM

Map p249 (☎011-4702-9920; www.espaciomemoria.ar; Av del Libertador 8151, Nuñez; ⏰noon-5pm Wed-Sun; 🚌15, 29, 130) FREE The former naval campus known as the ESMA is the most notorious of some 600 secret detention centers in Argentina, where during the military dictatorship of 1976 to 1983 tens of thousands of 'disappeared' people were taken to be tortured and killed. The actual building where the secret detention center was located, the Casino de Oficiales (officers' club), is now an excellent – though harrowing – museum. Due to the disturbing subject matter, children under 12 are not permitted.

The loft space where more than 5000 detainees were kept hooded and chained has been preserved, as has the 'nursery' where some 30 pregnant women gave birth to babies that were then taken and secretly given to families (often with military links) to raise as their own. Also part of the museum is the basement where detainees selected for a 'transfer' were taken before being put onto a plane and thrown alive into the Río de la Plata. Guided tours in English are given at 3pm on Saturday and Sunday with a minimum group size of seven people.

CASA POR LA IDENTIDAD MUSEUM

Map p249 (Abuelas de Plaza de Mayo; ☎011-4702-9920; www.abuelas.org.ar; Av del Libertador 8151, Nuñez; ⏰10am-5pm Mon-Fri; 🚌15, 29, 130) FREE This building at the Espacio Memoria y Derechos Humanos has photographs and explanatory texts (in Spanish) that celebrate the work of the Abuelas (grandmothers) of the Plaza de Mayo, an organization dedicated to uncovering the identities of the estimated 500 children born to mothers that were 'disappeared' by the Military Dictatorship of 1976 to 1983. No records were kept of the secret adoption of these children, who usually grew up with no knowledge of their true identity.

MUSEO MALVINAS MUSEUM

Map p249 (☎011-5280-0750; www.museomalvinas.gob.ar; Av del Libertador 8151, Nuñez; ⏰9am-5pm Mon-Fri, noon-8pm Sat & Sun; 🚌15, 29, 130) FREE This well-executed museum, opened by Cristina Kirchner in 2014, is dedicated to the history of the Islas Malvinas (Falkland Islands) and Argentina's claim to sovereignty of them, as well as the 1982 war with Britain over the islands. The history and geography of the islands are explored in an introductory film on a 360-degree cinema screen, interactive exhibits and innovative displays.

It's located at the Espacio Memoria y Derechos Humanos in Nuñez.

Costanera Norte

PARQUE DE LA MEMORIA PARK

Map p249 (☎011-4787-0999; http://parquedelamemoria.org.ar; Av Rafael Obligado 6745; ⏰10am-6pm Mon-Fri, to 8pm Sat & Sun; 🚌33, 42, 37) FREE On the edge of the river on the Costanera Norte is this landscaped park and gallery that serves as a memorial to the victims of the military dictatorships of 1969 to 1983. There is a monument dedicated to the disappeared and assassinated, with enough plaques for 30,000 names (9000 of them are inscribed), and a number of sculptures including a piece by Dennis Oppenheim and 53 road signs depicting the recent history of Argentina. A visitors center houses a gallery and archive.

Despite the darkness of the events the park memorializes, it's a pleasant place where families come to picnic, roller skate and enjoy the river views.

TIERRA SANTA AMUSEMENT PARK

Map p249 (☎011-4784-9551; www.tierrasanta.com.ar; Av Costanera R Obligado 5790; adult/child AR$130/55; ⏰9am-9pm Fri, noon-10pm Sat & Sun Apr-Nov, 4pm-midnight Fri-Sun Dec-Mar; 👪; 🚌33, 42, 160) Though many people who visit this religious theme park are devout Catholics, others go for the kitschy spectacle of the animatronic dioramas of Adam and Eve and the Last Supper among others; photo opportunities abound. Tierra Santa's pièce de résistance is a giant Jesus rising from a fake mountain – aka the resurrection – every half-hour.

The wonderfully tacky theme park is roughly based on Jerusalem. Head straight to the manger scene, where colorful lights and minimally animatronic figures swoon over baby Jesus. Better yet is the creation of the world, which features real rushing waters and life-size fake animals. From here it's a 30-second walk to witness the 12m-tall animatronic Jesus rise from the Calvary mound, open his eyes and finally turn his palms toward the emotional devoted below. Missed the show? Don't fret: another resurrection is just around the corner.

The park isn't just for Christians – there are reproductions of the Wailing Wall, along with a synagogue and a mosque. So regardless of religious affiliation, enjoy nibbling on a shawarma or take in an Arabic dancing show. It's a spectacle you won't find anywhere else on earth – especially not in Jerusalem.

EATING

Ask around to get the locals' recommendations for their favorite neighborhood eatery – the food is bound to be excellent and the atmosphere relaxed and friendly.

LA PACEÑA EMPANADAS $

Map p249 (☎011-4788-2282; www.lapacena.com; Echeverría 2570; empanadas AR$20; ⏰noon-3:30pm & 8pm-midnight Mon-Sat, 8pm-midnight Sun; Ⓢ Línea D Juramento) With thick, golden pastry and spicy fillings, the Bolivian-style *empanadas* sold at this family-run joint are some of Buenos Aires' best. Also on the menu are pizzas and traditional Argentine soups and stews.

DRINKING & NIGHTLIFE

There are plenty of neighborhood bars and cafes serving the locals of these residential areas, so you won't need to search far and wide for a drink around here. The Constanera Norte is home to some of the city's biggest clubs.

JET CLUB

Map p249 (☎011-4872-5599; www.jet.com.ar; Av Rafael Obligado 4801; ⏰10pm-6am Thu-Sat; 🚌33, 45, 160) Jet definitely has an exclusive vibe that attracts celebrities and fashionistas, so put on your best get-up or you won't make the dress code. Early on you can hang in the swanky cocktail lounge, nibble on tapas or sushi and enjoy the marina view. As the night progresses, however, the hip young clubbers start making their appearance.

Music runs toward house and electro.

ENTERTAINMENT

LA GLORIETA TANGO

Map p249 (glorietadebelgrano@yahoo.com.ar; Echeverría 1800, Barrancas de Belgrano; ⏰7-11pm Sat & Sun; 🚌15, 29, 42) FREE It's hard to imagine a more romantic setting for an outdoor *milonga* than the park bandstand at the Barrancas de Belgrano, where every Saturday and Sunday evening dancers of all ages and levels come to tango. There's usually a free lesson beforehand from 6pm to 7pm.

EL MONUMENTAL FOOTBALL

Map p249 (Estadio Monumental; ☎011-4789-1200; www.cariverplate.com; Alcorta 7597; museum admission AR$140-180; ⏰museum 10am-7pm; 🚌42, 29) Known as El Monumental, River Plate *fútbol* (soccer) club's home ground is the largest stadium in Argentina, with a capacity of 76,000. Check the website for tickets to upcoming games or swat up on the history of the club at the stadium museum.

Argentina's national team also plays here, and the stadium has hosted concerts by the likes of Paul McCartney, Roger Waters of Pink Floyd and the Rolling Stones.

SHOPPING

FERIA PLAZA BELGRANO MARKET

Map p249 (www.facebook.com/Feria.Plaza.Belgrano/; Juramento 2200; ⏰10am-8pm Sat & Sun; Ⓢ Línea D Juramento) Belgrano's artisan market is a great spot on a sunny weekend. Browse the stalls for handmade jewelry, *mate* (tea-like beverage) gourds, clothes and leather goods, mostly sold by the artisans who made them.

SPORTS & ACTIVITIES

PARQUE NORTE SWIMMING

Map p249 (☎011-4787-1382; www.parquenorte.com; Avs Cantilo & Guiraldes; adult/child pool & park Mon-Fri AR$160/85, Sat AR$190/110, Sun AR$210/110; ⏰pool 9am-8pm, park to midnight; 👪; 🚌33, 42, 160) When the temperatures and humidity skyrocket, head to this large water park. It's great for families with huge shallow pools, plus a large waterslide and lots of umbrellas and lounge chairs (both cost extra). There are plenty of grassy areas in which to enjoy a picnic or *mate*. Bring your own towels, and make sure you're clean – quick 'health' inspections are done to check for such unpleasantries as athlete's foot or lice.

Palermo

Neighborhood Top Five

❶ **Museo de Arte Latinoamericano de Buenos Aires** (p129) Checking out the contemporary artwork at this modern glassy museum where you can commune with Diego Rivera and Frida Kahlo.

❷ **Parque 3 de Febrero** (p130) Cycling, jogging and rollerblading around the lakes or just walking along the paths at this attractive park.

❸ **Restaurants** (p136) Eating your way around Palermo's fabulous restaurants, such as La Mar Cebicheria.

❹ **Museo Evita** (p131) Getting the scoop on Argentina's iconic former first lady at the museum housed in an elegant mansion.

❺ **Shopping** (p142) Rifling through designer clothing boutiques such as Blackmamba and browsing the homewares stores in Palermo Viejo.

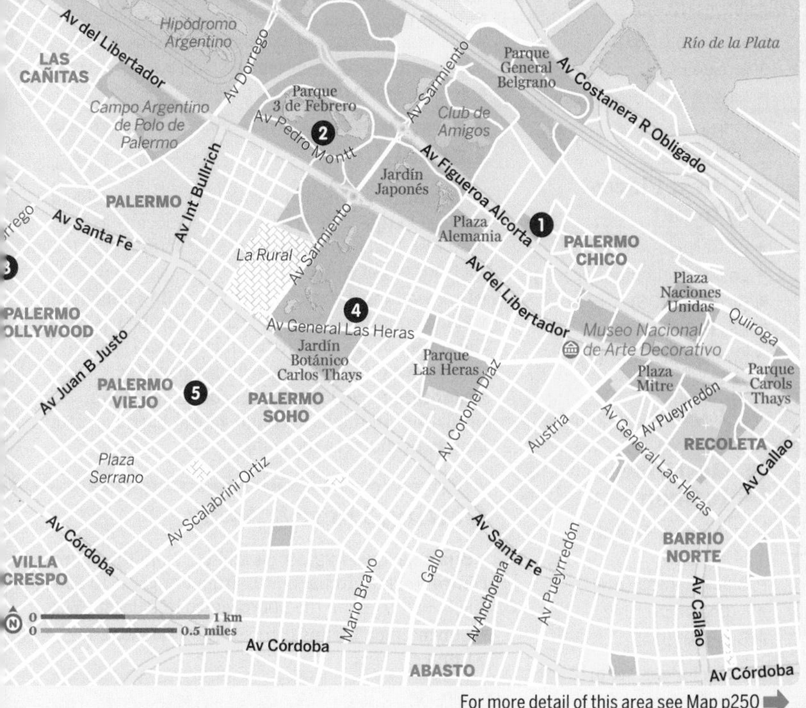

For more detail of this area see Map p250

Lonely Planet's Top Tip

Grab a bike and make use of the kilometers of protected bike paths along Palermo's green parks. It's a great way to see the area's many spread-out sites while breathing in some fresh air and getting exercise. The bike paths also exist within Palermo Soho and Hollywood. Bike rentals are available at a few bike-touring companies and on nice weekends near Av de la Infanta Isabel and Av Pedro Montt. Or sign up to use the yellow city bikes for free!

Best Museums

- Museo de Arte Latinoamericano de Buenos Aires (p129)
- Museo Nacional de Bellas Artes (p131)
- Museo Nacional de Arte Decorativo (p131)
- Museo Evita (p131)
- Museo Xul Solar (p131)

For reviews, see p131.

Best Places to Eat

- La Carnicería (p136)
- La Mar Cebicheria (p136)
- Proper (p136)
- Las Pizarras (p134)
- Sunae Asian Cantina (p136)

For reviews, see p133.

Best Places to Shop

- Elementos Argentinos (p142)
- Blackmamba (p142)
- Humawaca (p142)
- Bosque (p142)

For reviews, see p142.

Explore: Palermo

Most of Palermo's museums are located near its green parks. They're spread out over this large neighborhood, so give yourself plenty of time to see them. Museo Evita, Museo Nacional de Arte Decorativo and Museo de Arte Latinoamericano de Buenos Aires (MALBA) all have pleasant cafe-restaurants with outdoor areas.

Palermo Viejo is roughly bounded by Santa Fe, Scalabrini Ortiz, Córdoba and Dorrego. It's further divided into Palermo Hollywood (north of the train tracks) and Palermo Soho (south of the tracks), both full of old buildings, leafy sidewalks and cobbled streets. These areas have some of BA's best restaurants, along with plenty of bars and nightclubs; Plaza Serrano has dozens of sidewalk tables and attracts a young crowd on weekends.

Buenos Aires' most famous fashion designers have opened up dozens of boutiques here, and there are many designer housewares stores and other themed shops. It's not the cheapest place to shop, but likely the most fun – wear comfortable shoes as you'll be walking a lot.

The more low-key area immediately south of Scalabrini Ortiz is home to a crop of hip new restaurants and bars; keep an eye on what's new in this emerging neighborhood hot spot.

Further north is Las Cañitas; it occupies a wedge of blocks close to the polo grounds. It's mostly a residential area on the border with Belgrano and named after the fields of sugar cane that used to grow here. Just a few blocks long, it's densely packed with eateries, bars, cafes and even a club or two.

Local Life

Hangouts On sunny weekends Palermo's residents flock to Parque 3 de Febrero (known locally as the *bosques*). Don't forget to bring your *mate,* yerba tea and thermos of hot water.

Dog walking To catch a glimpse of BA's famous dog walkers and their charges, head to Parque Las Heras, at the corner of Avs Las Heras and Coronel Díaz. The best time to see them is late morning during the week.

Nightlife *Porteños* (residents of Buenos Aires) wait until after midnight to congregate at bars, and after 2am to head out to the clubs.

Getting There & Away

Bus Take buses 29, 59, 64 and 152 from the Microcentro to Plaza Italia; bus 39 from Congreso to Palermo Viejo; bus 111 from the Microcentro to Palermo Viejo.

Subte Línea D runs through Palermo along Av Santa Fe.

TOP SIGHT
MUSEO DE ARTE LATINOAMERICANO DE BUENOS AIRES (MALBA)

Housed in an elegant building with glass and cement walls is this airy modern-art museum, one of BA's finest. It contains some of the best works by classic and contemporary Argentine artists, such as Xul Solar and Antonio Berni, plus some pieces by other Latin American painters like Mexican duo Diego Rivera and Frida Kahlo.

The Collection

Opened in 2001, the MALBA is home to the private art collection of Eduardo F Costantini, a millionaire and philanthropist who has gathered together more than 200 of Latin America's best artworks from the 20th century. Well-known Argentine painters represented here include Lino Enea Spilimbergo, Jorge de la Vega, Emilio Pettoruti and Guillermo Kuitca. Many of these artists confront social issues in their works. If they're on display, check out figurative artist Antonio Berni's *nuevo realismo* (new realism) oeuvres.

Among the collection is the work of Tarsila do Amaral, one of Brazil's most famous painters; look for her *Abaporu* (1928), one of Brazil's most important paintings. Colombian Fernando Botero depicts human figures in cartoonish, overly plump sizes, as in his *Los Viudos* (1968). And Frida Kahlo's charming *Self-Portrait with Monkey and Parrot* (1942) cost Costantini nearly US$3.2 million.

World-class temporary exhibits are shown in several rooms.

DON'T MISS

- Frida Kahlo's *Self-Portrait with Monkey and Parrot*
- Diego Rivera's *Retrato de Ramón Gómez de la Serna*
- Temporary exhibitions
- Art-house cinema

PRACTICALITIES

- Map p250, H3
- 011-4808-6500
- www.malba.org.ar
- Av Figueroa Alcorta 3415
- AR$100, Wed AR$50
- noon-8pm Thu-Mon, to 9pm Wed
- 102, 130, 124

TOP SIGHT
PARQUE 3 DE FEBRERO

Also known as Bosques de Palermo, this sweeping green space abounds with small lakes and paddleboats, pretty gazebos, a monument to literary greats called El Jardín de los Poetas (the Garden of Poets) and the pleasant Rosedal (rose garden). On weekends it's filled with families picnicking, friends playing *fútbol* (soccer), lovers smooching and strolling, and outdoor enthusiasts jogging and cycling.

DON'T MISS

- Rosedal (p133)
- El Jardín de los Poetas
- Museo de Artes Plásticas Eduardo Sívori (p132)

PRACTICALITIES

- Map p250, F2
- cnr Avs del Libertador & de la Infanta Isabel
- 10, 34, 130

Private Gardens

The area around Parque 3 de Febrero was originally the private retreat of 19th-century dictator Juan Manuel de Rosas and became public parkland only after his fall from power – on February 3, 1852. Ironically for Rosas, the man who overthrew him – former ally Justo José de Urquiza – sits on his mount in a mammoth equestrian monument at the corner of Avs Sarmiento and Presidente Figueroa Alcorta.

Public Park

In 1875, Parque 3 de Febrero was inaugurated by Argentina's president, Nicolás Avellaneda. It was designed by Carlos Thays, a French botanist and landscape architect who also worked on Plaza de Mayo, Barracas de Belgrano and Parque Lezama. Thays used London's Hyde Park and Paris' Bois de Boulogne as inspiration for his work here.

SIGHTS

MUSEO DE ARTE LATINOAMERICANO DE BUENOS AIRES — MUSEUM

See p129.

PARQUE 3 DE FEBRERO — PARK

See p130.

★MUSEO NACIONAL DE BELLAS ARTES — MUSEUM

(☎011-5288-9900; www.mnba.gob.ar; Av del Libertador 1473; ⏰11am-8pm Tue-Fri, 10am-8pm Sat & Sun; 🚌130, 92, 63) FREE This is Argentina's most important fine-arts museum and contains many key works by Benito Quinquela Martín, Xul Solar, Eduardo Sívori and other Argentine artists, including a whole room of works by Antonio Berni. There are also pieces by European masters such as Cézanne, Degas, Picasso, Rembrandt, Toulouse-Lautrec and van Gogh, all well displayed. Worthwhile free tours in English (focusing on Argentinian art) are given on Tuesday, Wednesday and Friday at 1pm.

The museum's building is a former pump house for the city waterworks, and was designed by architect Julio Dormala. It was later modified by Alejandro Bustillo, famous for his alpine-style civic center in the northern Patagonian city of Bariloche.

MUSEO EVITA — MUSEUM

Map p250 (☎011-4807-0306; www.museoevita.org; Lafinur 2988; AR$75; ⏰11am-7pm Tue-Sun; Ⓢ Línea D Plaza Italia) Argentina's iconic first lady and wife of President Juan Domingo Perón has this fine museum devoted to her. Housed in a gorgeous 1923 mansion that from 1948 belonged to Eva Perón's social foundation, Museo Evita celebrates the Argentine heroine with videos, historical photos, books and posters. However, the prize memorabilia has to be her wardrobe: dresses, shoes, handbags, hats and blouses are all on display. Look for the picture of her kicking a soccer ball – in heels.

Attached to the museum is the pleasant Museo Evita Restaurante (p135) with a wonderfully leafy patio, perfect for relaxing on a warm day.

MUSEO NACIONAL DE ARTE DECORATIVO — MUSEUM

Map p250 (☎011-4802-6606; www.mnad.org; Av del Libertador 1902; AR$20, Tue free, tours AR$40; ⏰2-7pm Tue-Sun, closed Sun in Jan; 🚌130, 63, 92) This museum is housed in the stunning beaux-arts Residencia Errázuriz Alvear (1917) mansion, once the residence of Chilean aristocrat Matías Errázuriz and his wife, Josefina de Alvear. It now displays their art collection and other extravagant belongings, and is worth visiting for a glimpse into the world of Argentina's wealthy aristocratic families in the early 20th century, for whom these grand palaces with their elaborate marble staircases and ballrooms inspired by the Palace of Versailles were a status symbol.

Everything from renaissance religious paintings and porcelain dishes to Italian sculptures and period furniture was owned by Errázuriz, and some artwork by El Greco, Manet and Rodin can also be seen. Don't miss the wood-paneled Gothic-style central hall, created to complement the style of the religious tapestries it houses; concerts are sometimes held here. There are guided tours in English Tuesday to Saturday at 2:30pm.

MUSEO XUL SOLAR — MUSEUM

Map p250 (☎011-4824-3302; www.xulsolar.org.ar; Laprida 1212; AR$30; ⏰noon-8pm Tue-Fri, to 7pm Sat; Ⓢ Línea D Agüero) Xul Solar was a painter, inventor, poet and friend of Jorge Luis Borges. This museum (located in his old mansion) showcases over 80 of his unique and colorful, yet muted, paintings. Solar's Klee-esque style includes fantastically themed, almost cartoonish figures placed in surreal cubist landscapes. It's great stuff, and bizarre enough to put him in a class of his own.

MUSEO CASA DE RICARDO ROJAS — MUSEUM

Map p250 (☎011-4824-4039; www.cultura.gob.ar/museos/museo-casa-de-ricardo-rojas/; Charcas 2837; AR$20, Wed free; ⏰11am-7pm Tue-Sat; Ⓢ Línea D Agüero, Pueyrredón) Walk under the facade, modeled after the Casa de Independencia in Tucumán, and behold a quaint courtyard surrounded by European and Incan architectural motifs. Argentine educator and writer Ricardo Rojas lived here from 1929 to 1957, and in his office wrote his renowned work *El santo de la espada* (1933). Worthwhile guided tours in Spanish are given on Wednesdays at 4pm.

JARDÍN BOTÁNICO CARLOS THAYS — GARDENS

Map p250 (Botanical Gardens; ⏰8am-6:45pm Tue-Fri, 9:30am-6:45pm Sat & Sun Oct-Apr, to 5:45pm May-Sep; Ⓢ Línea D Plaza Italia) FREE

WALKING THE DOG

Buenos Aires supports a legion of *paseaperros* (professional dog walkers), who can be seen with up to a dozen canines on leashes. They'll stroll through Palermo's parks, Recoleta and even downtown with a variety of dogs ranging from scruffy mongrels to expensive purebreds, each of their tails happily a-waggin'.

Paseaperros are employed by busy apartment dwellers who either can't or prefer not to take the time to exercise their animals, and are willing to pay for this unique walking service.

Every day thousands of canines deposit tonnes (almost literally) of excrement in the streets and parks of the capital. You'll be aware of this fact soon after stepping onto the streets of Buenos Aires. Cleaning up after one's pooch is already a city requirement, but enforcement is nil, so be very careful where you tread – you'll see dog piles on almost every sidewalk.

Still, the capital's leashed packs are a remarkably orderly and always entertaining sight, and make great snapshots to bring back home.

Escape the frenzied traffic and packed sidewalks around Plaza Italia by dipping inside this lush botanical garden, designed by renowned landscape architect Carlos Thays and opened in 1898. It blooms with over 3000 tree and plant species, Roman-style sculptures, floating lily pads on still ponds and an antique iron-and-glass greenhouse originally shown at the 1900 Paris Exhibition.

BIBLIOTECA NACIONAL — LIBRARY

(☎011-4808-6000; www.bn.gov.ar; Agüero 2502; ⏱9am-9pm Mon-Fri, noon-7pm Sat & Sun; 🚌10, 59, 60) FREE Argentina's national library dates back to 1810 and was founded in the wake of the May revolution by the country's first government, for whom access to books and the ideas they contained was one of the ideals on which the new republic was founded. These days the library is housed in a striking, brutalist concrete building. Tours in English are offered on Monday and Thursday at 4pm. Bring photo ID.

MUSEO DE ARTES PLÁSTICAS EDUARDO SÍVORI — MUSEUM

Map p250 (☎011-4774-9452; www.buenosaires.gob.ar/museosivori; Av de la Infanta Isabel 555; AR$10, Wed & Fri free; ⏱noon-8pm Tue-Fri, 10am-8pm Sat & Sun; 🚌10, 34) Named for an Italo-Argentine painter who studied in Europe, this modern museum of Argentine art has open spaces allowing frequent and diverse exhibitions. Sívori's Parisian works reflect European themes, but later works returned to Argentine motifs, mainly associated with rural life in the Pampas. Most works on display are by other Argentine artists, such as Benito Quinquela Martín, Antonio Berni and Fernando Fader.

The texts accompanying the paintings are in Spanish, but guided tours in English are offered on Saturdays at 4pm. There's also a sculpture garden and slick cafe on the premises, and occasional theater, concerts, courses and workshops are offered.

JARDÍN JAPONÉS — GARDENS

Map p250 (☎011-4804-4922; www.jardinjapones.org.ar; Av Casares 2966; adult/child AR$70/free; ⏱10am-6pm; 🚌67, 102, 130) First opened in 1967, these well-maintained Japanese gardens are a peaceful spot for a stroll, unless you're averse to the gentle chimes of Japanese music that emanate from speakers around the grounds. Inside there's a Japanese restaurant along with ponds filled with koi and spanned by pretty bridges. Japanese gift shops and tea rooms are scattered around the gardens and a visitor center hosts occasional cultural exhibitions and workshops on origami and *taiko* (Japanese drumming).

PLAZA SERRANO — PLAZA

Map p250 (Jorge Luis Borges; 🚌141, 110, 111) The heart of Palermo Soho is Plaza Serrano, a small but popular plaza surrounded by bars and restaurants, and host to a small weekend arts fair (p144).

CENTRO ISLÁMICO REY FAHD — MOSQUE

Map p250 (☎011-4899-0201; www.ccislamicoreyfahd.org.ar; Av Int Bullrich 55; ⏱tours noon Tue, Thu & Sat; Ⓢ Línea D Palermo) FREE This landmark mosque, built by Saudis on land donated by former president Carlos Menem, is southeast of Las Cañitas. Free tours in Spanish are offered three times a week (bring your passport, dress conservatively and enter via Av Int Bullrich).

These visits are lengthy and concentrate on religious explanations rather than the history of the building or Argentina's Islamic community, but they do provide a chance to see inside the complex – which includes a school – and the prayer hall.

ROSEDAL GARDENS

Map p250 (Rose Garden; Av de la Infanta Isabel 900; 130, 160, 34) FREE Within the Parque 3 de Febrero is this gorgeous garden with more than 18,000 roses.

MUSEO DE ARTE POPULAR JOSÉ HERNÁNDEZ MUSEUM

Map p250 (011-4803-2384; www.buenosaires.gob.ar/museojosehernandez; Av del Libertador 2373; AR$10, Wed free; 1-7pm Tue-Fri, 10am-8pm Sat & Sun; 130, 93, 37) This small museum exhibits both traditional and contemporary arts and crafts, mostly from Argentina. Expect to see intricate gaucho-related silverwork such as knives and *mate* sets, Mapuche textiles including ponchos, and folk crafts from the country's northern regions.

PLANETARIO GALILEO GALILEI PLANETARIUM

Map p250 (011-4771-9265; www.planetario.gob.ar; cnr Avs Sarmiento & Belisario Roldán; 160, 130, 33) This planetarium has reasonably priced shows (mostly for kids) and free celestial viewings, including moon observations. Check the website for current offerings.

EATING

Palermo is where you'll find some of the most innovative cuisine in Buenos Aires. In Palermo Viejo, dozens of upmarket restaurants serve creative cuisine in a contemporary setting, but it's important to be discerning – a new eatery opens every week, and while quality is generally high, only a few places are truly special.

Some of Palermo's most interesting new restaurants are clustered in the area south of Av Scalabrini Ortiz, where the young chefs at Gran Dabbang (p134), Proper (p136) and NoLa are bringing fresh ideas and new flavors to the BA food-scene.

CHORI ARGENTINE $

Map p250 (011-3966-9857; www.facebook.com/Xchorix/; Thames 1653; choripan AR$70-95; 7pm-midnight Tue-Fri, 12:30-5pm & 7pm-midnight Sat & Sun; ; 55, 39) Elevating the humble Argentine *chori* (sausage) to new heights is this hip new joint in Palermo, its bright yellow walls decorated with smiling cartoon sausages. The quality, 100% pork *choris* and *morcillas* (blood sausages) hang on display – choose from a range of gourmet toppings and homemade breads for a *choripan* sandwich.

BURGER JOINT BURGERS $

Map p250 (011-4833-5151; www.facebook.com/BurgerJointPalermo/; Jorge Luis Borges 1766; burgers AR$80; noon-midnight; Línea D Plaza Italia) For some of the juiciest burgers in BA, head to this popular, graffiti-covered spot. NYC-trained chef Pierre Chacra offers just four kinds to choose from, but they're all stellar. Try the Mexican (jalapeños, guacamole and hot sauce) or Jamaican (pineapple, cheddar and bacon) with a side of hand-cut fries.

NOLA CAJUN $

Map p250 (www.nolabuenosaires.com; Gorriti 4389; mains AR$85-140; 5pm-midnight Mon-Fri, 1pm-midnight Sat & Sun; 140, 141, 110) The brainchild of American Lisa Puglia is this small, popular place serving New Orleans Cajun cuisine. Everything is homemade, from the fried chicken sandwich to the *chorizo* gumbo and the spicy, vegetarian red beans and rice. The jalapeño cornbread and bourbon-coffee pecan pie are the bomb, as is the microbrewed beer. Happy hour is from 5pm to 8pm (pints AR$50).

BIG SUR BURGERS $

Map p250 (011-4806-7264; www.facebook.com/BigSurBA/; Av Cerviño 3596; mains AR$50-190; noon-midnight Tue-Sun; Línea D Scalabrini Ortiz) This casual, industrial-style joint serves great hamburgers, fried chicken, hot dogs and fries in baskets, as well as quality craft beer.

UN ALTRA VOLTA ICE CREAM $

Map p250 (www.unaltravolta.com.ar; Av del Libertador 3060; 250g AR$80; 8am-midnight Sun-Thu, to 1am Fri & Sat; 111, 93, 130) Branch of the upmarket ice-cream parlor serving Italian-style *gelato*. Be sure to try the *dulce de leche* (caramel).

LOCAL KNOWLEDGE

BEHIND CLOSED DOORS

A popular Buenos Aires culinary offshoot are 'closed-door restaurants' or *puertas cerradas*. These places are open only a few days per week, have timed seatings and are generally prix fixe (and mostly cash only). They're not marked with signs and you have to ring a bell to enter. They won't even tell you the address until you make reservations (mandatory, of course). But for that tingly feeling brought on by discovering something off the beaten path – with some of the city's best food to boot – these are the places.

There are two kinds of *puertas cerradas:* the first is where you dine in the chef's actual home, and usually sit at a large communal table. This is a great way to meet other people, often interesting travelers or expats; it's ideal for folks traveling alone. The second kind has more of a restaurant feel and tables are for separate groups – just like a regular restaurant, but not open to walk-ins. Many *puertas cerradas* are located in Palermo.

Some of BA's best *puertas cerradas* include iLatina (p152), serving exquisite Colombian food; Casa Saltshaker (p117), where you'll sample ex–New Yorker Dan Perlman's culinary creations; Casa Felix (p152), a pescatarian's delight; and Casa Coupage (p136), specialising in modern Argentine cuisine and wine pairings.

FUKURO NOODLE BAR — JAPANESE $

Map p250 (☎011-4773-6810; www.fukuronoodlebar.com; Costa Rica 5514; noodles AR$145; ⏲8pm-midnight Tue-Thu, to 1am Fri & Sat; Ⓢ Línea D Palermo) For a change from all that meat, check out this comfort-food eatery. Four kinds of ramen are on offer, along with a good selection of *bao* (steamed buns) and *gyoza* (dumplings). Gluten-free noodles available, plus sake and microbrew draft beer. Counter seating only.

PETIT GREEN — DELI $

Map p250 (☎011-4806-8958; Jerónimo Salguero 3069; mains AR$60-120; ⏲10am-9pm Mon-Fri, to 6pm Sat; 📶🌿; 🚌102, 130, 124) A great little deli and juice bar selling freshly made vegetarian fare to take away. Pick up a salad, wrap, bagel or smoothie to have in one of the nearby parks or plazas.

★GRAN DABBANG — FUSION $$

Map p250 (☎011-4832-1186; www.facebook.com/grandabbang/; Av Scalabrini Ortiz 1543; small plates AR$40-150; ⏲8pm-midnight Mon-Sat; 🚌141, 15, 160) The rule-breaking, experimental fusion food conjured up by Mariano Ramón, one of the rising stars of the BA food scene, can be sampled in the small, packed dining room of this unassuming restaurant. Choose three small plates to share between two and get ready for a wild-eyed blend of Indian, Thai and Paraguayan flavors (among others), drawn from Ramón's travels.

★LAS PIZARRAS — INTERNATIONAL $$

Map p250 (☎011-4775-0625; www.laspizarrasbistro.com; Thames 2296; mains AR$185-300; ⏲8pm-midnight Tue-Sun; Ⓢ Línea D Plaza Italia) At this simple, unpretentious, excellent restaurant, Chef Rodrigo Castilla cooks up a changing rainbow of eclectic dishes such as grilled venison or rabbit stuffed with cherries and pistachios. Those with meeker stomachs can choose the asparagus and mushroom risotto or any of the homemade pastas. The chalkboard menu on the wall adds to the casual atmosphere.

★DON JULIO — PARRILLA $$

Map p250 (☎011-4832-6058; www.parrilladonjulio.com.ar; Guatemala 4691; mains AR$245-490; ⏲noon-4pm & 7:30pm-1am; Ⓢ Línea D Plaza Italia) Classy service and a great wine list add an upscale bent to this traditional – and very popular – corner steakhouse. The *bife de chorizo* (sirloin steak) is the main attraction here, but the baked goat cheese provolone, *bondiola de cerdo* (pork shoulder) and gourmet salads are a treat as well, and portions are large. Reserve ahead.

SIAMO NEL FORNO — PIZZA $$

Map p250 (☎011-4775-0337; Costa Rica 5886; pizzas AR$190-230; ⏲8pm-midnight Tue-Thu & Sun, to 1am Fri & Sat; 🚌111, 93, 39) Possibly the city's best Naples-style pizzas, made with quality ingredients and finished in a hot wood-fired oven so the thin crusts char beautifully. Try the margherita, with tomatoes, fresh mozzarella, basil and olive oil; the champignon and prosciutto comes with mushrooms, ham and goat cheese. Also bakes excellent calzone.

EL PREFERIDO DE PALERMO ARGENTINE $$

Map p250 (☎011-4774-6585; Jorge Luis Borges 2108; mains AR$110-200; ⌚9am-11:30pm Mon-Sat; S Línea D Plaza Italia) You can't get much more traditional than this atmospheric, family-run joint. Order tapas, meat platters, homemade pastas and seafood soups, or try one of its specialties – the tortillas, *milanesas* (breaded meat cutlets) and Cuban rice with veal and polenta. Hanging hams, jars of olives and high tables with blocky wood stools add to the charm.

EL TEJANO BARBECUE $$

Map p250 (☎011-4833-3545; www.facebook.com/ElTejanoBA; Honduras 4416; mains AR$150-180; ⌚8-11pm Tue-Sat, 12:30-4:30pm Wed-Sun; 🚌15, 140, 141) Missing Texas-style barbecue from back home? Here's the place to scratch that itch. Texan Larry Rogers grills up the city's best beef and pork ribs, along with smoked brisket, pulled pork and chicken wings. The offerings may change by the day, but you can always expect amazingly tender and delicious meats.

IL BALLO DEL MATTONE ITALIAN $$

Map p250 (☎011-4776-4247; www.facebook.com/ballodelmattone; Gorriti 5737; lunch mains AR$190, dinner AR$130-300; ⌚noon-4pm & 9pm-1:30am Mon-Sat; 🚌111, 93, 39) This artsy, eclectic trattoria attracts artists, musicians and tourists, among others, with its delicious homemade pastas. Cute little patio for warm days. Its annex is two blocks away at **Gorriti 5893** (Map p250; ☎011-4776-8648; www.facebook.com/ballodelmattone/; Gorriti 5893; lunch mains AR$190, dinner mains AR$130-300; ⌚noon-4pm & 9pm-1:30am Mon-Sat; 🚌111, 93, 39).

MUSEO EVITA RESTAURANTE ARGENTINE $$

Map p250 (☎011-4800-1599; JM Gutiérrez 3926; mains AR$160-280; ⌚9am-midnight Mon-Sat, to 7pm Sun; S Línea D Plaza Italia) This restaurant's charming tiled courtyard is a pretty spot for an alfresco lunch, and the cuisine is thoroughly sophisticated, too. Locals and visitors come for the gourmet sandwiches, steaks and salads, or try Evita's favorite, the *milanesa* with salad, followed by flan.

ARTEMISIA VEGETARIAN $$

Map p250 (☎011-4773-2641; www.artemisianatural.com; Costa Rica 5893; mains AR$145-240; ⌚10am-12:30am Tue-Sat, to 5pm Sun; 🌶; S Línea D Ministro Carranza) At this gorgeous corner restaurant you'll want to linger over the tasty organic, vegetarian food (there are a few fish options available, too). The large windows let in tonnes of light, and local artwork and a sunny, internal patio packed with plants add to the ambience. Meals come with a basket of excellent, freshly baked bread.

OUI OUI INTERNATIONAL $$

Map p250 (☎011-4778-9614; www.ouioui.com.ar; Nicaragua 6068; mains AR$85-240; ⌚8am-9pm Tue-Fri, 10am-8pm Sat & Sun; 📶; S Línea D Ministro Carranza) *Pain au chocolat* and shabby chic? *Oui*. This French-style cafe produces the goods – dark coffee, buttery croissants and jars of tangy lemonade – and has a small and cozy interior. Creative salads, gourmet sandwiches and luscious pastries are also on offer. Its annex, **Almacén Oui Oui** (Map p250; ☎011-4776-4442; www.ouioui.com.ar; Nicaragua 6099; mains AR$85-240; ⌚8am-9pm; 📶; S Línea D Ministro Carranza), is on the same block.

BIO VEGETARIAN $$

Map p250 (☎011-4774-3880; www.biorestaurant.com.ar; Humboldt 2192; mains AR$125-260; ⌚10am-midnight; 🌶; S Línea D Palermo) 🍃 Tired of meat? Then make a beeline for this casual family-run restaurant, which specializes in healthy, organic and vegetarian fare. Try the quinoa hamburgers, Mediterranean couscous or lentil *milanesa*, washed down with refreshing ginger lemonade. Also caters to celiacs, vegans and raw foodists. Cooking classes held on Tuesday afternoons.

BUENOS AIRES VERDE VEGETARIAN $$

Map p250 (☎011-4775-9594; www.bsasverde.com; Gorriti 5657; mains AR$145-215; ⌚9am-12:30am Mon-Sat; 🌶; 🚌111, 140, 39) Long-running organic, vegetarian restaurant serving wraps, salads, soups and sandwiches; wash them down with a wheatgrass juice or fruit smoothie. Small grocery too.

MIRANDA PARRILLA $$

Map p250 (☎011-4771-4255; www.parrillamiranda.com; Costa Rica 5602; mains AR$200-260; ⌚9am-1am Sun-Thu, to 2am Fri & Sat; 📶; 🚌111, 39, 93) Fashionable Miranda is the *parrilla* (steakhouse) of choice for those looking for both style and substance. It's a pleasant modern steakhouse with concrete walls, high ceilings and rustic wooden furniture, but high-quality grilled beef is the main attraction here – try the popular *ojo de bife* (rib eye). If you score a sidewalk table on a warm day, life doesn't get much better.

SOCIAL LA LECHUZA — ARGENTINE $$

Map p250 (☎011-4773-2781; Uriarte 1980; mains AR$95-230; ⏰8pm-midnight Tue, noon-3:30pm & 8pm-midnight Wed-Sun; Ⓢ Línea D Plaza Italia) A world away from its hip neighbors, this classic joint holds on to tradition and has a loyal, local clientele. Quirky art adorns the walls including amateur owl paintings (*lechuza* means 'owl'). Meats and pastas are served in abundant portions, but don't miss the desserts such as chocolate mousse and tiramisu.

★LA MAR CEBICHERIA — PERUVIAN $$$

Map p250 (☎011-4776-5543; http://lamarcebicheria.com.ar/; Arévalo 2024; mains AR$250-420; ⏰8pm-midnight Mon, 12:30pm-midnight Tue-Sun; 📶; Ⓢ Línea D Ministro Carranza) For lovers of fresh fish, this upmarket Peruvian *cebicheria* is a welcome addition to the meat-dominated BA food scene. The team at La Mar traveled across Argentina to source their ingredients, and the quality of the fish is evident in the eating. The menu is lengthy, with a choice of Peruvian dishes, and there's plenty of outdoor seating.

★PROPER — ARGENTINE $$$

Map p250 (☎011-4831-0027; www.properbsas.com.ar; Aráoz 1676; small plates AR$60-290; ⏰8:30pm-midnight Tue-Sat; 📶; 🚌111, 160, 141) Bringing new life to the BA food scene, the young chefs behind Proper pack flavor into seasonal produce cooked in a wood-fired oven at their roughly finished restaurant in a former car-repair shop. Order several small plates to share and delight in dishes such as perfectly cooked lamb chops or sweet potato with Patagonian blue cheese, fried almonds and kale.

★LA CARNICERÍA — PARRILLA $$$

Map p250 (☎011-2071-7199; www.facebook.com/xlacarniceriax/; Thames 2317; mains AR$275-295; ⏰8pm-midnight Tue-Fri, 1-3:30pm & 8pm-midnight Sat & Sun; Ⓢ Línea D Plaza Italia) This modern *parrilla* caused a buzz when it opened in 2014. The menu is limited but everything on it is spectacular, from the crispy *provoleta* (barbecued cheese) to the tenderloin and rib cuts. This is a place for serious meat lovers who won't be put off by the butcher-themed decor. Creativity runs rampant, and portions are huge. Reserve ahead.

★SUNAE ASIAN CANTINA — ASIAN $$$

Map p250 (☎011-4776-8122; www.sunaeasiancantina.com; Humboldt 1626; mains AR$235-300; ⏰8-11:30pm Mon-Thu, to midnight Fri & Sat; 📶; 🚌111, 108, 140) After honing her skills at her popular closed-door restaurant, chef Christina Sunae has moved on to open a sophisticated Asian *cantina* in Palermo Hollywood. The menu spans Southeast Asia, featuring Malaysian *rendang* (meat curry), Filipino pork buns, Vietnamese dishes, tangy Thai salads and fiery curries from the Chiang Mai region.

LA CABRERA — PARRILLA $$$

Map p250 (☎011-4832-5754; www.lacabrera.com.ar; José Antonio Cabrera 5099; mains AR$244-400; ⏰12:30-4:30pm & 8:30pm-midnight Sun-Thu, to 1am Fri & Sat; 🚌140, 34) Hugely popular for grilling up BA's most sublime meats, so soft they can be cut with a spoon. Steaks weigh in at 400g or 800g and arrive with many little complimentary side dishes. Come at 7pm for happy hour, when everything is 40% off – arrive early to score a table; reservations are taken from 8:30pm only.

Has a **second location** (Map p250; ☎011-4832-5754; http://lacabrera.com.ar/; José Antonio Cabrera 5127; mains AR$244-400; ⏰12:30-4:30pm & 8:30pm-midnight Sun-Thu, to 1am Fri & Sat; 🚌140, 34) nearby.

CASA COUPAGE — INTERNATIONAL $$$

Map p250 (☎011-4777 9295; www.casacoupage.com; Soler 5518; 6-course tasting menu AR$650; ⏰8:30-11pm Wed-Sat; Ⓢ Línea D Palermo) Wine lovers will love this closed-door restaurant run by two friendly sommeliers, Santiago Mymicopulo and Inés Mendieta. The gourmet food is gorgeously presented and will be some of the best you'll experience in BA. The wine pairings are excellent and the pours generous; expect to try some of Argentina's tastiest malbec, pinot, torrontés and chardonnay. Reserve ahead.

OVIEDO — ARGENTINE $$$

Map p250 (☎011-4822-5415; www.oviedoresto.com.ar; Beruti 2602; mains AR$290-390; ⏰noon-1am Mon-Sat, to 4pm Sun; Ⓢ Línea D Pueyrredón) This smart restaurant offers reliably good,

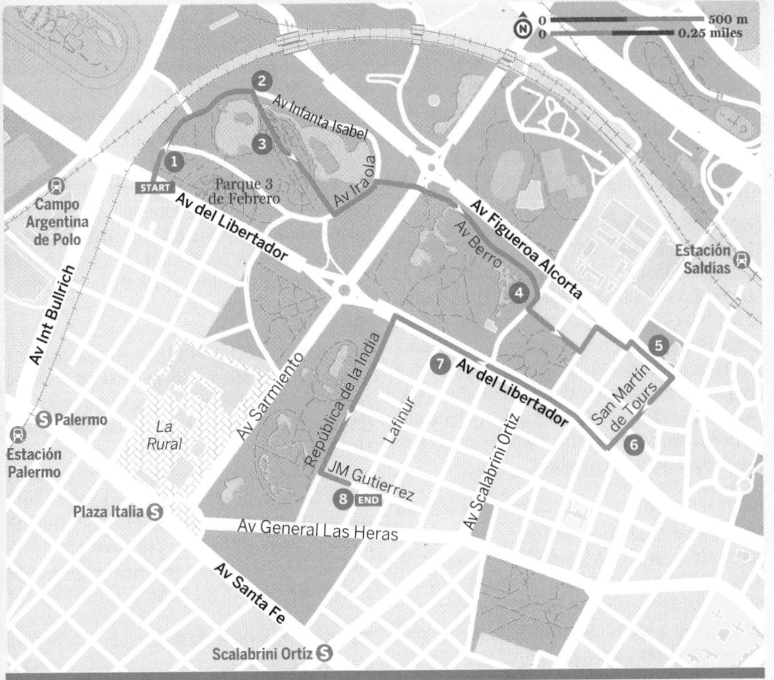

Neighborhood Walk
Walking the Green

START PARQUE 3 DE FEBRERO
END MUSEO EVITA
LENGTH 4.5KM; THREE TO FOUR HOURS

Start in 1 **Parque 3 de Febrero** (p130); these expansive green spaces were once the aristocracy's stomping ground. It's best on weekends, when locals come to jog, cycle and rollerblade around the lake, and is a great place for people-watching.

Those interested in modern art can peek into the contemporary 2 **Museo de Artes Plásticas Eduardo Sívori** (p132), which showcases Argentine works. There's a relaxing cafe here as well. If you like flowers, head across the road and cross the bridge to the 3 **Rosedal** (p133), where you can stop to smell the roses. Continue across the garden, then turn left on Av Iraola, continuing on for about a block before veering to the right to reach Av Sarmiento.

Cross Av Sarmiento (carefully!), and head along Av Berro for about 500m to BA's 4 **Jardín Japonés** (p132). This little paradise is meticulously maintained with koi ponds, pretty bridges and a tea shop, making it a welcome break from roads and traffic.

Now skim around Plaza Alemania and jog around a few residential streets to reach 5 **Museo de Arte Latinoamericano de Buenos Aires** (p129), an airy museum that's home to some excellent paintings. For more culture, go two blocks south to the much more modest 6 **Museo de Arte Popular José Hernández** (p133), which exhibits handicrafts and folkloric items.

On Av del Libertador, stop in at luscious ice-cream shop 7 **Un Altra Volta** (p133) for a peaked cone of *dulce de leche granizado* (milk caramel with chocolate chips). Now head down Lafinur to 8 **Museo Evita** (p131), where you can check out the collected memorabilia of Argentina's most famous woman and pick up an Evita souvenir in the gift shop. There's a good cafe-restaurant here where you can end your long walk.

classic dishes including braised rabbit, duck, squid and langoustine risotto, and trout along with the usual beef and pasta. The same menu is served all day with no break in service, making it a good option if you find yourself hungry at an odd time. Desserts are homemade, as are the breads.

SUDESTADA ASIAN **$$$**

Map p250 (☎011-4776-3777; Guatemala 5602; set lunch AR$145-160, mains AR$280-310; ⌚noon-3:30pm & 8pm-midnight Mon-Thu, to 1am Fri & Sat; Ⓢ Línea D Palermo) Sudestada's tasty curries, stir-fries and noodle dishes are inspired by the cuisines of Thailand, Vietnam, Malaysia and Singapore – and if you order them spicy, they're actually spicy. Don't forgo an exotic cocktail or delicious lychee *licuado* (smoothie). The popular set-lunch special is great value.

GREEN BAMBOO VIETNAMESE **$$$**

Map p250 (☎011-4775-7050; www.greenbamboo.com.ar; Costa Rica 5802; mains AR$230-310; ⌚8:30pm-midnight Sun-Thu, to 1am Fri & Sat; 🚌111, 93, 39) This sultry Vietnamese eatery offers just a small selection of dishes, but all are well prepared and flavorful. Sample dishes such as seafood curry, marinated sirloin in lemongrass and 'traditional' *pho* (well, Argentine-style – so don't expect much tradition). The atmosphere is dim and romantic, with a few low candle-lit tables, and the tropical cocktails are excellent.

STEAKS BY LUIS ARGENTINE **$$$**

Map p250 (☎011-4776-0780; www.steakbuenosaires.net; Malabia 1300; 5 courses with wine US$85; ⌚8:45pm Mon, Tue & Thu, 8:30pm Fri; 🚌140, 15, 168) An upscale *asado* (barbecue grill) experience where you'll nibble on cheese and sip boutique wine while watching large hunks of meat being grilled. Advance reservations essential.

DRINKING & NIGHTLIFE

With bars on every corner – from craft-beer pubs to coffee bars to speakeasy-style cocktail lounges – Palermo is the best place to go out for a drink in Buenos Aires. Buzzing at any time of the day or night, there's a party spot for everyone in this neighborhood.

★VERNE COCKTAIL BAR

Map p250 (☎011-4822-0980; http://vernecocktailclub.com; Av Medrano 1475; ⌚9pm-2am Sun-Tue, 8pm-2am Wed, to 3am Thu, to 4am Fri, 9pm-4am Sat; 🚌160, 15) This upscale yet casual bar has a vague Jules Verne theme. Cocktails are the house specialty, whipped up by one of BA's best bartenders, Fede Cuco. A few tables, some cushy sofas and an airy outdoor patio offer a variety of seating options, but plant yourself at the bar to watch the mixologists work their magic.

★ON TAP CRAFT BEER

Map p250 (☎011-4771-5424; www.ontap.com.ar; Costa Rica 5527; ⌚6pm-midnight Tue-Wed & Sun, to 1am Thu-Sat) This popular pub has 20 Argentine microbrews on tap, including IPAs, pilsners, stouts, wheat porters and honey beers. It's more of a place to enjoy beers than to hang out – there's only counter seating and a communal table, though a few burgers and other pub food are available. Bring a growler for refills; happy hour runs from 6pm to 8:30pm.

★LAB TRAINING CENTER & COFFEE SHOP CAFE

Map p250 (☎011-4843-1790; www.labcafe.com.ar; Humboldt 1542; ⌚8am-8pm Mon-Fri, 10am-8pm Sat; 🚌111, 140, 39) The high ceilings, exposed brick wall and industrial aesthetic here are such hallmarks of a hipster coffee joint that the place borders on self-parody, but the coffee *is* excellent. Choose your house-roasted beans and have them run through a Chemex, AeroPress, V60, Kalita, syphon or Clever Dripper. Mostly counter seating.

Brewing and espresso classes also on offer.

★NICETO CLUB CLUB

Map p250 (☎011-4779-9396; www.nicetoclub.com; Niceto Vega 5510; ⌚Thu-Sat; 🚌111, 140, 34) One of the city's biggest crowd-pullers, the can't-miss event at Niceto Club is Thursday night's Club 69, a subversive DJ extravaganza featuring gorgeously attired showgirls, dancing drag queens, futuristic video installations and off-the-wall performance art. On weekend nights, national and international spin masters take the booth to entertain lively crowds with blends of hip-hop, electronic beats, cumbia and reggae.

★**GLAM** CLUB

Map p250 (☎011-4963-2521; www.glambsas.com.ar; José Antonio Cabrera 3046; ⏰midnight-7am Thu & Sat; 🚌29, 109) Housed in an old mansion with tall brick hallways, this maze-like gay club brings in a crowd of young, good-looking guys here to dance. There are no shows to distract, just casual lounges, pretty bars and a fun atmosphere that makes this BA's top gay party. Saturday is the biggest night here.

BLUEDOG BAR

Map p250 (☎011-4832-3226; www.facebook.com/bluedogbeerstation/; Gorriti 4758; ⏰6pm-midnight Tue-Thu & Sun, to 1am Fri & Sat; 📶) Surf the wave of BA's craft beer revolution at this small bar with an exposed brick, polished concrete and wooden interior. The 12 ales on tap are produced by some of the best local breweries including Grunge, Berlina and Cheverry. Happy hour until 8:30pm. Bar snacks also available.

BENAIM BAR

Map p250 (www.facebook.com/BenaimBA/; Gorriti 4015; ⏰6pm-12:30am Mon-Thu, to 3am Fri, noon-3am Sat, noon-12:30am Sun; 🚌140, 39, 99) Order a pint of IPA or golden ale from the caravan bar and drink it under the fairy lights and hanging plants in Benaim's attractive beer garden. There's also a kitchen serving good-value Jewish street food, such as hummus and falafel, kebabs and pastrami. Happy hour is from 6pm to 8pm.

FRANK'S COCKTAIL BAR

Map p250 (www.facebook.com/FranksBar.ar; Arévalo 1445; ⏰9pm-4am Wed-Sat; 🚌111, 140, 39) This plush and elegant speakeasy bar requires a password (via telephone booth) to get in – follow the clues on the Facebook page. Inside it's a beautiful space with crystal chandeliers, billowy ceiling drapes and an exclusive feel. Classic cocktails from before the 1930s are stirred – never blended – and served to a crowd of locals and foreigners.

SUSPIRIA RESPLENDORIS COCKTAIL BAR

Map p250 (☎011-4832-2774; www.suspiriaresplendoris.com; Nicaragua 4346; ⏰8pm-2am Tue-Thu, to 4am Fri, 9pm-4am Sat; Ⓢ Línea D Scalabrini Ortiz) Look for this classy cocktail joint behind an unmarked, art-deco-style door. Inspired by the film *The Shining*, inside the dimly-lit place is all mirrors and velvet, with the bar taking central stage. With a creative menu of expertly mixed drinks, this is a bar for serious cocktail aficionados. Also serves a selection of meals and bar snacks.

VIVE CAFÉ CAFE

Map p250 (☎011-4774-5461; www.facebook.com/ViveCafeTienda/; Costa Rica 5722; ⏰9:30am-8pm Mon-Fri, 11am-8pm Sat, 2-7pm Sun; 📶; Ⓢ Línea D Palermo) If you're fussy about coffee, head to Vive for your flat white or cold brew fix – it'll be made with quality Colombian beans and prepared with a smile by the friendly owners, a young Colombian-Argentine couple. There are a few pastries available too, but the coffee is the star of the show.

LATTENTE ESPRESSO & BREW BAR CAFE

Map p250 (☎011-4833-1676; www.cafelattente.com; Thames 1891; ⏰9am-8pm Mon-Sat, 10am-8pm Sun; Ⓢ Línea D Plaza Italia) Riding on BA's java boom is this modern coffee shop serving house-roasted beans. Order your espresso, cappuccino, Americano or latte (via AeroPress or V60) and have a seat at one of the tall communal tables along with other hipster caffeine junkies. A few cookies and brownies are also on offer.

VICTORIA BROWN COCKTAIL BAR

Map p250 (☎011-4831-0831; www.victoriabrownbar.com; Costa Rica 4827; ⏰9pm-4am Tue-Sat; Ⓢ Línea D Plaza Italia) Secreted behind a large draped door inside a cute coffee shop, this atmospheric speakeasy lounge serves up quality cocktails. It's a popular place so dress up and come early to snag a sofa or curvy table-booth. The industrial-style interior decor is sophisticated; even the bathroom fittings are creative.

CARNAL BAR

Map p250 (☎011-4772-7582; www.carnalbar.com.ar; Niceto Vega 5511; ⏰7pm-5:30am Tue-Sat; 🚌151, 140, 168) See and be seen on the rooftop terrace at this ever-popular watering hole – preferably with an icy vodka tonic in hand. With its bamboo lounges and billowy curtains, the place can't be beat for a cool chill-out on a warm summer night. Early in the week reggae rocks, while Thursday to Saturday means pop and '80s tunes.

ANTARES BAR

Map p250 (☎011-4833-9611; www.cervezaantares.com; Armenia 1447; ⏰7pm-4am; 🚌140, 15, 110) BA might be surfing the wave of a craft beer revolution, but Antares has been brewing ales at its Mar del Plata factory since the current crop of beer-makers were in diapers. Its Palermo branch is a modern but relaxed space serving the brewery's famous porters, stout and barley wine.

Order a beer flight, sample the brewmaster's special-edition selection or just enjoy the two-for-one pints during happy hour. Also at **Las Cañitas** (Map p250; ☎011-4772-2133; www.cervezaantares.com; Arévalo 2876; ⏰6pm-2am Mon-Fri, 7pm-4am Sat & Sun; Ⓢ Línea D Ministro Carranza).

KIKA CLUB

Map p250 (www.kikaclub.com.ar; Honduras 5339; ⏰doors open 1am Tue-Sun; 🚌111, 34, 140) Being supremely well located near the heart of Palermo's bar scene makes Kika's popular Tuesday-night 'Hype' easily accessible for those up for a party. It's a mix of electro, rock, hip-hop, drum and bass, and dubstep, all spun by both local and international DJs. Other nights see electronica, raggaeton, Latin beats and live bands ruling the roost.

POST STREET BAR BAR

Map p250 (www.facebook.com/Poststretbar/; Thames 1885; ⏰5pm-1am Sun, Mon, Wed & Thu, to 4am Fri & Sat; Ⓢ Línea D Plaza Italia) Colorful stencils and murals cover the walls of this casual place, making it feel like you're hanging out in a grungy, artsy squat. It might lack the gloss of some of its Palermo neighbors but promotions such as free pizza on Thursdays keep the place buzzing.

CROBAR CLUB

Map p250 (☎011-4778-1500; www.crobar.com.ar; cnr Av de la Infanta Isabel & Freyre; ⏰11:30pm-7am Fri & Sat; 🚌10, 33, 111) Stylish and spacious Crobar remains one of BA's most popular clubs. On Fridays international DJs mash up the latest techno selections at Be Techno, while on Saturdays there's a mix of electro-pop and Latin beats at Keek in the main room, as well as the gay party Rheo. Bring a full wallet – this is a top-end spot.

The main levels are strewn with mezzanines and catwalks that allow views from above.

CONGO BAR

Map p250 (☎011-4833-5857; www.barcongo.com; Honduras 5329; ⏰7pm-3am Wed-Thu, 8pm-5am Fri & Sat; 🚌34, 111) The highlight here is the beautiful back patio which comes into its own on hot summer nights, with its slick bar, leafy surroundings and comfy wood booths. The music is great, too, with DJs spinning from Wednesday to Saturday, and inside there are elegant low lounges in romantic spaces. A full food menu is available, along with strong cocktails.

MUNDO BIZARRO COCKTAIL BAR

Map p250 (☎011-4773-1967; www.facebook.com/MundoBizarroCocktail/; Serrano 1222; ⏰8pm-3am Tue-Thu, 9pm-5am Fri & Sat; 🚌55, 140, 141) This red-lit, futuristically retro lounge bar is open pretty much all through the night on weekends, when everything from old-time American music to hip DJs to jazz stirs up the airwaves. If you're feeling peckish, check out the American-inspired bar food, which ranges from Tex-Mex to burgers to hot apple pie with ice cream.

HOME HOTEL BAR

Map p250 (☎011-4779-1006; www.homebuenosaires.com; Honduras 5860; ⏰8am-11:30pm; 🚌111, 93) Some of Palermo's best cocktails can be found at Home Hotel's intimate bar-restaurant. During the day, relax in the grassy garden next to the slick infinity pool. At night, settle down at the polished cement bar with a house cocktail, created by some of BA's best-known bartenders. A wide variety of vodkas, along with tapas are available.

SITGES GAY

Map p250 (www.facebook.com/SitgesBuenosAires; Av Córdoba 4119; ⏰11pm-4am Thu & Sun, midnight-6am Fri & Sat; 🚌140, 109, 24) One of BA's oldest gay clubs, with fun drag shows on Thursdays. Saturday night's Julepe party is *the* place to be seen.

BACH BAR GAY & LESBIAN

Map p250 (☎011-5184-0137; www.facebook.com/bach.bar/; José Antonio Cabrera 4390; ⏰11pm-6am Fri & Sat, 10pm-6am Sun; 🚌140, 141, 110) This popular lesbian club hosts karaoke nights and raucous live drag shows on weekends.

SHANGHAI DRAGON PUB

Map p250 (☎011-4778-1053; www.theshanghaidragon.com; Aráoz 1199; ⏰5pm-3am Mon-Wed, to 4am Thu & Fri, 6pm-5am Sat, to 2am Sun; 🚌141,

110, 15) Corner pub with mellow vibe, sports on TV and vague Asian theme. Come for dinner if you want Chinese food such as vegetable stir-fries and Kung Pao chicken, while happy hour means cheap drinks from 5pm to 10pm.

CLUB ARÁOZ CLUB

Map p250 (011-4832-9751; www.clubaraoz.com.ar; Aráoz 2424; Fri & Sat; S Línea D Scalabrini Ortiz) This multi-level club plays a mix of Latin, reggaeton and dance music and pulls in a young crowd. There's no dress code – a good thing, since it tends to get hot and sweaty in here.

ENTERTAINMENT

HIPÓDROMO ARGENTINO HORSE RACING

Map p250 (011-4778-2800; www.palermo.com.ar; Av del Libertador 4101; 29, 152, 160) FREE Even if you're not usually a fan, a few hours at the races in the glamorous grandstand of the historic Hipódromo Argentino is a fabulous afternoon outing (with first-rate people-watching, to boot). The big race of the season is the Gran Premio Nacional in November.

The tango singer Carlos Gardel was a racehorse owner and regular at the tracks. One of his most famous songs, *Por una Cabeza* (By a Head), is about a compulsive gambler and womanizer who compares his addictions to horses and women.

CAMPO ARGENTINO DE POLO SPECTATOR SPORT

Map p250 (www.aapolo.com; Arévalo 3065; S Línea D Ministro Carranza) Located just across from the Hipódromo Argentino in Palermo, this stadium holds up to 30,000 spectators and hosts polo's most important events, including the Argentine Open Polo Championship in November and December; tickets are sold via Ticketek (p35). Entrance to other more low-key, local tournaments is usually free; check the website for upcoming matches.

SALON CANNING TANGO

Map p250 (011-15-5738-3850; www.parakultural.com.ar; Av Scalabrini Ortiz 1331; 141, 140, 15) Some of BA's finest dancers (no wallflowers here) grace this traditional venue with its great dance floor. Well-known tango company Parakultural stages good events on Monday, Tuesday and Friday, involving orchestras, singers and dance performances; check the website for class times and the *milonga* musical line-up. Expect big crowds and plenty of tourists.

LA VIRUTA TANGO

Map p250 (011-4774-6357; www.lavirutatango.com; Armenia 1366; 141, 15, 110) Popular basement venue. Good beginner tango classes are available before the *milongas* – translating into many inexperienced dancers on the floor earlier on – so if you're an expert get here late (after 2am). Music can run the gamut from tango to rock to cumbia to salsa earlier in the evening, with more traditional tunes later.

If you're still there when the breakfast *medialunas* (croissants) are brought out at 4am it's probably been a good night.

THELONIOUS BAR JAZZ

Map p250 (011-4829-1562; www.thelonious.com.ar; Jerónimo Salguero 1884, 1st fl; 8:45pm-12:45am Wed & Thu, to 2:45am Fri & Sat; S Línea D Bulnes) Upstairs in an old mansion lies this dimly lit jazz bar, with high brick ceilings and a good sound system. Come early to snag a seat (or reserve one ahead of time) and choose something from the typically Argentine food menu and good range of cocktails.

LOS CARDONES LIVE MUSIC

Map p250 (011-4777-1112; www.cardones.com.ar; Jorge Luis Borges 2180; 9pm-5am Wed-Sat; S Línea D Plaza Italia) Come to this friendly, low-key *peña* (folk club) for mellow guitar shows, audience-participatory jam sessions (and possible dancing), hearty regional cuisine from northern Argentina and free-flowing red wine. A great place to hear traditional Argentine folklore music. Check the website for details on the current line-up and reserve ahead for a good table.

LA PEÑA DEL COLORADO FOLK

Map p250 (011-4822-1038; www.lapeniadelcolorado.com; Güemes 3657; 5pm-5am Mon-Sat; S Línea D Bulnes) The nightly music shows (mostly folkloric) are memorable at this rustic restaurant, and after midnight audience members pick up nearby guitars to make their own entertainment. There's also northern Argentine food on offer, including *locro* (a corn and meat stew), *chipá* (chewy cheese balls) and *humitas de Chala* (like tamales) – the spicy *empanadas* are excellent.

SHOPPING

Palermo Viejo, a large sub-neighborhood of Palermo, is a shopper's paradise. These days, the barrio hosts a wide range of designers selling high-end wares from home accessories and books to fancy stationery, soaps, candles, souvenirs, kids' toys and gourmet chocolate. It's easy to spend hours or even days shopping in Palermo; many design-minded travelers consider an afternoon here part of the sightseeing circuit.

★ELEMENTOS ARGENTINOS — HOMEWARES

Map p250 (011-4832-6299; www.elementosargentinos.com.ar; Gurruchaga 1881; 11am-7pm Tue-Sat; Línea D Plaza Italia) The high-quality carpets, rugs and blankets sold here are hand-dyed, hand-woven on a loom and fair trade; the owners work with cooperatives and NGOs to help the communities in northwestern Argentina where the textiles are produced. Have larger items mailed home, or pick up a super soft llama wool blanket to squeeze into your suitcase.

★BOSQUE — ARTS & CRAFTS

Map p250 (011-2071-0737; https://bosque2.mitiendanube.com/; Av Dorrego 2086; 11am-7pm Mon-Fri, noon-7pm Sat; Línea D Ministro Carranza) A charming range of arts and crafts with a botanical bent are sold in this tiny boutique. The woodland theme is evident in the forest scenes of the limited-edition illustrations, hand-painted decorative plates, ceramics and cushions, as well as geometric wooden lamps and decorative objects, all by independent local designers.

BLACKMAMBA — FASHION & ACCESSORIES

Map p250 (011-4832-5083; www.beblackmamba.com; Soler 4502; 11am-8pm Mon-Sat; Línea D Scalabrini Ortiz) Bianca Siconolfi's sultry designs for her label Blackmamba include menswear, womenswear and unisex pieces with a dark, gothic edge. Her leather jackets are particularly covetable (and cost around AR$15,000).

LO DE JOAQUÍN ALBERDI — FOOD & DRINKS

Map p250 (011-4832-5329; www.lodejoaquinalberdi.com; Jorge Luis Borges 1772; wine tastings AR$350; 11am-9:30pm Mon-Sat, noon-9:30pm Sun; Línea D Plaza Italia) Nationally produced wines for every taste and budget line the racks and cellar of this attractive wine shop; ask friendly owner Joaquín for his recommendations. Tastings happen Thursdays and Fridays at 7:30pm (book online ahead of time) and include four wines and some cheeses.

MONTE ARTE ÉTNICO ARGENTINO — HOMEWARES

Map p250 (011-4832-0516; www.monteargentino.com; El Salvador 4656; 11am-6pm Mon-Fri, 11am-4pm Sat; 15, 111, 141) Bright and beautiful woven *mantas* (blankets) from Santiago del Estero are the main attraction at this upscale shop, located in an old house. All are made from wool and natural dyes, and can also be used as light rugs.

HUMAWACA — FASHION & ACCESSORIES

Map p250 (011-4832-2662; www.humawaca.com; El Salvador 4692; 11am-8pm Mon-Sat, 2-7pm Sun; 141, 15, 39) Award-winning designer handbags, tote bags and wallets made with Argentine leather, all with clean modernist lines and colorful hues. Visit this tiny boutique – with the tagline 'todo cow' – and you'll always find something different and eye-catching. Bags cost around AR$2000 to AR$5000.

JUANA DE ARCO — FASHION & ACCESSORIES

Map p250 (011-4833-1621; www.juanadearco.net; El Salvador 4762; 10:30am-8pm Mon-Sat, 1-8pm Sun; 141, 15, 39) Mariana Cortés has designed adorable printed fabrics sewn into girly sets that would be best showcased during a pillow fight – think brightly colored T-shirts, flowery boxer shorts and tight leggings. Descend the staircase to discover more treasures.

MERCADO DE LAS PULGAS — MARKET

Map p250 (www.facebook.com/mercadodelaspulgascaba/; cnr Álvarez Thomas & Av Dorrego; 10am-7pm Tue-Sun; 39, 140, 168) This large covered warehouse is full of caged booths selling antiques, vintage objects and some modern items – precious things such as wooden furniture, glass soda bottles, chandeliers, clocks, silver trays, mirrors and ironwork. The building itself is a canvas for local graffiti artists – even if you don't want to shop, it's worth coming by to see the latest murals.

GALERIA PATIO DEL LICEO — MALL

Map p250 (Av Santa Fe 2729; most stores 2-8pm Mon-Sat; Línea D Agüero) Eclectic little shopping mall with a bohemian vibe. In the past few years, young independent artisans have

BA'S EMERGING DESIGNERS

One of the most notable transitions in Buenos Aires fashion in the last few years is the growing prominence of emerging designers. Based mostly out of private homes and apartments, known locally as 'showrooms,' a young community of recent fashion-school grads and 20-somethings with an entrepreneurial spirit are taking over BA's inventive design world. Initiatives by the Buenos Aires City government, such as competitions including IncuBA and La Ciudad de Moda (which allowed several of the most promising emerging designers to stage runway shows at Buenos Aires Fashion Week), have given the industry the boost it desperately needs to make BA one of the most intriguing fashion hot spots in Latin America. Whether you're on the hunt for casual street wear, luxurious leather or innovative jewelry design, BA's best emerging designers take pride in their originality and skilled craftsmanship.

When it comes to clothing design, names like **Belén Amigo** (www.underboutique.com) and **Bianca Siconolfi** of Blackmamba (p142) are capturing stylish locals with their alternative, street-chic designs that range from Siconolfi's exquisite leather pieces to Amigo's tailored pants and drapey silk organza tops. For more comfy casual wear, stop in at **Deleon's** (www.deleonba.com) Palermo Hollywood showroom, a destination for young fashionable locals looking to expand their collection of urban cool garments that scream sophistication.

Yet another exciting fresh face in BA's emerging fashion scene is **Julia Schang-Viton** (www.schangviton.com), a young design prodigy whose structured, architectural cuts and neutral color palette draw upon her Asian heritage.

In the world of jewelry, **Inés Bonadeo** (www.inesbonadeo.com.ar), a metal-working craftswoman who has shown her work in New York at the international design fair NY Now, can't be missed.

While popular among locals, shopping in showrooms can prove intimidating for visitors. To gain access to these hidden treasures, it takes some local knowledge and the right connections. Thankfully, a few ambitious expats are giving tourists the chance to discover the exciting world of BA's emerging design through personalized shopping tours that will take you to some of the most notable showrooms in town, as well as the hippest open-door boutiques. Sophie Lloyd at **ShopHopBA** (www.shop-buenosaires.com) is the perfect option for those looking to get inside the city's exclusive showrooms. Warm, welcoming and knowledgeable, Sophie's tours include champagne toasts and privately catered lunches, and she also offers personal color consultations to those in need of a wardrobe makeover. Vanessa Bell at **Creme de la Creme** (www.cremedelacreme.com.ar) is known for her extensive contacts and excellent taste.

Natalie Schreyer is a fashion writer and resident of Buenos Aires. She is the creator of www.bashopgirl.com, a fashion blog covering BA's best emerging designers. In addition to her blog, she has written for LandingPadBA.com.

taken over and created an artistic hub here, filling it with various small boutiques, exhibition spaces and workshops. You'll find a couple of bookshops, **Los Hermanos** ukulele store and some great design stores, including **Greens** and sustainable specialists **Tienda Raiz**. Hours vary.

HERMANOS ESTEBECORENA CLOTHING

Map p250 (☎011-4772-2145; www.hermanosestebecorena.com; El Salvador 5960; ⏲11am-8pm Mon-Sat; Ⓢ Línea D Ministro Carranza) The Estebecorena brothers apply their highly creative skills toward smartly designed tops, jackets that fold into bags, polo-collar work shirts and even seamless underwear. The focus is on original, highly stylish, very functional men's clothing that makes the artsy types swoon. Selection is limited, but what's there really counts.

LIBROS DEL PASAJE BOOKS

Map p250 (☎011-4833-6637; www.librosdelpasaje.com.ar; Thames 1762; ⏲10am-10pm Mon-Sat, 2-9pm Sun; Ⓢ Línea D Plaza Italia) This literary sanctuary offers history, culture and art books. They're mostly in Spanish, but look for the small English section near the front door. There's a cute cafe in back, with a small indoor patio, for a snack or cup of coffee.

RAPSODIA — FASHION & ACCESSORIES

Map p250 (011-4831-6333; www.rapsodia.com; Honduras 4872; 10am-9pm; 140, 110, 15) With gorgeous printed fabrics and details such as fringe and sequins, this large and popular boutique is a must for fashion mavens. Old and new are blended into creative, colorful styles with exotic and bohemian accents. Locals covet the dresses and jeans. There are over a dozen branches in the city.

BOLIVIA — CLOTHING

Map p250 (011-4832-6284; www.boliviadivina.com; Gurruchaga 1581; 10:30am-8:30pm Mon-Sat, 3-8:30pm Sun; 141, 110, 15) There's almost nothing here that your young, hip brother wouldn't love, from the fitted shirts to the skin-tight jeans and the military-style jackets. Metrosexual to the hilt, and paradise for the man who isn't afraid of patterns, plaid or pastels. Four other branches in the city.

MISHKA — SHOES

Map p250 (011-4833-6566; www.mishka.com.ar; El Salvador 4673; 10:30am-8:30pm Mon-Sat, 2-8pm Sun; 111, 141, 15) Wonderfully unique footwear with a retro-hip, feminine and slightly conservative vibe. Try on a pair of patent leather sandals for size, or go for more traditional suede moccasins (though styles are always changing). Check the website for other locations around the city.

28 SPORT — SHOES

Map p250 (011-4833-4287; www.28sport.com; Gurruchaga 1481; 11am-7pm Mon-Sat; 110, 141, 15) For the retro-sports fanatic, there's nothing better than this unique shop, with its sense of humor and vintage twist. Focusing on only one product and one style – men's '50s sport-style shoes – the cobblers here can concentrate on quality and craftsmanship. Inspiration comes from football, boxing and bowling shoes.

CALMA CHICHA — HOMEWARES

Map p250 (011-4831-1818; www.calmachicha.com; Honduras 4909; 10am-8pm; 15, 141, 140) Calma Chicha specializes in creative housewares and accessories that are locally produced from leather, faux leather, sheepskin, cowhide and brightly hued fabric. Look for butterfly chairs, throw rugs, leather place mats, bright pillows and cowskin bags.

PANORAMA — CLOTHING

Map p250 (011-4806-0282; www.pnrm.com.ar; República de la India 2905; 10am-9pm Mon-Sat; Línea D Plaza Italia) About 20 emerging young designers are showcased at this small, upscale store in Palermo Chico. Peruse the clothing racks for one-of-a-kind, eclectic tops, pants, dresses and coats that can be definite show-stoppers. Small sizes dominate, though custom orders are possible. There are also a few accessories and shoes.

PASEO ALCORTA — MALL

Map p250 (Alcorta Shopping; 011-5777-6500; www.alcortashopping.com.ar; Jerónimo Salguero 3172; 10am-10pm; 130, 33, 93) At this large, upscale shopping mall all the popular Argentine women's clothing shops are represented, as are international brands such as Adidas, Nike and Lacoste. Other stores sell leather goods, kids' clothes, men's designs, sportswear and accessories. There's also a large food court and a children's play area.

FERIA PLAZA SERRANO — MARKET

Map p250 (cnr Honduras & Jorge Luis Borges; 10am-8pm Sat & Sun; 140, 141, 34) Costume jewelry, hand-knit tops, hippie bags, *mate* gourds, leather accessories and much more fill the craft booths at this popular street fair on Plaza Serrano (also known as Plaza Cortázar). It's not huge, but the plaza is close to Palermo's nightlife and surrounded by bars, restaurants and stores.

HARAPOS PATAGONIA — GIFTS & SOUVENIRS

Map p250 (011-2058-7810; www.harapospatagonia.com.ar; Serrano 1542; 11am-7:30pm Mon-Sat, 2-7:30pm Sun; 140, 141, 110) Can't make it all the way to Patagonia? Just visit this small store to grab a southern souvenir. There are woolen goods (sheep are big down there), handmade ceramics, wooden utensils and silver and alpaca jewelry. All products are made by Patagonian craftspeople.

ALTO PALERMO — MALL

Map p250 (011-5777-8000; www.altopalermo.com.ar; Av Santa Fe 3253; 10am-10pm; Línea D Bulnes) Smack bang on bustling Av Santa Fe, this popular, shiny mall offers dozens of clothing shops, bookstores, jewelry boutiques, and electronics and housewares stores. Look for local brands Complot, Ayres and Ay Not Dead. Services include a food court, a cinema complex and a good kids' area on the 3rd floor.

SPORTS & ACTIVITIES

★BAR DU MARCHÉ WINE

Map p250 (☎011-4778-1050; www.bardumarchepalermo.com; Nicaragua 5946; tasting AR$195; ⏰9:30am-midnight Mon-Sat; Ⓢ Línea D Ministro Carranza) This small, upscale and French-inspired bistro is a great place for wine by the glass; the sommelier can fill you in on the 50 varieties on offer. Wine tastings are from 5pm to 8pm daily and – at AR$195 for three small glasses paired with specialty cheeses – are good value.

★BUENOS AIRES FÚTBOL AMIGOS FOOTBALL

Map p250 (BAFA; www.fcbafa.com; El Salvador 5301; per game AR$100; ⏰games 5-9pm Wed-Mon; Ⓢ Línea D Plaza Italia) Friendly five-aside soccer games for men and women with a mixture of locals and foreigners at pitches in Palermo and Villa Crespo. All levels are welcome and it's a great way to meet people and counteract all the meat consumption while playing the city's best-loved sport. Sign up for games in advance via the website. Game times and locations vary.

PAIN ET VIN WINE

Map p250 (☎011-4832-5654; www.facebook.com/painevin/; Gorriti 5132; tastings per person AR$400; ⏰noon-10pm Tue-Sat, to 7pm Sun; 🚌140, 34, 111) An inviting spot to try some wines by the glass in a contemporary, airy setting. Book in advance for tastings (in English) which include a detailed talk about the wines, four tasting glasses and a cheese and charcuterie board with freshly baked bread. A few gourmet sandwiches are available, too. Check the Facebook page for special tastings from particular vineyards.

ARGENTINE EXPERIENCE FOOD

Map p250 (☎011-4778-0913; www.theargentineexperience.com; Fitz Roy 2110; US$89-115; ⏰6:30-11:30pm Mon-Sat; Ⓜ Línea D Palermo) Learn the meaning of local hand gestures, the story of Argentina's beef and how to make *empanadas* (a pastry turnover filled with a variety of savoury ingredients and baked or fried) and *alfajores* (cookie sandwiches) at an interactive dinner party where the main course is a supremely tender steak. Book in advance.

NORMA SOUED COOKING

(☎011-15-4470-2267; www.argentinecookingclasses.com; Palermo; per person US$65-85; ⏰10:30am-1pm Tue & Thu, 11am-2pm Sat; Ⓢ Línea D Olleros) At her Palermo home, Norma will teach you the basics of how to prepare typical Argentine food such as *empanadas*, traditional stews and *alfajores*. The exact address is given when you book.

BUENA ONDA YOGA YOGA

Map p250 (www.buenaondayoga.net; Thames 1916; class US$14; Ⓢ Línea D Plaza Italia) Vinyasa flow and yin yoga classes taught in English; see the website for the current schedule. Classes also held in San Telmo and Villa Crespo.

1

2

GRAFFITIMUNDO ©

ɹral by Martin Ron **2.** Mural by Gaia & Nanook **3.** Graffiti in Street Bar (p140), Palermo

Street Art

Buenos Aires' turbulent history, its passion and its creativity have driven the growth of an internationally acclaimed street-art scene.

In the years following the 2001 economic crisis a generation of artists took to the streets to reclaim public spaces. At first graffiti and stencils delivered scathing criticisms of the government, then gradually a new style began to emerge, bringing humor, color and creative experimentation. Stencil artists, graffiti writers, activists and art collectives began to work together, giving the city walls a new role: channeling artistic expression. Out of a dark period of political and social upheaval, a vibrant new art movement was born.

Graffiti in Buenos Aires incorporates a dizzying array of techniques and styles and is found everywhere from sidewalks and shutters to garbage cans and towering walls. Huge-scale murals reflect both the talents of local artists and the tolerance their work enjoys. It's not unusual to find artists creating enormous, detailed pieces in broad daylight, and they travel from across the world to experience the freedom of painting BA's streets. Look out for works by Martin Ron, including his surrealist work *The Parrots' Tale* in Villa Urquiza and *Pedro Lujan and his Dog* in the southern neighborhood of Barracas.

To check out works from some of the scene's leading artists head to **Post Street Bar** (p140), a Palermo bar covered in stencils. There's a gallery at the back that specializes in street art.

To learn more and see some of the city's most impressive art, why not take a graffiti tour? **Graffitimundo** (p208) and **Buenos Aires Street Art** (p209) are two organizations that work closely with leading local artists. Reserve a spot on one of their tours and venture off the beaten track to discover spectacular murals and the hidden history of this remarkable scene.

South of Palermo

Neighborhood Top Five

1 Museo Casa Carlos Gardel (p150) Learning about tango's most famous singer via his old recordings, news clippings and personal items at this small museum located at the very house he used to live in.

2 La Bomba de Tiempo (p153) Dancing it up at Monday night's drumming parties at the Ciudad Cultural Konex.

3 La Catedral (p153) Dancing tango at BA's most bohemian *milonga* (dance hall), after taking a class at DNI Tango nearby.

4 Mercado de Abasto (p150) Visiting this impressive, gorgeously remodeled shopping center.

5 Museo Argentino de Ciencias Naturales (p150) Wandering among old skeletons, taxidermy rooms and natural-science exhibits.

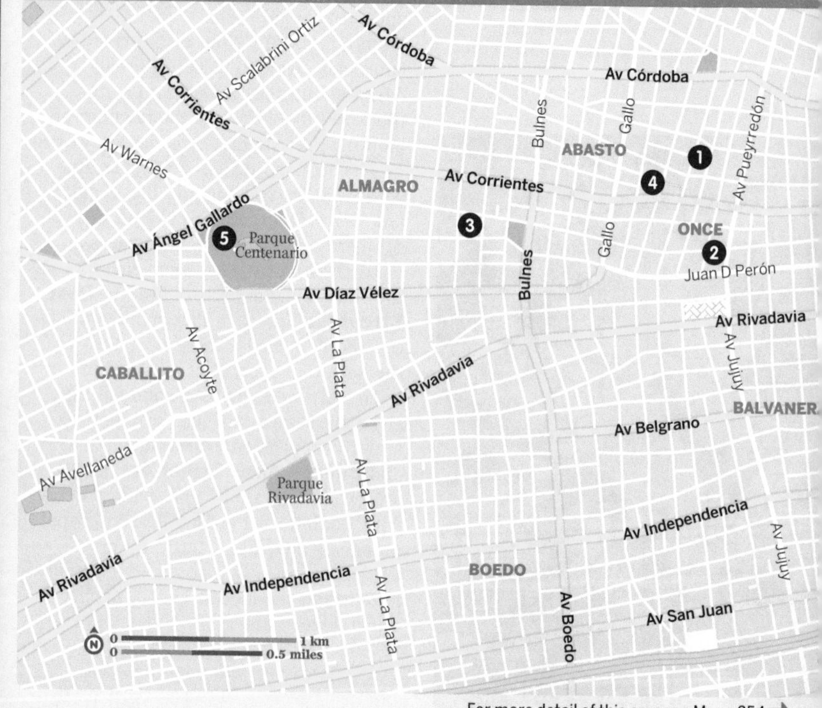

For more detail of this area see Map p254

Explore: South of Palermo

There are just a few interesting sights dotting the map in these refreshingly local neighborhoods. Start in Villa Crespo, a good area for outlet shopping that's also home to several casual but excellent restaurants. A short walk south is Caballito, a pleasant neighborhood that's home to the circular Parque Centenario. The main sight here is the Museo Argentino de Ciencias Naturales, a good natural-science museum that's worth a peek for its musty taxidermy and cool skeleton room.

East of Villa Crespo are the Abasto and Once (pronounced 'ohn-seh') neighborhoods, both melting-pot destinations that have attracted sizable populations of Jews, Peruvians and Koreans – and their respective ethnic cuisines as well. The main attraction in Abasto is the Mercado de Abasto, one of the city's most attractive shopping malls. On a side street just east of the mall, look for a small statue of Carlos Gardel, the famous tango singer who lived in this neighborhood; four blocks northeast is the Museo Casa Carlos Gardel, a museum in his former home. Many alternative theaters can also be found in this area.

East of Abasto is Once and its bustling train station, surrounded by hundreds of street vendors selling all manner of garments and cheap electronic devices. There's a colorful feel to this gritty, commercial pocket. Nearby Once are the bohemian neighborhoods of Almagro and Boedo. The intersection of Av San Juan and Boedo is especially historic and right on the Subte line.

Local Life

- **Parklife** For a condensed dose of local life head to Parque Centenario, the circular park at the geographical center of the city. It's always busy here; you'll see families out with their dogs, people jogging and doing yoga, and plenty of guitars.
- **Hangouts** Local *señoras* take a break at Las Violetas (p152), quite possibly the most beautiful traditional cafe in Buenos Aires.
- **Eating** Classic neighborhood eateries such as Café Margot (p151) will take you back in time.
- **Theater** Artsy *porteños* (residents of Buenos Aires) head to one of the many alternative theater productions going on in Almagro.

Getting There & Away

- **Bus** From Plaza de Mayo take bus 140 to Villa Crespo and Almagro, bus 26 to Once, bus 132 to Caballito and bus 126 to Boedo.
- **Subte** Líneas A, B and E are the fastest way to these neighborhoods.

Lonely Planet's Top Tip

Consider finding a place to stay in Villa Crespo or Almagro, the neighborhoods just south of Palermo. New restaurants, bars and guesthouses are opening here as rents become too expensive for many businesses in Palermo, but the nightlife and sights of the better-known neighborhood are often within walking distance.

Best Places to Eat

- i Latina (p152)
- Guarda la Vieja (p151)
- Sarkis (p151)
- Café Crespin (p151)

For reviews, see p151.

Best Places to Drink

- Las Violetas (p152)
- 878 (p152)
- El Bandarín (p152)

For reviews, see p152.

Best Entertainment

- La Catedral (p153)
- La Bomba de Tiempo (p153)
- Complejo Tango (p153)

For reviews, see p153.

SIGHTS

These neighborhoods aren't packed with must-see sights, but there are a few interesting galleries and museums and some impressive architecture to see. The real attraction here is the local flavor – soak it up by exploring the streets on foot or by bike.

MERCADO DE ABASTO NOTABLE BUILDING

Map p254 (011-4959-3400; www.abasto-shopping.com.ar; Av Corrientes 3247; 10am-10pm; Línea B Carlos Gardel) The historic Mercado de Abasto (1895) has been turned into one of the most beautiful shopping centers in the city. The building, once a large vegetable market, received an architectural prize in 1937 for its Av Corrientes facade. It holds more than 200 stores, a large cinema, a food court and the only kosher McDonald's outside Israel (the one upstairs and next to Burger King). It's great for families, with a good children's museum and even a small amusement park.

MUSEO CASA CARLOS GARDEL MUSEUM

Map p254 (011-4964-2071; www.facebook.com/carlitosrgardel/; Jean Jaurés 735; AR$10; 11am-6pm Mon & Wed-Fri, 10am-7pm Sat & Sun; Línea B Carlos Gardel) Small but noteworthy is this tribute to tango's most famous voice. Located in Gardel's old house, this museum traces his partnership with José Razzano and displays old memorabilia including photos, records and news clippings. There isn't a whole lot to see inside but the house itself – a typical chorizo-style residence with rooms leading off a central patio – is worth a look.

CARLOS GARDEL STATUE MONUMENT

Map p254 (Av Anchorena; Línea B Carlos Gardel) The Abasto neighborhood was once home to tango legend Carlos Gardel, and on this cobbled street off Av Anchorena is a statue of the singer.

CASA BRANDON CULTURAL CENTER

Map p254 (011-4858-0610; www.brandongayday.com.ar; Luis Maria Drago 236; 8pm-3am Wed-Sun; Línea B Ángel Gallardo) Located in Villa Crespo, this meeting spot is so much more than a bar. The concept at Casa Brandon is to promote art in the context of sexual diversity. There's an art gallery that showcases paintings and photographs, and you can watch movies or take in a live music performance. And for those who need a bit more excitement, there are karaoke and drag party nights.

MUSEO ARGENTINO DE CIENCIAS NATURALES MUSEUM

Map p254 (Natural Science Museum; 011-4982-6595; www.macn.gov.ar; Av Ángel Gallardo 490; AR$25; 2-7pm; ; Línea B Ángel Gallardo) In the geographical center of the city at circular Parque Centenario is this excellent natural-science museum. On display are large collections of meteorites, rocks and minerals, Argentine seashells, insects and dinosaur-skeleton replicas. The taxidermy and skeleton rooms are especially good. Bring the kids; they can mingle with the hundreds of children who visit on school excursions.

CARLOS GARDEL

In June 1935 a Cuban woman committed suicide in Havana; meanwhile, in New York and Puerto Rico two other women tried to poison themselves. It was all over the same man – tango singer Carlos Gardel, who had just died in a plane crash in Colombia.

Gardel was born in France, and when he was three his destitute single mother brought him to Buenos Aires. In his youth he entertained neighbors with his rapturous singing, then went on to establish a successful performing career.

Gardel played an enormous role in creating the tango *canción* (song) and almost single-handedly took the style out of Buenos Aires' tenements and brought it to Paris and New York. His crooning voice, suaveness and overall charisma made him an immediate success in Latin American countries – a rising star during tango's golden years of the 1920s and 1930s. Unfortunately, Gardel's later film career was tragically cut short by that fatal plane crash.

His devoted followers cannot pass a day without listening to him; as the saying goes, 'Gardel sings better every day.'

OBSERVATORIO ASTRONÓMICO OBSERVATORY

Map p254 (☎011-4863-3366; www.asaramas.com.ar; Av Patricias Argentinas 550; guided observation AR$50; Ⓢ Línea B Ángel Gallardo) This observatory offers one-hour telescopic stargazing sessions. Call or check the website before your visit, as observation hours change depending on the season.

EATING

Hip Villa Crespo is the place to go for brunch, while Almagro and Boedo have some fantastic old-time bars and restaurants, some of them neighborhood classics. Once is a good place to hunt for ethnic foods with Jewish, Peruvian or Korean flavors.

GUARDA LA VIEJA ARGENTINE $$

Map p254 (☎011-4863-7923; Billinghurst 699; mains AR$94-205; ⊙6pm-2am Sun-Thu, to 5am Fri & Sat; 📶; Ⓢ Línea B Carlos Gardel) With a reliable menu of tasty pizzas, salads, pastas and *milaneses* (breaded meat cutlets), it's no surprise that this corner restaurant-bar in Abasto is so popular. Sit at one of the pavement tables and order a few *raciones* (snacks) or share a *picada* (shared appetizer plate) – they come laden with calamari, ham, cheeses, olives, sweet potato and homemade bread.

CAFÉ MARGOT ARGENTINE $$

Map p254 (☎011-4957-0001; Av Boedo 857; mains AR$57-200; ⊙8am-2am; 📶; Ⓢ Línea E Boedo) Opened in 1904, this classic cafe in the bohemian neighborhood of Boedo is a typically *porteño* spot to relax with a *picada* and a bottle of wine, or a frosty mug of beer and a sandwich piled high with sliced turkey.

SARKIS MIDDLE EASTERN $

Map p254 (☎011-4772-4911; Thames 1101; mains AR$60-170; ⊙noon-3pm & 8pm-1am; 🚌140, 111, 34) The food is fabulous and well-priced at this long-standing Middle Eastern restaurant – come with a group to sample many exotic dishes. Start with the roasted eggplant hummus, *boquerones* (marinated sardines) or *parras rellenas* (stuffed grape leaves), then follow up with kebabs or lamb in yogurt sauce. Less busy at lunchtime; there's usually a wait for a table at dinner.

PAN Y ARTE ARGENTINE $

Map p254 (☎011-4957-6922; www.panyarte.com.ar; Av Boedo 880; mains AR$90-240; ⊙9am-1am; 📶; Ⓢ Línea E Boedo) There's a wonderful old-time atmosphere at this bohemian eatery. The menu includes a range of sandwiches, *empanadas* (a pastry turnover filled with a variety of savoury ingredients and baked or fried) and *picadas* and there's also an organic bakery and products such as cheese and crackers to purchase. It's in a great, local neighborhood. Often has piano concerts and tango nights.

There's also a theater here offering some interesting independent productions; see the website for upcoming events.

CAFÉ CRESPIN CAFE $$

Map p254 (☎011-4855-3771; www.cafecrespin.com.ar; Vera 699; mains AR$130-210, set brunches AR$290-600; ⊙8am-8pm Tue-Fri, 9am-8pm Sat, noon-7pm Sun; 📶; Ⓢ Línea B Malabia) Cute corner cafe in Villa Crespo. Stock up on pancakes, French toast and bagel sandwiches for breakfast, or go for the quesadillas, salmon salad or ham-and-cheese *tostados* (toasted sandwiches) at lunchtime. Tasty brunches, and there are also good pastries and a bakery on the premises.

MALVÓN CAFE $$

Map p254 (☎011-4774-2563; www.malvonba.com.ar; Serrano 789; mains AR$150-285; ⊙8am-8:30pm Sun & Mon, to midnight Tue-Thu, 9pm-12:30am Fri & Sat; Ⓢ Línea B Medrano) Famous for its US-style weekend brunch – which features pancakes, French toast and eggs Benedict – Malvón has a wonderfully rustic yet upscale atmosphere. The gourmet sandwiches are tasty, but there are also great bagels, burgers, tapas and baked treats including scones, muffins and pecan pie. Expect a wait on the weekend.

BI WON KOREAN $$

Map p254 (☎011-4372-1146; Junín 548; mains AR$150-230; ⊙noon-3pm & 7:30-11:30pm Mon-Fri, 7:30-11:30pm Sat; Ⓢ Línea B Pasteur) Korean food can't be beat at this simple restaurant. Go for the *bulgogi* (grill the meat yourself at the table), *bibimbap* (rice bowl with meat, veggies, egg and hot sauce) or *kim chee chigue* (kimchi soup with pork – for adventurous, spice-loving tongues only!). And don't forget to say *kamsamnida* (thank you) to your server at the end.

WORTH A DETOUR

FERIA DE MATADEROS

In the working-class barrio of Mataderos is this excellent **folk market and fair** (☎011-4342-9629; www.facebook.com/fmatadero/; cnr Avs Lisandro de la Torre & de los Corrales; ⏰11am-8pm Sun Apr–mid-Dec, 6pm-midnight Sat late Jan–mid-Mar; 🚌126, 55). Merchants offer handmade crafts and regional cuisine including *locro* (a corn and meat stew) and *humita* (a savory corn and cheese mixture wrapped in husks). Folk singers, dancers and gauchos on horseback entertain, and nearby there's a small **museum** (Gaucho Museum; ☎011-4687-1949; Av de los Corrales 6436, Mataderos; AR$15; ⏰11am-7:30pm Sun; 🚌143, 91, 101) containing exhibits on gaucho life and the history of the meat-packing area of Mataderos.

Call ahead in between seasons to make sure it's open. From downtown take bus 126 or from Palermo take bus 55; the journey takes about one hour. You can also take a taxi to and from Mataderos if you're pinched for time.

★I LATINA SOUTH AMERICAN **$$$**

Map p254 (☎011-4857-9095; www.ilatinabuenosaires.com; Murillo 725; 7-course tasting menu AR$1400; ⏰8-11pm Tue-Sat; Ⓢ Línea B Malabia) Located south of Palermo in Villa Crespo is one of BA's best restaurants: i Latina. The set menu consists of seven courses, all exquisitely prepared and presented. Flavors are incredibly stimulating and complex; this isn't a place to simply fill your tummy, but rather to savor a gustatory experience that will dazzle your taste buds. Reservation required.

★CASA FELIX SEAFOOD **$$$**

(http://colectivofelix.com/buenos-aires/cenas/; 5-course tasting menu AR$600; ✍) At his closed-door restaurant in the Chacarita neighborhood, chef Diego Felix welcomes his guests with a cocktail in the candle-lit patio area, next to the herb and vegetable garden where many of his ingredients are grown. The five-course menu changes seasonally, but the dishes are always fresh, inventive, largely vegetarian and inspired by Felix's travels around South America.

The exact address is given when you make a reservation.

DRINKING & NIGHTLIFE

These neighborhoods are home to some fabulous old-time cafes (in Almagro and Boedo), as well as some hipper bars (in Villa Crespo and Abasto).

LAS VIOLETAS CAFE

Map p254 (☎011-4958-7387; http://lasvioletas.com/; Av Rivadavia 3899; ⏰8am-2am; Ⓢ Línea A Castro Barros) Dating back to 1884, this historic coffeehouse's stained-glass awnings, high ceilings and gilded details make it one of the most beautiful cafes in the capital. Come for the luxurious afternoon tea and be sure to pick something up in the cake shop on the way out.

878 COCKTAIL BAR

Map p254 (☎011-4773-1098; www.878bar.com.ar; Thames 878; ⏰7pm-3am Mon-Thu, to 4:30pm Fri, 8pm-4:30am Sat & Sun; 🚌55) Hidden behind an unsigned door is this 'secret' bar, but it's hardly exclusive. Enter a wonderland of elegant, low lounge furniture and red-brick walls; for whiskey lovers there are over 80 kinds to try, but the cocktails are tasty too. If you're hungry, tapas are available (reserve for dinners). Vermouth happy hour is 7pm to 9pm Monday to Friday.

EL BANDARÍN BAR

Map p254 (☎011-4862-7757; http://elbanderin.com.ar; Guardia Vieja 3601; ⏰8:30am-midnight Mon-Wed, to 2am Thu & Fri; Ⓢ Línea B Medrano) This traditional neighborhood cafe and bar has been serving the locals their morning *cafe con leche* (milky coffee) and afternoon beers since 1923. Inside the old brick walls are covered with soccer memorabilia (*el bandarín* means 'the flag').

COSSAB PUB

Map p254 (☎011-2060-5023; Carlos Calvo 4199; ⏰6:30pm-1am Wed-Thu, to 3am Fri, 7:30pm-3am Sat, to 1am Sun; Ⓢ Línea E Boedo) This pub in Boedo was serving the needs of BA's beer lovers long before hip new craft-beer bars starting popping up across the city. It has one of BA's best selections of world beers, with a good choice of German, Dutch and Belgian brews available, as well as Cossab's own IPA, Scotch, Stout and others on tap.

Also serves a selection of sandwiches and pizzas.

AMERIKA CLUB

Map p254 (☎011-4865-4416; www.ameri-k.com.ar; Gascón 1040; ⏰Fri-Sun; Ⓢ Línea B Medrano) BA's largest and feistiest gay nightclub, long-running Amerika attracts all kinds of folks – but Saturdays are especially popular with gay guys. There are two music floors, one electronica and one Latina, plus *canilla libre* (all-you-can-drink) on Fridays and Saturdays. Large video screens, stripper shows, four bars and a wild dark room keep things interesting.

ENTERTAINMENT

★LA BOMBA DE TIEMPO LIVE MUSIC

Map p254 (www.labombadetiempo.com; Sarmiento 3131, Ciudad Cultural Konex; AR$70; ⏰7-10pm Mon; Ⓢ Línea B Carlos Gardel) One of BA's most unique events takes place every Monday when the long-running percussion group La Bomba de Tiempo plays at Konex (p194). You'll find it impossible not to dance to the rhythms when the drummers get into their stride.

★LA CATEDRAL MILONGA

Map p254 (☎011-15-5325-1630; www.lacatedralclub.com; Sarmiento 4006; Ⓢ Línea B Medrano) This grungy warehouse space is very casual, with unusual art on the walls, thrift-store furniture, dim, atmospheric lighting and the occasional cat wandering among the tables. It's very bohemian and there's no implied dress code – you'll see plenty of jeans. A great place for beginners since even non-expert dancers can feel comfortable on the dance floor.

The most popular night here is Tuesday.

ESQUINA CARLOS GARDEL TANGO

Map p254 (☎011-4867-6363; www.esquinacarlosgardel.com.ar; Carlos Gardel 3200; show from US$96, show & dinner from US$140; Ⓢ Línea B Carlos Gardel) One of the fanciest tango shows in town plays at this impressive 430-seat theater right next to the lovely Mercado de Abasto (p150) shopping mall. This fine show highlights passionate, top-notch musicians and performers in period costumes, though a modern segment involving a skin suit is cutting-edge, athletic and memorable.

The Abasto neighborhood was once Carlos Gardel's stomping ground, and he even hung out at this locale.

COMPLEJO TANGO TANGO

Map p254 (☎011-4941-1119; www.complejotango.com.ar; Av Belgrano 2608; show US$55, dinner & show from US$125; Ⓢ Línea A Plaza Miserere) For those who wish to not only

LOCAL KNOWLEDGE

AVANT-GARDE THEATER

Get off-the-beaten-play path and go for something out of the ordinary – there's plenty of choice in this creative city for unique and worthwhile theater.

Actors Studio Teatro (Map p254; ☎011-4983-9883; www.actors-studio.org; Av Díaz Vélez 3842; Ⓢ Línea A Castro Barros) Offers new interpretations of old classics, along with cutting-edge productions in its 120-seat theater. Also has occasional acting classes.

El Camarín de las Musas (Map p254; ☎011-4862-0655; www.elcamarindelasmusas.com.ar; Mario Bravo 960; Ⓢ Línea B Medrano) Offers contemporary dance and theater. There are also workshops and classes available, and a trendy restaurant-cafe provides affordable snacks.

El Cubo (Map p254; ☎011-4963-2568; www.cuboabasto.com.ar; Pasaje Zelaya 3053; Ⓢ Línea B Carlos Gardel) A hip small Abasto space, it hosts gutsy theater pieces and offbeat performances such as queer musicals.

Espacio Callejón (Map p254; ☎011-4862-1167; http://espaciocallejon.com/; Humahuaca 3759; Ⓢ Línea B Medrano) A small independent venue that showcases edgy new theater, music and dance, and offers a few classes (including 'clown' acting).

watch tango but also experience it, there's this classy venue in Once. The first hour is a free beginners' tango lesson, which you can follow with a tasty dinner, then an excellent tango show – be warned that performers go around toward the end, picking out audience members to dance with them (usually badly).

CLUB GRICEL TANGO

Map p254 (☎011-4957-7157; www.clubgriceltango.com.ar; La Rioja 1180; Línea E General Urquiza) This old classic in the San Cristóbal neighborhood (take a taxi) often has big crowds. It attracts an older, well-dressed, mostly local clientele – avoid Sundays if you're alone as it's mostly for couples. There's a wonderful springy dance floor and occasionally live orchestras.

SAN LORENZO DE ALMAGRO SOCCER

(☎011-4918-4237; www.sanlorenzo.com.ar; Varela 2680; 143, 101) One of Argentina's top five clubs and recent winners of the Copa Libertadores, San Lorenzo's home ground is currently in the less than salubrious area of Nueva Pompeya in the south of the city. However, plans are underway for the club to move back to its home neighborhood of Boedo soon.

Game tickets are sold at Av La Plata 1782 in Boedo and Av de Mayo 1373 in Congreso.

ESQUINA HOMERO MANZI TANGO

Map p254 (☎011-4957-8488; www.esquinahomeromanzi.com.ar; Av San Juan 3601; show AR$330, show & dinner from AR$550; Línea E Boedo) This tango venue in a remodeled old-time cafe is located right on the historic intersection of San Juan and Boedo. It has the capacity for 300 spectators and offers a decent show that's a mix of glitzy high-kicks and more traditional *milonga*-type dancing.

SHOPPING

Villa Crespo is the place to head for discount outlet stores and some specialist leather shops, as well as shoe shops selling the wares of local designers; you'll find these shops along Aguirre and Layolo along the three blocks between Serrano and Malabia. Further east, Abasto Shopping is a large, air-conditioned mall with plenty of chain fashion and sports stores, all housed in the striking Mercado de Abasto (p150) building.

CENTRICO SHOES

Map p254 (☎011-4773-9129; www.centricocentrica.com.ar; Loyola 531; 11am-8pm Mon-Sat; Línea B Malabia) Leonardo Mancuso designs these handmade leather shoes with a classic, traditional styling that emphasizes simplicity over showiness. Both men's and women's shoes are available, and some have unisex looks; there are also a few ankle and knee-high boots.

SPORTS & ACTIVITIES

★DNI TANGO DANCING

Map p254 (☎011-4866-6553; https://dni-tango.com/; Bulnes 1101; group class per person AR$100; Línea B Medrano) This excellent tango school offers group and private classes in English and Spanish for all levels. For those starting out, the Saturday afternoon *práctica* is a friendly place to dance with different partners without the pressure of taking to the floor at a more formal *milonga*. DNI is located in a beautiful old building in the neighborhood of Almagro.

ACATRAZ BOWLING

Map p254 (☎011-4982-4818; www.facebook.com/acatrazmultiespacio/; Av Rivadavia 3636; 4pm-4am Wed & Thu, to 6am Fri & Sat, to 3am Sun; Línea A Loria) Unusual restaurant-bar-bowling-alley-billiards-hall destination. You can do it all here; a great place to come with a group of friends. There are two bowling alleys, various pool tables, sports on TVs, plenty of tables to eat at and bars to drink at. Spread out over several floors, this place is huge and takes entertainment to a new level.

Day Trips from Buenos Aires

Tigre & the Delta p156

Take laid-back boat rides along the peaceful backwaters of the Paraná Delta. Interesting museums and a nearby outdoor market are pluses.

San Isidro p158

Enjoy spectacular river views and visit several worthwhile museums in this affluent city suburb that's steeped in history.

San Antonio de Areco p159

Explore this serene pampas village and its historic buildings, and perhaps visit a nearby *estancia* (ranch). If you're lucky, you might spot a gaucho or two.

Colonia p162

Located across the Río de la Plata in Uruguay, this pleasant little colonial town is lined with cobbled streets and charming old buildings.

Tigre & the Delta

Explore

The city of Tigre (35km north of Buenos Aires) and the surrounding delta region is a popular weekend getaway for weary *porteños* (residents of Buenos Aires). Latte-colored waters, tinted by sediment that results from large quantities of water from South America's great rivers being forced through smaller tributaries, flow through what is the third-largest river delta in the world. Glimpse into how locals live along peaceful canals, with boats as their only transportation. All along the shorelines are signs of water-related activity, from kayaking to canoeing to sculling.

The Best...

- **Sight** Museo de Arte Tigre
- **Place to Eat** Boulevard Sáenz Peña
- **Place to Drink** Maria Luján

Top Tip

Kayak or canoe tours are a good way to explore the peaceful back waterways of the delta. Try El Dorado Kayak or Bonanza Deltaventura.

Getting There & Away

- **Train** You can take the Tigre branch of the Mitre line train (with/without SUBE AR$6/12) from Retiro (one hour) or Belgrano C (45 minutes). The most scenic way to reach Tigre is via the **Tren de la Costa** (0800-222-8736; www.trendelacosta.com.ar; tickets AR$20), whose southernmost station (Maipú) is in the suburb of Olivos. The Mitre train from Retiro will take you to Maipú (get off at Mitre station at the end of the line and cross the pedestrian bridge to Maipú). You can also reach Maipú station on the 152 bus, which stops at Plaza Italia in Palermo.
- **Boat Sturla Viajes** (Map p236; in BA 011-4314-8555, in Tigre 011-4731-1300; www.sturlaviajes.com.ar; Ceclilia Grierson 400; one-way/return AR$450/590; 92, 106) You can take the Sturla boat straight to Tigre from Puerto Madero. Boats leave Puerto Madero at 10am (journey time two hours) and make the return trip from Tigre's Estación Fluvial at 4pm.

Need to Know

- **Area Code** 011
- **Location** 35km northwest of Buenos Aires
- **Tourist Office** (011-4512-4497; www.vivitigre.gov.ar; Bartolomé Mitre 305; 9am-6pm)

SIGHTS

Tigre city itself is very walkable and its main sights are easily reached on foot.

MUSEO DE ARTE TIGRE MUSEUM

(011-4512-4528; www.mat.gov.ar; Paseo Victorica 972; AR$40; 9am-7pm Wed-Fri, noon-7pm Sat & Sun) Tigre's grandest museum is located in a magnificent 1912 social club. Inside, it showcases the work of famous Argentine artists from the 19th and 20th centuries. Perched on the river bank in glorious grounds, the building in itself is worth a visit. Guided tours in Spanish are given at 11am and 5pm Wednesday to Friday and more frequently on weekends.

MUSEO NAVAL MUSEUM

(Naval Museum; 011-4749-0608; Paseo Victorica 602; AR$20; 8:30am-5:30pm Mon-Fri, 10:30am-6:30pm Sat & Sun) This worthwhile museum traces the history of the Argentine navy with an eclectic mix of historical photos, old maps, artillery displays and pickled sea critters. The intricate scale models of various naval ships are particularly impressive.

PUERTO DE FRUTOS MARKET

(Sarmiento 160; 10am-6pm) At this popular market, vendors sell homewares, furniture, wicker baskets, souvenirs and knickknacks; there are restaurants too. Weekends are busiest.

PARQUE DE LA COSTA AMUSEMENT PARK

(011-4002-6000; www.parquedelacosta.com.ar; Vivanco 1509; AR$285; 11am-6pm Fri, to 7:15pm Sat & Sun) Near to Puerto de Frutos is Tigre's amusement park with some fun attractions including roller-coaster rides and waterslides.

DELTA BOAT TRIPS

To explore the swampy waters of the delta, you'll need to get out in a boat. Frequent commuter launches depart from Estación Fluvial, behind the tourist office (p156), for various destinations in the delta (AR$70 to AR$190 one-way). A popular destination is the **Tres Bocas** neighborhood, a half-hour boat ride from Tigre, where you can take residential walks on thin paths connected by bridges over narrow channels. There are several restaurants and accommodations here. The **Rama Negra** area has a quieter and more natural setting with fewer services, but is an hour's boat ride away.

Several companies offer inexpensive boat tours, but commuter launches give you flexibility if you want to go for a stroll or stop for lunch at one of the delta's restaurants.

MUSEO DEL MATE MUSEUM

(011-4506-9594; www.elmuseodelmate.com; Lavalle 289; AR$50; 11am-6pm Wed-Sun) This niche museum with over 2000 items (mostly *mate* gourds) is dedicated to the national drink. The visit begins with a short film explaining the history of *mate* and Argentinian yerba production.

EATING

★BOULEVARD SÁENZ PEÑA INTERNATIONAL $$

(011-5197-4776; www.boulevardsaenzpena.com.ar; Blvd Sáenz Peña 1400; mains AR$155-190; 10:30am-7pm Wed-Sat, to 5pm Sun) Occupying a prime corner spot is this appealing cafe serving salads, sandwiches, coffee and cakes. Inside, it's spacious, modern and airy with plenty of contemporary design touches, but you'll want to bag a table on the outdoor patio, beneath the ivy and surrounded by plants. There's also a shop here, selling art, books and homewares.

ALMACÉN DE TIGRE ARGENTINE $$

(011-5197-4009; www.facebook.com/almacendeflorescafeboutiquetigre; Blvd Sáenz Peña 1336; mains AR$98-185; 9:30am-7pm Sun-Thu, to midnight Fri & Sat) Serves a tempting range of healthy soups, salads, sandwiches and bigger mains such as lasagne and *milanesas* (breaded meat cutlets).

MARIA LUJÁN ARGENTINE $$$

(011-4731-9613; www.ilnovomariadellujan.com; Paseo Victorica 611; mains AR$190-355; 8:30am-midnight) For an upscale meal on Paseo Victorica, the city's pleasant riverside avenue, try Maria Luján, which has a gorgeous shady patio. Serves the usual Argentinian fare – grilled meats, homemade pastas – as well as a number of seafood dishes.

SPORTS & ACTIVITIES

EL DORADO KAYAK KAYAKING

(011-4039-5858; www.eldoradokayak.com; full day AR$900) Kayaking tours deep inside the delta; all equipment and lunch included. Also offers full-moon night kayaking trips.

BONANZA DELTAVENTURA ADVENTURE

(011-4409-6967; www.deltaventura.com; Stand 16, Estación Fluvial, Bartolomé Mitre 305; 9am-5pm) Adventures include canoe trips, guided nature walks and horseback rides. Also offers overnight accommodations. Located a one-hour boat ride from Tigre.

SLEEPING

POSADA DE 1860 HOTEL $

(011-4749-4034; http://hotelposada1860.com.ar; Av Libertador San Martín 190; d Mon-Thu US$65, Fri-Sun US$78, extra bed US$10;) This well-run hotel has eight simple but good-value rooms. Spacious common areas give the place a homey feel; there's a kitchen, plenty of dining space indoors and out on the deck, and a *parrilla* (grill) in the garden for *asados* (barbecues). Rooms can sleep up to six people, making this a good choice for families or small groups.

CASONA LA RUCHI GUESTHOUSE $$

(011-4749-2499; www.casonalaruchi.com.ar; Lavalle 557; d/tr with shared bath US$80/90;) This family-run guesthouse is in a beautiful old 1893 mansion. Most of the four romantic bedrooms have balconies; all have shared bathrooms with original tiled floors. There's a pool and large garden out back.

San Isidro

Explore

About 20km north of Buenos Aires is peaceful and residential San Isidro, a salubrious suburb of leafy cobblestone streets lined with some luxurious mansions, as well as more modest houses. The historic center is at Plaza Mitre with its beautiful neo-Gothic cathedral; on weekends the area buzzes with a crafts fair. There are a number of worthwhile museums with sweeping river views that make for a pleasant day trip from the city. The suburb is easily reached by train from Buenos Aires; it's also possible to stop here on the way to or from Tigre.

San Isidro is steeped in history dating back to the first settlement of Buenos Aires in 1580, when Juan de Garay divided a 20km stretch of coastline into narrow strips of land that were divvied up among the group of 40 who had made the journey from Spain.

The Best...

- **Sight** Villa Ocampo
- **Place to Eat** Bruna
- **Place to Drink** Perú Beach

Top Tip

Don't miss the views of the Río de la Plata from the gardens of Quinta Los Ombúes.

Getting There & Away

- **Train** The Tigre branch of the Mitre line train from Retiro stops at San Isidro and Beccar stations (with/without SUBE card AR$5/12, 35 minutes). The most scenic way to reach San Isidro is via the Tren de la Costa (p156), whose southernmost station (Maipú) is in the suburb of Olivos. The Mitre train from Retiro will take you to Maipú (get off at Mitre station at the end of the line and cross the pedestrian bridge to Maipú).
- **Bus** Certain branches of the 60 bus go to San Isidro via Plaza Italia in Palermo; the route you need is 'Alto Tigre por Bajo San Isidro'; check with the driver.

Need to Know

- **Area Code** 011
- **Location** 20km north of Buenos Aires

SIGHTS

★VILLA OCAMPO — MUSEUM

(011-4732-4988; www.villaocampo.org/web/; Elortondo 1837; AR$50; 12:30-7pm Wed-Sun, guided tours 3pm & 4:30pm; Beccar) This beautifully restored mansion and Unesco-protected site was once the home of Victoria Ocampo (1890–1979), a feminist writer, publisher and intellectual who founded the magazine *Sur*. It's worth timing your visit to coincide with one of the excellent guided tours (in English and Spanish) of the property, which once hosted the likes of Graham Greene, Albert Camus, Le Corbusier and Pablo Neruda. There's also a pleasant cafe serving lunch until 3:30pm and then afternoon tea.

★MUSEO PUEYRREDON — MUSEUM

(011-4512-3131; www.museopueyrredon.org.ar; Rivera Indarte 48; 10am-6pm Tue-Thu, 2-8pm Sat & Sun; San Isidro) FREE This colonial villa was once the home of revolutionary hero General Juan Martín de Pueyrredón. Inside the building has been beautifully preserved and contains historical displays and recreations of the colonial-era kitchen, living room, bedroom and dining room complete with period furniture and historical portraits. The glorious gardens have sweeping views down to the river. Note the *algarrobo* (carob tree) under which Pueyrredón and José de San Martín planned battle strategies against the Spanish during the wars of independence.

To get here from the cathedral, walk five blocks south down Av Libertador, turn left onto Sáenz Peña and after two blocks turn right onto Rivera Indarte.

QUINTA LOS OMBÚES — MUSEUM

(www.quintalosombues.com.ar; Adrián Beccar Varela 774; 10am-6pm Tue & Thu, 2-6pm Sat & Sun; San Isidro) FREE This beautiful *quinta* (country house) is now a museum that's worth a look. The rooms leading off the Spanish-style central patio contain period furniture and antiques as well as a few of the personal belongings of the house's

WORTH A DETOUR

PERÚ BEACH

If you're keen to do some water sports – or simply sit by the river and watch – head to **Perú Beach** (011-4798-4642; www.peru-beach.com.ar; Sebastián Elcano 794; water sports 10am-6pm Tue-Sun; Tren de la Costa Barrancas). This riverside sports complex offers windsurfing, kitesurfing, stand-up paddle and kayaking equipment hire and instruction (book online in advance). There's also a grassy lawn and outdoor tables for refreshments – great on a sunny day. Perú Beach is located in Acassuso, just across from the Tren de la Costa's Barrancas station. This is the station before San Isidro as you travel from Buenos Aires on the Tren de la Costa, making it a convenient place to stop. It's more of a social scene than anything else, and families are welcome.

most celebrated former resident, Mariquita Sánchez de Thompson. It was here in 1813 that Sánchez is said to have sung the first ever rendition of the Marcha Patriótica (now the Argentinian national anthem). Don't miss the impeccably maintained gardens with river views.

EATING

BRUNA INTERNATIONAL **$$**

(011-4743-3390; www.facebook.com/BrunaDelBajo/; Juan Bautista de Lasalle 433; mains AR$90-200; 9:30am-midnight Tue-Sat, to 5pm Sun; ; San Isidro) Bright and sunny restaurant with beachy white furniture and a pretty outdoor patio serving decent burgers, sandwiches, salads and classic mains such as *milanesas* and grilled salmon. Portion sizes are generous. Good in-house lemonade too.

San Antonio de Areco

Explore

San Antonio de Areco is the prettiest town in the pampas. Located 113km northwest of Buenos Aires, it welcomes many day-tripping *porteños* (residents of the capital) who come for the peaceful atmosphere and picturesque colonial streets. The town dates from the early 18th century and preserves many gaucho and criollo traditions, including the fine silverwork and saddlery of its artisans. Gauchos from all over the pampas gather here for November's **Día de la Tradición** (www.sanantoniodeareco.com; Nov), when you can catch them, and their horses, strutting the cobbled streets in all their finery.

San Antonio de Areco's compact town center and quiet streets are very walkable. Around the Plaza Ruiz de Arellano, named in honor of the town's founding *estanciero* (ranch owner), are several historic buildings, including the **iglesia parroquial** (parish church).

Like many other small towns in this part of Argentina, Areco shuts down during the afternoon siesta.

The Best...

- **Sight** Museo Gauchesco Ricardo Güiraldes (p160)
- **Place to Eat** Almacén Ramos Generales (p161)
- **Place to Drink** Boliche de Bessonart (p161)

Top Tip

If you're here in early to mid-November, don't miss the Día de la Tradición, when the town puts on the country's biggest gaucho celebration.

Getting There & Away

- **Bus** Areco's **bus terminal** (Av Dr Smith & Gral Paz) is five blocks east of the central square. **Chevallier** (02326-453904; www.nuevachevallier.com; Av Dr Smith & Gral Paz) runs frequent buses to/from Buenos Aires (AR$130, two hours).
- **Shuttle** A useful option if you're trying to connect to one of the area's *estancias* (ranches) is the shuttle services operated by independent companies like **Areco Bus** (www.arecobus.com.ar; round-trip AR$650; Sat & Sun). Check the website for the latest itineraries and to make reservations.

San Antonio de Areco

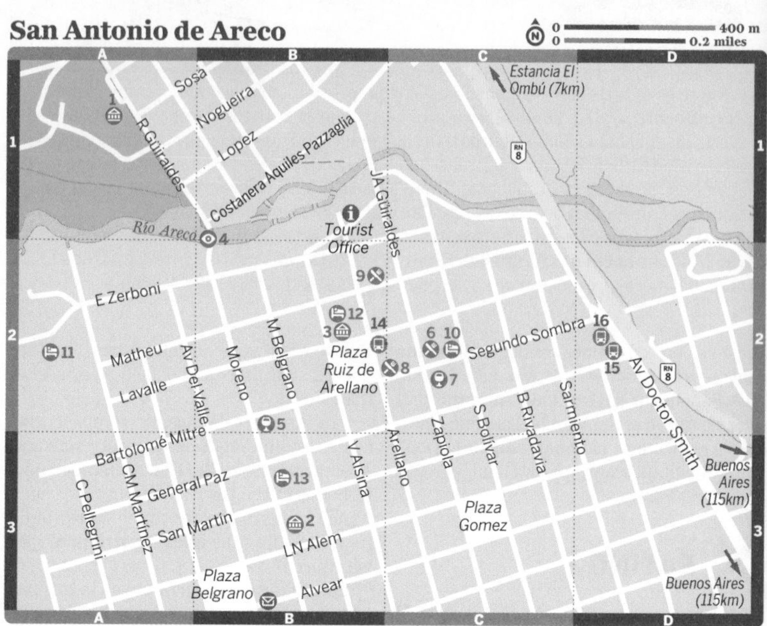

San Antonio de Areco

Top Sights
1 Museo Gauchesco Ricardo Güiraldes A1

Sights
2 Museo Las Lilas de Areco B3
3 Museo y Taller de Platería Draghi B2
4 Puente Viejo B1

Eating & Drinking
5 Almacén Los Principios B2
6 Almacén Ramos Generales C2
7 Boliche de Bessonart C2
8 La Esquina de Merti C2
9 La Olla de Cobre B2

Sleeping
10 Antigua Casona C2
11 Estancia La Cinacina A2
12 Paradores Draghi B2
13 Patio de Moreno B3

Transport
14 Areco Bus B2
15 Chevallier D2
16 Terminal de Ómnibus D2

Need to Know

- **Area Code** ☎02326
- **Location** 115km northwest of Buenos Aires
- **Tourist Office** (☎02326-453165; www.sanantoniodeareco.com; cnr Zerboni & Arellano; ⏰8am-8pm)

SIGHTS

★MUSEO GAUCHESCO RICARDO GÜIRALDES MUSEUM

(☎02326-455839; www.facebook.com/museoguiraldes/; Camino Ricardo Güiraldes; ⏰10am-5pm) FREE This sprawling museum in Parque Criollo dates from 1936 and is largely dedicated to Ricardo Güiraldes, author of the novel *Don Segundo Sombra*, and local gaucho history and culture in general. The entrance is in a re-created *pulpería* (tavern), set up as it would have been when it first opened in 1850, while the museum's main displays are housed in a 20th-century reproduction of an 18th-century *casco* (ranch house). Guided tours are offered at 11am and 3pm.

MUSEO LAS LILAS DE ARECO MUSEUM
(☎02326-456425; www.museolaslilas.org; Moreno 279; AR$100; ⊙10am-6pm Thu, to 8pm Fri-Sun) Florencio Molina Campos is to Argentines what Norman Rockwell is to Americans – a folk artist whose themes are based on comical caricatures. This pretty courtyard museum displays an extensive collection of his famous works. As well as the gallery there is also a Sala de Carruajes (carriage room) to look at and a gaucho-themed sound-and-light show.

Stop for a coffee or a slice of homemade cake at the museum's cafe.

MUSEO Y TALLER DE PLATERÍA DRAGHI MUSEUM
(www.draghiplaterosorfebres.com; Lavalle 387; AR$75; ⊙10am-2:30pm & 4-6:30pm Mon-Sat, 10am-2.30pm Sun) This small museum contains an exceptional collection of 19th-century silver *facones* (gaucho knives), beautiful horse gear and intricate *mate* paraphernalia. It's attached to the silversmith workshop of the locally renowned Draghi family. Tours in English and Spanish of the museum and workshop are on Friday, Saturday and Sunday at 11am. Mariano Draghi's jewelry and silverwork are for sale in the attached shop.

PUENTE VIEJO BRIDGE
(Old Bridge) The pink *puente viejo* (old bridge) spanning the Río Areco dates from 1857 and follows the original cart road to northern Argentina. Once a toll crossing, it's now a pedestrian bridge leading to San Antonio de Areco's main attraction, the Museo Gauchesco Ricardo Güiraldes.

EATING & DRINKING

★BOLICHE DE BESSONART BAR
(cnr Zapiola & Segundo Sombra; ⊙11am-3pm & 6pm-late Tue-Sun) This weather-beaten corner building full of dusty bottles was originally a general store and is more than 200 years old. These days it's a family-run bar popular with gauchos and young people alike, who come for the excellent *picadas* (sharing boards of cold cuts and cheese) washed down with copious beers, red wine or Fernet (a bitter aromatic spirit).

LA ESQUINA DE MERTI ARGENTINE $
(www.esquinademerti.com.ar; cnr Arellano & Segundo Sombra; mains AR$100-155; ⊙9am-midnight) Located right on the plaza, this corner bar and restaurant is one of San Antonio de Areco's most traditional and atmospheric. Stop in for coffee, *empanadas* (a pastry turnover filled with a variety of savoury ingredients and baked or fried), sandwiches, a glass of wine, or a steak grilled on the *parrilla*. When the weather's nice the outdoor tables are a prime spot for gaucho-watching.

LA OLLA DE COBRE CAFE $
(www.laolladecobre.com.ar; Matheu 433; snacks AR$20-55; ⊙10am-1pm & 2:30-7:30pm Wed-Sun, 10am-1pm Mon) This cozy cafe specializes in artisanal chocolates and *alfajores* (cookie-type sandwiches usually stuffed with *dulce de leche*) to go with coffee, tea and hot chocolate. It's also a great place to pick up an edible gift.

ALMACÉN RAMOS GENERALES ARGENTINE $$
(www.ramosgeneralesareco.com.ar; Zapiola 143; mains AR$100-270; ⊙noon-3pm & 8pm-midnight; 🛜) Another of San Antonio's historic dining venues, this elegantly restored space was once a general store. Today, it offers a quaintly rustic setting and quality, traditional Argentine fare – grilled meats from the *parrilla, milanesas* and some specialty rabbit dishes.

ALMACÉN LOS PRINCIPIOS BAR
(Moreno 151; ⊙8:30am-1pm & 5-9:30pm Mon-Sat) Stop for a beer at this charming general store and bar, which remains much as it was when it first opened in 1922. Dusty jars and tins line the wooden shelves and vintage advertisements adorn the walls (it's a look many hipster bars aim for, but this place is the real deal).

SLEEPING

While San Antonio is a popular destination for day trips out of Buenos Aires, it's worth hanging around as there are some lovely places to stay. Book ahead on weekends, when prices go up.

HOME ON THE RANGE

One of the best ways to spend a few days in the region – and soak up a bit of traditional gaucho culture while remaining within easy reach of Buenos Aires – is to visit an *estancia* (ranch). Once the private homes of wealthy landowners, many of the province's grandest mansions are now open to the public. Choose between a *día de campo* (country day; an access pass to the ranch that typically includes an elaborate lunch and afternoon tea, plus horseback riding and other outdoor activities) or stay for a night or two.

Upscale **Estancia El Ombú de Areco** (☎02326-492080, in Buenos Aires 011-4737-0436; www.estanciaelombu.com; RP31, Cuartel VI, Villa Lía; día de campo US$100, s/d incl full board US$325/410; ❄📶🏊) is a 300-hectare ranch with a gorgeous colonial mansion that dates from 1880. It's named after the massive *ombú* (*Phytolacca dioica*) tree casting shade over the gardens. At El Ombú, it's old-fashioned hospitality all the way. In addition to horseback riding, you can watch (and even take part in) rounding up cattle herds. The *estancia* also provides complimentary bicycles, or you can just relax in the gardens or linger over an alfresco lunch or tea. It's located about 20km outside of San Antonio de Areco.

A slightly more affordable option – and one that's also, conveniently, closer to town – is **Estancia La Cinacina** (☎02326-452045; www.lacinacina.com.ar; Zerboni & Martínez; d from US$170; ❄📶🏊). With thematic gaucho shows, the *estancia* is on the touristy side, but it's popular with travelers.

Several other *estancias* in the area offer similar experiences. Check www.sanantoniodeareco.com/donde-dormir/estancias for a full list. Private transfers directly from Buenos Aires to most *estancias* are available for an extra charge. Another option is Areco Bus (p159), a shuttle that offers transportation from Buenos Aires.

★PARADORES DRAGHI GUESTHOUSE **$$**
(☎02326-455583; www.paradoresdraghi.com.ar; Matheu 380; s/d/tr from US$75/95/110; ❄@📶🏊) It's worth staying over in Areco just so you can check in here. Lovingly run by a mother-daughter team and conveniently located near the main plaza, this nine-room boutique guesthouse has spacious rooms, breezy patios, a grassy garden with a beautiful pool, a lovely continental breakfast, and a private silver workshop and museum (p161) where you can learn about silverware-making.

ANTIGUA CASONA GUESTHOUSE **$$**
(☎02325-15-416030; www.antiguacasona.com; Segundo Sombra 495; d from US$112; ❄📶🏊) A wonderful place to stay in Areco, this restored traditional home offers five high-ceilinged rooms with wooden floors; all are set around covered tile hallways and leafy patios. There's a communal *parrilla*, should you be tempted to grill your own steak, and a small but picturesque swimming pool set in a brick-lined courtyard.

PATIO DE MORENO BOUTIQUE HOTEL **$$$**
(☎02326-455197; www.patiodemoreno.com; Moreno 251; d US$165-215; ❄📶🏊) This chic hotel looks traditional on the outside, but step through the doors to enter a bright, contemporary space with a successful blend of old and new furnishings, a well-stocked bar and a gorgeous leafy garden and plunge pool. The spacious rooms have king-sized beds; some have double rain showers.

Colonia

Explore

On the east bank of the Río de la Plata, 180km west of Montevideo, but only 50km from Buenos Aires by ferry, Colonia is an irresistibly picturesque Uruguayan town enshrined as a Unesco World Heritage site. Its Barrio Histórico, an irregular colonial-era nucleus of narrow cobbled streets, occupies a small peninsula jutting into the river. Pretty rows of sycamores offer protection from the summer heat, and the riverfront is a venue for spectacular sunsets (it's a Uruguayan custom to applaud the setting sun). Colonia's charm and its proximity to Buenos Aires draw thousands of Argentine visitors; on weekends, especially in summer, prices rise and it can be difficult to find a room.

The Best...

- **Sight** Faro (p165)
- **Place to Eat** Charco Bistró (p165)
- **Place to Drink** El Drugstore (p166)

Top Tip

To avoid the crowds and more expensive accommodations prices, consider visiting Colonia midweek. If you want US dollars, use ATMs in Uruguay – those in Argentina do not give them out.

Getting There & Away

- **Boat** Buquebus (p205) runs three or more fast boats daily between Buenos Aires and Colonia. The same company owns Seacat (p205), which runs less frequent but more affordable high-speed ferry services. Crossings take one hour. The most economical service is offered by Colonia Express (p205), which runs three fast ferries a day (1¼ hours). Immigration for both countries is handled at the port before boarding.

Getting Around

Walking is enjoyable in compact Colonia, but motor scooters, bicycles and gas-powered buggies are popular alternatives. **Thrifty** (☎4522-2939; www.thrifty.com.uy; Av General Flores 172; bicycle/scooter/golf cart per hr US$6/12/18, per 12hr US$18/30/60; ⏰9am-8pm) rents everything from high-quality bikes to scooters to golf carts.

Local COTUC buses go to the beaches and bullring at Real de San Carlos (UR$19) from along Av General Flores.

Need to know

- **Area Code** ☎452
- **Location** 50km east of Buenos Aires by ferry.
- **Tourist Office** (☎4522-8506; www.coloniaturismo.com; Manuel Lobo 224; ⏰9am-6pm)

SIGHTS

A single UR$50 ticket covers admission to Colonia's eight historical museums. All keep the same hours, but closing day varies by museum. Tickets are sold at Museo Municipal.

CASA NACARELLO — MUSEUM

(☎4523-1237; www.museoscolonia.com.uy; Plaza Mayor 25 de Mayo 67; admission incl in historical museums ticket UR$50; ⏰11:15am-4:45pm Wed-Mon) One of the prettiest colonial homes in town, with period furniture, thick whitewashed walls, wavy glass and original lintels (duck if you're tall!).

MUSEO PORTUGUÉS — MUSEUM

(☎4523-1237; www.museoscolonia.com.uy; Plaza Mayor 25 de Mayo 180; admission incl in historical museums ticket UR$50; ⏰11:15am-4:45pm Sat-Tue & Thu) In this beautiful old house, you'll find Portuguese relics including porcelain, furniture, maps, Manuel Lobo's family tree and the old stone shield that once adorned the Portón de Campo.

MUSEO MUNICIPAL — MUSEUM

(☎4522-7031; www.museoscolonia.com.uy; Plaza Mayor 25 de Mayo 77; admission incl in historical museums ticket UR$50; ⏰11:15am-4:45pm Wed-Mon) Houses an eclectic collection of treasures including a whale skeleton, a re-creation of a colonial drawing room, historical timelines and a scale model of Colonia (c 1762).

MUSEO ESPAÑOL — MUSEUM

(☎4523-1237; www.museoscolonia.com.uy; San José 164; admission incl in historical museums ticket UR$50; ⏰11:15am-4:45pm Fri-Mon & Wed) Scheduled to reopen in 2017 after a long period of restoration, this museum has a varied collection of Spanish artifacts, including colonial pottery, engravings, clothing and maps.

MUSEO INDÍGENA — MUSEUM

(☎4523-1237; www.museoscolonia.com.uy; cnr Del Comercio & Av General Flores; admission incl in historical museums ticket UR$50; ⏰11:15am-4:45pm Fri-Sun, Tue & Wed) Houses Roberto Banchero's personal collection of Charrúa stone tools, exhibits on indigenous history, and an amusing map upstairs showing how many European countries could fit inside Uruguay's borders (it's at least six!).

MUSEO PALEONTOLÓGICO — MUSEUM

(☎4523-1237; www.museoscolonia.com.uy; José Roger Balet, Real de San Carlos; admission incl in historical museums ticket UR$50; ⏰11:15am-4:45pm Thu-Sun) This two-room museum displays glyptodon shells, bones and other locally excavated finds from the private collection of self-taught paleontologist Armando Calcaterra.

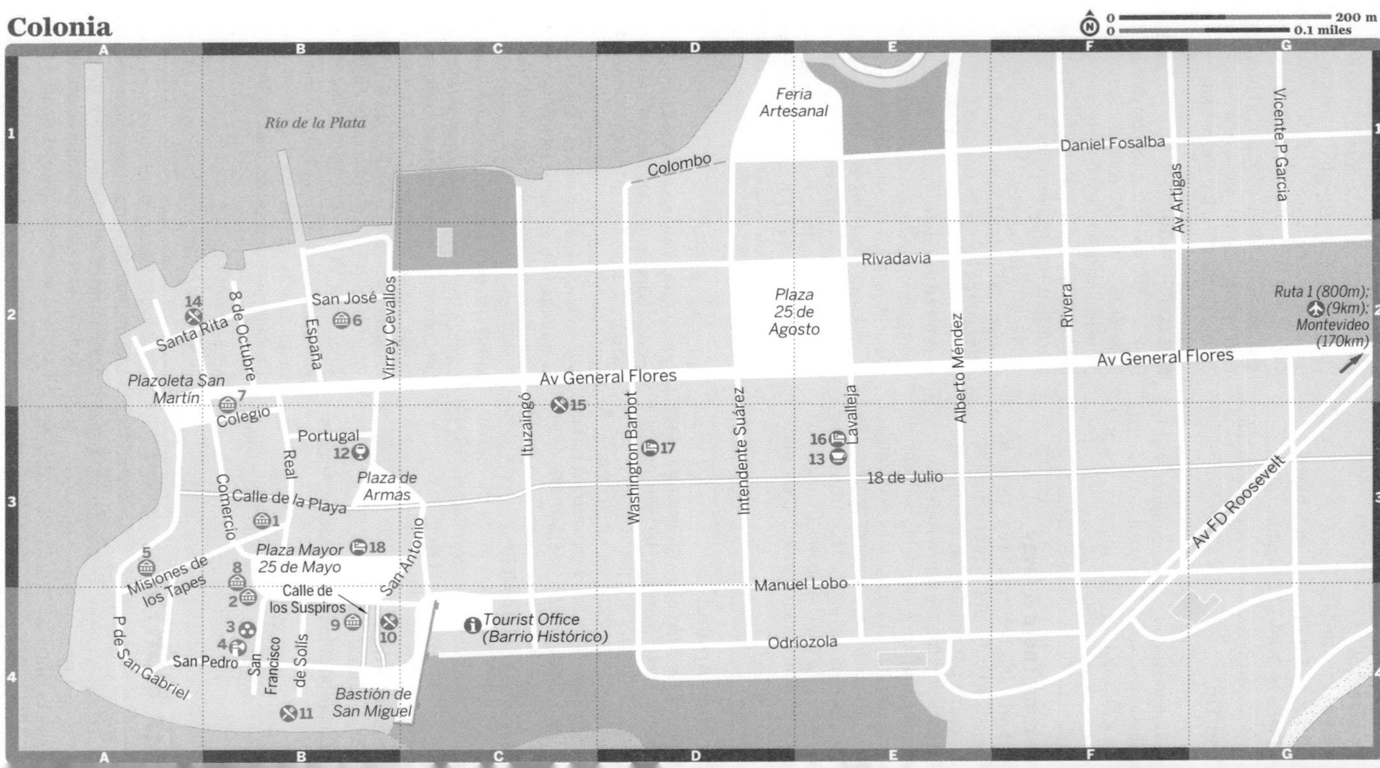
Colonia
0 200 m
0 0.1 miles
Río de la Plata
Feria Artesanal
Colombo
Daniel Fosalba
Av Artigas
Vicente P Garcia
Rivadavia
Plaza 25 de Agosto
Ruta 1 (800m); (9km); Montevideo (170km)
14
8 de Octubre
San José
6
España
Virrey Cevallos
Santa Rita
Rivera
Alberto Méndez
Av General Flores
Plazoleta San Martín
7
Colegio
Itzaingó
15
Washington Barbot
17
Intendente Suárez
16
13
Lavalleja
Portugal
12
Real
Plaza de Armas
18 de Julio
Comercio
Calle de la Playa
1
Av FD Roosevelt
5
Plaza Mayor 25 de Mayo
18
San Antonio
Misiones de los Tapes
8
2
Calle de los Suspiros
Manuel Lobo
3
9
10
Tourist Office (Barrio Histórico)
4
P de San Gabriel
San Pedro
San Francisco
de Solís
Odriozola
Bastión de San Miguel
11

Sleeping

Buenos Aires may be the city that never sleeps – but really, who doesn't need a bit of rest once in a while? You'll find a wide range of places to rest your head here, from hostels to boutique hotels, guesthouses, rental apartments and international five-star hotels. Just remember to book ahead – or pay in cash – for the best deals.

Rates, Discounts & Payments

Buenos Aires is decent value compared to the USA or Europe. However, inflation has been running at 25% to 30% annually. To avoid sticker shock, double check the prices we list before reserving.

The prices we list – particularly for the four- or five-star hotels – are generally the rack or high-season rates from November through January. Rates for top-end hotels can vary widely on any particular day, as many are dependent on how empty or full the hotel is that day. Rates can also skyrocket during holidays such as Easter, Christmas or New Year. Some places lower their rates during slow periods, while others don't. But whatever the season, you don't always have to pay the official posted price.

Your best bet for getting a cheaper rate is to book in advance. You can do this via most hotels' websites. Calling ahead and talking to a salesperson with the power to negotiate prices can also be fruitful, especially if you plan on staying more than a few days. Offering to pay in cash can also bring about a discount.

The most expensive hotels will take credit cards, but budget or midrange places may not – or they may levy a surcharge (about 10%).

Hostels

Buenos Aires' hostels range from basic no-frills deals to beautiful, multi-perk buildings more luxurious than your standard cheap hotel. Most fall in between, but all have common kitchens, living areas, shared bathrooms and dorm rooms (bring earplugs). Most have a few private rooms (with or without bathroom) and provide some traveler services. BA has a few **Hostelling International** (☎011-4511-8723; www.hostels.org.ar; Av Florida 835, 1st fl; ⌚9am-7pm Mon-Fri; Ⓢ Línea C San Martín) hostels, where members can get a small discount.

Hotels

As in many cities, BA's hotels vary from utilitarian holes-in-the-wall to luxurious five-star hotels with all the usual top-tier services. In general, hotels provide a room with private bathroom, cable TV and sometimes a phone. Cheap hotels might also have cheaper rooms with shared bathroom. Higher-end hotels may have safe boxes, a refrigerator and a desk. Some hotels have a cafe or restaurant. Staff members at tourist-oriented hotels will usually speak some English.

Boutique Hotels & B&Bs

The neighborhood of Palermo has dozens of boutique hotels; most are pricey but beautiful, with a handful of hip, elegant rooms and decent service. In BA, B&Bs are sometimes (but not always) run by the owners, and usually have fewer rooms than boutique hotels – but often offer a better breakfast.

NEED TO KNOW

Price Ranges

The following price ranges refer to a double room with bathroom. Unless otherwise stated, breakfast is included in the price.

$ less than US$75

$$ US$75–US$150

$$$ more than US$150

Reservations

It's a good idea to make a reservation during any holidays or the busy summer months of November through February.

Breakfast

Some kind of breakfast, whether it be continental or buffet, is usually included at most accommodations. Unless you're staying somewhere fancy, however, don't expect too much – a typical breakfast will often consist of toast or *medialunas* (croissants), with some jam or butter if you're lucky, plus coffee or tea.

Lonely Planet's Top Choices

Poetry Building (p174) Lovely apartments decorated with vintage-reproduction furniture.

Faena Hotel + Universe (p171) Unique luxury hotel located in Puerto Madero.

Cabrera Garden (p177) Peaceful B&B boasting just three gorgeous rooms and a grassy garden.

Magnolia Hotel (p176) Fine boutique hotel with a very relaxing rooftop terrace.

Casa Calma (p173) Ecologically minded luxury hotel providing a paradise in BA's busy downtown.

Best by Budget

$

América del Sur (p172) Five-star boutique hostel with awesome rooms and services.

Reina Madre Hostel (p175) Very comfortable, well-run and intimate hostel.

Palermo Viejo B&B (p175) Friendly B&B in a classic *chorizo* (sausage) house.

$$

Le Petit Palais (p176) Charming French-run little palace in a great location.

Imagine Hotel (p171) Peaceful guesthouse with plenty of designer touches and outdoor space.

Patios de San Telmo (p173) Historic building turned stylish boutique hotel.

$$$

Faena Hotel + Universe (p171) Supremely elegant and over the top – this is where celebrities stay.

Palacio Duhau – Park Hyatt (p174) Gorgeous remodeled mansion with a stunning courtyard.

Alvear Palace Hotel (p174) Buenos Aires' most traditional and luxurious five-star hotel.

Best Boutique Hotels

Magnolia Hotel (p176) Splendid boutique hotel with a very relaxing rooftop terrace.

Imagine Hotel (p171) Cozy interior design touches and spacious gardens.

Mansión Vitraux (p173) San Telmo's slickest spot to lay your head.

Patios de San Telmo (p173) Plenty of outdoor space and nicely decorated rooms.

Duque Hotel (p176) Elegant and beautiful, and there's a spa too.

Best Hostels

América del Sur (p172) Well-run hostel with excellent facilities.

Reina Madre Hostel (p175) Character-filled place with resident cat.

V & S Hostel Club (p170) Centrally located hostel in a beautiful old building.

Portal del Sur (p170) Laid-back place to stay with a roof terrace.

Milhouse Youth Hostel (p170) BA's premiere party hostel.

Best for Families

Poetry Building (p174) Upscale apartments, all with kitchen, plus a soaking pool.

Novotel Hotel (p172) Especially family-friendly services – including two kiddie pools.

Hotel Lyon (p172) Simple budget lodgings with tonnes of space for large families.

Where to Stay

NEIGHBORHOOD	FOR	AGAINST
THE CENTER	Great transportation options; fairly close to all neighborhoods except Palermo; offers many services.	Limited eating, shopping and nightlife options; noisy and crowded during the day and impersonal after dark.
PUERTO MADERO	Very safe, calm, quiet and upscale; great strolling opportunities, both in a natural reserve and along the pleasant restaurant-lined dikes.	Expensive: many restaurants are overpriced; very limited public transportation, accommodations, shopping and service options and not much interesting nightlife.
CONGRESO & TRIBUNALES	Reasonably central, with plenty of traditional theater and other cultural options; interesting local flavor, tending toward classic architecture and governmental vibe.	Certain sections are desolate and less safe at night; limited shopping and eating possibilities.
SAN TELMO	Endearing traditional atmosphere, reasonable shopping and nightlife, a good range of restaurants and many decent hostels.	Far from Palermo; some areas can be edgy at night; public transportation is somewhat limited.
LA BOCA		Not recommended and practically no accommodations options.
RETIRO	Beautiful upscale neighborhood within walking distance of Recoleta and the Center; convenient for public transportation.	Very expensive; limited accommodations options; not many affordable restaurants or shops.
RECOLETA & BARRIO NORTE	Buenos Aires' most upscale neighborhood; gorgeous architecture, good transportation options and fairly safe.	Most accommodations, restaurants and shopping are very expensive.
BELGRANO, NUÑEZ & COSTANERA NORTE	Plenty of excellent restaurants in Belgrano and Nuñez. Great shopping in Belgrano and nightlife in Costanera Norte.	These areas are light on accommodations options.
PALERMO	Many boutique hotels to choose from; the city's widest range of interesting restaurants, by both cuisine and budget; great shopping and nightlife.	A bit of a trek to the Center and San Telmo; might be too touristy for some.
SOUTH OF PALERMO	Up-and-coming neighborhoods with local atmosphere and some decent accommodations, restaurants and shops; quick access via Subte to the Center.	Fewer traveler services; some neighborhoods are not central.

The Center

Buenos Aires' Center, being right in the middle of things, has the most business-type accommodations in the city. The recent pedestrianization of most of the neighborhood has made the area more pleasant to walk around and it's close to the upscale neighborhoods of Puerto Madero, Retiro and Recoleta. The Plaza de Mayo area contains the bustling banking district and many historic buildings, and is within walking distance of San Telmo.

★PORTAL DEL SUR HOSTEL **$**

Map p234 (011-4342-8788; www.portaldelsurba.com.ar; Hipólito Yrigoyen 855; dm from US$13, r with/without bath from US$44/39; ; Línea A Piedras) Located in a charming old building, this is one of the city's best hostels. Beautiful dorms and hotel-quality private rooms surround a central common area, which is rather dark but open. The highlight is the lovely rooftop deck with views and attached bar. A relaxed but sociable place with plenty of activities on offer including *asados* (barbecues) and free tango classes.

MILHOUSE YOUTH HOSTEL HOSTEL **$**

Map p234 (011-4345-9604; www.milhousehostel.com; Hipólito Yrigoyen 959; dm from US$15, r from US$47; ; Línea A Av de Mayo) BA's premiere party hostel, this popular spot offers a plethora of activities and services. Dorms are good and private rooms can be very pleasant; most surround an appealing open patio. Common spaces include a bar-cafe (with pool table) on the ground floor, a TV lounge on the mezzanine and a rooftop terrace. A gorgeous annex building nearby offers similar services.

V & S HOSTEL CLUB HOSTEL **$**

Map p234 (011-4322-0994; www.hostelclub.com; Viamonte 887; dm from US$15, d from US$42; ; Línea C Lavalle) This attractive, central hostel is located in a pleasant older building. The common space, which is also the dining and lobby area, is good for socializing, and there's a kitchen for guests. The spacious dorms are carpeted and the private rooms are excellent; all have their own bathroom. A nice touch is the tiny outdoor patio in back.

GOYA HOTEL HOTEL **$**

Map p234 (011-4322-9269; www.goyahotel.com.ar; Suipacha 748; s US$39-45, d US$55-60; ; Línea C Lavalle) This family-run hotel is a good budget choice with 42 modern, comfortable and carpeted rooms. 'Classic' rooms are older and have open showers; 'superior' rooms are slicker and come with bathtubs. Pleasant breakfast room with patio; good breakfast too.

GRAN HOTEL HISPANO HOTEL **$**

Map p234 (011-4345-2020; www.hhispano.com.ar; Av de Mayo 861; s/d/tr/q US$48/64/74/87; ; Línea A Piedras) The tiny stairway lobby here isn't an impressive start, but upstairs there's a sweet atrium area with covered patio. Most rooms are carpeted; those in front are biggest, and those on the top floor are brightest and have air-con. It's a popular, central and well-tended place, so reserve ahead. Pay in cash for a 10% discount.

HOTEL FACÓN GRANDE HOTEL **$$**

Map p234 (011-4312-6360; www.hotelfacongrande.com; Reconquista 645; d/tr/q US$84/103/123; ; Línea B Florida) For those seeking a touch of the country in Buenos Aires, there's this (slightly) gaucho-themed hotel. The lobby has rustic furniture and cowhide-covered pillows, and rooms are modern and comfortable. The location is good and there's an intimate vibe that's rare in hotels of this size. Get a top-floor room for views. Overall, a good deal for the price.

HOTEL LAFAYETTE HOTEL **$$**

Map p234 (011-4393-9081; www.lafayettehotel.com.ar; Reconquista 546; d US$90; ; Línea B Florida) Spacious, elegant rooms are on offer at this comfortable, well-run downtown hotel that attracts a largely business clientele. The bathrooms are small but efficient, while double-glazed windows guarantee peace and quiet. Hotel amenities include a sauna and gym. Book ahead for the best rates.

CLARIDGE HOTEL HOTEL **$$**

Map p234 (011-4314-2020; www.claridge.com.ar; Tucumán 535; d/ste from US$100/150; ; Línea C Lavalle) Behind the Claridge's grand entrance is a less high-end hotel than you might expect. Standard rooms are fine but go for a suite (some with balcony and Jacuzzi) if you want something special. The pool is only open in summer. Prices vary widely, so check beforehand.

Puerto Madero

Puerto Madero is home to a few luxury chain hotels as well as the unique Faena Hotel + Universe, but is woefully short of midrange and budget sleeping options. The neighborhood is within walking distance of the Center, which has a wider range of accommodations choices.

★**FAENA HOTEL + UNIVERSE** HOTEL **$$$**
Map p236 (☎011-4010-9000; www.faenahotelanduniverse.com; Martha Salotti 445; r from US$500; ❄@📶🏊; 🚌111, 43, 143) Located in a renovated storage mill, this Philippe Starck–designed fantasy hotel is more than just a place to stay. Traipse through the plush main hallway, lined with two top-notch restaurants, a sultry bar-lounge, a basement cabaret and – outside – a slick swimming pool. The luxurious rooms feature claw-foot beds and glass-walled bathrooms. Also has a Turkish bath and spa.

Congreso & Tribunales

Congreso's hotels tend to be low-cost and often rather musty and old-fashioned, reflecting the slightly gritty, bureaucratic atmosphere of the streets around Avs Callao, Rivadavia and Corrientes.

There are a couple of lovely boutique hotels in the area south of Av de Mayo in the non-touristy, local-feeling neighborhood of Montserrat. Bear in mind that some of the smaller streets in Congreso can feel a little desolate at night; take a taxi if you feel uncomfortable.

HOSTEL ESTORIL HOSTEL **$**
Map p238 (☎011-4382-9684; www.hostelestoril3.com; Av de Mayo 1385, 1st & 6th fl; dm/s/d from US$15/33/46; ❄@📶; S Línea A Sáenz Peña) This well-run hostel is located across two floors in a beautiful old building. It's stylish and clean, with pleasant, good-sized dorms and hotel-quality doubles. There's also a decent kitchen for guests, but the hostel's biggest draw has to be the awesome rooftop terrace overlooking the Palacio Barolo and Av de Mayo; the owners organize regular *asados* and yoga classes.

The same family runs a cheaper hostel on the 3rd floor.

HOTEL BONITO BOUTIQUE HOTEL **$**
Map p238 (☎011-4381-2162; www.bonitobuenosaires.com; Chile 1507, 3rd fl; r US$50-70; ❄@📶; S Línea E Independencia) Lovely boutique hotel with just five artsy, gorgeous rooms mixing the traditional and contemporary. Some have loft beds and small balconies; floors are wooden or acid-finished concrete. There's a warm, homey atmosphere, with a small bar area and a good breakfast. It's in a non-touristy, very local neighborhood within walking distance of Congreso and San Telmo.

SABATICO HOSTEL HOSTEL **$**
Map p238 (☎011-4381-1138; www.sabaticohostel.com.ar; México 1410; dm from US$15, d with shared/private bath from US$45/60; ❄@📶; S Línea E Independencia) This friendly hostel is located off the beaten tourist path in an atmospheric neighborhood. Rooms are small but fine, and the pleasant common areas include a nice kitchen, dining and living room, airy patio hallways and a great rooftop terrace with hammocks, *parrilla* (grill) and soaking tub. There's also a ping-pong table, bike rentals and a daily schedule of group activities.

HOTEL MARBELLA HOTEL **$**
Map p238 (☎011-4383-8566; www.hotelmarbella.com.ar; Av de Mayo 1261; s/d/tr from US$38/50/60; ❄@📶; S Línea A Lima) The carpeted rooms at this hotel are basic and rather worn, but clean – if you can stand a bit of traffic noise, try to secure one with a balcony. From here it's an easy tramp to either Plaza del Congreso or Plaza de Mayo. Pay in cash and save 10%.

GRAN HOTEL ORIENTAL HOTEL **$**
Map p238 (☎011-4951-6427; www.granhoteloriental.com; Bartolomé Mitre 1840; s/d US$25/32; ❄📶; S Línea A Congreso) Despite its name this hotel is not grand, but it is reasonably priced. Downstairs rooms are a bit dark and have fans only (get one upstairs), and showers are small, but the simple, high-ceilinged rooms are fine for non-fussy travelers – just don't expect many services.

★**IMAGINE HOTEL** BOUTIQUE HOTEL **$$**
Map p238 (☎011-4383-2230; www.imaginehotelboutique.com; México 1330; d/tr from US$100/145; ❄@📶; S Línea E Independencia) This beautiful guesthouse in a traditional

chorizo-style house (a long, narrow sausage-like building) offers nine appealing rooms, all individually decorated with rustic, yet upscale, furniture. The rooms open onto three outdoor patios with original tiles and leafy plants; the last one has a grass lawn. It's a peaceful little place in a non-touristy neighborhood. Fully wheelchair accessible. Reserve ahead; dog on premises.

LIVIN' RESIDENCE APARTMENT **$$**

Map p238 (011-5258-0300; www.livinresidence.com; Viamonte 1815; studio from US$75, 1-bedroom apt US$150, 2-bedroom apt US$175; S Línea D Callao) All of these studios and one- or two-bedroom apartments have a simple, contemporary feel, with tasteful furniture, flat-screen TVs, small kitchens and balconies. There's a tiny rooftop terrace with Jacuzzi, *asado* and nearby gym room. Security is good; reserve ahead.

HOTEL LYON HOTEL **$$**

Map p238 (011-4372-0100; www.hotel-lyon.com.ar; Riobamba 251; s/d/tr/q US$60/80/90/110; @; S Línea B Callao) If you're a traveling family or group on a budget, consider this old-school, French-style place. The two- and three-bedroom apartments are basic and no-frills but very spacious, and all include large bathrooms and separate dining areas with fridges (but no kitchens). There are plans to build a fitness room and sauna.

NOVOTEL HOTEL HOTEL **$$$**

Map p238 (011-4370-9500; www.novotel.com; Av Corrientes 1334; r from US$150; @; S Línea B Uruguay) This large, contemporary French chain hotel is tastefully designed. Rooms are comfortable, but the highlight is out back, where a beautiful deck surrounds three pools – one for adults and two for the kids – along with a living wall of vegetation and a bar.

This Novotel is family-friendly, offering kid discounts, a playroom and Xbox rental; it's located smack in the middle of Corrientes' entertainment district.

San Telmo

Located within walking distance of the Center and surrounded by bars and restaurants, San Telmo is a popular place to stay. Some of the city's best hostels are located here, as well as a few good guesthouses and boutique hotels.

★AMÉRICA DEL SUR HOSTEL **$**

Map p240 (011-4300-5525; www.americahostel.com.ar; Chacabuco 718; dm from US$15, d from US$50; @; S Línea C Independencia) This gorgeous boutique-like hostel – the smartest of its kind in BA – was built especially to be a hostel. Beyond reception is a fine bar area with a large wood-decked patio. Sparklingly clean dorms with four beds all have well-designed bathrooms, while private rooms are tastefully decorated and better than those at many midrange hotels. Wide range of services on offer.

CIRCUS HOSTEL & HOTEL HOSTEL **$**

Map p240 (011-4300-4983; www.hostelcircus.com; Chacabuco 1020; dm from US$13, r from US$47; @; S Línea C Independencia) From the flash lounge at the front to the wooden deck–surrounded wading pool in back, this hotel-hostel exudes hipness. Both dorms and private rooms, all small and simple, have basic furniture and their own bathrooms. There's a pool table and slick TV area too, but no kitchen.

ART FACTORY HOSTEL HOSTEL **$**

Map p240 (011-4343-1463; www.artfactoryba.com.ar; Piedras 545; dm from US$17, d from US$47; @; S Línea E Belgrano) Friendly and uniquely art-themed, this fine hostel offers more private rooms than most – and all feature huge murals, painted and decorated by different artists. Even the hallways and water tanks have colorful cartoonish themes, and the 1850s rambling mansion adds some charm. There's a large rooftop terrace with hammocks and separate bar-lounge area with pool table.

L'ADRESSE BOUTIQUE HOTEL **$$**

Map p240 (011-4307-2332; www.facebook.com/ladressehotelbuenosaires/; Bolívar 1491; r from US$75; 29, 33, 159, 130) French couple Clara and Romain spent more than three years painstakingly restoring an 1880s mansion turned run-down tenement house into this character-filled boutique hotel. The 15 rooms are simple but comfortable and lead off the house's original tiled passageways; much of the furniture was salvaged and upcycled by the owners themselves. Great bar and breakfast area, too.

BOHEMIA BUENOS AIRES HOTEL **$**

Map p240 (011-4115-2561; www.bohemiabuenosaires.com.ar; Perú 845; d/tr/q from US$50/68/86; @; S Línea C Independencia)

With its upscale-motel feel, this good-value San Telmo hotel offers 22 simple and neat rooms, most good-sized, if a bit antiseptic with their white-tiled floors. The peaceful grassy backyard and small interior patios are a plus. Cash discount.

LUGAR GAY GUESTHOUSE **$**

Map p240 (011-4300-4747; www.lugargay.com.ar; Defensa 1120; dm US$25, s US$45-60, d US$65-80; ; 29, 24, 111) Head up a long flight of stairs to this intimate guesthouse, where only gay men can book a stay. Just four of the eight small but elegant rooms have a private bathroom, but most have stunning views of the pretty church out back. It's a maze of catwalks, spiral staircases and sunny terraces, plus a tango salon and a cafe.

PATIOS DE SAN TELMO BOUTIQUE HOTEL **$$**

Map p240 (011-4307-0480; http://patiosdesantelmo.com.ar/; Chacabuco 752; r US$70-150; @; Línea C Independencia) Located in an 1860 former *conventillo* (tenement house) is this pleasant boutique hotel with 30 spacious, elegant rooms surrounding several patios. There's a lovely 'library' room decorated with artwork, a back patio with hanging basket chairs and a tiny rooftop pool with wood deck.

MANSIÓN VITRAUX BOUTIQUE HOTEL **$$**

Map p240 (011-4878-4292; www.mansionvitraux.com; Carlos Calvo 369; r from US$143-164; @; Línea C Independencia) Almost too slick for San Telmo, this glass-fronted boutique hotel offers 12 beautiful rooms, all in different designs. All have either flat-screen or projection TV, and bathrooms have a contemporary design. The breakfast buffet is in the basement wine bar. There is also a large Jacuzzi, a sauna, an indoor pool and a slick rooftop terrace with a second pool.

MUNDO BOLÍVAR BOUTIQUE HOTEL **$$**

Map p240 (011-4300-3619; www.mundobolivar.com; Bolívar 1701; studio & apt US$60-90; ; 29) Fourteen spacious studios and loft apartments with kitchenettes have been renovated into attractive modern spaces – some with original details such as carved doorways or painted ceilings – at this gorgeous mansion. Separate entrances join with hallways connecting through the complex, and there are lovely garden patios in which to relax. No breakfast; long-term stays available.

SCALA HOTEL HOTEL **$$**

Map p240 (011-4343-0606; www.scalahotelbuenosaires.com; Bernardo de Irigoyen 740; d US$80-150; @; Línea C Independencia) A grand lobby awaits you at this business-oriented, four-star hotel. All rooms are lovely and spacious; standard ones have wooden floors, while higher categories come with carpets and sitting rooms. Some have views of Av 9 de Julio. There's a pleasant, large patio in back that's good for kids, plus a gym, restaurant and two business salons.

Retiro

Retiro is a great, central place to be, if you can afford it – many of BA's most expensive hotels, along with some of its richest inhabitants, are settled in here. Close by are leafy Plaza San Martín, the Retiro train and bus stations, and many upscale stores and business services.

HOTEL TRES SARGENTOS HOTEL **$**

Map p246 (011-4312-6082; www.hotel3sargentos.com.ar; Tres Sargentos 345; s/d/tr US$45/52/65; ; Línea C San Martín) A good deal for the location, this simple budget hotel has an interesting history – author Julio Cortázar once stayed here. The carpets are a bit worn but the plainly decorated rooms are comfortable enough. Some rooms higher up and facing out even offer a bit of a view. Five-person apartment available.

★CASA CALMA BOUTIQUE HOTEL **$$$**

Map p246 (011-4312-5000; www.casacalmahotel.com.ar; Suipacha 1015; r from US$200; @; Línea C San Martín) Hidden behind a living wall of greenery is this eco-conscious hideaway in central BA. The 17 rooms are pristine and relaxing with Jacuzzi baths and a serene ambience; some have small balconies. Yoga mats and bamboo bikes available; discount without breakfast.

HOTEL PULITZER BOUTIQUE HOTEL **$$$**

Map p246 (011-4316-0800; www.hotelpulitzer.com.ar; Maipú 907; r from US$150; @; Línea C San Martín) In a good location, this sleek boutique hotel has a contemporary lobby with minimalist decor. Rooms are spacious and stylish with great monochrome bathrooms and plenty of design touches; some have a balcony. The highlight is the beautiful rooftop terrace with attached bar offering great views over the city.

Recoleta & Barrio Norte

Most of the accommodations in Recoleta and Barrio Norte are expensive; what cheap hotels there are tend to be full much of the time. Buildings here are grand and beautiful, befitting the city's richest barrio, and you'll be close to Recoleta's famous cemetery, along with its lovely parks, museums and boutiques.

HOTEL LION D'OR HOTEL $

Map p244 (011-4803-8992; www.hotel-liondor.com.ar; Pacheco de Melo 2019; s/d/tr from US$35/45/63; ; Línea D Pueyrredón) These digs have their charm (it's an old embassy), but rooms vary widely – some are small, basic and dark, while others are grand. Despite some rough edges, all are good value and most have been modernized for comfort. The old marble staircase and elevator are fabulous, and there's a nice rooftop area. Air-con costs extra; breakfast not included.

PETIT RECOLETA HOSTEL HOSTEL $

Map p244 (011-4823-3848; www.petitrecoleta.com; José Uriburu 1183; dm US$14-16, s from US$28, d from US$35; @; Línea D Facultad de Medicina) This hostel is comfortable enough and in a good location. It's in an old building that has character but is showing its age in places, though the communal areas – which include an interior patio, TV room, kitchen and pool-table area – are fine. There are two dorms, one for men and one for women. Only two rooms have air-con.

AYRES DE RECOLETA APARTMENT $$

Map p244 (011-4801-0505; www.ayresderecoleta.com; José Uriburu 1756; studios from US$120; @; Línea H Las Heras) The studio apartments here all come with king-size beds or two twins and are spacious and well-equipped, though the deco is a little dull. There are also simple kitchenettes with fridges and microwaves, plus a small pool. And the location can't be beat – you're a block from Recoleta cemetery. A good option for families. Breakfast served on request.

★**POETRY BUILDING** APARTMENT $$$

Map p244 (011-4827-2772; www.poetrybuilding.com; Junín 1280; apt US$280-390; ; Línea D Pueyrredón) These gorgeous studios and one-bedroom apartments are perfect for families. Each one is different, eclectically decorated with reproduction antique furniture, and all come with plenty of mod cons and a fully equipped kitchen (stocked with groceries on request). Some apartments have a private outdoor balcony or patio, but there's also a beautiful common terrace with soaking pool.

Best of all is the rooftop vegetable garden, where guests can help themselves to home-grown kale, hot peppers, chard, beans and tomatoes.

ALVEAR PALACE HOTEL HOTEL $$$

Map p244 (011-4808-2100; www.alvearpalace.com; Av Alvear 1891; r from US$620; @; 130, 93, 62) The classiest, most traditional hotel in BA oozes old-world sophistication and has the service and all the facilities you would expect of a five-star hotel, with in-room luxuries such as Hermès toiletries and Egyptian-cotton bed sheets. The recently added top-floor suites have stunning views across Recoleta to the river; the new roof garden and indoor pool are equally impressive.

There's also an excellent restaurant, wine-tasting room, elegant tea room, champagne bar and fine spa.

FOUR SEASONS HOTEL $$$

Map p244 (011-4321-1200; www.fourseasons.com/buenosaires; Posadas 1086; d from US$770; @; 130, 62, 93) No surprise here – the Four Seasons offers all the perks that define a five-star hotel, such as free-standing bathtubs facing TVs hidden in the bathroom mirror. Rooms are spacious with contemporary furnishings and views of Av 9 de Julio; the finest suites are located in an old mansion next door (go for the presidential – it's US$10,000 per night).

There's also a gorgeous spa, an outdoor heated swimming pool and a top-notch restaurant.

PALACIO DUHAU – PARK HYATT HOTEL $$$

Map p244 (011-5171-1234; www.buenosaires.park.hyatt.com; Av Alvear 1661; d from US$675; @; 130, 111, 62) If it's good enough for presidents, diplomats and Tom Cruise, it's good enough for us. The luxurious Park Hyatt takes up a city block and consists of two wings, including the Palacio Duhau, a renovated mansion with a separate reception. There's a gorgeous terraced garden with fountains and patios, plus a fine spa, indoor pool, classy bar and art gallery.

ART SUITES APARTMENT $$$

Map p244 (011-4821-6800; www.artsuites.com.ar; Azcuénaga 1465; 1- & 2-bedroom apt US$250-290; ; Línea D Pueyrredón) The 15 luxurious, modern and spacious apartments here are all bright, with minimalist decor, full kitchens or kitchenettes, sunny balconies and slick, hip furniture. Windows are double-paned, staff speak English and security is excellent. Long-term discounts are available; reserve ahead. An annex offers more apartments.

Belgrano, Nuñez & the Costanera Norte

Most areas of the residential northern neighborhoods of Belgrano and Nuñez are too far from BA's main sights in the Center, San Telmo and Recoleta to hold much of an appeal as a place to stay, and they are light on accommodations options. The exception is the area of Belgrano around busy Av Cabildo, where the Subte Línea D provides easy access to the Center. The Costanera Norte has no houses, let alone hotels, so forget about looking for a bed around here.

PAMPA HOSTEL HOSTEL $

Map p249 (011-4544-2273; www.hostelpampa.com; Iberá 2858; dm/s/d/tr with shared bath from US$12/45/55/63; ; Línea D Congreso de Tucumán) This colorful hostel in a traditional *chorizo*-style house is located in a residential part of Belgrano. Pluses include the sunny roof terrace and guest kitchen. Special rates for stays of one month or longer. Some rooms have air-con and private bathrooms.

Palermo

About a 20-minute taxi ride from the city center (and also well connected by bus and Subte lines), Palermo is the top choice for many travelers. Not only is it full of extensive parklands – which are great for weekend jaunts and sporting activities – but you'll have heaps of cutting-edge restaurants, designer boutiques and dance clubs at your door. Most of these places are located in the extensive sub-neighborhoods of Palermo Soho and Palermo Hollywood.

★**REINA MADRE HOSTEL** HOSTEL $

Map p250 (011-4962-5553; www.rmhostel.com; Av Anchorena 1118; dm US$15-20, s/d US$40/44; @; Línea D Pueyrredón) This wonderful hostel is clean, safe and well run. It's in an old building that has plenty of personality, with high ceilings and original tiles, and all rooms are comfortable (and share bathrooms). There's a cozy living room and small kitchen, plus lots of dining tables, but the highlight is the wooden-deck rooftop with *parrilla*. Pet cat on premises.

★**PALERMO VIEJO B&B** GUESTHOUSE $

Map p250 (011-4773-6012; www.palermoviejobb.com; Niceto Vega 4629; s US$55, d US$60-75, tr US$85; @; 140) This friendly B&B is located in a remodeled *casa chorizo* dating from 1901, that was once the owner's father's clothes factory. The six rooms all front a leafy outdoor patio and are decorated with local artwork; two have lofts. All come with a fridge and a good breakfast. Call ahead.

RUGANTINO HOTEL GUESTHOUSE $

Map p250 (011-6379-5113; www.rugantinohotelboutique.com; Uriarte 1844; r US$50-85; @; Línea D Palermo) This intimate, homey guesthouse is located in a 1920s building and run by an Italian family. Various terraces and catwalks connect the seven simple rooms, all decked out in hardwood floors and modern styling, combined with a few antiques. The climbing vine and greenery in the small central courtyard is soothing, and you can expect espresso for breakfast. Reserve ahead.

ART FACTORY PALERMO HOSTEL $

Map p250 (011-2004-4958; www.artfactorypalermo.com.ar; Costa Rica 4353; dm US$11-15, r with shared/private bath US$57/67; @; Línea D Scalabrini Ortiz) This decent, no-frills hostel is well located close to Palermo's restaurants and nightlife. Like its sister hostel in San Telmo, it's in an old house and decorated with artsy murals and stencils. There's a small kitchen, ping-pong table and living room area, and a limited number of bathrooms – so their use can get tight.

ECO PAMPA HOSTEL HOSTEL $

Map p250 (011-4831-2435; www.hostelpampa.com.ar; Guatemala 4778; dm US$13-17, s/d US$46/60; @; Línea D Plaza Italia) Buenos Aires' first 'green' hostel is this casual spot sporting vintage and recycled furniture, low-energy light bulbs and a recycling system. The rooftop is home to a small veggie garden, compost pile and solar panels. Dorms are a good size and each of the eight private rooms comes with bathroom and flat-screen TV (most have air-con). Also has a kitchen.

MANSILLA 3935 B&B B&B $

Map p250 (011-4833-3821; www.mansilla3935.com; Mansilla 3935; s/d US$35/50; ; S Línea D Scalabrini Ortiz) Family-run B&B in a homey, darkish house, offering a great deal. Each of the six simple rooms comes with its own bathroom. Ceilings are high, and a few tiny patios add charm.

★LE PETIT PALAIS B&B $$

Map p250 (011-4962-4834; www.lepetitpalais-buenosaires.com; Gorriti 3574; s/d from US$70/80; ; S Línea D Agüero) Small but charming, this French-run B&B offers just five simple but pleasant rooms, all with private bathroom. The highlight is the pretty little terrace on the 2nd floor, where possibly BA's best breakfast is served in warm weather – fresh yogurt, jams and breads (all homemade), along with eggs, *medialunas* and cereals. Friendly cats on premises.

★MAGNOLIA HOTEL BOUTIQUE HOTEL $$

Map p250 (011-4867-4900; http://magnoliahotelboutique.com/palermo-buenosaires/; Julián Álvarez 1746; r US$100-160; ; S Línea D Scalabrini Ortiz) This classy boutique hotel is in a gorgeously restored old house. Its eight impeccably groomed rooms are bathed in muted colors and fitted with elegant furniture; some have a patio or balcony. Other pluses include a welcome drink and a little patio for breakfast.

DUQUE HOTEL BOUTIQUE HOTEL $$

Map p250 (011-4832-0312; www.duquehotel.com; Guatemala 4364; d US$125-175; ; S Línea D Scalabrini Ortiz) All 14 rooms at this charming boutique hotel are well designed, though some can be a bit small – go for a superior or deluxe if you need more space. Pluses include a large Jacuzzi, sauna, basement spa, buffet breakfast, afternoon tea with pastries and a great little backyard garden with a tiny pool. Online discounts available.

HOTEL CLASICO HOTEL $$

Map p250 (011-4773-2353; www.hotelclasico.com; Costa Rica 5480; r US$120-170; ; S Línea D Palermo) Attractive hotel with 33 tasteful 'classic' rooms, some with tiny balconies but all with wood floors, modern conveniences and earthy color schemes; a local photographer was specially commissioned to take the photos of BA that adorn the walls. Go for the penthouse with terrace for something special. Creative elevator with one glass wall facing an artsy mural.

THE 5TH FLOOR B&B $$

Map p250 (011-4827-0366; www.the5thfloorba.com; near Vidt & Santa Fe; r US$90-170; ; S Línea D Scalabrini Ortiz) This upscale B&B offers six elegant rooms, two with private balcony. All are tastefully decorated with art-deco furniture and modern amenities. The common living room is great for chatting with the English owner, a polo enthusiast, and there's also a pleasant back patio with lovely tile details. Excellent breakfast. Address given upon reservation; three-night minimum stay.

PALERMITANO BOUTIQUE HOTEL $$

Map p250 (011-4897-2100; www.palermitano.biz; Uriarte 1648; r US$100-180; ; 39, 55) Located in the middle of Palermo's nightlife, this boutique hotel has 16 tastefully decorated, contemporary rooms. In the summer, the rooftop terrace bar with its small pool is the perfect place for an early evening cocktail. A branch of the excellent Peruvian restaurant Sipan is on the ground floor; meals can be ordered as room service.

LIVIAN GUESTHOUSE GUESTHOUSE $$

Map p250 (011-4862-8841; www.livianguesthouse.com; Palestina 1184; r US$75-94; ; 140, 109) Located in an attractive old building in a hip section of Palermo is this artsy guesthouse, which used to be the owner Lisandra's family home. There are 10 colorful rooms on offer, two with their own semi-private terrace and most with air-con and private bathroom. There are pleasant living-room spaces, a pretty back garden, communal deck and rental bikes.

INFINITO HOTEL BOUTIQUE HOTEL $$

Map p250 (011-2070-2626; www.infinitohotel.com; Arenales 3689; r US$70-90, ste US$120-150; ; S Línea D Scalabrini Ortiz) Starting at its small lobby cafe-reception, this hotel exudes a certain hipness. Rooms are small but good, with flat-screen TVs, fridges, wooden floors and a purple color scheme, and there's a Jacuzzi on the sunny rooftop terrace. An effort is made to be ecologically conscious, mostly by recycling. Located near the parks but still within walking distance of Palermo's nightlife.

RENDEZVOUS HOTEL BOUTIQUE HOTEL **$$**

Map p250 (011-3964-5222; www.rendezvoushotel.com.ar; Bonpland 1484; r from US$135; ; 111, 140, 39) This boutique hotel is located in a beautiful four-story French-style building. Each of the 11 rooms is unique, styled with either antique or modern furnishings and bright colors; two have private balcony and outdoor Jacuzzi. There's a tiny rooftop deck and cute patio at the entrance.

ABODE GUESTHOUSE **$$**

Map p250 (011-4774-3331; www.abodebuenosaires.com; Costa Rica 5193; d/tr from US$100/150; ; S Línea D Palermo) A very intimate and homey guesthouse. Each of the four simple yet comfortable rooms comes with its own bathroom, and the largest has a balcony. By reservation only; no walk-ins.

VAIN BOUTIQUE HOTEL BOUTIQUE HOTEL **$$$**

Map p250 (011-4776-8246; www.vainuniverse.com; Thames 2226; r US$145-230; ; S Línea D Plaza Italia) Fifteen elegant rooms, most with high ceilings and wooden floors, can be found at this nicely renovated building. All are modern in that white, minimalist way, with sofas and small desks. The highlight is the wonderfully airy, multilevel living room with attached wooden-decked terrace and Jacuzzi. Discounts available online.

CABRERA GARDEN GUESTHOUSE **$$$**

Map p250 (011-4777-7668; www.cabreragarden.com; José Antonio Cabrera 5855; r US$145-250; ; 140, 111, 93) One of BA's loveliest places to stay is this three-room B&B run by a Polish-German gay couple. The remodeled 1920s building has a beautiful grassy garden with small patio and pool, and there's a wonderful living room in which to hang out. The spacious rooms are very comfortable, with rug-covered wooden floors, and are decorated with interesting artwork. Reserve ahead.

MINE HOTEL BOUTIQUE HOTEL **$$$**

Map p250 (011-4832-1100; www.minehotel.com; Gorriti 4770; d US$236-315; ; 140, 110, 55) This hip boutique hotel offers 20 good-sized rooms; some come with Jacuzzi and balcony and all have a desk and natural decor touches. Get one overlooking the highlight of the hotel: the peaceful backyard with a small wading pool. There's a small bistro for the buffet breakfast. Discounted rates available online.

MIRAVIDA SOHO GUESTHOUSE **$$$**

Map p250 (011-4774-6433; www.miravidasoho.com; Darregueyra 2050; r US$250-290; ; S Línea D Plaza Italia) This gorgeous guesthouse comes with six elegant rooms, one with a private terrace. There's a wine cellar, bar-lounge area for evening wine tastings, a small and relaxing patio, and even an elevator. It serves good, full breakfasts; reserve ahead.

CASASUR HOTEL **$$$**

Map p250 (011-4770-9452; http://casasurhotel.com/palermo/; Costa Rica 6032; r US$200-320; ; S Línea D Ministro Carranza) Beginning with its airy, contemporary lobby fitted with oversized bookshelves, the CasaSur is a stylish place to stay. The elegant rooms have graphic wallpaper and a monochrome color scheme; those on floors one to four have balconies. There's a small outdoor pool, spa and gym and – best of all – a spacious roof terrace with great views.

BA SOHOTEL BOUTIQUE HOTEL **$$$**

Map p250 (011-4831-1844; www.basohotel.com; Paraguay 4485; r US$160-200; ; S Línea D Plaza Italia) This 33-room boutique hotel is a safe bet, with good service and an attached restaurant. The rooms are spacious and come with wooden floors, desk, large balconies, double-paned windows, Jacuzzi tubs and bathroom mirrors that don't fog (it's important!). There's also a tiny pool and Jacuzzi on the roof terrace. Reserve ahead for discounts.

248 FINISTERRA BOUTIQUE HOTEL **$$$**

Map p250 (011-4773-0901; www.248finisterra.com; Av Báez 248; r US$120-200; ; S Línea D Ministro Carranza) Smack in the middle of Las Cañitas' nightlife strip lies this elegant, Zen-like boutique hotel. There are 11 minimalist rooms, all beautifully contemporary, though the smallest are a bit tight. There's a dining area for breakfast and a small grassy garden in back, but the highlight has to be the rooftop terrace, with wooden lounges and a Jacuzzi. Reserve ahead.

South of Palermo

With the popularity of Palermo raising property values and rents, more places to stay have popped up in the neighborhoods immediately to the south. This large area is a good choice if you don't mind being a bit further from the main sights (but not *too* far away); public transportation is good.

CHILL HOUSE GUESTHOUSE **$**

Map p254 (011-4861-6175; www.chillhouse.com.ar; Agüero 781; s/d from US$35/48; ; Línea B Carlos Gardel) This relaxed and friendly guesthouse is in a remodeled old house with high ceilings and a rustic artsy style, and has 10 private rooms (number 6, with a balcony and air-con, is especially nice). There's also an awesome rooftop terrace where *asados* take place, as well as occasional live music.

Well-located close to public transportation and within easy reach of Palermo and the Center.

POP HOTEL HOTEL **$$**

Map p254 (011-4776-6900; www.pophotelsbuenosaires.com; Juan Ramírez de Velasco 793; r US$90-130; ; Línea B Malabia) Located near Villa Crespo's outlet stores is this bright and colorful hotel. Halls are carpeted and rooms are modern and comfy, all with fridge and flat-screen TV; the ones on the 4th floor are larger and have balconies. Breakfast not included. Rates vary widely; prepay for discounts that can put the hotel into the budget category.

RACÓ DE BUENOS AIRES BOUTIQUE HOTEL **$$**

Map p254 (011-3530-6075; Yapeyú 271; d/ste from US$90/170; ; Línea A Castro Barros) This Italian-designed building in a non-touristy neighborhood offers 12 lovely rooms with different styling, from virgin white classic to subdued masculine to animal print. All are spacious and have wooden floors, high ceilings and modern amenities. There's a small plant-strewn patio for breakfast. Located in the Almagro neighborhood, just three blocks from the Subte.

Understand Buenos Aires

Buenos Aires Today

Whether life in Buenos Aires is on the up or not depends on who you ask. In 2015 a new president was sworn in after 12 years under the Kirchners, signaling a significant shift to the political center. For many, Mauricio Macri's victory was a welcome change; others were distraught at the defeat of *Kirchnerismo*. And while homelessness and unemployment in the capital are on the increase, there is a feeling of optimism among many. After all, *porteños* are nothing if not resilient.

Best on Film

La historia oficial (*The Official Story*; 1985) Oscar-winning film on the military dictatorship.

Nueve reinas (*Nine Queens*; 2000) Two con men chasing the big score.

El secreto de sus ojos (*The Secret in Their Eyes*; 2009) 2010 Oscar-winning thriller.

Pizza, birra, faso (*Pizza, Beer, Cigarettes*; 1998) Four BA gangster youths try to survive on the city streets.

Esperando la Carroza (*Waiting for the Hearse*; 1985) Cult comedy about a *porteña* family.

Best in Print

Kiss of the Spider Woman (Manuel Puig; 1976) Two prisoners and their developing relationship in a Buenos Aires prison.

The Tango Singer (Tomás Eloy Martínez; 2006) An American graduate student travels to Buenos Aires and tracks down a legendary tango singer.

The Aleph (Jorge Luis Borges; 1974) Collection of short stories set in the author's home city.

And the Money Kept Rolling In (and Out) (Paul Blustein; 2005) How the IMF helped bankrupt Argentina.

On Heroes and Tombs (Ernesto Sábato; 1961) A complex plunge into Buenos Aires' society, aristocracy and family dynamics in the 1950s.

Enter Macri

Since narrowly winning the 2015 presidential election as the candidate for Cambiemos (Let's Change'), a coalition of three political parties, Mauricio Macri has set about implementing his plans to encourage foreign investment, a pro-business, free-market reform stance that sets him apart from his leftist, pro-government predecessor.

Macri had been Buenos Aires' mayor since 2007 and was a former president of the Boca Juniors soccer club. His victory came on the back of his promise to improve international relations and loosen economic controls; for many *porteños* (residents of Buenos Aires), it was Macri's pledge to relax restrictions on the buying of US dollars that decided their vote. President Obama's visit to Buenos Aires in March 2016 made him the first US president to hold high-level talks with an Argentine leader for 20 years, and was a great boost for Macri less than six months into his presidential term.

But already, *porteños* are feeling the pinch of Macri's policies, particularly the end of government subsidies of utility bills. Sky-rocketing heat and electricity bills, and rising unemployment, have dampened any optimism surrounding the new political order, and only time will tell if Argentina's new president can kick-start the sluggish economy. Argentina's problems of high inflation and economic instability may not be over just yet.

A Taste of the Future

Despite a discouraging economy and a downturn in tourism in the last few years, Buenos Aires' culinary culture continues to evolve. Intrepid young chefs are providing creative twists to the restaurant scene with relatively new-to-BA concepts such as molecular gastronomy. Chefs Gonzalo Aramburu at Aramburu p83) and Soledad Nardelli at Chila (p74) are haking up the BA food scene with their experimental cooking, while the likes of Leo Lanussol and Augusto Mayer at Proper (p136) and Mariano Ramón at Gran Dabbang (p134) offer a fresh approach to cooking at more accessible prices.

Buenos Aires was named the 2017 Ibero-American Capital of Gastronomy, prompting the city government to stage a series of events throughout the year. Add to that a few new exciting food fairs, such as the **Feria Masticar** (www.feriamasticar.com.ar; cnr Concepción Arenal & Conde; admission AR$80, dishes AR$50-80; May; 39, 140, 168), and BA is well on its way to becoming a foodie destination.

Meanwhile, BA has embraced craft beer with an almost revolutionary fervor, with a new bar opening practically every week. There's a real sense of camaraderie among local brewers, who get together to exchange tips, and it shows – the IPAs, golden ales and Scotch they produce are improving all the time.

Going Green

Buenos Aires' public transportation is evolving. The final implementation of the SUBE card meant that obtaining enough coins for the bus was no longer a source of friction and stress in *porteños'* daily lives (really – it was *that* bad). And new bus-only Metrobus lanes down big avenues (including 9 de Julio and Juan B Justo) have eased traffic somewhat, though people continue to purchase private cars as an investment against inflation (nobody trusts banks with their savings any more). Congestion in the Center has been relieved by the pedestrianization of more than 100 blocks; making walking around the area a decidedly more pleasant experience. Bicycle use has also increased, as the bike-lane system keeps expanding, and the city's free bike-share program has been deemed a success. In 2014, these efforts were rewarded when Buenos Aires won the Sustainable Transport Award.

Finally, Buenos Aires is at last making serious efforts at recycling its waste. The Ciudad Verde campaign educates *porteños* on separating waste. Thirty Punto Verdes (green stations) are located in the city's parks and plazas where recyclable materials are collected and information is distributed.

population per sq mile

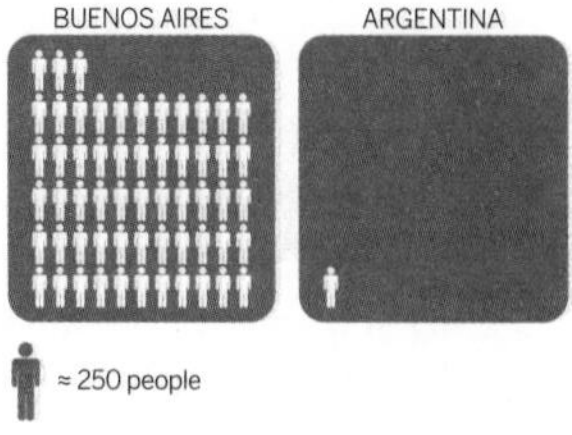

belief systems
(% of population)

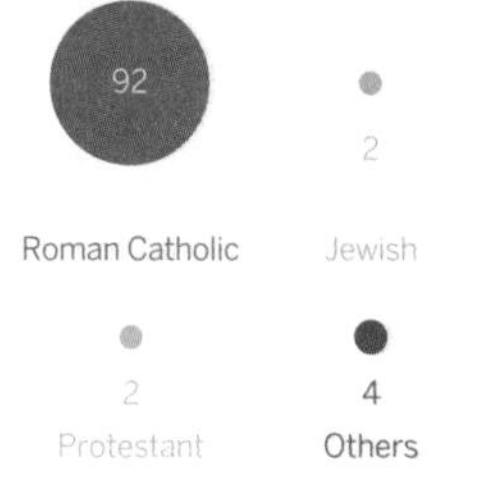

if Buenos Aires were 100 people

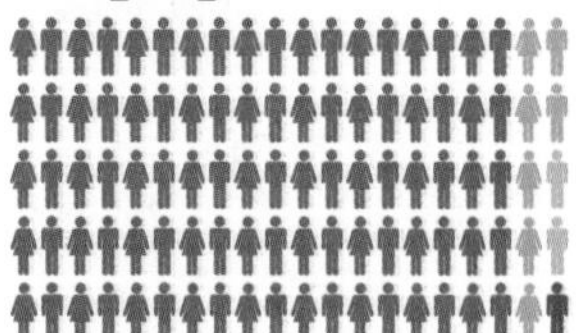

90 would be white
7 would be indigenous
2 would be Asian
1 would be black

History

Like all Latin American countries, Argentina has a tumultuous history, one tainted by periods of despotic rule, corruption and hard times. But its history is also illustrious, the story of a country that fought off Spanish colonial rule and was once among the world's economic powerhouses. It's a country that gave birth to international icons such as the gaucho, Eva Perón and Che Guevara. Understanding Argentina's past is paramount to understanding its present and, most importantly, to understanding Argentines themselves.

The Spanish Arrive

Although the banks of the Río de la Plata had been populated for tens of thousands of years by nomadic hunter-gatherers, the first attempt at establishing a permanent settlement was made by Spanish aristocrat Pedro de Mendoza in 1536. His verbose name for the outpost, Puerto Nuestra Señora Santa María del Buen Aire (Port Our Lady Saint Mary of the Good Wind) was matched only by his extravagant expedition of 16 ships and nearly 1600 men – almost three times the size of Hernán Cortés' forces that conquered the Aztecs. In spite of his resources and planning, Mendoza unfortunately arrived too late in the season to plant adequate crops. The Spanish soon found themselves short on food and in typical colonialist fashion tried to bully the local Querandí indigenous groups into feeding them. A bitter fight and four years of struggle ensued, which led to such an acute shortage of supplies that some of the Spanish resorted to cannibalism. Mendoza himself fled back to Spain, while a detachment of troops who were left behind retreated upriver to Asunción (now the capital of Paraguay).

With Francisco Pizarro's conquest of the Inca empire in present-day Peru as the focus of the Spanish crown, Buenos Aires was largely ignored for the next four decades. In 1580 Juan de Garay returned with an expedition from Asunción and attempted to rebuild Buenos Aires. The Spanish had not only improved their colonizing skills since Mendoza's ill-fated endeavor but also had some backup from the cities of Asunción and Santa Fe.

TIMELINE

1536

Spanish aristocrat Pedro de Mendoza reaches the Río de la Plata and attempts to set up a permanent settlement, only to return to Spain within four years.

1580

Buenos Aires is reestablished by Spanish forces, but for years the city remains a backwater in comparison to growing strongholds in central and northwestern Argentina.

1660

Buenos Aires' population is around 4000; it will take another century for it to double.

Still, Buenos Aires remained a backwater in comparison to Andean settlements such as Tucumán, Córdoba, Salta, La Rioja and Jujuy. With the development of mines in the Andes and the incessant warfare in the Spanish empire swelling the demand for both cattle and horses, ranching became the core of the city's early economy. Spain maintained harsh restrictions on trade out of Buenos Aires and the increasingly frustrated locals turned to smuggling contraband.

The city continued to flourish and the crown was eventually forced to relax its restrictions and co-opt the growing international trade in the region. In 1776 Madrid made Buenos Aires the capital of the new Viceroyalty of the Río de la Plata, which included the world's largest silver mine in Potosí (in present-day Bolivia). For many of its residents, the new status was recognition that the adolescent city was outgrowing Spain's parental authority.

Although the new viceroyalty had internal squabbles over trade and control issues, when the British raided the city twice – in 1806 and 1807 – the response was unified. Locals rallied against the invaders without Spanish help and chased them out of town. These two battles gave the city's inhabitants confidence and an understanding of their self-reliance. It was just a matter of time until they broke with Spain.

One of the best-known contemporary accounts of post-independence Argentina is Domingo Faustino Sarmiento's *Life in the Argentine Republic in the Days of the Tyrants* (1868). He also wrote *Facundo, Or Civilization and Barbarism* (1845).

Smuggling in Buenos Aires

It's not a coincidence that one of the most popular whiskeys served in Buenos Aires is called Old Smuggler. The city's history of trading in contraband goes all the way back to its founding. Some argue that the culture of corruption, so pervasive in Argentina, is tolerated because the historical role of smuggling in Buenos Aires led to a 'tradition' of rule bending.

The Spanish empire kept tight regulations on its ports and only certain cities were allowed to trade goods with other countries. Buenos Aires, originally on the periphery of the empire, was hard to monitor and therefore not allowed to buy from or sell to other Europeans. Located at the mouth of the Río de la Plata, the settlement was an ideal point of entry to the continent for traders. Buenos Aires merchants turned to smuggling everything from textiles and precious metals to weapons and slaves. Portuguese-manufactured goods flooded the city and made their way inland to present-day Bolivia, Paraguay and even Peru.

Later, the British and high-seas pirates found a ready and willing trading partner in Buenos Aires (and also introduced a taste for fine whiskeys). An increasing amount of wealth passed through the city and much of the initial growth of Buenos Aires was fueled by the trade in contraband. As smuggling was an open game, without favored imperial merchants, it offered a chance for upward social mobility and gave birth to a commercially oriented middle class.

1776

Buenos Aires becomes capital of the new Spanish Viceroyalty of the Río de la Plata, which included what are today Bolivia, Argentina, Paraguay and Uruguay.

1806 & 1807

British troops raid the city but are beaten back by the people of Buenos Aires in two battles, now celebrated as La Reconquista (the Reconquest) and La Defensa (the Defense).

May 25, 1810

Buenos Aires declares its independence from Spain, although actual independence is still several years off. The city renames its main square Plaza de Mayo to commemorate the occasion.

1829

Federalist *caudillo* Juan Manuel de Rosas takes control of Buenos Aires and becomes its governor; BA's influence increases dramatically during his 23-year reign.

Independence

When Napoleon conquered Spain and put his brother on the throne in 1808, Buenos Aires became further estranged from Madrid and finally declared its independence on May 25, 1810.

Six years later, on July 9, 1816, outlying areas of the viceroyalty also broke with Spain and founded the United Provinces of the River Plate. Almost immediately a power struggle arose between Buenos Aires and the provincial strongmen: the Federalist landowners of the interior provinces were concerned with preserving their autonomy, while the Unitarist businessmen of Buenos Aires tried to consolidate power in the city with an outward orientation toward overseas commerce and European ideas. Some of the interior provinces decided to go their own way, forming Paraguay in 1814, Bolivia in 1825 and Uruguay in 1828.

The Argentinian beer Quilmes is named after the now decimated indigenous group of northwest Argentina. It's also the name of a city in the province of Buenos Aires.

After more than a decade of violence and uncertainty, Juan Manuel de Rosas become governor of Buenos Aires in 1829. Although he swore that he was a Federalist, Rosas was more of an opportunist – a Federalist when it suited him and a Unitarist once he controlled the city. He required that all international trade be funneled through Buenos Aires rather than proceeding directly to the provinces, and he set ominous political precedents, creating the *mazorca* (his ruthless political police) and institutionalizing torture.

The Fleeting Golden Years

Rosas' overthrow came in 1852 at the hands of Justo José de Urquiza, a rival governor who tried to transfer power to his home province of Entre Rios. In protest, Buenos Aires briefly seceded from the union, but it was reestablished as the capital when Bartolomé Mitre crushed Urquiza's forces in 1861. From there, Buenos Aires never looked back and became the undisputed power center of the country.

A fascinating, fictionalized version of the life of ex-president Juan Perón, culminating in his return to Buenos Aires in 1973, is Tomás Eloy Martínez's *The Perón Novel* (1998).

The economy boomed and Buenos Aires became a port town of 90,000 people in the late 1860s. Immigrants poured in from Spain, Italy and Germany, followed by waves of newcomers from Croatia, Ireland, Poland and Ukraine. Its population grew nearly sevenfold from 1869 to 1895, to over 670,000 people. The new residents worked in the port, lived tightly in crammed tenement buildings, developed tango, and jump-started the leftist labor movement. The onslaught of Europeans not only expanded Buenos Aires into a major international capital but gave the city its rich multicultural heritage, famous idiosyncrasies and sharp political differences.

By Argentina's centennial in 1910, Buenos Aires was a veritable metropolis. The following years witnessed the construction of the subway, while British companies built modern gas, electrical and sewer systems.

1852

Federalist and former Rosas ally Justo José de Urquiza defeats Rosas at the Battle of Caseros and, in 1853, draws up Argentina's first constitution.

1862

Bartolomé Mitre, governor of Buenos Aires province, poet and founder of *La Nación* newspaper, becomes president after defeating Urquiza's federal forces.

1868

Intellectual Domingo Faustino Sarmiento is elected president. He encourages immigration, ramps up public education and pushes to Europeanize the country.

1869–95

The Argentine economy booms, immigration skyrockets as Italian and Spanish immigrants flood in, and Buenos Aires' population grows from 95,000 to 670,000.

Buenos Aires was at the height of a golden age, its bustling streets full of New World businesses, art, architecture and fashion. Argentina grew rich during this time based on its meat production. Advances in refrigeration and the country's ability to ship beef to distant lands was key to its economic success. In fact, by the beginning of WWI, Argentina was one of the world's 10 richest countries, and ahead of France and Germany.

Conservative forces dominated the political sphere until 1916, when Radical Party leader Hipólito Yrigoyen took control of the government in a move that stressed fair and democratic elections. After a prolonged period of elite rule, this was the first time Argentina's burgeoning middle class obtained a political voice.

It was also at this time that Argentina's fortunes started to change, but unfortunately not for the better. Export prices dropped off, wages stagnated and workers became increasingly frustrated and militant. La Semana Trágica (Tragic Week), when over 100 protesters were killed during a metalworkers' strike, was the culmination of these tensions; some say this radical reaction was due to the government being pressured by moneyed interests. The Wall Street crash of 1929 dealt the final

ESMA SECRET DETENTION CENTER

Along a busy road in the BA neighborhood of Nuñez is an imposing building officially called the Naval Mechanics School but better known as ESMA. During Argentina's 1976 to 1983 military rule it served as an infamous detention center where some 5000 people were brutally tortured and killed. Truckloads of blindfolded prisoners were unloaded outside the building, taken to the basement, sedated and killed. Some were murdered by firing squads and others were drugged and dropped from planes into the Río de la Plata on twice-weekly 'death flights.' The building also served as a clandestine maternity center that housed babies taken from their mothers (many of whom were subsequently killed) to be given to police and military couples without children.

In 2004, as part of president Néstor Kirchner's effort to revisit the crimes committed by the military junta, the building was designated a memorial museum, handed over to a human rights group and named the Space for Memory and Promotion and Defense of Human Rights. But reviving the memory was like opening Pandora's box. A public debate ensued on how to tackle the museum: whether to make it educational, poignant, moralizing or realistic. This debate – together with the human rights group's insistence that all campus buildings, some of which were still occupied by the Navy, be vacated – delayed the museum's launch. (In the end, the Navy did move to another locale.)

Eventually, it was agreed that it was best to leave the space bare, with few explanatory signs, and so commemorate the victims. On the public tours (p124) through the bleak rooms, guides tell the stories of detainees' tragic lives.

1869–95

Tango emerges in Buenos Aires.

1871

Serious shortages of water and inadequate sewerage systems lead to a severe outbreak of yellow fever that kills more than 10% of the city's population.

1887

Construction of Puerto Madero begins.

1888

The first Teatro Colón, located on Plaza de Mayo, is demolished.

blow to the export markets and a few months later, in 1930, the military took over the country in a coup led by General José Félix Uriburu. The golden age rapidly became a distant memory.

This was the first of many military coups that blemished the rest of the century and served to shackle the progress of the nation. Scholars have argued that the events that culminated in the 2001 economic collapse can be traced back to the 1930 military takeover.

The Age of the Peróns

During WWII the rural poor migrated into Buenos Aires in search of work. The number of people living in the city nearly tripled and it soon held a third of the national population (which is similar to the percentage today). The growing strength of these urban working classes swept populist Lieutenant-General Juan Domingo Perón into the presidency in 1946. Perón quickly nationalized large industry, including the railways, and created Argentina's first welfare state, cultivating his image at massive popular rallies in Plaza de Mayo.

Hectór Olivera's 1983 film *Funny Dirty Little War* is an unsettling black comedy set in a fictitious town just before the 1976 military coup.

The glamorous Eva Duarte, a onetime radio soap-opera star who married Perón in 1945, became the celebrity first lady and an icon who would eclipse Perón himself. Known as Evita, her powerful social-assistance foundation reached out to lower-class women through give-aways of such things as baby bottles and strollers, and the construction of schools and hospitals. The masses felt a certain empathy with Evita, who was also born into the working class. Her premature death in 1952 came just before things went sour and her husband's political power plummeted.

After Evita's death Perón financed payouts to workers by simply printing new money, bungled the economy, censored the press and cracked down on opposition. He was strikingly less popular without Evita, and was deposed by the military in 1955 after two terms in office. Perón lived in exile in Spain while a series of military coups ailed the nation. When he returned in 1973, there were escalating tensions from left and right parties; even if he'd lived to serve his term of re-election, Perón would have had too much on his plate. His successor, his hapless third wife Isabel, had even less staying power and her overthrow by a military junta in 1976 came as no surprise.

Although the effects of Perón's personal political achievements are debatable, the Peronist party, based largely on his ideals, has endured.

1897

Puerto Madero is completed, but Eduardo Madero – the businessman contracted for the project – died four years earlier.

1908

After 20 years of construction, the second Teatro Colón opens with a presentation of Giuseppe Verdi's opera *Aida*.

1916

Hipólito Yrigoyen, leader of the Radical Party popular with the middle classes, is elected president and introduces minimum wage to counter inflation; he's re-elected in 1928.

1930

Hipólito Yrigoyen is overthrown in a military coup led by General José Félix Uriburu, who stays in power for two years, after which civilian rule is restored.

The Military Dictatorship 1976 to 1983

The new military rulers instituted the Process of National Reorganisation, known as El Proceso, and this was headed by the notorious Jorge Rafael Videla. Ostensibly an effort to remake Argentina's political culture and modernize the flagging economy, El Proceso was nothing less than an attempt to kill off or intimidate all leftist political opposition in the country.

Based in Buenos Aires, a left-wing guerrilla group known as the Montoneros bombed foreign buildings, kidnapped executives for ransom and robbed banks to finance its armed struggle against the government. The Montoneros were composed mainly of educated, middle-class youths; they were hunted down by the military government. An estimated 30,000 civilians died – many of them simply 'disappeared' while walking down the street or sleeping in their beds; some victims had no links to the Montoneros. Many were tortured to death, or sedated and dropped from planes into the Río de la Plata. Anyone who seemed in any way suspicious or sympathetic to the Montoneros could be whisked off the streets and detained, tortured or killed. A great number of the 'disappeared' are still unaccounted for today.

Nunca Más (Never Again; 1984), the official report of the National Commission on the Disappeared, systematically details military abuses from 1976 to 1983 during the military dictatorship.

The military leaders let numerous aspects of the country's well-being slip into decay, along with the entire national economy. When Ronald Reagan took power in the USA in 1981, he reversed Jimmy Carter's condemnation of the junta's human rights abuses and invited the generals to visit Washington, DC. Backed by this relationship with the USA, the military was able to solicit development loans from international lenders, but endemic corruption quickly drained the funds into their Swiss bank accounts.

The Return to Democracy

The military dictatorship that ruled the country with an iron fist lasted from 1976 to 1983. General Leopoldo Galtieri took the reins of the draconian military junta in 1981, but its power was unraveling: the economy was in recession, interest rates skyrocketed and protesters took to the streets of Buenos Aires. A year later, Galtieri tried to divert national attention by goading the UK into a war over control of the Falkland Islands (known in Argentina as Las Islas Malvinas). The British had more resolve than the junta had imagined and Argentina was easily defeated. The greatest blow came when the British nuclear submarine *Conqueror* torpedoed the Argentine heavy cruiser *General Belgrano*, killing 323 men. Argentina still holds that the ship was returning to harbor.

The Falklands War is a sensitive subject in Argentina. If the topic comes up, try to call the islands the Malvinas instead of the Falklands; nearly all Argentines believe that the islands have always belonged to Argentina.

1946	1952	1955	1976–83
Populist Lieutenant-General Juan Domingo Perón is elected president; Perón and his young wife Eva Perón ('Evita') make sweeping changes to the political structure.	Evita dies of cancer on July 26 at age 33, one year into Juan Perón's second term as president. Her death severely weakens the political might of her husband.	After the economy slides into recession, Perón loses further political clout; he is thrown from the presidency and exiled to Spain after a military coup.	Argentina is ruled by a military junta under the leadership of General Jorge Videla. In eight years, up to 30,000 people 'disappear.'

Embarrassed and proven ineffectual, the military regime fell apart and a new civilian government under Raúl Alfonsín was elected in 1983. Alfonsín enjoyed a small amount of success and was able to negotiate a few international loans, but he could not limit inflation or constrain public spending. By 1989 inflation was out of control and Alfonsín left office five months early, when Carlos Menem took power.

Menem & the Boom Years

Under the guidance of his shrewd economic minister, Domingo Cavallo, Carlos Menem introduced free-market reforms to stall Argentina's economic slide. Many of the state-run industries were privatized and, most importantly, the peso was fixed by law at an equal rate to the American dollar. Foreign investment poured into the country. Buenos Aires began to thrive again: buildings were restored and new businesses boomed. The capital's Puerto Madero docks were redeveloped into an upscale leisure district, tourism increased and optimism was in the air. People in Buenos Aires bought new cars, talked on cell phones and took international vacations.

Carlos Menem's Syrian ancestry earned him the nickname 'El Turco' (The Turk). In 2001 he married Cecilia Bolocco, a former Miss Universe 35 years his junior; they're now separated.

Although the Argentine economy seemed to be booming to the casual observer, by Menem's second term (1995–99) some things were already amiss. The inflexibility imposed by the economic reforms made it difficult for the country to respond to foreign competition, and Mexico's 1995 currency collapse jolted a number of banks in Buenos Aires. Not only did Menem fail to reform public spending, but corruption was so widespread that it dominated daily newspaper headlines.

The Economic Crisis

As an economic slowdown deepened into a recession, voters turned to the mayor of Buenos Aires, Fernando de la Rúa, and elected him president in 1999. He was faced with the need to cut public spending and hike taxes during the recession.

The economy stagnated further, investors panicked, the bond market teetered on the brink of oblivion and the country seemed unable to service its increasingly heavy international debt. Cavallo was brought back in as the economic minister and in January 2001, rather than declaring a debt default, he sought over US$20 million more in loans from the IMF.

Argentina had been living on credit and it could no longer sustain its lifestyle. The facade of a successful economy had been ripped away, and the indebted, weak inner workings were exposed. As the storm clouds gathered, there was a run on the banks. Between July and November, Argentines withdrew around US$20 billion, hiding it under their mattresses or sending it abroad. In a last-ditch effort to keep money in the

1982

General Leopoldo Galtieri provokes the UK into a war over control of the Falkland Islands (Las Islas Malvinas), but Argentina is easily defeated by the British.

1983

The military regime collapses; civilian government is restored under Radical leader Raúl Alfonsín, but he leaves office early due to growing inflation problems.

1989

Peronist Carlos Menem succeeds Alfonsín as president and overcomes the hyperinflation that reached nearly 200% per month by instituting free-market reforms.

1992

A bomb attack at the Israeli embassy kills 29 and injures over 200.

country, the government imposed a limit of US$1000 a month on bank withdrawals. Called the *corralito* (little corral), the strategy crushed many informal sectors of the economy that function on cash (taxis, food markets), and rioters and looters inevitably took to the streets. As the government tried to hoard the remaining hard currency, all bank savings were converted to pesos and any remaining trust in the government was broken. Middle-class protesters joined the fray in a series of pot-and-pan-banging protests, and both Cavallo and de la Rúa bowed to the inevitable and resigned.

Two new presidents came and went in the same week and the world's greatest default on public debt was declared. The third presidential successor, former Buenos Aires province governor Eduardo Duhalde, was able to hold onto power. In order to have more flexibility, he dismantled the currency-board system that had pegged the peso to the American dollar for a decade. The peso devalued rapidly and people's savings were reduced to a fraction of their earlier value. In January 2002 the banks were only open for a total of six days and confidence in the government was virtually nonexistent. The economy ceased to function: cash became scarce, imports stopped and demand for nonessential items flatlined. More than half of the fiercely proud Argentine people found themselves below the national poverty line: the once-comfortable middle class woke up in the lower classes and the former lower classes were plunged into destitution. Businesspeople ate at soup kitchens and homelessness became rampant.

At least two idiomatic expressions stem from Argentina's economic crisis: *el corralito* (a little corral) refers to the cap placed on cash withdrawals from bank accounts during 'La Crisis,' while *cacerolazo* (from the word *cacerola*, meaning pan) is the street protest where angry people bang pots and saucepans.

Enter Néstor Kirchner

Duhalde, to his credit, was able to use his deep political party roots to keep the country together through to elections in April 2003. Numerous candidates entered the contest; the top two finishers were Menem (making a foray out of retirement for the campaign) and Néstor Kirchner, little-known governor of the thinly populated Patagonian province of Santa Cruz. Menem bowed out of the runoff election and Kirchner became president.

Kirchner was the antidote to the slick and dishonest Buenos Aires establishment politicians. He was an outsider, with his entire career in the provinces and a personal air of sincerity and austerity. The people were looking for a fresh start and someone to believe in – and they found that in Kirchner.

During his term Kirchner defined himself as a hard-nosed fighter. In 2003 he managed to negotiate a debt-refinancing deal with the IMF under which Argentina would only pay interest on its loans. In 2006 Argentina repaid its $9.5 billion debt, not a small feat, which drove his

1994

Eighty-five people are killed and over 100 are wounded when a Jewish community center is bombed.

1999

The mayor of Buenos Aires, Fernando de la Rúa, is voted president of Argentina as a result of dissatisfaction with the corrupt Menem administration; he inherits $114 billion in public debt.

2001–02

Argentina commits the largest debt default in world history; Argentina's economy is ruined, which sparks massive riots and looting around the country.

2003

Néstor Kirchner – a governor from Patagonia's province of Santa Cruz – is sworn in as Argentina's president after Carlos Menem bows out of the race, despite winning more first-round votes.

approval rating up to 80%. Annual economic growth was averaging an impressive 8%, the poverty rate dropped to about 25% and unemployment nose-dived. A side effect of the 2001 collapse was a boom in international tourism, as foreigners enjoyed cosmopolitan Buenos Aires at bargain prices, injecting tourist money into the economy.

But not everything was bread and roses. The fact that Argentina had repaid its debt was fantastic news indeed, but economic stability didn't necessarily follow. In fact, a series of problems ensued during Kirchner's presidency: high inflation rates caused by a growing energy shortage, unequal distribution of wealth, and a rising breach between rich and poor that was slowly obliterating the middle class.

On the foreign policy front, Kirchner's belligerence became aimed at outside forces. In November 2005, when George Bush flew in for the 34-nation Summit of the Americas, his presence sparked massive demonstrations around the country. Although anti-US sentiment unites most Argentines, some feared that Kirchner's schmoozing with Venezuelan president Hugo Chávez alienated potential investors in the United States and Europe.

Kirchner made admirable strides toward addressing the human rights abuses of the military dictatorship. In 2005 the Supreme Court lifted an amnesty law that protected former military officers suspected of human rights abuses, and this led to a succession of trials that put several of them away for life.

The Trials & Tribulations of Cristina

When Néstor Kirchner stepped aside in July 2007 in favor of his wife's candidacy for the presidential race, many started wondering: would Cristina be just a puppet for her husband, who intended to rule behind the scenes?

In the October 2007 presidential election, Cristina Fernández de Kirchner succeeded in her ambition to move from first lady to president. Weak opposition and her husband's enduring clout were some of the reasons for her clear-cut victory. While this was not the first time Argentina had had a female head of state (Isabel Perón held a brief presidency by inheriting her husband's term), Cristina was the first woman to be elected president by popular vote in Argentina.

Cristina's first term was marked by roller-coaster approval ratings. In March 2008 she significantly raised the export tax on soybeans, infuriating farmers, who went on strike and blockaded highways. Soon after, she enacted a law set to break apart Clarín, a media conglomerate that opposed her presidency. All the while, Argentina was hounded by inflation unofficially estimated at up to 25%. There were plenty of positives,

2005

An amnesty law that protected military officers suspected of human rights abuses during the 1976 to 1983 dictatorship is abolished.

2007

Lawyer, senator and former first lady Cristina Fernández de Kirchner becomes Argentina's first female president elected by popular vote.

May 2010

Argentina celebrates its bicentennial with a bang; BA's Av 9 de Julio shuts down for many colorful festivities, and the Teatro Colón reopens after four years of restoration.

Oct 27, 2010

Néstor Kirchner dies suddenly of heart failure.

however. The economy grew strongly during the first part of her tenure, and Cristina implemented a wide range of social programs to beef up the pension system, benefit impoverished children and help fight cases related to crimes against humanity. And in July 2010 she signed a bill that legalized same-sex marriage in Argentina, making it Latin America's first country to do so.

On October 27, 2010, Cristina was dealt a serious blow when Néstor Kirchner died suddenly of a heart attack. The country rallied around Cristina's sorrow, and her popularity in early 2011 remained high enough that she ran for office again and was easily re-elected. She had run on a platform that appealed to the populist vote, promising to raise incomes, restore industry and maintain Argentina's economic boom. But her popularity wasn't to last.

By 2015, Argentina was ready for a change. Unable to contest a third term under the constitution, Cristina backed the candidacy of Daniel Scioli. The contest was close, but Scioli was narrowly defeated by former Buenos Aires mayor Mauricio Macri, leader of the political coalition 'Cambiemos' (Let's Change). How that change will be realized remains to be seen.

2011

Cristina Kirchner wins presidential election race.

2012

Inflation is running at about 25% (though government figures say it's less than 10%). Kirchner passes a law restricting the sale of US dollars, creating huge black-market demand.

2013

Kirchner loses major support during October's mid-term elections. Her dreams of changing the constitution to allow her to run for a third presidential term quickly evaporate.

2015

Former Buenos Aires mayor Mauricio Macri wins the presidential election against Daniel Scioli, in Argentina's first-ever presidential run-off vote.

Music

A variety of music genres are well represented in Buenos Aires, especially when it comes to the city's most famous export, the tango (see p44). But BA's music scene is also about hybrids of overlapping sounds and styles. Traditional kinds of folklore, tango and *cumbia* are melded with digital technology to create global tunes that are gaining recognition in living rooms and music festivals all around the world.

Folk Music

The folk music of Argentina spans a variety of styles, including *chacarera, chamamé* and *zamba*. The late Atahualpa Yupanqui was a giant of Argentine folk music, which takes much of its inspiration from the northwestern Andean region and countries to the north, especially Bolivia and Peru. Probably the best-known Argentine folk artist outside of South America, however, is Mercedes Sosa (1935–2009) of Tucumán.

Charly García's version of the Argentine national anthem does what Jimi Hendrix did for 'The Star-Spangled Banner,' but it earned García a court appearance for 'lacking respect for national symbols.'

Contemporary musicians to watch out for are Chango Spasiuk, an accordion player who popularized *chamamé* music abroad; Mariana Baraj, a singer and percussionist who experiments with Latin America's traditional folk music as well as elements of jazz, classical music and improvisation; and Soledad Pastorutti, whose first two albums have been Sony's top sellers in Argentina – ever!

Argentine music has experienced the hybrid phenomenom of blending electronic music with more traditional sounds. Onda Vaga's smooth harmonies add a jazzy feel to traditional *folklórica*.

Other big names in *folklórica* are Eduardo Falú, Victor Heredia, Los Chalchaleros and León Gieco. To hear *folklórica* in Buenos Aires, head to the Feria de Mataderos (p152).

Rock & Pop

Murga is a form of athletic musical theater composed of actors and percussionists. Primarily performed in Uruguay, *murga* in Argentina is more heavily focused on dancing than singing. You're most likely see this exciting musical art form at Carnaval celebrations.

Argentine rock started in the late 1960s with a trio of groups – Almendra (great melodies and poetic lyrics), Manal (urban blues) and Los Gatos (pop) – leading the pack. Evolution was slow, however; the 1966 and 1976 military regimes didn't take a shine to the liberalism and freedom that rock represented. Emerging in the 1980s, musicians like Charly Garciá (formerly a member of the pioneering group Sui Generis) and Fito Páez (a socially conscious pop-hippie) are now icons of *rock nacional*. The late poet-songwriter Alberto Luis Spinetta of Almendra fame also had an early influence on the Argentine rock movement, and another mythical figure is Andrés Calamaro, frontman of the popular 1970s band Los Abuelos de la Nada.

More recent Argentine groups that have played *rock nacional* include Soda Stereo; cult-like Patricio Rey y sus Redonditos de Ricota (its legendary leader Indio Solari now has a solo career); versatile Los Piojos (mixing rock, blues, ska and the Uruguayan music styles *murga* and *candombe*); and Los Ratones Paranóicos, who in 1995 opened for the Rolling Stones' spectacularly successful five-night stand in Buenos Aires.

Los Fabulosos Cadillacs have popularized ska and reggae, along with groups such as Los Auténticos Decadentes, Los Pericos and Los Cafres. Almafuerte, descended from the earlier Hermética, is Buenos Aires' leading heavy-metal band. The bands Dos Minutos and Expulsados seek to emulate punk-rock legends the Ramones, who are popular in Argentina. Other classic bands include hippyish Los Divididos (descendants of the famous group Sumo), Mendozan trio Los Enanitos Verdes and the wildly unconventional Babasónicos.

Today some of Argentina's most popular bands include Bersuit Vergarabat (utilizing multigenre tunes with political, offensive and wave-making lyrics), La Portuaria, who collaborated with David Byrne (rock fusion influenced by jazz and R&B), and Valentin y Los Volcanes (indie-pop with great guitar music). And don't miss the multicultural, alternative and eclectic Kevin Johansen.

Jazz & Blues

The high degree of crossover between Buenos Aires' blues and rock scenes is illustrated by the path of the late guitar wizard Pappo (1950–2005). An elder statesman, Pappo was in the groundbreaking rock group Los Abuelos de la Nada and became involved with the seminal blues-rock band Pappo's Blues, as well as Los Gatos and others. He played hard-driving, full-tilt rockin' blues and was especially great when covering such American masters as Howlin' Wolf, BB King and Muddy Waters.

Guitarist-singer Miguel 'Botafogo' Vilanova is an alumnus of Pappo's Blues and an imposing figure in his own right. Also worth checking out is La Mississippi, a seven-member group that has been performing rock-blues since the late 1980s. Memphis La Blusera was around BA's blues scene for a long time until it broke up in 2008; it once worked with North American legend Taj Mahal.

Lalo Schifrin is an Argentine pianist, composer and conductor with a jazz background; he's most famous for writing the *Mission: Impossible* theme. He's also won four Grammy awards and has been nominated for six Oscars. In the late 1950s, Schifrin performed with Gato Barbieri, another notable composer and jazz saxophonist. Carlos Alberto Franzetti is a big-band composer who wrote *The Mambo Kings* (1992) and won a Latin Grammy in 2001 for his *Tango Fatal* album.

Guitarist Luis Salinas is known for his mellow and melodic tunes that run along George Benson lines but are a bit less poppy; be sure to check out his jazz takes on such traditional Argentine forms as the *chacarera, chamamé* and tango. Dino Saluzzi, a *bandoneón* player originally from Salta who began recording in the '70s, was one of the first Argentine musicians to mix folklore, tango and jazz. Dino's son José is a renowned guitarist in his own right.

Born in Córdoba in the early 1940s, *cuarteto* is Argentina's original pop music. Despised by the middle and upper classes for its arresting rhythm and offbeat musical pattern (called the '*tunga-tunga*'), as well as its working-class lyrics, it's definitely music from the margins. Although definitively *cordobés* (from Córdoba), it's played in working-class bars, dance halls and stadiums throughout the country.

BUENOS AIRES PLAYLIST

- **Estaciones Porteñas** (Ástor Piazzolla; 1965–70) Four tango compositions, one for each season in Buenos Aires.
- **Mi Buenos Aires Querido** (Carlos Gardel; 1934) Once of the tango crooner's most famous songs.
- **Sur** (Aníbal Troilo and Homero Manzi; 1948) Tango song about the city's southern neighborhoods of Boedo, Parque Patricios and Pompeya.
- **Puerto Madero** (Kevin Johansen; 2002) Pokes fun at the tourist's view of Buenos Aires.

Another musician and son of an Argentine jazz legend is Javier Malosetti, whose group Electrohope blends jazz, blues, rock and swing with Latin rhythms and funk. Drummer Sebastián Peyceré, who favors a funk-tinged fusion, has played with the likes of Paquito D'Rivera, BB King and Stanley Jordan. Finally, BA's own version of the Sultans of Swing is the Caoba Jazz Band, who for years have been playing 1920s and '30s New Orleans–style jazz for the love of it.

Latin & Electronica

Electrónica exploded in Argentina in the 1990s and has taken on various forms in popular music. Heavyweights in DJ-based club and dance music include Aldo Haydar (progressive house), Bad Boy Orange (drum n bass), Diego Ro-K (the 'Maradona' of Argentine DJs) and Gustavo Lamas (blending ambient pop and electro house). Hernán Cattáneo has played with Paul Oakenfold and at Burning Man.

In 2007 electronic musicians from Zizek Records, a homegrown BA label, created 'digital *cumbia*' by fusing various forms of *cumbia* and Argentine traditional music with reggaeton, dance-hall, hip-hop and electronic beats.

Buenos Aires' young clubbers have embraced the *música tropical* trend that's swept Latin America in recent years. Many a BA booty is shaken to the lively, Afro-Latin sounds of salsa, merengue and especially *cumbia*. Originating in Colombia, *cumbia* combines an infectious dance rhythm with lively melodies, often carried by brass. An offshoot is *cumbia experimental* or *cumbia villera,* a fusion of *cumbia* and gangsta posturing with a punk edge and reggae overtones.

One of BA's most interesting music spectacles is La Bomba de Tiempo (p153), a collective of drummers that features some of Argentina's leading percussionists. Its explosive performances are conducted by Santiago Vázquez, who communicates with the musicians through a language of mysterious signs – the result is an incredible improvisational union that simulates electronic dance music and sounds different every time. During the summer it plays open-air at **Ciudad Cultural Konex** (Map p254; ☎011-4864-3200; www.ciudadculturalkonex.org; Av Sarmiento 3131; Ⓢ Línea B Carlos Gardel) every Monday evening; it's also featured at various happenings and parties in BA's clubs.

Literature & Cinema

Argentina has a strong literary heritage, with many writers using the country's darkest moments as inspiration for their complex and sometimes disturbing fiction. Leading the pack are writers Jorge Luis Borges, Julio Cortázar and Ernesto Sábato. Buenos Aires is also home to Argentina's vibrant, thriving film industry. The country has won two Oscars for best foreign-language film (in 1985 and 2010) – the only Latin American country to have won the award – and continues to produce excellent directors and movies.

Literary Classics

One of Argentina's most influential pieces of classic literature is the epic poem by José Hernández, *Martín Fierro* (1872). Not only did this story about a gaucho outlaw lay the foundations of the Argentine *gauchesco* literary tradition but also it inspired the name of the short-lived but important literary magazine of the 1920s that published avant-garde works based on the 'art for art's sake' principle.

Julio Cortázar (1914–84) is an author well known to readers outside Argentina. He was born in Belgium to Argentine parents, moved to Buenos Aires at age four and died in self-imposed exile in Paris at the age of 70. His stories frequently plunge their characters out of everyday life into surrealistic situations. One such story was adapted into the film *Blow-Up* by Italian director Michelangelo Antonioni. Cortázar's novel *Hopscotch* takes place simultaneously in Buenos Aires and Paris and requires the reader to first read the book straight through, then read it a second time, 'hopscotching' through the chapters in a prescribed but nonlinear pattern for a completely different take on the story.

Argentines are pretty well read – their literacy rate is over 97% – and Buenos Aires is home to some fabulous bookstores, including El Ateneo Grand Splendid (p119) in Recoleta. Look for bargain titles at the shops on Av Corrientes near Av 9 de Julio, or at the stalls at Parque Rivadavia in the Caballito neighborhood.

Another member of Borges' literary generation is Ernesto Sábato (1911–2011), whose complex and uncompromising novels have been extremely influential on later Argentine literature. *The Tunnel* (1948) is Sábato's engrossing existentialist novella of a *porteño* painter so obsessed with his art that it distorts his relationship with everything and everyone else.

Adolfo Bioy Casares (1914–99) and Borges were close friends and occasional collaborators. Bioy's sci-fi novella *The Invention of Morel* (1940) gave Alain Resnais the plot for his classic film *Last Year at Marienbad* and also introduced the idea of the holodeck decades before *Star Trek* existed.

Post-Boom Literature

The contemporary, post-boom generation of Argentine writers is more reality-based, often reflecting the influence of popular culture and directly confronting the political angles of 1970s authoritarian Argentina. One of the most famous post-boom Argentine writers is Manuel Puig (1932–90), whose first love was cinema. Much of his writing consists solely of dialogue, used to marvellous effect. Puig's novel *The Buenos Aires Affair* (1973) is a page-turner delving into the relationship between murderer and victim (and artist and critic), presented as a

VICTORIA OCAMPO

In 1931 Victoria Ocampo (1890–1979) – a writer, publisher and intellectual – founded *Sur*, a renowned cultural magazine that introduced Virginia Woolf, Albert Camus and TS Eliot to Argentine readers. *Sur* also featured writers including Jorge Luis Borges, Adolfo Bioy Casares, Ernesto Sábato and Julio Cortázar.

Ocampo was an inexhaustible traveler and a pioneering feminist, and was loathed by some for her lack of convention. A ferocious opponent of Peronism, chiefly because of Perón's interference with intellectual freedom, Ocampo was arrested at her summer chalet, Villa Victoria, at the age of 63. She entertained her fellow inmates by reading aloud and acting out scenes from novels and cinema.

Ocampo never went to university, but her voracious appetite for knowledge and her love of literature led her to become Argentina's leading lady of letters. She hosted intellectuals from around the globe at Villa Victoria, in Mar del Plata, creating a formidable literary and artistic salon. (The villa is now a cultural center.)

Today, you can also visit Victoria Ocampo's restored mansion in San Isidro, Villa Ocampo (p158), for a reminder of a bygone era.

If Victoria is remembered as a lively essayist and a great patroness of writers, her younger sister, Silvina, was the literary talent, writing both short stories and poetry. Silvina won several literary prizes for her work, and in 1940 she married Casares, the famous Argentine writer and friend of Jorge Luis Borges.

deconstructed crime thriller. His most famous work is *Kiss of the Spider Woman* (1976), a captivating story of a relationship that develops between two men inside an Argentine prison; it was made into the 1985 Oscar-winning film starring William Hurt. Being openly gay and critical of Perón did not help his job prospects in Argentina, and Puig spent many years in exile.

Another prolific writer was Tomás Eloy Martínez (1934–2010). His *The Perón Novel* (1988), a fictionalized biography of the controversial populist leader, and its sequel, *Santa Evita* (1996), which traces the worldwide travels of Evita's embalmed corpse, were both huge hits.

Ricardo Piglia (b 1941) is one of Argentina's most well-known contemporary writers. He pens hard-boiled fiction and is best known for his socially minded crime novels with a noir touch, such as *The Absent City* (1992), *Money to Burn* (1997) and *Nocturnal Target* (2010).

Osvaldo Soriano (1943–97), perhaps Argentina's most popular contemporary novelist, wrote *Funny Dirty Little War* (1986) and *Winter Quarters* (1989). Juan José Saer (1937–2005) penned short stories and complex crime novels, while Rodrigo Fresán (b 1963), the youngster of the post-boom generation, wrote the international bestseller *Argentine History* (1991).

The first novel of Federico Andahazi (b 1963), *The Anatomist*, caused a stir when it was published in 1997. Its theme revolves around the 'discovery' of the clitoris by a 16th-century Venetian who is subsequently accused of heresy. Andahazi based his well-written book on historical fact, and manages to have some fun while still broaching serious subjects. His prize-wining *El Conquistador* (2006) is a historical novel about an Aztec youth who 'discovers' Europe before Columbus reaches America, while his latest book, *Pecar como Dios manda* (To Sin Like You Mean It; 2008), hypothesizes that to understand the essence of a society you have to understand the web of sexual relations on which it's built.

Two of the younger generation of Argentine writers are Washington Cucurto and Gabriela Bejerman. Cucurto runs **Eloísa Cartonera** (www.eloisacartonera.com.ar), a small publishing house that releases books by young authors made of recycled cardboard collected by the city's *cartoneros*. Bejerman, a multimedia artist who launched a music career as Gaby Bex, released an album in 2007 that incorporates some of her poetry with electro music. Other names to watch out for are Andrés Neuman, Oliverio Coelho and Pedro Mairal.

Cinema

Buenos Aires is at the center of the Argentine film industry and New Argentine Cinema. While this movement can't be called a school of cinema, as it includes a hodgepodge of themes and techniques, it's certainly a new wave of film-making that has been attracting international attention.

The film that's considered to have spearheaded the New Argentine Cinema is *Rapado* by Martín Rejtman, a minimalist 1992 feature that for the first time pushed the boundaries in a country where films were generally heavy with bad dialogue. In the late 1990s the government withdrew subsidies pledged to film schools and the movie industry. Despite this, two films ignited 'the new wave' – the low-budget *Pizza, birra, faso* (Pizza, Beer, Cigarettes; 1998) by Adrián Caetano and Bruno Stagnaro, and Pablo Trapero's *Mundo grúa* (Crane World; 1999), a black-and-white portrait of Argentina's working-class struggles.

Trapero went on to become one of Argentina's foremost filmmakers, whose credits include *El bonaerense* (2000), the ensemble road movie *Familia rodante* (Rolling Family; 2004), *Nacido y criado* (Born and Bred; 2006) – a stark story about a Patagonian man's fall from grace – and the 2010 noir film *Carancho,* a love story whose protagonist is a sleazy opportunist who frequents emergency rooms and accident scenes to find new clients for his legal firm. Trapero's 2012 film *Elefante blanco* (White Elephant) was screened at Cannes; his most recent film is *El clan* (The Clan; 2015).

JORGE LUIS BORGES

Many of the greatest lights of Argentine literature called Buenos Aires home, and the one that burned brightest was without doubt Jorge Luis Borges (1899–1986), one of the foremost writers of the 20th century. A prolific author and an insatiable reader, Borges possessed an intellect that seized on difficult questions and squeezed answers out of them. Though super-erudite in his writing, he was also such a jokester that it's a challenge to tell when he's being serious and when he's pulling your leg (though often it's a case of both at once). From early on one of his favorite forms was the scholarly analysis of nonexistent texts, and more than once he found himself in trouble for perpetrating literary hoaxes and forgeries. A few of these are contained in his *Universal History of Iniquity* (1935), a book that some point to as the origin of magic realism in Latin American literature.

Borges' dry, ironic wit is paired (in his later work) with a succinct, precise style that is a delight to read. His paradoxical *Ficciones* (1944) – part parable, part fantasy – blurs the line between myth and truth, underscoring the concept that reality is only a matter of perception and the number of possible realities is infinite. Other themes that fascinated Borges were the nature of memory and dreams, labyrinths, and the relationship between the reader, the writer and the written piece. *Collected Fictions* (1999) is a complete set of his stories.

Though he received numerous honors in his lifetime – including the Cervantes Prize, the Legion of Honor and an OBE – Borges was never conferred the Nobel. He joked of this in typical fashion: 'Not granting me the Nobel Prize has become a Scandinavian tradition. Since I was born they have not been granting it to me.'

Pilgrims can head to his **last residence** (Map p246; Maipú 994; S Línea C San Martín) in BA: a private apartment building near the corner of Florida and Santa Fe in Retiro. Look for a plaque on the wall.

One of the brightest stars of the New Argentine Cinema is Daniel Burman, who deals with the theme of identity in the character of a young Jew in modern-day Buenos Aires. His films include *Esperando al mesíah* (Waiting for the Messiah; 2000), *El abrazo partido* (Lost Embrace; 2004) and *Derecho de familia* (Family Law; 2006). Burman's other claim to fame is his co-production of Walter Salles' Che Guevara–inspired *The Motorcycle Diaries*.

Another director to have made a mark on Argentine cinema is the late Fabián Bielinsky. He left behind a small but powerful body of work that includes his award-winning feature *Nueve reinas* (Nine Queens; 2000), which inspired a 2004 Hollywood remake, *Criminal*. His last film, the 2005 neo-noir flick *El Aura*, screened at Sundance and was the official Argentine entry for the 2006 Oscars.

Argentina's biggest film event is the Buenos Aires International Festival of Independent Film (Festival Internacional de Cine Independiente; http://festivales.buenosaires.gob.ar/en/bafici), held in April. Fims are shown at cinemas around the city.

Lucrecia Martel has left an indelible trace on Argentina's contemporary cinema. Her 2001 debut, *La ciénaga* (The Swamp), and the 2004 follow-up, *La niña santa* (The Holy Girl), both set in Martel's native Salta province, deal with themes of social decay, the Argentine bourgeois and sexuality in the face of Catholic guilt. Another acclaimed director, Carlos Sorín, takes us to the deep south of Argentina in two of his neorealist flicks, the 2002 *Historias mínimas* (Minimal Stories) and the 2004 *Bombón el perro* (Bombón the Dog).

Juan José Campanella's *El hijo de la novia* (Son of the Bride) received an Oscar nomination for best foreign-language film in 2001. His 2004 film *Luna de avellaneda* (Moon of Avellaneda) is a masterful story about a social club and those who try to save it. And in 2010 Campanella won the Oscar for best foreign-language film with his *El secreto de sus ojos* (The Secret in Their Eyes).

An up-and-coming director is Lucía Puenzo (daughter of Luis Puenzo). Her *XXY* (2007) won multiple awards at Cannes that year; it follows the travails of a 15-year-old hermaphrodite. In 2013 Puenzo directed *Wakolda* (The German Doctor), a true story about the family who unknowingly lived with Josef Mengele during his exile in South America. Finally, Damián Szifron's black comedy *Relatos salvajes* (Wild Tales; 2014) was Oscar-nominated for Best Foreign Language Film.

Art & Architecture

Over the years, Argentina has produced some fine artists, notably Antonio Berni, Benito Quinquela Martín and Marta Minujín, each with their own style and ability to break the mold in the art world. The buildings of Buenos Aires reflect many styles that were in vogue at various times throughout the city's life. You'll find old and new juxtaposed in sometimes jarring and often enchanting ways.

Visual Arts

Eduardo Sívori (1847-1918) was one of Argentina's first notable artists and celebrated realist painters. He depicted pampas landscapes, painted portraits and helped found one of Argentina's first artist guilds. Other early artists included Cándido López (1840–1902) – a soldier who learned to paint with his left hand after losing his right arm in war – and Ernesto de la Cárcova, who depicted social issues such as poverty.

Lino Enea Spilimbergo (1896–1964) was a diverse painter and engraver whose subjects ranged from classical to post-impressionism to stark and surreal human figures. His contemporary, Antonio Berni (1905–81), would sometimes visit shantytowns and collect materials to use in his works. Various versions of his theme *Juanito Laguna bañándose* (Juanito Laguna Bathing) – a protest against social and economic inequality – have commanded wallet-busting prices at auctions. You can see both artists' work in the restored ceiling murals of the Galerías Pacífico shopping center (p61).

Street art – which is not illegal in Buenos Aires – has become more and more prominent in neighborhoods such as Barracas, San Telmo, La Boca, Colegiales and Palermo. Colorful murals, political stencils and graffiti-inspired creations cover public and private walls, sometimes commissioned by the city and property owners.

Other famous Argentine artists of this era are Juan Carlos Castagnino, a realist and figurative painter; Jorge de la Vega, who dabbled not only in various styles of visual art but also became a popular singer and songwriter; and Emilio Pettoruti, who affronted Buenos Aires with his 1924 cubist exhibition. Roberto Aizenberg was one of Argentina's top surrealists.

One of the more interesting contemporary artists is Roberto Jacoby (b 1944), who has been active in diverse fields since the 1960s, from organizing socially flavored multimedia shows to setting up audiovisual installations. His most famous work, *Darkroom*, is a video performance piece with infrared technology meant for a single spectator.

Guillermo Kuitca (b 1961) is known for his imaginative techniques that include the use of digital technology to alter photographs, maps and other images and integrate them into larger-themed works. His work is on display at major international collections and he's had solo and group shows at key art expos around the world.

Other internationally recognized artists who experiment with various media are Buenos Aires–born, New York–based Liliana Porter, who imaginatively plays with video, paintings, 3D prints, photos and an eclectic collection of knickknacks; Graciela Sacco, whose politically and socially engaging installations often use public space as their setting; and the photographer Arturo Aguiar, known for playing with light and shadow in his mysterious works. Also watch out for highly eclectic Argentine pop artist Marta Minujín.

SAIKO3P / SHUTTERSTOCK ©

Top: Palacio Barolo (p79), Congreso & Tribunales
Bottom: Puente de la Mujer (p73), Puerto Madero

Buenos Aires has also seen a rise in urban art interventions, a movement of diverse activist artists whose work calls attention to social and urban issues in the city's public spaces. The most prominent figure is Marino Santa María, whose award-winning *Proyecto Calle Lanín* is a series of colorful murals along the narrow Calle Lanín in the southern neighborhood of Barracas.

The late Benito Quinquela Martín, who put the working-class barrio of La Boca on the artistic map, painted brightly colored oils of life in the factories and on the waterfront. Xul Solar, a multitalented phenomenon who was a good friend of Jorge Luis Borges, painted busy, Klee-inspired dreamscapes. The former homes of both Quinquela (p101) and Solar (p131) are now museums showcasing their work.

Architectural History

Little trace remains of the modest one-story adobe houses that sprang up along the mouth of the Riachuelo following the second founding of Buenos Aires in 1580. Many of them were occupied by traffickers of contraband, as the Spanish crown forbade any direct export or import of goods from the settlement. For an idea of how BA's first settlements used to be, visit El Zanjón de Granados (p88) in San Telmo.

Buenos Aires' Cabildo (p61) is a fair example of colonial architecture, although its once plaza-spanning colonnades were severely clipped by the construction of Av de Mayo and the diagonals feeding into it. Most of the other survivors from the colonial era are churches. In Plaza de Mayo, the Catedral Metropolitana (p59) was begun in 1752 but not finished until 1852, by which time it had acquired its rather secular-looking neoclassicist facade.

Many examples of post-independence architecture (built after 1810) can be found in the barrios of San Telmo and Montserrat. San Telmo also holds a wide variety of vernacular architecture such as *casas chorizos* (sausage houses) – so called for their long, narrow shape (some have a 2m frontage on the street). The perfect example is Casa Mínima (at San Lorenzo 380).

In the latter half of the 19th century, as Argentina's agricultural exports soared, a lot of money accumulated in Buenos Aires. Wealth was demonstrated with the construction of elaborate mansions, public buildings and wide Parisian-style boulevards. In the first few decades of the boom, buildings were constructed mostly in Italianate style, but toward the end of the 19th century a French influence began to exert itself. Mansard roofs and other elements gave a Parisian look to parts of the city, and by the beginning of the 20th century art nouveau was all the rage.

Among the highlights of the building boom's first five decades is the presidential palace, the Casa Rosada (p63), created in 1882 by joining a new wing to the existing post office. Others include the showpiece Teatro Colón (p78), the magnificent Palacio de las Aguas Corrientes (p79) and the imposing Palacio del Congreso (p79).

The 1920s saw the arrival of the skyscraper, in the form of the 100m-high, 22-story Palacio Barolo (p79). This building was the tallest in Argentina (and one of the tallest in South America) from its opening in 1923 until the completion of the 30-story art-deco Edificio Kavanagh (p107) in 1936. The Kavanagh, when finished, was the largest concrete building in the world and remains an impressive piece of architecture.

Buenos Aires continued to grow during Juan Perón's spell in power (1946 to 1955), during which time utilitarian housing and office blocks were built. Bucking the trend were such oddball buildings as the Banco de Londres on Reconquista, designed in 1959 by Clorindo Testa. The bank was finished by 1966, but Testa's brutalist Biblioteca Nacional (p132) – which must've looked pretty groovy to him on the drawing board in 1962 – was dated by the time it opened (following many delays) in 1992.

Discover the art world of Buenos Aires during the Arte BA (p20) festival and the annual Noche de los Museos (Night of the Museums).

A heartening trend of 'architectural recycling' took off in Buenos Aires in the latter 20th century and continues today, helping to preserve the city's glorious old structures. Grand old buildings have been remodeled (and sometimes augmented) to become luxury hotels, museums and cultural centers; notable examples include the Centro Cultural Kirchner (p59), which used to be the city's main post office, and the Usina del Arte (p102), a concert hall that used to be an old electricity factory. Old markets have also been restored to their original glory to live again as popular shopping malls, such as the Mercado de Abasto (p150) and Galerías Pacífico (p61).

Modern Architecture

The first decade of the 21st century has seen an increasingly modern skyline develop in Buenos Aires. Soaring structures of glass and steel tower above earlier efforts, many innovative and quite striking, such as the Edificio República in Buenos Aires' downtown. It was designed by César Pelli, who also did Kuala Lumpur's Petronas Towers.

The renovation of Puerto Madero turned dilapidated brick warehouses into offices, upscale restaurants and exclusive lofts. Contrasting with these charming low, long buildings is one of the city's tallest structures, the 170m-high Torres El Faro, standing at the eastern section of Puerto Madero. It's a pair of joined towers that now house fancy apartments. Other architectural gems here include Calatrava's Puente de la Mujer (p73) and the glass-domed Museo Fortabat (p73) by Uruguayan-born architect Rafael Viñoli.

Survival Guide

Transportation

ARRIVING IN BUENOS AIRES

Buenos Aires is well connected by air, with direct international flights to cities all over the world including New York, Miami, London, Madrid, Frankfurt, Amsterdam and Auckland, as well as most major cities within South America.

If you are traveling overland, you'll most likely arrive by bus at Retiro bus station, from where long-distance buses depart for destinations across Argentina as well as Chile and Paraguay.

A small number of infrequent trains link the capital with Rosario, Córdoba, Tucumán, Bahía Blanca, Tandil and Mar del Plata. Tickets are cheap but often sell out well in advance.

Ferries link Buenos Aires with Colonia and Montevideo in Uruguay.

Flights, cars and tours can be booked online at lonelyplanet.com/bookings.

Ezeiza Airport

Most international flights arrive at Buenos Aires' **Aeropuerto Internacional Ministro Pistarini** (Ezeiza; ☎011-5480-6111; www.aa2000.com.ar), about 35km south of the Center. Ezeiza is a modern airport with ATMs, restaurants, a pharmacy, duty-free shops and a small **post office** (Ezeiza Airport; ⏲9am-5pm Mon-Fri, to noon Sat).

Airport Shuttle

If you're traveling alone, the best option is to catch a shuttle with a transfer company such as **Manuel Tienda León** (MTL; Map p246; ☎011-4315-5115; www.tiendaleon.com; Av Eduardo Madero 1299; Ⓢ Línea C Retiro). You'll see its stand immediately as you exit customs, in the transport 'lobby' area. Frequent shuttles cost AR$190 per person to the Center, run all day and night, and take 40 to 60 minutes, depending on traffic. They'll deposit you at the MTL office in Retiro (from where you can take a taxi).

Another shuttle service, directed at independent travelers, is **Hostel Shuttle** (☎011-4511-8723; www.hostelshuttle.com.ar; US$13). Check the website for schedules and drop-off destinations (only at certain hostels), and try to book ahead.

Taxi

To catch a taxi, go past the transport 'lobby' area immediately outside customs, walk past the taxi touts, and you'll see the freestanding city taxi stand with a blue sign saying **Taxi Ezeiza** (☎011-5480-0066; www.taxiezeiza.com.ar; from Ezeiza to Center one-way AR$630; ⏲24hr).

Chauffeur-Driven Car

For a special treat, reserve a luxury car from **Silver Star**

CLIMATE CHANGE & TRAVEL

Every form of transport that relies on carbon-based fuel generates CO_2, the main cause of human-induced climate change. Modern travel is dependent on aeroplanes, which might use less fuel per kilometre per person than most cars but travel much greater distances. The altitude at which aircraft emit gases (including CO_2) and particles also contributes to their climate change impact. Many websites offer 'carbon calculators' that allow people to estimate the carbon emissions generated by their journey and, for those who wish to do so, to offset the impact of the greenhouse gases emitted with contributions to portfolios of climate-friendly initiatives throughout the world. Lonely Planet offsets the carbon footprint of all staff and author travel.

EZEIZA ARRIVAL & DEPARTURE TIPS

➡ Australian and Canadian passport holders have to pay a reciprocity fee before arriving in Argentina; ideally you'll be reminded of this when you buy your plane ticket. You'll need to pay this fee online with a credit card before arriving in Argentina; see www.migraciones.gov.ar/accesibleingles and click on 'tourism fees.' These fees are US$100 for Australians (good for one year) and US$92 for Canadians (multiple entry). In 2016 President Macri revoked the reciprocity fees for US citizens.

➡ There's a **tourist information booth** (☎011-5480-6111; Terminal A arrivals, 1st fl, Ezeiza airport; ⏰24hr) just beyond the city's Taxi Ezeiza stand.

➡ When departing Buenos Aires, get to Ezeiza at least two to three hours before your international flight out; security and immigration lines can be long. And be aware that traffic is often bad *getting* to Ezeiza; it can take an hour or more.

Transport (☎in Argentina 011-15-6826-8876, in the USA 214-502-1605; www.silverstarcar.com); you'll be driven by native English speakers to the destination of your choice.

Aeroparque Airport

Most domestic flights arrive at **Aeroparque airport** (☎011-5480-6111; www.aa2000.com.ar; Av Rafael Obligado; 🚌33, 45), a short distance from downtown Buenos Aires.

Bus

Manuel Tienda León (MTL; Map p246; ☎011-4315-5115; www.tiendaleon.com; Av Eduardo Madero 1299; Ⓢ Línea C Retiro) does hourly transfers from Ezeiza to Aeroparque. To get from Aeroparque to the Center, take public bus 33 or 45 (don't cross the street; take them going south); you'll need a loaded SUBE transport card, though, as the buses no longer accept cash.

Taxi

A taxi to the Center costs around AR$160.

Boat

There's a regular ferry service to and from Colonia and Montevideo, both in Uruguay. **Buquebus** (Map p236; ☎011-4316-6530; www.buquebus.com; Av Antártida Argentina 821; 🚌92, 106) and **Seacat** (Map p236; ☎011-4314-5100; www.seacatcolonia.com; Av Antártida Argentina 821; Ⓢ Línea B Alem) ferries leave from the same terminal in Puerto Madero. The terminal is a 15-minute walk from Alem Subte station on Línea B.

Colonia Express (Map p242; ☎011-4317-4100; www.coloniaexpress.com; Av Don Pedro de Mendoza 330; ⏰9am-8pm; 🚌130, 8, 86) is the cheapest company but has limited departures; its terminal is in an industrial neighborhood near La Boca; take a taxi. Book online in advance for the best prices.

Bus

Buenos Aires' modern **Retiro bus terminal** (Retiro; Map p246; ☎011-4310-0700; www.tebasa.com.ar; Av Antártida Argentina; Ⓢ Línea C Retiro) is 400m long and has bays for 75 buses. The bottom floor is for cargo shipments and luggage storage, the top for purchasing tickets, and the middle for everything else.

There's an **information booth** (Map p246; ☎011-4310-0700; ⏰24hr) that provides general bus information and schedules, plus a **tourist office** (Map p246; Retiro Bus Station; ⏰9am-6pm; Ⓢ Línea C Retiro) near Puente 3 on the main floor, on the same level as bus bay 36. Other services include ATMs, telephone offices (some with internet access), cafes and many small stores. There's also a booth where you can buy a **SUBE card** (☎0800-777-7823; www.sube.gob.ar).

You can buy a ticket to practically anywhere in Argentina and departures are fairly frequent to the most popular destinations. You can buy tickets online using the booking services **Omnilíneas** (☎0810-999-0210; www.omnilineas.com; ⏰9am-9pm Mon-Sat, 11am-7pm Sun) or **Plataforma 10** (www.plataforma10.com.ar), or from the bus company's website (depending on your route).

Transport Options

Retiro is connected to the local bus system, but you'll need a SUBE card to use it. There's also a nearby Subte station (Retiro, on Línea C). To find out the best public-transport options check http://comollego.ba.gob.ar.

Be careful wandering around looking lost with your phone out in and around the bus station, as this area is a hot spot for petty crime.

Various *remise* (call-taxi) booths are also available; the one near bay 54 is open 24 hours. If you're arriving into Buenos Aires at night this is your best transport option.

SUBE CARD

➡ To use BA's public-transport system, you'll need a **SUBE card** (☎0800-777-7823; www.sube.gob.ar); it's no longer possible to pay for buses with cash.

➡ Purchase one at any of the city tourist information booths, some *kioskos* and Correo Argentino or OCA post offices around the city; check the website for locations or look for the SUBE logo at businesses.

➡ Ezeiza airport and Retiro bus station also have SUBE booths where you can purchase and recharge this card.

➡ To purchase a SUBE card, you'll need your passport or a copy of it.

➡ Charging the card itself is easy, and can be done at many kiosks or Subte stations.

Train

There is a limited train service connecting Buenos Aires with nearby provinces. Book ahead; tickets often sell out in advance.

➡ Tigre, Rosario, Córdoba and Tucumán are served by **Línea Mitre** (☎0800-222-8736; www.sofse.gob.ar) trains from Retiro.

➡ The southern suburbs and La Plata are served by **Línea Roca** (☎0800-222-8736; www.sofse.gob.ar) trains from Constitución.

➡ Bahía Blanca, Tandil and Mar del Plata are served by **Ferrobaires** (☎011-4304-0028; www.ferrobaires.gba.gov.ar) trains from Constitución.

➡ The southwestern suburbs and Luján are served by **Línea Sarmiento** (☎0800-222-8736; www.sofse.gob.ar) trains from Once.

Take Subte Línea C to Retiro and Constitución and Línea A to Plaza Miserere for Once.

GETTING AROUND BUENOS AIRES

Subte (Underground)

BA's Subte opened in 1913 and is the quickest way to get around the city, though it can get mighty hot and crowded during rush hour. It consists of *líneas* (lines) A, B, C, D, E and H. Four parallel lines run from downtown to the capital's western outskirts, while Línea C runs north–south and connects the two major train stations of Retiro and Constitución. Línea H runs from Las Heras south to Hospitales, with plans to expand it.

To use the Subte you'll need a **SUBE card** (☎0800-777-7823; www.sube.gob.ar). The best place to get one of these cards is at any of the city tourist booths; bring your passport. Each journey costs AR$7.50.

Trains operate from 5am to around 10:30pm Monday to Saturday and 8am to around 10pm on Sundays and holidays, so don't rely on the Subte to get you home after dinner. Service is frequent on weekdays; on weekends you'll wait longer. At some stations platforms are on opposite sides, so be sure of your direction *before* passing through the turnstiles.

Bus

Buenos Aires has a huge and complex bus system. Luckily the city government has set up the website Como Llego (http://comollego.ba.gob.ar) to help you plot your journey; there's also a free app you can download to your smartphone.

To use the buses, you must have a SUBE card (coins are no longer accepted). The best place to get one of these cards is at any of the city tourist booths; bring your passport.

Most bus routes (but not all) run 24 hours; there are fewer buses at night. Seats up front are offered to the elderly, pregnant women and those with young children.

Taxi

The city's numerous (about 40,000) and relatively inexpensive taxis are conspicuous by their black-and-yellow paint jobs. They click every 200m (or every minute of waiting time) and cost 20% more after 6pm. Make sure that the meter's set to the current price when you start your ride. Drivers do not expect a big tip, but it's customary to let them keep small change. Taxis looking for passengers will have a red light lit on the upper right corner of their windshield.

Most cab drivers are honest workers making a living, but there are a few bad apples in the bunch. Try to have an idea of where you're going or you might be taking the 'scenic' route (though also be aware there are many one-way streets in BA, and your route to one place may be quite different on the way back).

Finally, make an attempt to snag an 'official' taxi. These are usually marked by a roof light and license number printed on the doors; the words *radio taxi* are usually a good sign. Official drivers must display their license on the back of their seat or dashboard.

Many locals will recommend you call a *remise* instead of hailing cabs off the street. A *remise* looks like a regular car and doesn't have a meter. It costs a bit more than a street taxi but is considered more secure, since an established company sends them out. Most hotels and restaurants will call a *remise* for you; expect a short wait for them to show up.

Bicycle

For those comfortable with the trials of cycling in a major city, bicycle is often the fastest and most pleasant way of getting around Buenos Aires. The city is almost completely flat, most streets are one-way, and you can use the 130km network of interconnected bike lanes. Just remember to watch out for traffic (if in doubt, always give way, be prepared for the odd running of a red traffic light and be especially careful of buses – assume they haven't seen you). If you are cycling on one of the main, one-way avenues (eg Av Corrientes), use the lane on the far left (but watch out for motorcycles).

The city government has a free **city bike** (EcoBici; ☎0800-333-2424; www.buenosaires.gob.ar/ecobici/sistema-ecobici/turistas; ⊙24hr) **FREE** scheme, called EcoBici, which tourists can use. Complete the registration form online or via the app – you'll need to upload a photo of your passport. Once you're registered, you can use the EcoBici app to hire a bike by entering an access code at any of the (unmanned) bike stations. You'll need data on your cell phone to use the app while at the bike stations. The free bike hire period is one hour on weekdays and two hours at weekends.

Ask in any of the city tourist offices for a copy of the city government cycle map (*mapa de ciclovías de la Ciudad de Buenos Aires*), which shows the bike lanes and location of city bike stations and repair shops (*bicicletarías*). You can also use http://comollego.ba.gob.ar to plot your route.

You can also join city bike tours – try **Biking Buenos Aires** (Map p240; ☎011-4300-5373; www.bikingbuenosaires.com; Perú 988; ⊙9am-6pm; Ⓢ Línea C Independencia) or **Urban Biking** (Map p246; ☎011-4314-2325; www.urbanbiking.com; Esmeralda 1084; ⊙9am-6pm Mon-Fri, noon-6pm Sat & Sun; Ⓢ Línea C San Martín) – which include bicycle and guide.

Car & Motorcycle

Anyone considering driving in Buenos Aires should know that driving in the city can be challenging. Problems include aggressive drivers, unpredictable buses, potholes, traffic, difficulty parking and the fact that pedestrians cross the road haphazardly. Reconsider your need to have a car in this city; public transportation will often get you anywhere faster, cheaper and with much less stress.

Rental

If you want to rent a car, expect to pay US$30 to US$50 or more per day. International chains can be more expensive than local rental agencies; call around. You'll need to be at least 21 years of age and have a valid driver's license; having an international driver's license wouldn't be a bad idea, though you don't necessarily need one. A credit card and passport are also necessary.

Avis (☎011-4326-5542; www.avis.com.ar; Cerrito 1535; ⊙8am-7:45pm Mon-Sat, to 5:45pm Sun; 🚌130, 62, 93)

Hertz (☎011-4816-0899, 0810-222-43789; www.hertz.com.ar; Paraguay 1138; Ⓢ Línea D Tribunales)

New Way (☎011-4515-0331; www.new-wayrentacar.com;

HANDY BUS ROUTES

ROUTE	BUS
Microcentro to Palermo Viejo	111
Microcentro to Plaza Italia (in Palermo)	29, 59, 64
Once to Plaza de Mayo to La Boca	64
Plaza de Mayo to Ezeiza airport (placard says 'Ezeiza')	8
Plaza Italia to Microcentro to San Telmo	29
Plaza Italia to La Boca via Retiro & Plaza de Mayo	152, 29
Plaza Italia to Recoleta to Microcentro to Constitución	59
Plaza San Martín to Aeroparque airport	33, 45
Recoleta to Congreso to San Telmo to La Boca	39
Retiro to Plaza de Mayo to San Telmo	22

WATCH THAT POCKET!

When traveling on BA's crowded bus or Subte lines, watch for pickpockets. They can be well dressed, men or women, often with a coat slung over their arm to hide nefarious activities going on near your bag or pocket. Occasionally there are several of them, working as a team, and they'll try to shove or distract you. The best thing to do is not look like a tourist, keep your wallet well ensconced in your front pocket, wedge your purse under your arm and wear your backpack in front – like the locals do. Don't make yourself an easy target and they'll move on – and you might not even notice they exist.

Marcelo T de Alvear 773; SLínea C San Martín)

For motorcycle rentals, head to **Motocare** (☎011-4761-2696; www.motocare.com.ar/rental; Esteban Echeverría 738, Vicente López). You must be at least 25 years of age; bring your own helmet and riding gear. Crossing into Chile, Uruguay, Paraguay and Brazil is possible.

Automobile Associations

If you drive in Argentina – especially in your own car – it may be worth joining the **Automóvil Club Argentino** (ACA; ☎011-4808-4040; www.aca.org.ar; Av del Libertador 1850; ⏲9am-4pm Mon-Fri; 🚌130, 62, 93), which has many nationwide offices. ACA recognizes members of overseas affiliates, such as the American Automobile Association (AAA), and often grants them similar privileges, including discounts on maps, accommodations, camping, tours and other services.

TOURS

A guided tour is a great way to glimpse beneath the surface and gain an insight into Buenos Aires' turbulent history and distinctive culture. A wealth of stories lie behind every monument and public square and a guided tour can help bring the city's sights to life.

Being compact and flat, Buenos Aires is easily explored on foot, and a walking tour is a good way for first-time visitors to get their bearings in the city. Alternatively, take advantage of BA's growing network of cycle lanes on a bike tour.

Those with specialist interests should sign up for one of the excellent tours focused on a particular theme, including street art, food, photography and tango.

Walking Tours

Buenos Tours (www.buenostours.com; full-day/half-day tour for 1-3 people US$235/125) Well-run private walking tours guided by friendly, knowledgeable and responsible native English speakers living long-term in Buenos Aires.

Cultour (☎15-5624-7368, 011-15-6365-6892; www.cultour.com.ar) Good tours run by teachers and students from UBA (University of Buenos Aires). Prepare to learn the historical and cultural facets of Buenos Aires.

BA Free Tour (Map 238; ☎011-4495-3832; www.bafreetour.com; cnr Av Rivadavia & Rodríguez Peña; donation recommended; ⏲11am Mon-Sat) Free (actually, donation) walking tours given by enthusiastic young guides who love their city. Even if you can't give anything you're welcome to join.

BA Walking Tours (☎011-5773-1001; www.ba-walking-tours.com; 2hr group tour per person US$30) Group and private tours covering all the main sights on day tours, night tours, historic tours and tango tours.

Cycling Tours

★**Biking Buenos Aires** (Map p240; ☎011-4300-5373; www.bikingbuenosaires.com; Perú 988; ⏲9am-6pm; SLínea C Independencia) Friendly American and Argentine guides take you on various tours of Buenos Aires; tour themes include graffiti and architecture. Recommended.

Urban Biking (Map p246; ☎011-4314-2325; www.urbanbiking.com; Esmeralda 1084; ⏲9am-6pm Mon-Fri, noon-6pm Sat & Sun; SLínea C San Martín) One- and two-day cycling tours, along with bike and kayak excursions to Tigre. Also rents out bamboo bikes.

Bus Tour

Buenos Aires Bus (Map p234; ☎011-4018-0055; www.buenosairesbus.com; Av Diagonal Roque Sáenz Peña 728; 24hr ticket AR$350; ⏲9am-5pm; SLínea C Diagonal Norte) Hop-on, hop-off bus that runs every 20 minutes to 35 stops, from La Boca to Palermo (see website).

Specialist Tours

Graffitimundo (☎011-15-3683-3219; www.graffitimundo.com; group tours US$18-30) Excellent tours of some of BA's best graffiti are offered by this nonprofit organization that upports the local urban art scene. Learn artists' history and the local graffiti culture. Several tours available; stencil workshops too.

Buenos Aires Street Art (www.buenosairesstreetart.com; group tours US$20-30) Group and private walking tours with knowledgeable guides highlighting some of BA's most interesting street art in the northern and southern city suburbs. Supports local artists too.

Tango Trips (☎011-5235-4923; http://tangotrips.com/; private tour for 1-3 people from US$170) Private tours to *milongas* with experienced and passionate *tangueros* (tango dancers). The venues visited depend on where the best place to go on any particular night is. Start with a private tango lesson to gain confidence before hitting the salons; if you're not a dancer, just sit back and watch tango danced in its most authentic form.

Foto Ruta (☎011-15-3331-7980; www.foto-ruta.com; streetscape tour per person US$120) On Foto Ruta's 'streetscape' workshops a professional photographer offers pro tips before sending folks out into neighborhoods with a few 'themes' to photograph – afterwards everyone watches the slide show over a glass of wine. The company also offers a number of private tours and photography workshops.

Seriema Nature Tours (☎011-5410-3235; www.seriematours.com) It does nature tours throughout South America, but around BA the most popular outings are birdwatching tours at the **Reserva Ecológica** (Map p236;☎011-4893-1588; visitasguiadas_recs@buenosaires.gob.ar; Av Tristán Achaval Rodríguez 1550; ⏲8am-7pm Tue-Sun Nov-Mar, to 6pm Apr-Oct; 🚌2) FREE in the Costanera Sur.

Directory A–Z

Bargaining

Bargaining is not acceptable in stores, except possibly for high-price items like jewelry and leather jackets (in some places). Some shops will give a *descuento* (discount) for cash payments. At street markets you can try negotiating, but keep in mind you may be talking to the artists themselves.

Be clear about whether the vendor is quoting in pesos or dollars. Always check your change before walking away.

Discount Cards

Travelers of any age can obtain a Hostelling International card at any HI Hostel or at the tiny HI office in **Retiro** (☎011-4511-8723; www.hostels.org.ar; Av Florida 835, 1st fl; ⏰9am-7pm Mon-Fri; Ⓢ Línea C San Martín). With this card you can obtain discounts at any HI hostel in Argentina, usually 10% to 15% off regular prices. International Student Identity Cards are also sold here; you'll need current student ID.

For non-HI hostels, check out **minihostels** (www.minihostels.com), a network of quality, 'good-vibe' hostels throughout Argentina and expanding to other places in Central and South America.

The **HoLa card** (www.holahostels.com) works in a similar way for a different network of hostels.

Travelers over the age of 60 can sometimes obtain discounts on museum admissions and the like. Usually a passport with date of birth is sufficient evidence of age.

Electricity

Argentina's electric current operates on 220V, 50 Hertz. Adapters are readily available from almost any *ferretería* (hardware store).

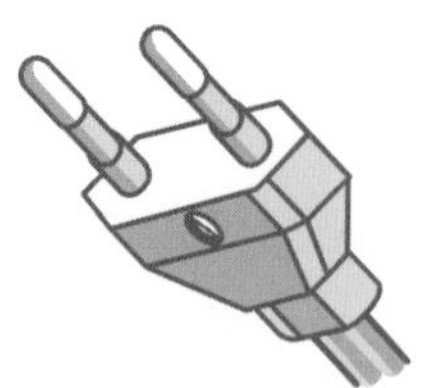

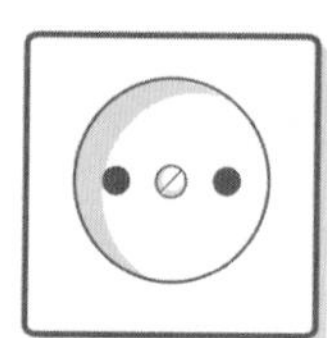

Type C
220V/50Hz

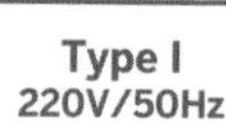

Type I
220V/50Hz

Embassies & Consulates

Australian Embassy (☎011-4779-3500; www.argentina.embassy.gov.au; Villanueva 1400; ⏰8:30am-5pm Mon-Fri; Ⓢ Línea D Olleros)

Bolivian Embassy (☎011-4394-1463; www.embajadadebolivia.com.ar; Av Corrientes 545; ⏰9:30am-5:30pm Mon-Fri; Ⓢ Línea B Florida)

Brazilian Consulate (☎011-4515-6500; www.conbrasil.org.ar; Carlos Pellegrini 1363, 5th fl; ⏰9am-1pm Mon-Fri; Ⓢ Línea C San Martín)

Canadian Embassy (☎011-4808-1000; www.embassy-canada.com; Tagle 2828; ⏲8:30am-12:30pm & 1:30-5:30pm Mon-Thu, 8:30am-2pm Fri; 🚌130, 62, 33)

Chilean Embassy (☎011-4808-8601; www.chile.gob.cl/argentina; Tagle 2762; ⏲9am-1pm & 2-5pm Mon-Fri; Ⓢ Línea H Las Heras)

French Embassy (☎011-4515-7030; www.embafrancia-argentina.org; Cerrito 1399; ⏲11am-1pm Mon-Fri; Ⓢ Línea C San Martín)

German Embassy (☎011-4778-2500; www.buenosaires.diplo.de; Villanueva 1055; ⏲8:30-11am Mon-Fri; Ⓢ Línea D Olleros)

Irish Embassy (☎011-4808-5700; www.dfa.ie/irish-embassy/argentina/; Edificio Bluesky 6th fl, Av del Libertador 1068; ⏲9am-1pm Mon-Fri; 🚌130, 93, 62)

Italian Consulate (☎011-4114-4800; www.consbuenosaires.esteri.it; Reconquista 572; Ⓢ Línea B Alem)

Netherlands Embassy (☎011-4338-0050; http://argentina.nlembajada.org; Olga Cossettini 831, 3rd fl; ⏲9am-5pm Mon-Thu, to 1pm Fri; Ⓢ Línea B Alem)

New Zealand Embassy (☎011-5070-0700; www.nzembassy.com/argentina; Carlos Pellegrini 1427, 5th fl; ⏲10am-noon Mon-Fri; Ⓢ Línea C San Martín)

Spanish Embassy (☎011-4809-4900; www.exteriores.gob.es/Embajadas/buenosaires; Av Figueroa Alcorta 3102; ⏲9am-2:30pm Mon-Fri; 🚌130, 62, 93)

UK Embassy (☎011-4808-2200; www.ukinargentina.fco.gov.uk; Dr Luis Agote 2412; ⏲9am-1pm Mon-Fri; 🚌63, 130, 93)

Uruguayan Embassy (☎011-6009-4020; www.embajadadeluruguay.com.ar; Paraguay 1571; ⏲8:30am-2:30pm Mon-Fri; Ⓢ Línea D Tribunales)

US Embassy (☎011-5777-4533; https://ar.usembassy.gov/; Colombia 4300; ⏲9am-5:30pm Mon-Fri; Ⓢ Línea D Plaza Italia)

CONCIERGE SERVICE

Madi Lang's **cultural concierge service** (☎15-3876-5937; www.baculturalconcierge.com) helps you plan itineraries, book flights, arrange airport transportation, run errands, get a cell phone, reserve theater tickets, scout out a potential apartment and do a thousand other things that'll help your trip run smoothly. She also offers customized day tours of Buenos Aires, tango tours and outings to Mataderos fair.

Emergencies

AMBULANCE	☎107
POLICE	☎911
FIRE	☎100

Gay & Lesbian Travelers

Argentina is a Catholic country with heavy elements of machismo. In Buenos Aires, however, there is a palpable acceptance of homosexuality. In 2010 Argentina became the first Latin American country to legalize same-sex marriage. In fact, gay tourism has become so popular that BA is now one of the world's top gay destinations.

Argentine men are more physically demonstrative than their North American and European counterparts, so behaviors such as kissing on the cheek in greeting or a vigorous embrace are considered innocuous even to those who express unease with homosexuals. Likewise, lesbians walking hand-in-hand should generally attract little attention. See also p32.

Health

Recommended Vaccinations

Before visiting Argentina, you should be up to date on routine vaccinations. Hepatitis A and typhoid vaccinations are recommended for most travelers.

For more specific information on vaccinations you should consider before traveling to Argentina, see wwwnc.cdc.gov/travel/destinations/argentina.htm.

Health Insurance

If you develop a life-threatening medical problem, you may want to be evacuated to your home country. Since this may cost thousands of dollars, be sure you have the appropriate insurance before you depart. Your embassy can also recommend medical services.

Availability & Cost of Health Care

Public health care in Buenos Aires is reasonably good and free, even if you're a foreigner. Waits can be long, however, and quality spotty. Those who can afford it usually opt for the superior private-care system, and here most doctors and hospitals will expect payment in cash. Many medical personnel speak English.

Dengue Fever

Dengue fever is a viral infection found throughout South America. It is transmitted by Aedes mosquitoes, which prefer to bite during the daytime and breed primarily in artificial water containers. It causes flu-like symptoms, including fever, muscle aches, joint pains, headaches, nausea and vomiting, often followed by a rash. The body aches may be uncomfortable, but most cases resolve uneventfully in a few days.

Tap Water

Tap water in Buenos Aires is generally safe to drink.

Internet Access

Wi-fi is available at nearly all hotels, hostels, restaurants, cafes and bars, and is generally fast and free.

Locutorios (telephone offices) with internet access are common; you can often find one by just walking a few blocks in any direction. Rates are cheap and connections are quick.

Medical Services

Hospitals

Highly regarded hospitals include **Hospital Italiano** (☎011-4959-0200; www.hospitalitaliano.org.ar; Juan D Perón 4190; ⓈLínea B Medrano), **Hospital Alemán** (☎011-4827-7000; www.hospitalaleman.org.ar; Pueyrredón 1640; ⏲appointments 8am-8pm Mon-Fri; ⓈLínea D Pueyrredón) and **Hospital Británico** (☎011-4309-6400; www.hospitalbritanico.org.ar; Perdriel 74; 🚌28, 50, 59). Another popular medical facility is **Swiss Medical** (☎0810-333-8876; www.swissmedicalcenter.com.ar; Av Pueyrredón 1441; ⏲clinic 8am-8pm Mon-Fri, emergency 24hr; ⓈLínea D Pueyrredón), with various branches around town.

Dentists

Dental Argentina (☎011-4828-0821; www.dental-argentina.com.ar; Laprida 1621, 2B; ⏲9am-7pm Mon-Fri; ⓈLínea D Agüero) provides modern facilities and good dental services with English-speaking professionals.

Pharmacies

Pharmacies are common in Buenos Aires. The biggest chain is **Farmacity** (www.farmacity.com; Av de Mayo 602; ⏲9am-7pm Mon-Fri, to 3pm Sat; ⓈLínea A Perú), with dozens of branches throughout the city; they're modern, bright and well-stocked with sundries. They have a prescription counter and some are open 24 hours. It's hard to miss their blue-and-orange color theme.

Money

Carrying cash and an ATM card is best; credit cards are also widely accepted.

ATMs

ATMs *(cajeros automáticos)* are everywhere in BA and are the handiest way to get money; they can also be used for cash advances on major credit cards. There's often an English-translation option if you don't read Spanish.

There may be limits per withdrawal, but you may be able to withdraw several times per day – just beware of per-transaction fees. A fee is charged on ATM transactions by the *local* bank (not including charges by your home bank, which are extra). Note that this is a *per transaction* fee, so consider taking out your maximum allowed.

Cash

Notes come in denominations of two, five, 10, 20, 50, 100, 200 and 500 pesos. One peso equals 100 centavos; coins come in denominations of five, 10, 25 and 50 centavos, as well as one and two pesos. The $ sign in front of a price is usually used to signify pesos.

Don't be dismayed if you receive dirty and hopelessly tattered banknotes; they will still be accepted everywhere. Some banks refuse worn or defaced US dollars, however, so make sure you arrive in Buenos Aires with pristine bills.

Counterfeiting of both local and US bills has become something of a problem in recent years, and merchants are very careful when accepting large denominations. You should be, too;

PRACTICALITIES

- **Smoking** Banned in most public spaces such as restaurants, cafes, bars and buses.
- **Weights & Measures** Argentina uses the metric system.

Media

- **Newspapers** Popular newspapers include leftist *Página 12* (www.pagina12.com.ar), right-leaning *Clarín* (www.clarin.com) and *La Nación* (www.lanacion.com.ar).
- **Buenos Aires Herald** (www.buenosairesherald.com) is the city's English-language newspaper, now published just once a week.
- **The Bubble** (www.thebubble.com) is a useful local English-language news website.

LANGUAGE COURSES

BA has become a major destination for students of Spanish. Good institutes are opening up all the time and private teachers are a dime a dozen. Cultural centers also offer language classes; the **Centro Cultural Ricardo Rojas** (Map p2; ☎011-4954-5521; www.rojas.uba.ar; Av Corrientes 2038; Ⓢ Línea B Callao) has an especially good range of offerings, from Korean to Russian to Yiddish.

Most private language institutes organize social activities, private classes and (usually) volunteer opportunities. Homestay programs are also available but often cost more than finding a place yourself. Check websites for fees and schedules.

Vamos (Map p250; ☎011-5984-2201; www.vamospanish.com; Av Coronel Díaz 1736; ⊙9:30am-5:30pm Mon-Fri; Ⓢ Línea D Bulnes) This Spanish language school in Palermo offers a crash course for travelers as well as group and private classes.

VOS (Map p244; ☎011-4812-1140; www.vosbuenosaires.com; Marcelo T de Alvear 1459; ⊙9am-7pm Mon-Fri; Ⓢ Línea D Callao) Offers a range of group and private classes as well as intensive courses and conversation classes.

University of Buenos Aires (Map p234; ☎011-4343-5981; www.idiomas.filo.uba.ar; 25 de Mayo 221; ⊙10am-7pm; Ⓢ Línea B Florida) Offers intensive, long-term classes (one to four months) in Spanish, Italian, German, French, Portuguese and Japanese. It's cheap, and great for serious students, but classrooms can be run-down.

Academia Buenos Aires (Map p234; ☎011-4345-5954; www.academiabuenosaires.com; Hipólito Yrigoyen 571, 4th fl, Microcentro; Ⓢ Línea A Perú) Located in an attractive old building near Plaza de Mayo this well-established Spanish-language school offers intensive courses.

Expanish (Map p234; ☎011-5252-3040; www.expanish.com; 25 de Mayo 457, 4th fl; Ⓢ Línea B Alem) Centrally located Spanish school offering a range of courses.

DWS (Map p250; ☎011-4963-4415; www.dwsba.com.ar; Billinghurst 1187; Ⓢ Línea D Agüero) Spanish language school located in Palermo offering Spanish group and private classes, as well as language and tango class packages.

Rayuela (Map p240; ☎011-4300-2010; www.spanish-argentina.com.ar; Chacabuco 852, 1st fl, No 11; Ⓢ Línea C Independencia) San Telmo–based language school offering a range of courses, with both group and private classes.

look for a clear watermark or running thread on the largest bills, and be especially careful when receiving change in dark nightclubs or taxis.

US dollars are accepted by many tourist-oriented businesses, but you should also carry some pesos.

Credit Cards

Many tourist services, larger stores, hotels and restaurants take credit cards such as Visa and MasterCard, especially for big purchases. Be aware, however, that some businesses add a *recargo* (surcharge) of up to 10% to credit-card purchases; ask ahead of time. Some lower-end hotels and private businesses will not accept credit cards, and tips can't usually be added to credit-card bills at restaurants. Many places will give you a small discount if you pay in cash, rather than use a credit card.

The following local representatives can help you replace lost or stolen cards:

American Express (☎011-4310-3000; Arenales 707; ⊙10am-4pm Mon-Fri; Ⓢ Línea C San Martín)

MasterCard (☎0800-444-5220)

Visa (☎011-4379-3333)

Traveler's Checks

Traveler's checks are very impractical in Argentina, and even in BA it's very hard to change them. Outside BA it's almost impossible to change traveler's checks. If you do decide to bring some, get them in US dollars.

The Blue Market

In December 2015 currency controls were abolished, decreasing demand for US dollars on Argentina's 'blue' (ie black) market, but you'll still hear people on Buenos Aires' Florida pedestrian strip calling out '*cambio, cambio, cambio.*' These folks are best avoided.

Tipping

Bartenders Usually not expected.

Delivery persons A small bill.

Hotel cleaning staff A few pesos per day (only at upscale hotels).

Hotel porters A small bill.

Restaurant servers 10%; 15% for fine restaurants with great service.

Spas 15%

Taxi drivers No tip unless they help with luggage; many people round up to nearest peso.

Tour guides 10% to 15%

Opening Hours

There are always exceptions, but the following are general opening hours:

Banks 8am to 3pm or 4pm Monday to Friday; some open till 1am Saturday.

Bars 8pm or 9pm to between 4am and 6am nightly (downtown, some open and close earlier).

Cafes 7am to midnight or much later; open daily.

Clubs 1am to 2am to between 6am and 8am Friday and Saturday.

Office business hours 8am to 5pm.

Post offices 8am to 6pm Monday to Friday, 9am to 1pm Saturday.

Restaurants Noon to 3:30pm, 8pm-midnight or 1am (later on weekends).

Shops 9am or 10am to 8pm or 9pm Monday to Saturday.

CULTURAL CENTERS

Buenos Aires has good cultural centers offering all sorts of art exhibitions, classes and events. They're listed in the neighborhood chapters. There are also several foreign cultural centers offering language classes, exhibitions, films and workshops.

Alianza Francesa (Map p234; 011-4322-0068; www.alianzafrancesa.org.ar; Av Córdoba 946; 9am-8pm Mon-Fri, 9am-1pm Sat; S Línea C Lavalle) Offers screenings of French films, exhibitions and a number of workshops and courses including French-language classes.

British Arts Centre (Map p246; 011-4393-6941; www.britishartscentre.org.ar; Suipacha 1333; S Línea C San Martín) Offers plays, dance performances, film screenings, art exhibitions and concerts that showcase British culture.

Instituto Cultural Argentino-Norteamericano (Map p234; 011-5382-1500; www.icana.org.ar; Maipú 672; S Línea C Lavalle) Focuses on English-language courses but also hosts occasional artistic talks and workshops.

Instituto Goethe (Map p234; 011-4318-5600; www.goethe.de/hs/bue; Av Corrientes 319; S Línea B Alem) German cultural center offering language classes and film screenings.

Post

The more-or-less reliable **Correo Argentino** (www.correoargentino.com.ar) is the government postal service, with numerous branches scattered throughout BA. Essential overseas mail should be sent *certificado* (registered). For international parcels weighing over 2kg, take a copy of your passport and go to the **Correo Internacional** (Map p246; 011-4891-9191; www.correoargentino.com.ar; Av Antártida Argentina 1100; 9am-3:30pm Mon-Fri; S Línea C Retiro) near the Retiro bus station. Check the website for all prices.

If a package is being sent to you, expect to wait awhile for it to turn up within the system (or to receive notice of its arrival). Unless you have a permanent address, your parcel will likely end up at the Correo Internacional. To collect the package you'll have to wait – first to get it and then to have it checked by customs. There might also be a small holding fee, charged per day. Don't expect any valuables to make it through.

Privately run international and national services are available including **Federal Express** (Map p234; 0810-333-3339; www.fedex.com; Maipú 753, Microcentro; 9am-6pm Mon-Fri; S Línea C Lavalle) and **DHL International** (Map p246; 0810-122-3345; www.dhl.com.ar; Av Córdoba 783; 9am-7pm Mon-Fri; S Línea C Lavalle). **OCA** (Map p234; 011-4311-5305; www.oca.com.ar; Viamonte 526; 8am-6pm Mon-Fri; S Línea C Lavalle) and **Andreani** (0810-122-1111; www.andreani.com.ar; Av Belgrano 1211; 9am-6pm Mon-Fri, to 1pm Sat; S Línea C Moreno) are good for domestic packages; both have many locations around town.

Public Holidays

Government offices and businesses are closed on the numerous national holidays.

Public-transportation options are more limited on holidays, when you should reserve tickets in advance.

January 1 Año Nuevo; New Year's Day

February or March Carnaval – dates vary; a Monday and Tuesday become holidays.

March 24 Día de la Memoria; anniversary of the military coup of 1976 and the subsequent dictatorship.

March/April Semana Santa (Easter week) – dates vary; most businesses close on Good Thursday and Good Friday; major travel week.

April 2 Día de las Malvinas; honors the fallen Argentine soldiers from the Islas Malvinas (Falkland Islands) war in 1829.

May 1 Día del Trabajor; Labor Day

May 25 Día de la Revolución de

Mayo; commemorates the 1810 revolution against Spain.

June 20 Día de la Bandera (Flag Day); anniversary of death of Manuel Belgrano, creator of Argentina's flag and military leader.

July 9 Día de la Independencia; Independence Day

August (third Monday) Día del Libertador San Martín; marks the anniversary of José de San Martín's death (1778–1850).

October (second Monday) Día del Respeto a la Diversidad Cultural; a day to respect cultural diversity.

November (fourth Monday) Día de la Soberanía Nacional; day of national sovereignty.

December 8 Día de la Concepción Inmaculada; celebrates the immaculate conception of the Virgin Mary.

December 25 Navidad; Christmas Day

Note that Christmas Eve and New Year's Eve are treated as semi-holidays, and you will find some businesses closed for the latter half of those days.

Safe Travel

Buenos Aires is generally pretty safe and you can comfortably walk around at all hours of the night in many places, even as a lone woman. Some areas where you should be careful at night, however, are around Constitución's train station, the eastern border of San Telmo, some parts of Once and La Boca – where, outside tourist streets, you should be careful even during the day. Using your head is good advice anywhere: don't flash any wealth (including expensive jewelry), always be aware of your surroundings and look like you know exactly where you're going (even if you don't).

Petty Crime

➡ Like all big cities, BA has its share of problems. As a tourist you're much more likely to be a target of petty crimes such as pickpocketing and bag-snatching than armed robbery or kidnapping.

➡ Be careful on crowded buses, on the Subte and at busy *ferias* (street markets). Don't put your bag down without your foot through the strap (especially at sidewalk cafes), and even then keep a close eye on it.

➡ Be especially careful at Retiro bus station.

➡ The **Tourist Police** (Comisaría del Turista; ☎0800-999-5000, 011-4346-5748; turista@policiafederal.gov.ar; Av Corrientes 436; ⏲24hr; Ⓢ Línea B Florída) can provide interpreters and help victims of robberies.

Police

➡ Police are generally helpful and courteous to tourists, though you're hardly likely to get involved with them if you follow the law.

➡ If you feel you're being patted down for a bribe (most often if you're driving), you can respond by tactfully paying up or asking the officer to accompany you to the police station to take care of it. The latter will likely cause the officer to drop it. Pretending you don't understand Spanish may also frustrate a potential bribe.

Pickets & Protests

Street protests have become part of daily life in Buenos Aires, especially around Plaza de Mayo and Av 9 de Julio. Generally these have little effect on tourists other than blocking traffic and making it difficult to see the sights.

ELECTRONICS WARNING

Buying a smartphone, especially an iPhone, is extremely expensive in Argentina due to import restrictions – and they are not widely available. If you do bring your smartphone, don't flash it around unnecessarily or leave it unprotected somewhere. This goes for tablets and laptop computers too.

Taxes & Refunds

One of Argentina's primary state revenue earners is the 21% value-added tax known as the Impuesto de Valor Agregado (IVA), which is included in the stated price of goods. Under limited circumstances, foreign visitors may obtain IVA refunds on purchases of Argentine products upon departing the country. A 'Tax Free' window decal (in English) identifies participants in this program, but always check that the shop is part of the tax-free program before making your purchase.

You can obtain tax refunds on purchases of AR$70 or more made at one of these participating stores. To do so, present your passport to the merchant, who will make out an invoice for you. On leaving the country keep the purchased items in your carry-on baggage. A customs official will check them and stamp your paperwork, then tell you where to obtain your refund. Be sure to leave yourself a bit of extra time at the airport to get this done.

In 2016 it was announced that IVA paid on hotel bills using foreign credit cards would also be refunded.

Telephone

Street phones require coins or *tarjetas telefónicas* (magnetic phone cards available at many *kioskos*, or small markets). You'll only be able to speak for a limited time before you get cut off, so carry enough credit.

Toll-free numbers in BA have '0800' before a seven-digit number.

Cell Phones

It's best to bring your own factory unlocked tri- or quad-band GSM cell phone, then buy an inexpensive SIM chip (you'll get a local number) and credits (or *cargo virtual*) as needed.

Both SIM chips and credits can be bought at many *kioskos* or *locutorios* (small telephone offices); look for the *'recarga facil'* signs. Many Argentines use this system with their cell phones, and you can buy SIM chips with data for wi-fi access as well. Phone-unlocking services are available; ask around.

You can also buy cell phones that use SIM chips; these usually include some credits for your first batch of calls.

If you plan to travel with an iPhone or other 3G smartphone, prepare yourself – you may need to purchase an international plan to avoid being hit by a huge bill for roaming costs. On the other hand, it's possible to call internationally for free or very cheaply using a VoIP (Voice over Internet Protocol) system such as Skype. This is a constantly changing field, so do some research before you travel.

Cell-phone numbers in Argentina are always preceded by '15.' If you're calling a cellular phone number from a landline, you'll have to dial 15 first. But if you're calling a cell phone from another cell phone, you don't need to dial 15 (at least within the same area code).

When calling cell phones from outside Argentina, dial your country's international access code, then 54 9 11 and then the eight-digit number, leaving out the 15.

Locutorios

One way to make a local or international phone call is to find a *locutorio*, a small telephone office with private booths from which you make your calls and then pay at the register. There's a *locutorio* on practically every other block in the Center.

When making international calls from *locutorios* ask about off-peak discount hours, which generally apply after 10pm and on weekends. Making international calls over the internet using Skype is a cheap option; many internet cafes have this system in place.

Phone Codes

The Buenos Aires area code is 011. You will need to dial this when calling BA from outside the city, but you don't need to dial it when calling from within BA.

Time

Argentina is three hours behind GMT and generally does not observe daylight-saving time (though this situation can easily change). Many *porteños* use the 24-hour clock to differentiate between am and pm.

Toilets

- ➡ Public toilets in BA are generally decent and usually stocked with toilet paper (carry some anyway), but soap and towels are rarer.
- ➡ If you're looking for a bathroom while walking around, note that the largest shopping malls (such as Galerías Pacífico) always have public bathrooms available, but in a pinch you can always walk into a large cafe.
- ➡ Changing facilities for babies are not always available.
- ➡ Some may find bidets a novelty; they are those strange shallow, ceramic bowls with knobs and a drain, often accompanying toilets in hotel bathrooms. They are meant for between-shower cleanings of nether regions. Turn knobs slowly, or you may end up spraying yourself or the ceiling.

LOCAL ETIQUETTE

Greetings Friends – including two men – always greet each other with a kiss on the cheek; if joining a small group, each person should be greeted and kissed. The gesture is repeated when saying goodbye.

Lines People in Buenos Aires are generally respectful of queues and you'll see orderly lines at bus stops. It's common to take a number in shops and doctors and wait to be called. In supermarkets and shops, people with babies and the elderly are often ushered to the front of the line.

Seats It's common for the young and fit to cede their seats on public transport to the elderly, children, pregnant women or anyone less able to stand.

Tourist Information

Ministerio de Turismo (Map p246; ☎011-4312-2232; www.turismo.gov.ar; Av Santa Fe 883; ⏰9am-7pm Mon-Fri; Ⓢ Línea C San Martín) Dispenses information on Buenos Aires but focuses on Argentina as a whole.

There are several tourist offices and kiosks in Buenos Aires. Staff speak English and can provide maps and information about free guided walks and other activities.

Ezeiza airport (☎011-5480-6111; Terminal A arrivals, 1st fl, Ezeiza airport; ⏰24hr)

Florida (Map p234; ☎for WhatsApp, 9am-6pm 011-2851-8074; cnr Florida & Roque Sáenz Peña; ⏰9am-6pm; Ⓢ Línea D Catedral)

La Boca (Map p242; ☎for WhatsApp messages 011-2851-8074; https://turismo.buenosaires.gob.ar; Av Don Pedro de Mendoza 1901; ⏰9am-6pm; wi-fi; bus 33, 64, 29)

Plaza San Martín (Map p246; ☎for WhatsApp 9am-6pm 011-2851-8074; cnr Av Florida & Marcelo T de Alvear; ⏰9am-6pm; Ⓢ Línea C San Martín)

Puerto Madero (Map p236; ☎for WhatsApp 9am-6pm 011-2851-8075; Dique 4, Juana M Gorriti 200; ⏰9am-6pm; Ⓢ Línea B Alem)

Recoleta (Map p244; ☎for WhatsApp 9am-6pm 011-2851-8047; https://turismo.buenosaires.gob.ar; Av Quintana 596; ⏰9am-6pm; bus 130, 62, 93)

Retiro (Map p246; Retiro Bus Station; ⏰9am-6pm; Ⓢ Línea C Retiro)

Travel Agencies

Say Hueque (☎011-5258-8740; www.sayhueque.com; Thames 2062; ⏰9am-6pm Mon-Fri, 10am-1pm Sat; Ⓢ Línea D Plaza Italia)

Tangol (☎011-4363-6000; www.tangol.com; Defensa 831; ⏰9am-6pm Mon-Sat, 10am-7pm Sun; Ⓢ Línea C Independencia)

Anda Responsible Travel (☎011-3221-0833; www.andatravel.com.ar; Billinghurst 1193, 3B; ⏰9am-6pm Mon-Fri; Ⓢ Línea D Agüero)

OFFICE SPACE

The brainchild of one of BA's many expat entrepreneurs, **Areatres** (☎011-5353-0333; www.areatresworkplace.com; Malabia 1720; ⏰8:30am-8pm Mon-Fri; Ⓢ Línea D Scalabrini Ortiz) is a secure working office where you can rent a desk or office. There are copy services, internet and wi-fi connections, networking social events, meeting rooms, a large presentation room and even a Zen-like patio for the stress-prone. Facilities are cutting-edge – it's like you never left Silicon Valley.

Travelers with Disabilities

Negotiating Buenos Aires as a disabled traveler is not the easiest of tasks. City sidewalks are narrow, busy and dotted with many broken tiles. Not every corner has a ramp, and traffic is ruthless when it comes to pedestrians (and wheelchair-users). A few buses do have *piso bajo* (they 'kneel' and have extra-large spaces), but the Subte (subway) does not cater to the mobility-impaired.

International hotel chains often have wheelchair-accessible rooms, as do other less fancy hotels – accessibility laws have changed for the better over the last few years. **Imagine Hotel** (Map p238; ☎011-4383-2230; www.imaginehotelboutique.com; México 1330; d/tr from US$100/145; air-con, internet, wi-fi; Ⓢ Línea E Independencia) in Congreso is fully accessible. Some restaurants and many important tourist sights have ramps, but BA is sorely lacking in wheelchair-accessible bathrooms – although the city's shopping malls usually have at least one, restaurants don't often have the appropriate installations.

In Buenos Aires, **QRV Transportes Especiales** (☎011-4306-6635, 011-15-6863-9555; www.qrvtransportes.com.ar) offers private transport and city tours in vans fully equipped for wheelchair users. **BA Cultural Concierge** (☎011-15-3876-5937; www.baculturalconcierge.com) offers service for low-mobility travelers, by helping with errands.

Other than the use of braille on ATMs little effort has been dedicated to bettering accessibility for the vision-impaired. Stoplights are rarely equipped with sound alerts. The **Biblioteca Argentina Para Ciegos** (Argentine Library for the Blind; BAC; ☎011-4981-0137; www.bac.org.ar; Lezica 3909; ⏰noon-7pm Mon-Fri; Ⓢ Línea A Castro Barros) FREE maintains a braille collection of over 3000 books, as well as other resources.

Download Lonely Planet's free Accessible Travel guide from http://lptravel.to/AccessibleTravel.

Visas

Nationals of the USA, Canada, European Union countries, Australia and New Zealand do not need visas to visit Argentina, but check current regulations. Most foreigners receive a 90-day visa upon arrival.

WORKING IN BUENOS AIRES

Unless you have a special skill, business and/or speak Spanish, it's hard to find work other than teaching English – or perhaps putting time in at a hostel or bar. And it's good to realize that you're not likely to get rich doing these things.

Native English-speakers usually work out of language institutes. Twenty hours a week of actual teaching is about enough for most people (note that you are not paid for travel time and prep time). Frustrations include dealing with unpleasant institutes, classes being spread throughout the day and canceled classes. Institute turnover is high and most people don't teach for more than a year.

A TEFL certification can certainly help but isn't mandatory for all jobs. You'll make more money teaching private students, but it takes time to gain a client base. And you should take into account slow periods like December through February, when many locals leave town on summer vacation.

To find a job, call up the institutes or visit expat bars and websites and start networking. March is when institutes are ramping up their courses, so it's the best time to find work. Many teachers work on tourist visas (which is not a big deal), heading over to Uruguay every three months for a new visa or visiting the **immigration office** (☎011-4317-0234; www.migraciones.gov.ar; Av Antártida Argentina 1355; ⏰7:30am-2pm Mon-Fri; 🚌92, 106) for a visa extension.

For general job listings check www.craigslist.org. You can also try posting on expat website forums such as www.baexpats.org.

For visa extensions, visit **immigration** (☎011-4317-0234; www.migraciones.gov.ar; Av Antártida Argentina 1355; ⏰7:30am-2pm Mon-Fri; 🚌92, 106). Set aside some time as this process can take an hour or two.

Another option if you're staying more than three months is to cross into Colonia or Montevideo (both in Uruguay; Colonia is an easy day trip) and return with a new three-month visa. This strategy is most sensible if you are from a country that does not require a visa to enter Uruguay.

Australians and Canadians need to pay a reciprocity fee before arriving in Argentina, see box on p205.

Women Travelers

Buenos Aires is a modern, sophisticated city, and women travelers – even those traveling alone – should not encounter many difficulties.

A few men feel the need to comment on a woman's attractiveness. This often happens when a woman is walking alone; it will never occur when she is with another man. Comments usually include whistles or *piropos*, which many Argentine males consider the art of complimenting a woman. *Piropos* are often vulgar, although some can be eloquent. The best thing to do is completely ignore the comments. After all, many *porteñas* are used to getting these 'compliments,' and most men don't necessarily mean to be insulting.

On the plus side of machismo, men will hold a door open for you and let you enter first, including getting on buses.

Language

Latin American Spanish pronunciation is easy, as most sounds have equivalents in English. Read our coloured pronunciation guides as if they were English, and you'll be understood. Note that kh is a throaty sound (like the 'ch' in the Scottish *loch*), v and b are like a soft English 'v' (between a 'v' and a 'b'), and r is strongly rolled. Also note that the letters *ll* (pronounced ly or simplified to y in most parts of Latin America) and *y* are pronounced like the 's' in 'measure' or the 'sh' in 'shut' in Buenos Aires, which gives the language its very own local flavor. In this chapter, we've used the symbol sh to represent this sound. You'll get used to this idiosyncracy very quickly listening to and taking your cues from the locals.

The stressed syllables are indicated with an acute accent in written Spanish (eg *días*) and with italics in our pronunciation guides.

The polite form is used in this chapter; where both polite and informal options are given, they are indicated by the abbreviations 'pol' and 'inf'. Where necessary, both masculine and feminine forms of words are included, separated by a slash and with the masculine form first, eg *perdido/a* (m/f).

BASICS

Hello.	*Hola.*	o·la
Goodbye.	*Adiós./Chau.*	a·dyos/chow
How are you?	*¿Qué tal?*	ke tal
Fine, thanks.	*Bien, gracias.*	byen gra·syas
Excuse me.	*Perdón.*	per·don
Sorry.	*Lo siento.*	lo syen·to
Please.	*Por favor.*	por fa·vor
Thank you.	*Gracias.*	gra·syas
You're welcome.	*De nada.*	de na·da
Yes./No.	*Sí./No.*	see/no

WANT MORE?

For in-depth language information and handy phrases, check out Lonely Planet's *Latin American Spanish phrasebook*. You'll find it at **shop.lonelyplanet.com**, or you can buy Lonely Planet's iPhone phrasebooks at the Apple App Store.

My name is ...
Me llamo ... — me sha·mo ...

What's your name?
¿Cómo se llama Usted? — ko·mo se sha·ma oo·ste (pol)
¿Cómo te llamas? — ko·mo te sha·mas (inf)

Do you speak English?
¿Habla inglés? — a·bla een·gles (pol)
¿Hablas inglés? — a·blas een·gles (inf)

I don't understand.
Yo no entiendo. — yo no en·tyen·do

ACCOMMODATIONS

I'd like a ... room.	*Quisiera una habitación ...*	kee·sye·ra oo·na a·bee·ta·syon ...
single	*individual*	een·dee·vee·dwal
double	*doble*	do·ble

How much is it per night/person?
¿Cuánto cuesta por noche/persona? — kwan·to kwes·ta por no·che/per·so·na

Does it include breakfast?
¿Incluye el desayuno? — een·kloo·she el de·sa·shoo·no

air-con	*aire acondicionado*	ai·re a·kon·dee·syo·na·do
bathroom	*baño*	ba·nyo
campsite	*terreno de cámping*	te·re·no de kam·peeng
guesthouse	*hostería*	os·te·ree·a
hotel	*hotel*	o·tel
youth hostel	*albergue juvenil*	al·ber·ge khoo·ve·neel
window	*ventana*	ven·ta·na

DIRECTIONS

Where's ...?
¿Dónde está ...? — don·de es·ta ...

What's the address?
¿Cuál es la dirección? — kwal es la dee·rek·syon

Could you please write it down?
¿Puede escribirlo, por favor? — pwe·de es·kree·beer·lo por fa·vor

Can you show me (on the map)?
¿Me lo puede indicar (en el mapa)? — me lo pwe·de een·dee·kar (en el ma·pa)

at the corner	*en la esquina*	en la es·kee·na
at the traffic lights	*en el semáforo*	en el se·ma·fo·ro
behind ...	*detrás de ...*	de·tras de ...
far	*lejos*	le·khos
in front of ...	*enfrente de ...*	en·fren·te de ...
left	*izquierda*	ees·kyer·da
near	*cerca*	ser·ka
next to ...	*al lado de ...*	al la·do de ...
opposite ...	*frente a ...*	fren·te a ...
right	*derecha*	de·re·cha
straight ahead	*todo recto*	to·do rek·to

EATING & DRINKING

Can I see the menu, please?
¿Puedo ver el menú, por favor? — pwe·do ver el me·noo por fa·vor

What would you recommend?
¿Qué me recomienda? — ke me re·ko·myen·da

Do you have vegetarian food?
¿Tienen comida vegetariana? — tye·nen ko·mee·da ve·khe·ta·rya·na

I don't eat (red meat).
No como (carne roja). — no ko·mo (kar·ne ro·kha)

That was delicious!
¡Estaba buenísimo! — es·ta·ba bwe·nee·see·mo

Cheers!
¡Salud! — sa·loo

The bill, please.
La cuenta, por favor. — la kwen·ta por fa·vor

Signs

Abierto	Open
Cerrado	Closed
Entrada	Entrance
Hombres/Varones	Men
Mujeres/Damas	Women
Prohibido	Prohibited
Salida	Exit
Servicios/Baños	Toilets

Question Words

How?	*¿Cómo?*	ko·mo
What?	*¿Qué?*	ke
When?	*¿Cuándo?*	kwan·do
Where?	*¿Dónde?*	don·de
Who?	*¿Quién?*	kyen
Why?	*¿Por qué?*	por ke

I'd like a table for ...	*Quisiera una mesa para ...*	kee·sye·ra oo·na me·sa pa·ra ...
(eight) o'clock	*las (ocho)*	las (o·cho)
(two) people	*(dos) personas*	(dos) per·so·nas

Key Words

appetisers	*aperitivos*	a·pe·ree·tee·vos
bottle	*botella*	bo·te·sha
bowl	*bol*	bol
breakfast	*desayuno*	de·sa·shoo·no
children's menu	*menú infantil*	me·noo een·fan·teel
(too) cold	*(muy) frío*	(mooy) free·o
dinner	*cena*	se·na
food	*comida*	ko·mee·da
fork	*tenedor*	te·ne·dor
glass	*vaso*	va·so
hot (warm)	*caliente*	ka·lyen·te
knife	*cuchillo*	koo·chee·yo
lunch	*almuerzo*	al·mwer·so
main course	*plato principal*	pla·to preen·see·pal
plate	*plato*	pla·to
restaurant	*restaurante*	res·tow·ran·te
spoon	*cuchara*	koo·cha·ra
with	*con*	kon
without	*sin*	seen

Meat & Fish

beef	*carne de vaca*	kar·ne de va·ka
chicken	*pollo*	po·sho
duck	*pato*	pa·to
fish	*pescado*	pes·ka·do
lamb	*cordero*	kor·de·ro
pork	*cerdo*	ser·do
turkey	*pavo*	pa·vo
veal	*ternera*	ter·ne·ra

Fruit & Vegetables

apple	*manzana*	man·sa·na
apricot	*damasco*	da·*mas*·ko
artichoke	*alcaucil*	al·*kow*·seel
asparagus	*espárragos*	es·*pa*·ra·gos
banana	*banana*	ba·*na*·na
beans	*chauchas*	*chow*·chas
beetroot	*remolacha*	re·mo·*la*·cha
cabbage	*repollo*	re·*po*·sho
carrot	*zanahoria*	sa·na·*o*·rya
celery	*apio*	*a*·pyo
cherry	*cereza*	se·*re*·sa
corn	*choclo*	*cho*·klo
cucumber	*pepino*	pe·*pee*·no
fruit	*fruta*	*froo*·ta
grape	*uvas*	*oo*·vas
lemon	*limón*	lee·*mon*
lentils	*lentejas*	len·*te*·khas
lettuce	*lechuga*	le·*choo*·ga
mushroom	*champiñón*	cham·pee·*nyon*
nuts	*nueces*	*nwe*·ses
onion	*cebolla*	se·*bo*·sha
orange	*naranja*	na·*ran*·kha
peach	*durazno*	doo·*ras*·no
peas	*arvejas*	ar·*ve*·khas
(red/green) pepper	*pimiento (rojo/verde)*	pee·*myen*·to (*ro*·kho/*ver*·de)
pineapple	*ananá*	a·na·*na*
plum	*ciruela*	seer·*we*·la
potato	*papa*	*pa*·pa
pumpkin	*zapallo*	sa·*pa*·sho
spinach	*espinacas*	es·pee·*na*·kas
strawberry	*frutilla*	froo·*tee*·sha
tomato	*tomate*	to·*ma*·te
vegetable	*verdura*	ver·*doo*·ra
watermelon	*sandía*	san·*dee*·a

Other

bread	*pan*	pan
butter	*manteca*	man·*te*·ka
cheese	*queso*	*ke*·so
egg	*huevo*	*we*·vo
honey	*miel*	myel
jam	*mermelada*	mer·me·*la*·da
oil	*aceite*	a·*sey*·te
pasta	*pasta*	*pas*·ta
pepper	*pimienta*	pee·*myen*·ta
rice	*arroz*	a·*ros*
salt	*sal*	sal
sugar	*azúcar*	a·*soo*·kar
vinegar	*vinagre*	vee·*na*·gre

LUNFARDO

Below are are some of the spicier *lunfardo* (slang) terms you may hear on your travels in Argentina.

boliche – disco or nightclub
boludo – jerk, asshole, idiot; often used in a friendly fashion, but a deep insult to a stranger
bondi – bus
buena onda – good vibes
carajo – asshole, prick; bloody hell
chabón/chabona – kid, guy/girl (term of endearment)
che – hey
diez puntos – OK, cool, fine (literally '10 points')
fiaca – laziness
guita – money
laburo – job
macanudo – great, fabulous
mango – one peso
masa – a great, cool thing
mina – woman
morfar – eat
pendejo – idiot
piba/pibe – cool young guy/girl
piola – cool, clever
pucho – cigarette
re – very, eg *re interestante* (very interesting)
trucho – fake , imitation , bad quality

¡Ponete las pilas! – Get on with it! (literally 'Put in the batteries!')

Me mataste. – I don't know; I have no idea. (literally 'You've killed me')

Le faltan un par de jugadores. – He's not playing with a full deck. (literally 'He's a couple of players short')

che boludo – The most *porteño* phrase on earth. Ask a friendly local youth to explain.

Drinks

beer	*cerveza*	ser·*ve*·sa
coffee	*café*	ka·*fe*

Numbers

1	*uno*	*oo*·no
2	*dos*	dos
3	*tres*	tres
4	*cuatro*	*kwa*·tro
5	*cinco*	*seen*·ko
6	*seis*	seys
7	*siete*	*sye*·te
8	*ocho*	*o*·cho
9	*nueve*	*nwe*·ve
10	*diez*	dyes
20	*veinte*	*veyn*·te
30	*treinta*	*treyn*·ta
40	*cuarenta*	kwa·*ren*·ta
50	*cincuenta*	seen·*kwen*·ta
60	*sesenta*	se·*sen*·ta
70	*setenta*	se·*ten*·ta
80	*ochenta*	o·*chen*·ta
90	*noventa*	no·*ven*·ta
100	*cien*	syen
1000	*mil*	meel

(orange) juice	*jugo (de naranja)*	*khoo*·go (de na·*ran*·kha)
milk	*leche*	*le*·che
tea	*té*	te
(mineral) water	*agua (mineral)*	*a*·gwa (mee·ne·*ral*)
(red/white) wine	*vino (tinto/ blanco)*	*vee*·no (*teen*·to/ *blan*·ko)

EMERGENCIES

Help!	*¡Socorro!*	so·*ko*·ro
Go away!	*¡Vete!*	*ve*·te

Call ...!	*¡Llame a ...!*	*sha*·me a ...
a doctor	*un médico*	oon *me*·dee·ko
the police	*la policía*	la po·lee·*see*·a

I'm lost.
Estoy perdido/a. es·*toy* per·*dee*·do/a (m/f)

I'm ill.
Estoy enfermo/a. es·*toy* en·*fer*·mo/a (m/f)

I'm allergic to (antibiotics).
Soy alérgico/a a (los antibióticos). soy a·*ler*·khee·ko/a a (los an·tee·*byo*·tee·kos) (m/f)

Where are the toilets?
¿Dónde están los baños? *don*·de es·*tan* los *ba*·nyos

SHOPPING & SERVICES

I'd like to buy ...
Quisiera comprar ... kee·*sye*·ra kom·*prar* ...

I'm just looking.
Sólo estoy mirando. *so*·lo es·*toy* mee·*ran*·do

Can I look at it?
¿Puedo verlo? *pwe*·do *ver*·lo

I don't like it.
No me gusta. no me *goos*·ta

How much is it?
¿Cuánto cuesta? *kwan*·to *kwes*·ta

That's too expensive.
Es muy caro. es mooy *ka*·ro

Can you lower the price?
¿Podría bajar un poco el precio? po·*dree*·a ba·*khar* oon *po*·ko el *pre*·syo

There's a mistake in the bill.
Hay un error en la cuenta. ai oon e·*ror* en la *kwen*·ta

ATM	*cajero automático*	ka·*khe*·ro ow·to·*ma*·tee·ko
credit card	*tarjeta de crédito*	tar·*khe*·ta de *kre*·dee·to
internet cafe	*cibercafé*	see·ber·ka·*fe*
market	*mercado*	mer·*ka*·do
post office	*correos*	ko·*re*·os
tourist office	*oficina de turismo*	o·fee·*see*·na de too·*rees*·mo

TIME & DATES

What time is it?	*¿Qué hora es?*	ke *o*·ra es
It's (10) o'clock.	*Son (las diez).*	son (las dyes)
It's half past (one).	*Es (la una) y media.*	es (la *oo*·na) ee *me*·dya

morning	*mañana*	ma·*nya*·na
afternoon	*tarde*	*tar*·de
evening	*noche*	*no*·che
yesterday	*ayer*	a·*sher*
today	*hoy*	oy
tomorrow	*mañana*	ma·*nya*·na
Monday	*lunes*	*loo*·nes
Tuesday	*martes*	*mar*·tes
Wednesday	*miércoles*	*myer*·ko·les
Thursday	*jueves*	*khwe*·ves
Friday	*viernes*	*vyer*·nes
Saturday	*sábado*	*sa*·ba·do
Sunday	*domingo*	do·*meen*·go

EL VOSEO

Spanish in the Río de la Plata region differs from that of Spain and the rest of the Americas, most notably in the use of the informal form of 'you'. Instead of *tuteo* (the use of *tú*), Argentines commonly speak with *voseo* (the use of *vos*), a relic from 16th-century Spanish requiring slightly different grammar. All verbs change in spelling, stress and pronunciation. Examples of verbs ending in *-ar*, *-er* and *-ir* are given below; the *tú* forms are included to illustrate the contrast. Imperative forms (commands) also differ, but negative imperatives are identical in *tuteo* and *voseo*.

The Spanish phrases in this chapter use the *vos* form. An Argentine inviting a foreigner to address him or her informally will say *Me podés tutear* (literally 'You can address me with *tú*'), even though they'll use the *vos* forms in subsequent conversation.

Verb	Tuteo	Voseo
hablar (speak): You speak./Speak!	*Tú hablas./¡Habla!*	*Vos hablás./¡Hablá!*
comer (eat): You eat./Eat!	*Tú comes./¡Come!*	*Vos comés./¡Comé!*
venir (come): You come./Come!	*Tú vienes./¡Ven!*	*Vos venís./¡Vení!*

TRANSPORTATION

boat	*barco*	bar·ko
bus	*colectivo/ micro*	ko·lek·tee·vo/ mee·kro
plane	*avión*	a·vyon
train	*tren*	tren

first	*primero*	pree·me·ro
last	*último*	ool·tee·mo
next	*próximo*	prok·see·mo

A ... ticket, please.	*Un boleto de ..., por favor.*	oon bo·lee·to de ... por fa·vor
1st-class	*primera clase*	pree·me·ra kla·se
2nd-class	*segunda clase*	se·goon·da kla·se
one-way	*ida*	ee·da
return	*ida y vuelta*	ee·da ee vwel·ta

I want to go to ...
Quisiera ir a ... kee·sye·ra eer a ...

Does it stop at ...?
¿Para en ...? pa·ra en ...

What stop is this?
¿Cuál es esta parada? kwal es es·ta pa·ra·da

What time does it arrive/leave?
¿A qué hora llega/sale? a ke o·ra she·ga/sa·le

Please tell me when we get to ...
¿Puede avisarme cuando lleguemos a ...? pwe·de a·vee·sar·me kwan·do she·ge·mos a ...

I want to get off here.
Quiero bajarme aquí. kye·ro ba·khar·me a·kee

airport	*aeropuerto*	a·e·ro·pwer·to
bus stop	*parada de colectivo*	pa·ra·da de ko·lek·tee·vo
platform	*plataforma*	pla·ta·for·ma
ticket office	*taquilla*	ta·kee·sha
timetable	*horario*	o·ra·ryo
train station	*estación de trenes*	es·ta·syon de tre·nes
I'd like to hire a ...	*Quisiera alquilar ...*	kee·sye·ra al·kee·lar ...
bicycle	*una bicicleta*	oo·na bee·see·kle·ta
car	*un coche/ auto*	oon ko·che/ aw·to
motorcycle	*una moto*	oo·na mo·to

helmet	*casco*	kas·ko
hitchhike	*hacer dedo*	a·ser de·do
mechanic	*mecánico*	me·ka·nee·ko
petrol/gas	*nafta*	naf·ta
service station	*estación de servicio*	es·ta·syon de ser·vee·syo
truck	*camion*	ka·myon

Is this the road to ...?
¿Se va a ... por esta carretera? se va a ... por es·ta ka·re·te·ra

Can I park here?
¿Puedo estacionar acá? pwe·do e·sta·syo·nar a·ka

The car has broken down.
El coche se ha averiado. el ko·che se a a·ve·rya·do

I've run out of petrol.
Me he quedado sin nafta. me e ke·da·do seen naf·ta

I have a flat tyre.
Tengo una goma pinchada. ten·go oo·na ·go·ma peen·cha·da

Behind the Scenes

SEND US YOUR FEEDBACK

We love to hear from travelers – your comments keep us on our toes and help make our books better. Our well-traveled team reads every word on what you loved or loathed about this book. Although we cannot reply individually to your submissions, we always guarantee that your feedback goes straight to the appropriate authors, in time for the next edition. Each person who sends us information is thanked in the next edition – the most useful submissions are rewarded with a selection of digital PDF chapters.

Visit **lonelyplanet.com/contact** to submit your updates and suggestions or to ask for help. Our award-winning website also features inspirational travel stories, news and discussions.

Note: We may edit, reproduce and incorporate your comments in Lonely Planet products such as guidebooks, websites and digital products, so let us know if you don't want your comments reproduced or your name acknowledged. For a copy of our privacy policy visit lonelyplanet.com/privacy.

OUR READERS

Many thanks to the travelers who used the last edition and wrote to us with helpful hints, useful advice and interesting anecdotes: Borja Garcia, Bryce Bui, Greg Smith, Laura Cavatorta, Lucia Ledesma, Núria Sugranyes, Olivia Butterman, Owen Jones, Stan Jones

WRITER THANKS

Isabel Albiston

Huge thanks to Alan and Liz Seabright-Grear for your help, to MaSovaida Morgan and to Stefan Arestis and Sebastien Chaneac aka the Nomadic Boys. *Muchísimas gracias* to Jazmin Arellano for accompanying me on my research missions and to Cesar Saenz for picking me up from Ezeiza early on a Monday morning. *Besos* to all my friends in Buenos Aires, especially Cecilia Martínez, Patricio Santos, Bárbaro Poey, Patricia Franco, Nano Aznarez and Facundo Santos Martínez; thanks for your friendship and support.

ACKNOWLEDGEMENTS

Climate map data adapted from Peel MC, Finlayson BL & McMahon TA (2007) 'Updated World Map of the Köppen-Geiger Climate Classification', Hydrology and Earth System Sciences, 11, 163344.

Cover photograph: View of El Caminito, La Boca, Karol Kozlowski/AWL©

HIS BOOK

his 8th edition of Lonely lanet's *Buenos Aires* guide-ook was researched and ritten by Isabel Albiston, ho also curated it. The revious edition was written y Sandra Bao, who also rote the 6th edition along with Bridget Gleeson. This guidebook was produced by the following:

Destination Editor MaSovaida Morgan
Product Editor Jenna Myers
Senior Cartographer Mark Griffiths
Book Designer Virginia Moreno
Assisting Editors Imogen Bannister, Anne Mulvaney, Lauren O'Connell
Assisting Cartographer Hunor Csutoros
Cover Researcher Naomi Parker
Thanks to Paul Harding, Liz Heynes, Kate Mathews, Vicky Smith, Tony Wheeler

See also separate subindexes for:
- EATING P229
- DRINKING & NIGHTLIFE P230
- ENTERTAINMENT P230
- SHOPPING P230
- SPORTS & ACTIVITIES P231
- SLEEPING P231

Index

Sights 000
Map Pages **000**
Photo Pages **000**

Sights 000
Map Pages **000**
Photo Pages **000**

ENTERTAINMENT

SHOPPING

Sights 000
Map Pages **000**
Photo Pages **000**

Buenos Aires Maps

Sights

- Beach
- Bird Sanctuary
- Buddhist
- Castle/Palace
- Christian
- Confucian
- Hindu
- Islamic
- Jain
- Jewish
- Monument
- Museum/Gallery/Historic Building
- Ruin
- Shinto
- Sikh
- Taoist
- Winery/Vineyard
- Zoo/Wildlife Sanctuary
- Other Sight

Activities, Courses & Tours

- Bodysurfing
- Diving
- Canoeing/Kayaking
- Course/Tour
- Sento Hot Baths/Onsen
- Skiing
- Snorkeling
- Surfing
- Swimming/Pool
- Walking
- Windsurfing
- Other Activity

Sleeping

- Sleeping
- Camping

Eating

- Eating

Drinking & Nightlife

- Drinking & Nightlife
- Cafe

Entertainment

- Entertainment

Shopping

- Shopping

Information

- Bank
- Embassy/Consulate
- Hospital/Medical
- Internet
- Police
- Post Office
- Telephone
- Toilet
- Tourist Information
- Other Information

Geographic

- Beach
- Gate
- Hut/Shelter
- Lighthouse
- Lookout
- Mountain/Volcano
- Oasis
- Park
- Pass
- Picnic Area
- Waterfall

Population

- Capital (National)
- Capital (State/Province)
- City/Large Town
- Town/Village

Transport

- Airport
- Border crossing
- Bus
- Cable car/Funicular
- Cycling
- Ferry
- Metro station
- Monorail
- Parking
- Petrol station
- Subway/Subte station
- Taxi
- Train station/Railway
- Tram
- Underground station
- Other Transport

Note: Not all symbols displayed above appear on the maps in this book

Routes

- Tollway
- Freeway
- Primary
- Secondary
- Tertiary
- Lane
- Unsealed road
- Road under construction
- Plaza/Mall
- Steps
- Tunnel
- Pedestrian overpass
- Walking Tour
- Walking Tour detour
- Path/Walking Trail

Boundaries

- International
- State/Province
- Disputed
- Regional/Suburb
- Marine Park
- Cliff
- Wall

Hydrography

- River, Creek
- Intermittent River
- Canal
- Water
- Dry/Salt/Intermittent Lake
- Reef

Areas

- Airport/Runway
- Beach/Desert
- Cemetery (Christian)
- Cemetery (Other)
- Glacier
- Mudflat
- Park/Forest
- Sight (Building)
- Sportsground
- Swamp/Mangrove

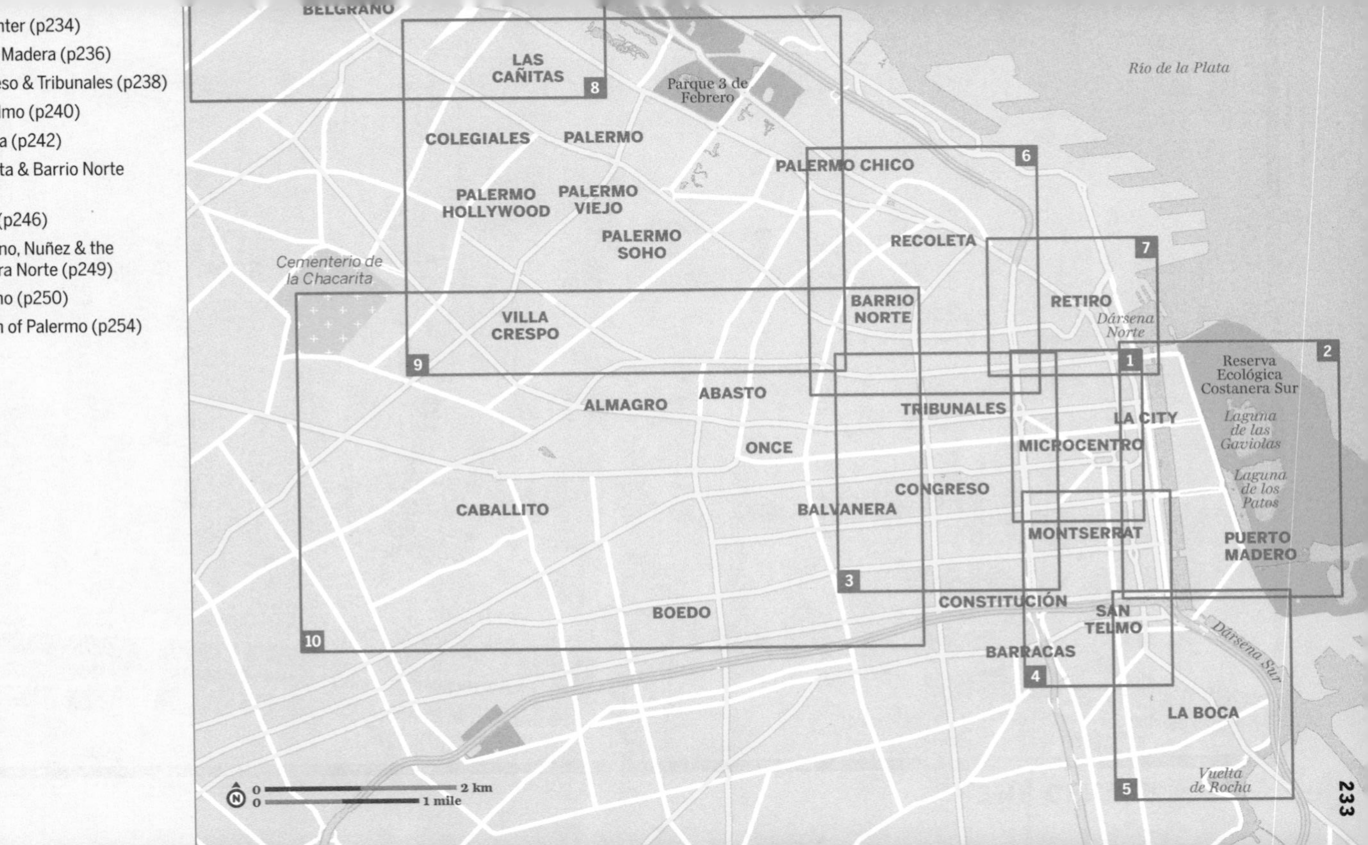
Río de la Plata
BELGRANO
LAS CAÑITAS
Parque 3 de Febrero
COLEGIALES
PALERMO
PALERMO CHICO
PALERMO HOLLYWOOD
PALERMO VIEJO
PALERMO SOHO
RECOLETA
Cementerio de la Chacarita
RETIRO
Dársena Norte
BARRIO NORTE
VILLA CRESPO
Reserva Ecológica Costanera Sur
ALMAGRO
ABASTO
TRIBUNALES
LA CITY
Laguna de las Gaviolas
ONCE
MICROCENTRO
Laguna de los Patos
CONGRESO
CABALLITO
BALVANERA
MONTSERRAT
PUERTO MADERO
CONSTITUCIÓN
BOEDO
SAN TELMO
Dársena Sur
BARRACAS
LA BOCA
Vuelta de Rocha
0 2 km
0 1 mile
1
2
3
4
5
6
7
8
9
10

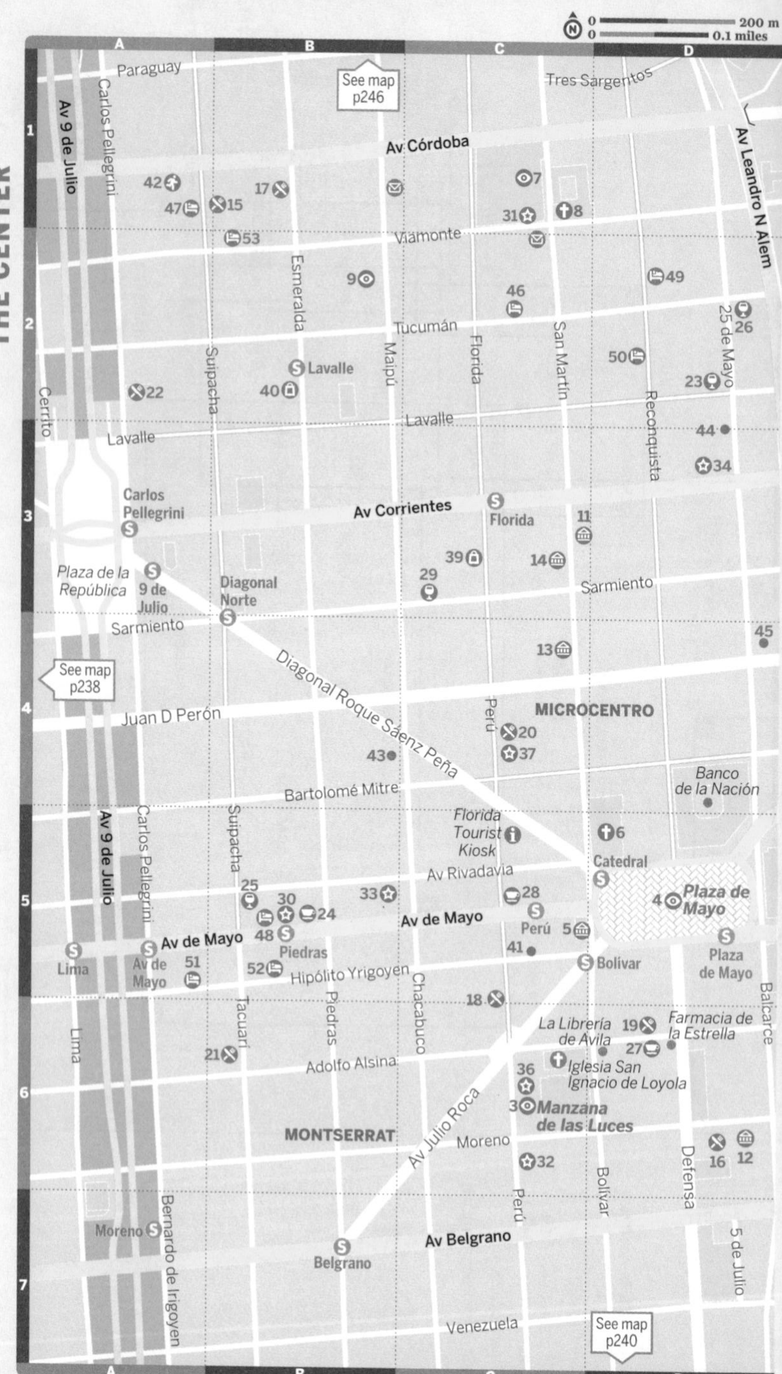

200 m
0.1 miles
See map p246
See map p238
See map p240
Paraguay
Tres Sargentos
Av Córdoba
Viamonte
Tucumán
Lavalle
Av Corrientes
Sarmiento
Juan D Perón
Bartolomé Mitre
Av Rivadavia
Av de Mayo
Hipólito Yrigoyen
Adolfo Alsina
Moreno
Av Belgrano
Venezuela
Av 9 de Julio
Carlos Pellegrini
Cerrito
Suipacha
Esmeralda
Maipú
Florida
San Martín
Reconquista
25 de Mayo
Av Leandro N Alem
Diagonal Roque Sáenz Peña
Perú
Tacuarí
Piedras
Chacabuco
Bolívar
Defensa
Balcarce
Lima
Bernardo de Irigoyen
Av Julio Roca
5 de Julio
MICROCENTRO
MONTSERRAT
Carlos Pellegrini
Plaza de la República
9 de Julio
Diagonal Norte
Lavalle
Florida
Catedral
Perú
Bolívar
Plaza de Mayo
Lima
Av de Mayo
Piedras
Moreno
Belgrano
Banco de la Nación
Florida Tourist Kiosk
Plaza de Mayo
La Librería de Avila
Farmacia de la Estrella
Iglesia San Ignacio de Loyola
Manzana de las Luces

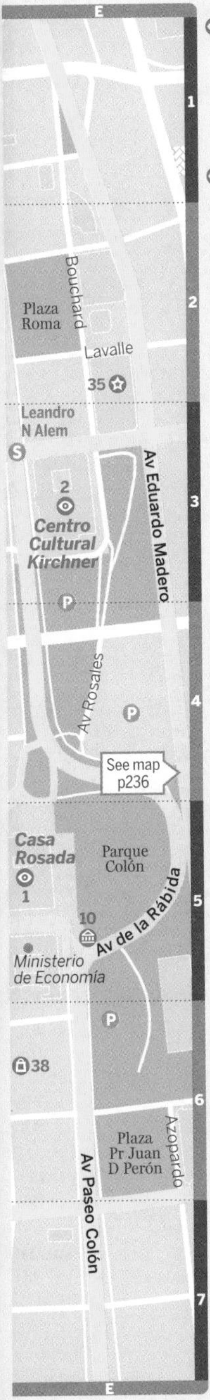

E
1
2
3
4
5
6
7
Bouchard
Plaza Roma
Lavalle
35
Leandro N Alem
Av Eduardo Madero
2
Centro Cultural Kirchner
Av Rosales
See map p236
Casa Rosada
1
Parque Colón
Av de la Rábida
10
Ministerio de Economía
38
Plaza Pr Juan D Perón
Azopardo
Av Paseo Colón
E

Top Sights (p58)

1 Casa Rosada........E5
2 Centro Cultural Kirchner.....E3
3 Manzana de las Luces........C6
4 Plaza de Mayo........D5

Sights (p59)

5 Cabildo........C5
6 Catedral Metropolitana........D5
7 Galerías Pacífico........C1
8 Iglesia Santa Catalina........C1
9 Instituto Cultural Argentino-Norteamericano........B2
10 Museo Casa Rosada........E5
11 Museo de la Policía Federal........C3
12 Museo Etnográfico Juan B Ambrosetti........D6
13 Museo Histórico y Numismático José Evaristo Uriburu........C4
14 Museo Mitre........C3
Museo Mundial del Tango........(see 30)

Eating (p63)

15 180 Burger Bar........B1
16 Aldo's Restoran & Vinoteca........D6
17 Broccolino........B1
18 D'Oro........C5
19 Furaibo........D6
20 Granix........C4
21 Latino Sandwich........B6
22 Tomo 1........A2
Vita........(see 41)

Drinking & Nightlife (p65)

23 Bahrein........D2
24 Café Tortoni........B5
25 Cocoliche........B5
26 La Cigale........D2
27 La Puerto Rico........D6
28 London City........C5
29 New Brighton........C3

Entertainment (p66)

30 Academia Nacional del Tango........B5
31 Centro Cultural Borges........C1
32 El Querandí........C6
33 Federación Argentina de Pato........B5
34 Instituto Goethe........D3
35 Luna Park........E2
36 Patio de Tango........C6
37 Piazzolla Tango........C4

Shopping (p67)

38 Arte y Esperanza........E6
39 El Ateneo........C3
40 El Coleccionista........B2

Sports & Activities (p208)

41 Academia Buenos Aires........C5
42 Alianza Francesa........A1
43 Buenos Aires Bus........B4
44 Expanish........D3
45 University of Buenos Aires........D4

Sleeping (p170)

46 Claridge Hotel........C2
47 Goya Hotel........A1
48 Gran Hotel Hispano........B5
49 Hotel Facón Grande........D2
50 Hotel Lafayette........D2
51 Milhouse Youth Hostel........A5
52 Portal del Sur........B5
53 V & S Hostel Club........B2

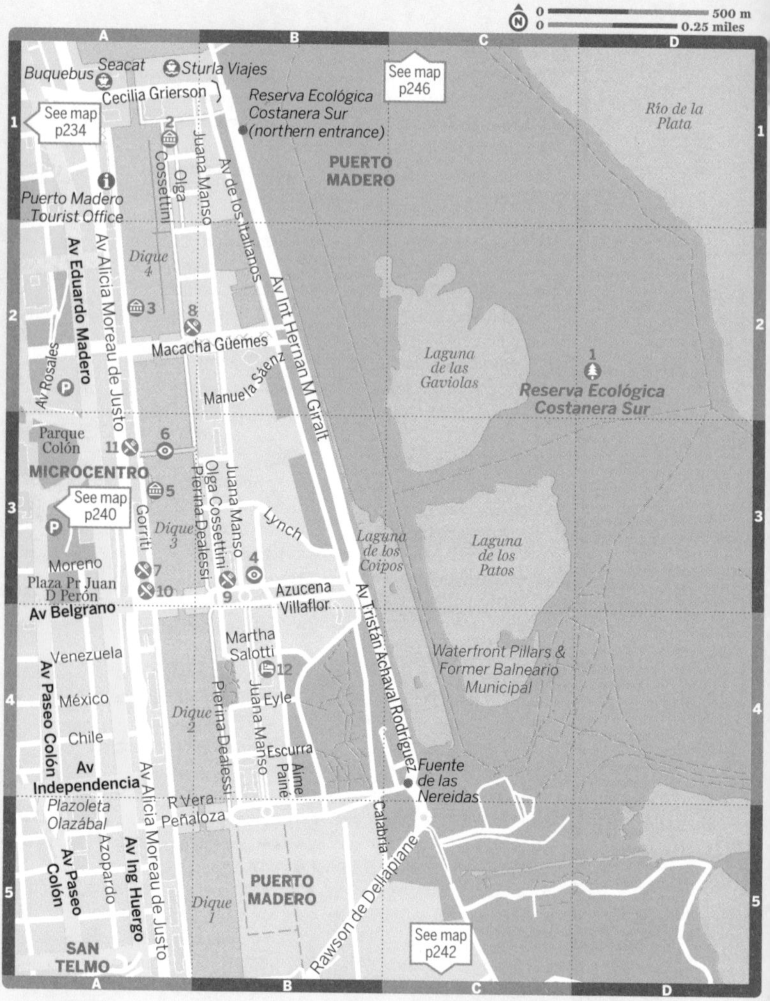

Top Sights (p72)

1 Reserva Ecológica Costanera Sur D2

Sights (p73)

2 Colección de Arte Amalia Lacroze de Fortabat A1
3 Corbeta Uruguay A2
4 Faena Arts Center B3
5 Fragata Sarmiento A3
6 Puente de la Mujer A3

Eating (p74)

7 Chila A3
8 i Central Market A2
9 i Fresh Market B3
La Parolaccia del Mare .... (see 10)
10 La Parolaccia Trattoria A3
11 Le Grill A3

Entertainment (p75)

Rojo Tango .... (see 12)

Sleeping (p171)

12 Faena Hotel + Universe B4

CONGRESO & TRIBUNALES *Map on p238*

Top Sights (p78)

1 Museo Botica del Ángel ... E7
2 Palacio Barolo ... E5
3 Teatro Colón ... F2

Sights (p79)

4 Centro Cultural San Martín ... D3
Museo del Agua y de la Historia Sanitaria ... (see 7)
5 Museo Judío de Buenos Aires ... F1
6 Obelisco ... F3
7 Palacio de las Aguas Corrientes ... C2
8 Plaza Lavalle ... E2
9 Teatro Nacional Cervantes ... F1

Eating (p80)

10 Aramburu ... F8
11 Aramburu Bis ... F8
12 Cadore ... D3
13 Chan Chan ... E5
14 Chiquín ... D3
15 El Cuartito ... E1
16 Parrilla Peña ... D2
17 Pizzería Güerrín ... E3
18 Plaza Asturias ... F4

Drinking & Nightlife (p83)

19 El Gato Negro ... D3
20 Los 36 Billares ... F4
21 Los Galgos ... C2

Entertainment (p83)

22 Café de los Angelitos ... B5
Centro Cultural Ricardo Rojas ... (see 23)
23 Cosmos-UBA ... B3
24 El Beso ... C3
25 Espacio INCAA Gaumont ... D4
26 Tango Porteño ... F2
27 Teatro Avenida ... F5
28 Teatro Paseo la Plaza ... D3
29 Teatro San Martín ... D3

Shopping (p84)

30 Zivals ... C3

Sports & Activities (p208

31 BA Free Tour ... D5

Sleeping (p171)

32 Gran Hotel Oriental ... C4
33 Hostel Estoril ... E4
34 Hotel Bonito ... E7
35 Hotel Lyon ... C4
36 Hotel Marbella ... F4
37 Imagine Hotel ... E7
38 Livin' Residence ... C2
39 Novotel Hotel ... E3
40 Sabatico Hostel ... E7

CONGRESO & TRIBUNALES

Congreso
Av Rivadavia
31
Av de Mayo
2
27
Alberti
Av Rivadavia
Pasco
22
Palacio del Congreso
Monumento a los Dos Congresos
Sáenz Peña
Palacio Barolo
13
Hipólito Yrigoyen
Plaza 1 de Mayo
Adolfo Alsina
CONGRESO
Adolfo Alsina
Moreno
Moreno
Belgrano
BALVANERA
Moreno
Av Belgrano
See map p254
Av Belgrano
Venezuela
MONTSERRAT
Virrey Cevallos
Luis Sáenz Peña
San José
Santiago del Estero
Salta
Lima
Av 9 de Julio
Bernardo de Irigoyen
Tacuarí
Combate de los Pozos
Av Entre Ríos
Solís
Museo Botica del Ángel
1
40
37
34
México
See map p240
Venezuela
Rincón
México
Sarandí
México
Pasco
Chile
Chile
Independencia
Av Independencia
Av Independencia
Estados Unidos
CONSTITUCIÓN
Salta
Virrey Cevallos
Estados Unidos
Carlos Calvo
10
11
Humberto Primo
5
6
7
8
A
B
C
D
E
F
G

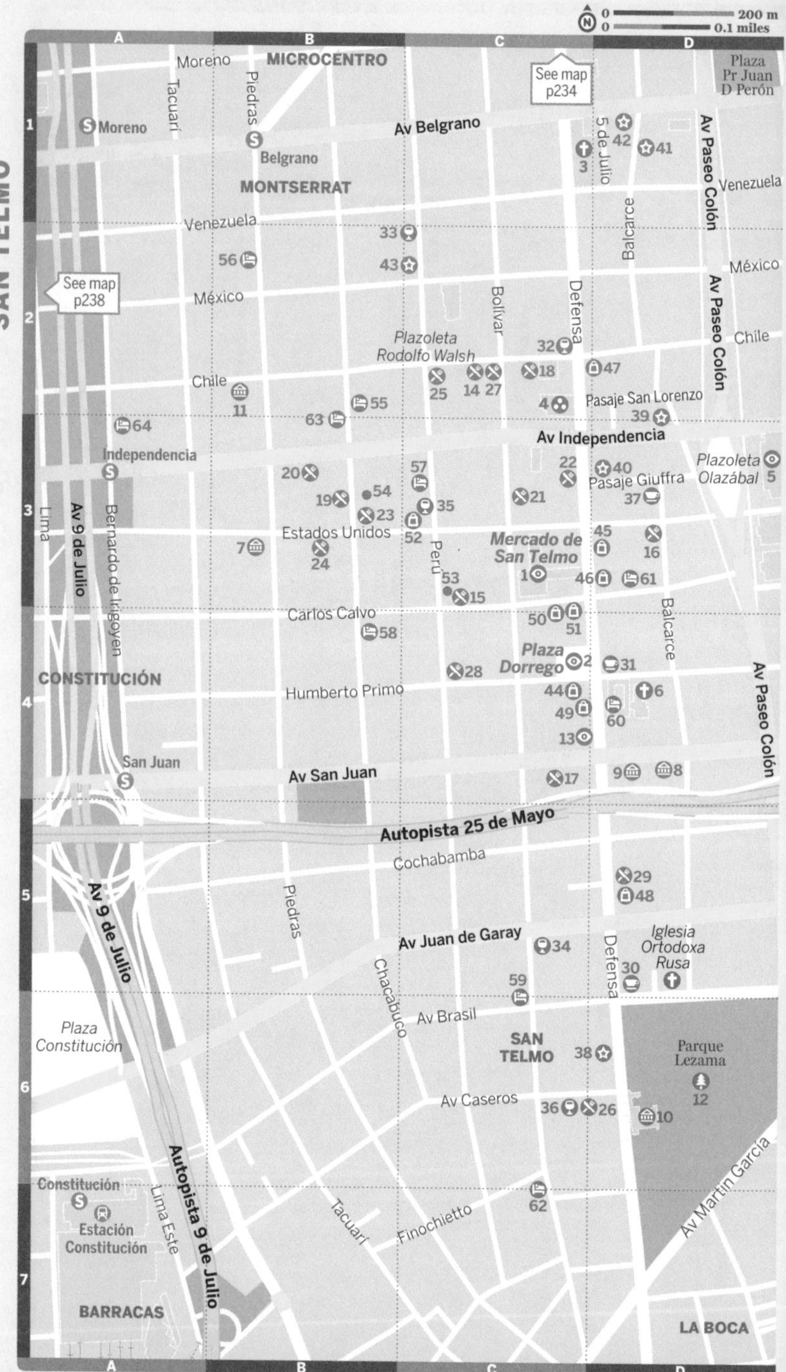

MICROCENTRO
MONTSERRAT
CONSTITUCIÓN
SAN TELMO
BARRACAS
LA BOCA
See map p234
See map p238
Moreno
Tacuarí
Piedras
Av Belgrano
Belgrano
5 de Julio
Av Paseo Colón
Venezuela
Balcarce
México
Bolívar
Defensa
Chile
Plazoleta Rodolfo Walsh
Pasaje San Lorenzo
Av Independencia
Independencia
Plazoleta Olazábal
Pasaje Giuffra
Lima
Av 9 de Julio
Bernardo de Irigoyen
Estados Unidos
Perú
Mercado de San Telmo
Carlos Calvo
Plaza Dorrego
Humberto Primo
San Juan
Av San Juan
Autopista 25 de Mayo
Cochabamba
Av Juan de Garay
Chacabuco
Iglesia Ortodoxa Rusa
Av Brasil
Plaza Constitución
Parque Lezama
Av Caseros
Av Martín García
Constitución
Estación Constitución
Lima Este
Autopista 9 de Julio
Tacuarí
Finochietto
Plaza Pr Juan D Perón
200 m
0.1 miles

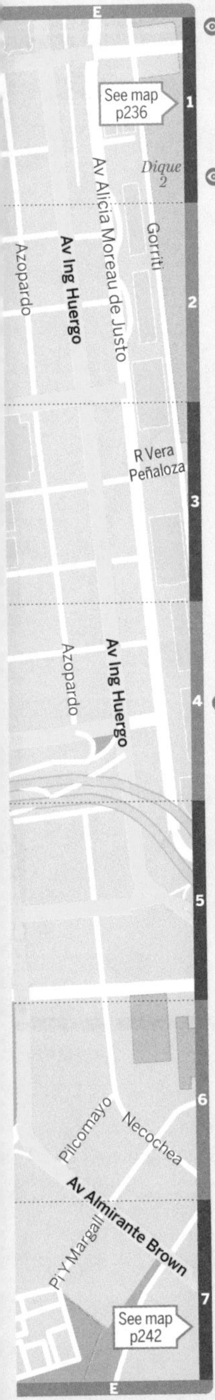
E
See map p236
1
Dique 2
Av Alicia Moreau de Justo
Gorriti
Azopardo
Av Ing Huergo
2
R Vera Peñaloza
3
Azopardo
Av Ing Huergo
4
5
6
Pilcomayo
Necochea
Av Almirante Brown
Pi Y Margall
7
See map p242
E

Top Sights (p87)

Feria de San Telmo........................(see 2)
1 Mercado de San Telmo....... C3
2 Plaza Dorrego........................ C4

Sights (p88)

3 Basílica de Nuestra Señora del Rosario C1
4 El Zanjón de Granados........ C2
5 Facultad de Ingeniería......... D3
6 Iglesia San Pedro González Telmo D4
7 Museo Argentino del Títere B3
8 Museo de Arte Contemporáneo Buenos Aires D4
9 Museo de Arte Moderno de Buenos Aires................ D4
10 Museo Histórico Nacional D6
11 Museo Nacional de la Historia del Traje................B2
12 Parque Lezama.................... D6
13 Pasaje de la Defensa C4

Eating (p91)

14 Abuela Pan........................... C2
15 Bar El Federal C3
16 Cafe Rivas D3
17 Café San Juan C4
18 Cantina San Juan.................. C2
19 Casal de Catalunya...............B3
20 Comedor Nikkai B3
21 El Banco Rojo C3
22 El Desnivel............................ C3
23 El Refuerzo Bar Almacen B3
24 El Refuerzo Provisiones B3
25 Gran Parrilla del Plata C2
26 Hierbabuena......................... D6
27 La Poesia.............................. C2
Lo de Freddy.....................(see 1)
28 Origen Café.......................... C4
29 Pulpería Quilapán D5

Drinking & Nightlife (p93)

30 Bar Británico D5
31 Bar Plaza Dorrego D4
32 Bar Seddón.............................C2
33 Club Museum..........................C2
Coffee Town ....(see 1)
34 Doppelgänger C5
35 Gibraltar..................................C3
36 On Tap.....................................C6
37 Pride Cafe D3

Entertainment (p94)

38 Centro Cultural Torquato Tasso D6
39 El Viejo Almacén...................D2
40 La Scala de San Telmo D3
41 La Trastienda D1
42 La Ventana D1
43 Maldita Milonga C2
Tango Queer...............(see 43)

Shopping (p94)

44 Gil Antiguedades C4
45 Imhotep...................................D3
46 L'Ago D3
47 Materia Urbana......................D2
48 Moebius D5
49 Punto Sur.................................C4
50 Puntos en el Espacio............C4
51 Signos C3
Vinotango ....(see 1)
52 Walrus Books C3

Sports & Activities (p95)

53 Biking Buenos Aires C3
54 Rayuela B3

Sleeping (p172)

55 América del Sur B2
56 Art Factory Hostel.................B2
57 Bohemia Buenos Aires C3
58 Circus Hostel & Hotel...........B4
59 L'Adresse................................C6
60 Lugar Gay D4
61 Mansión Vitraux.....................D3
62 Mundo Bolívar........................C7
63 Patios de San Telmo B3
64 Scala Hotel A3

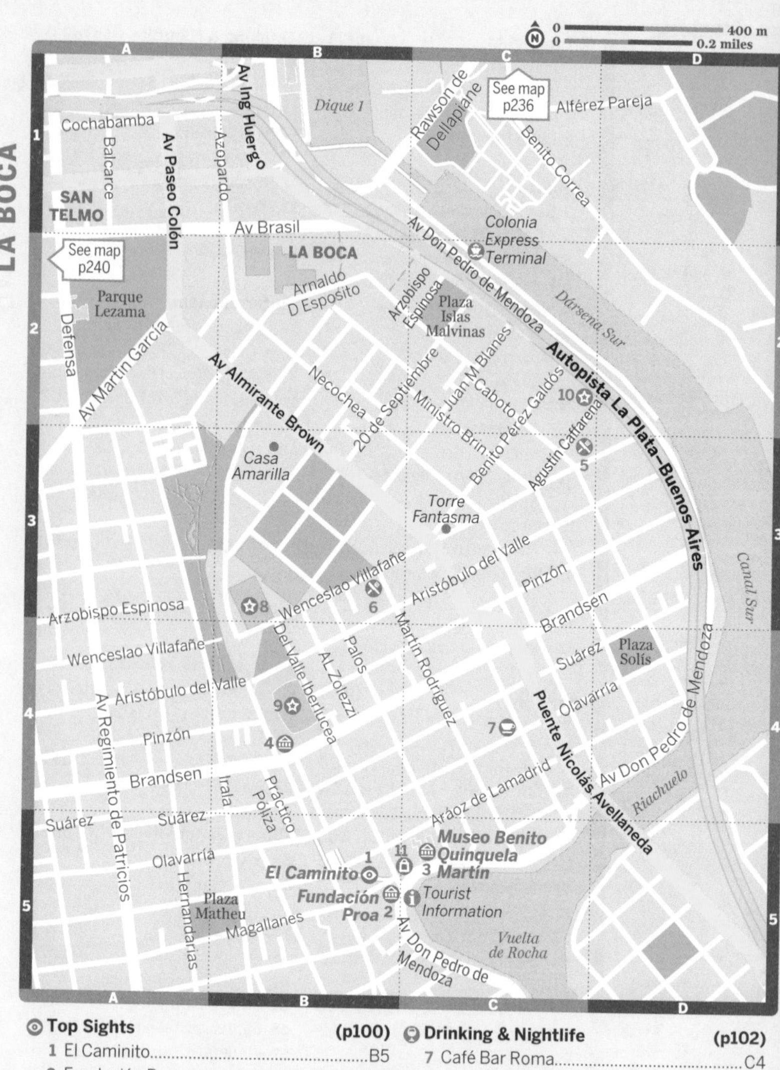

Top Sights (p100)
1 El Caminito ... B5
2 Fundación Proa ... B5
3 Museo Benito Quinquela Martín ... C5

Sights (p101)
4 Museo de la Pasión Boquense ... B4
Museo del Cine ... (see 10)

Eating (p101)
5 El Obrero ... C3
6 Il Matterello ... B3
Proa Cafe ... (see 2)

Drinking & Nightlife (p102)
7 Café Bar Roma ... C4

Entertainment (p102)
8 Estadio Luis Conde ... B3
9 La Bombonera Stadium ... B4
Teatro de la Ribera ... (see 3)
10 Usina del Arte ... C2

Shopping (p103)
11 Feria de Artesanos Caminito ... C5

RECOLETA & BARRIO NORTE *Map on p244*

Top Sights (p113)
1 Cementerio de la Recoleta D4
2 Centro Cultural Recoleta D4

Sights (p114)
3 Basílica de Nuestra Señora del Pilar D4
4 Facultad de Ingeniería C4
5 Floralis Genérica C2
6 Museo Participativo de Ciencias D4
7 Palais de Glace E3

Eating (p114)
8 Como en Casa C6
9 Cumaná D6
10 El Burladero C5
11 El Sanjuanino E4
Elena ..... (see 36)
L'Orangerie ..... (see 33)
12 Persicco D4
13 Rodi Bar D5
14 Un Altra Volta D4

Drinking & Nightlife (p117)
15 Buller Brewing Company D4
16 Clásica y Moderna D8
17 Gran Bar Danzón F6
18 La Biela D4
19 Milión E7
Pony Line Bar ..... (see 36)
20 Shamrock D6

Entertainment (p118)
21 Notorious D7
22 Teatro Coliseo F7
23 Unión de Rugby de Buenos Aires C5

Shopping (p119)
24 Buenos Aires Design D3
25 Comme Il Faut F6
26 El Ateneo Grand Splendid D7
27 Feria Artesenal Plaza Francia D4
28 Fueguia E5
29 Galería Bond Street D7
30 Memorabilia F6
31 Patio Bullrich F4

Sports & Activities (p213)
32 VOS E7

Sleeping (p174)
33 Alvear Palace Hotel E4
34 Art Suites B5
35 Ayres de Recoleta C4
36 Four Seasons G5
37 Hotel Lion D'or C5
38 Palacio Duhau – Park Hyatt E4
39 Petit Recoleta Hostel B6
40 Poetry Building C6

RECOLETA & BARRIO NORTE

Key on p243

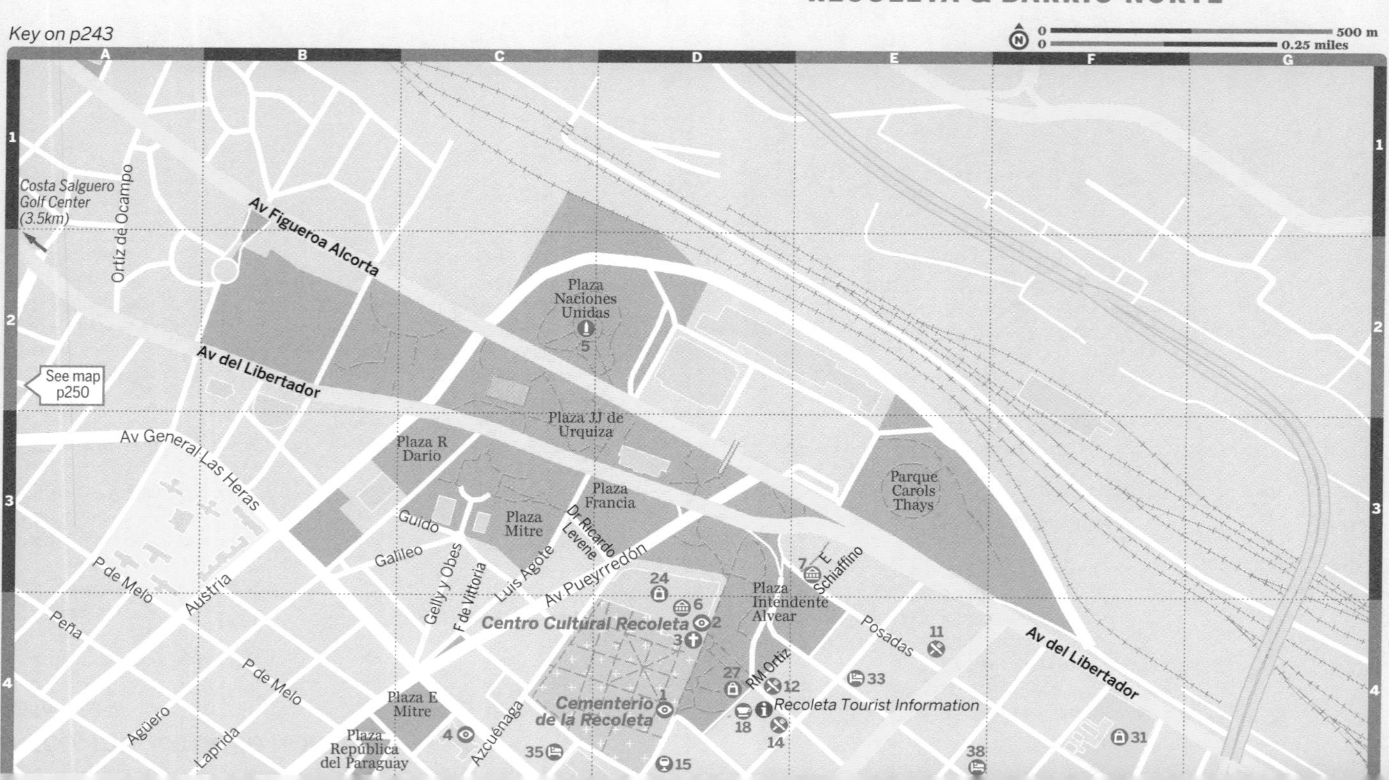

RECOLETA & BARRIO NORTE

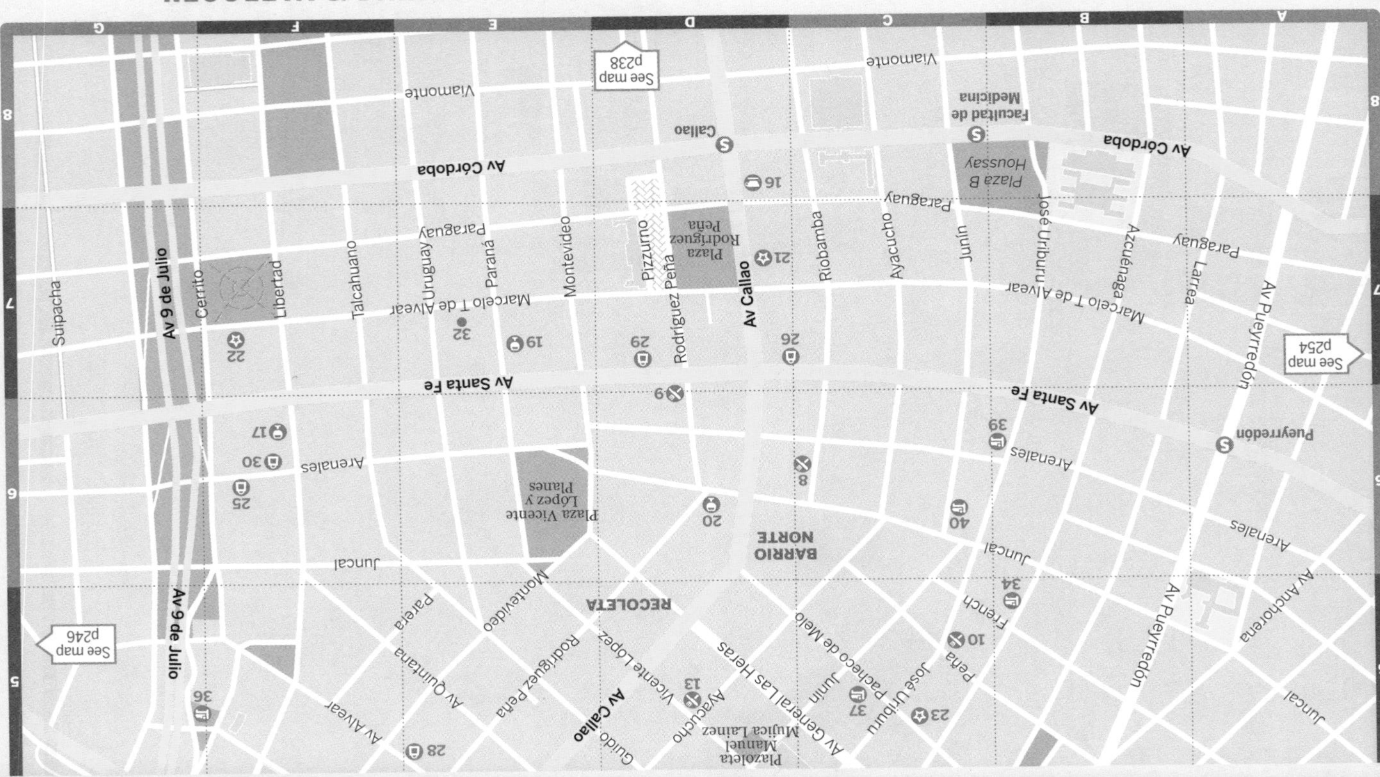

Key on p248

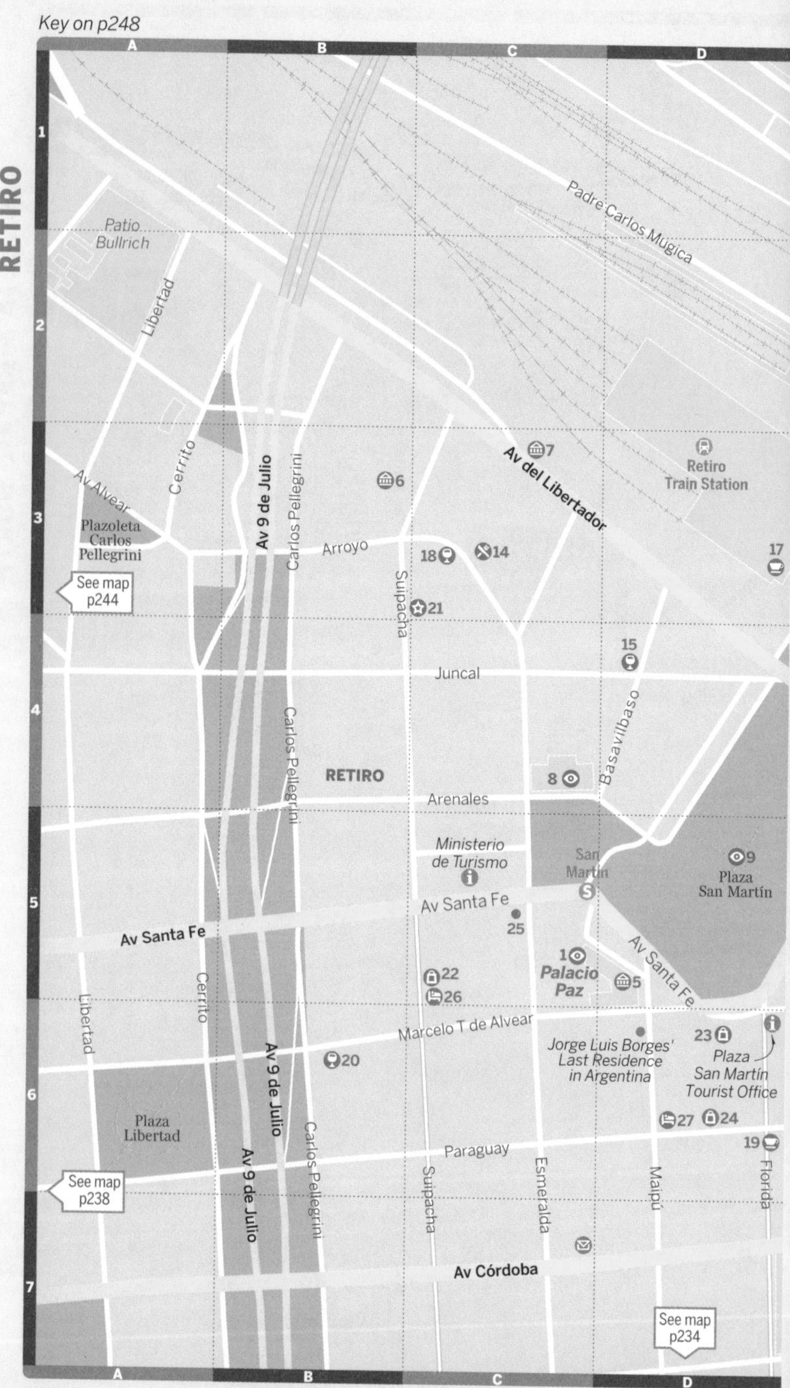

Patio Bullrich
Libertad
Padre Carlos Múgica
Cerrito
Av 9 de Julio
Carlos Pellegrini
Av Alvear
Plazoleta Carlos Pellegrini
Arroyo
Suipacha
Av del Libertador
Retiro Train Station
See map p244
Juncal
Basavilbaso
RETIRO
Arenales
Ministerio de Turismo
San Martín
Plaza San Martín
Av Santa Fe
Palacio Paz
Marcelo T de Alvear
Jorge Luis Borges' Last Residence in Argentina
Plaza San Martín Tourist Office
Plaza Libertad
Paraguay
Esmeralda
Maipú
Florida
See map p238
Av Córdoba
See map p234

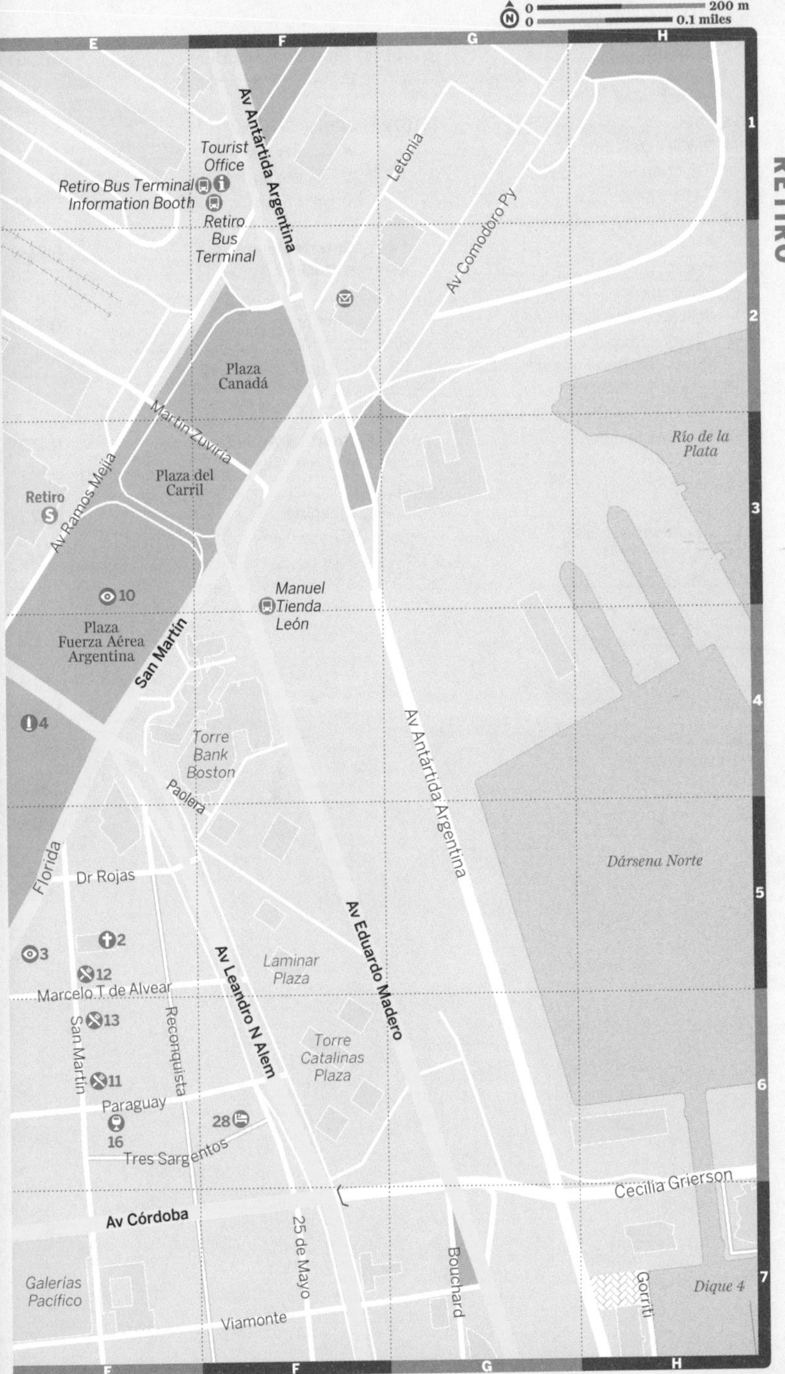

0 200 m
0 0.1 miles
RETIRO
Av Antártida Argentina
Tourist Office
Retiro Bus Terminal Information Booth
Retiro Bus Terminal
Letonia
Av Comodoro Py
Plaza Canadá
Martín Zuviría
Plaza del Carril
Retiro
Av Ramos Mejía
Río de la Plata
10
Manuel Tienda León
Plaza Fuerza Aérea Argentina
San Martín
4
Torre Bank Boston
Paolera
Av Antártida Argentina
Dársena Norte
Florida
Dr Rojas
2
3
12
Av Eduardo Madero
Laminar Plaza
Marcelo T de Alvear
13
Reconquista
Av Leandro N Alem
Torre Catalinas Plaza
San Martín
11
Paraguay
28
16
Tres Sargentos
Cecilia Grierson
Av Córdoba
25 de Mayo
Bouchard
Gorriti
Galerías Pacífico
Dique 4
Viamonte

RETIRO *Map on p246*

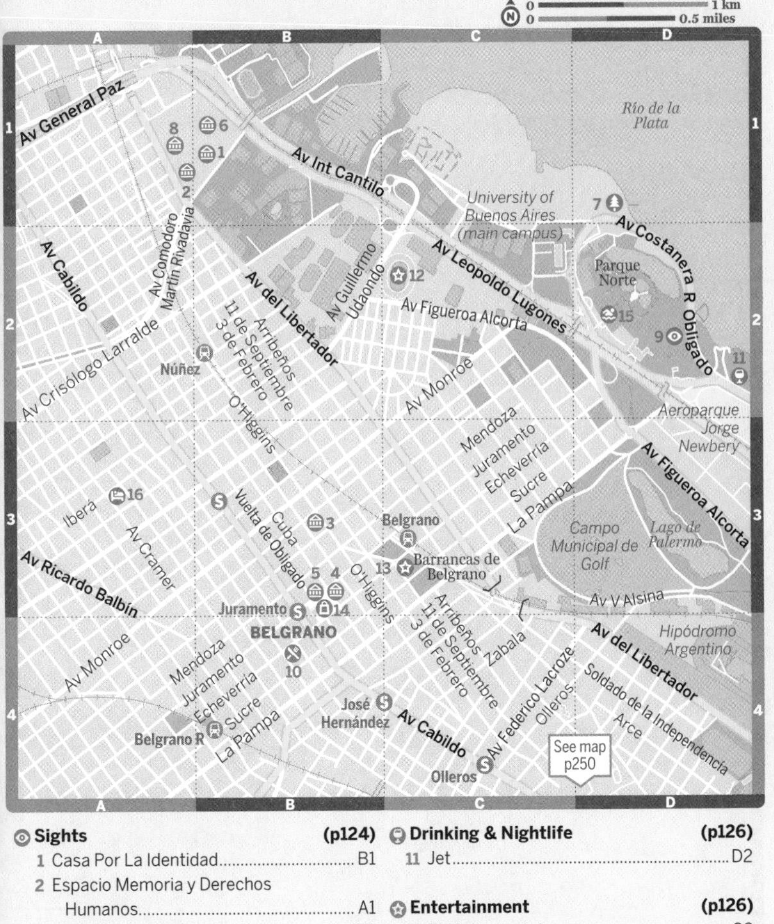

Sights (p124)

1 Casa Por La Identidad B1
2 Espacio Memoria y Derechos Humanos A1
3 Museo Casa de Yrurtia B3
4 Museo Histórico Sarmiento B3
5 Museo Larreta B3
6 Museo Malvinas B1
7 Parque de la Memoria D1
8 Sitio de Memoria ESMA A1
9 Tierra Santa D2

Eating (p125)

10 La Paceña B4

Drinking & Nightlife (p126)

11 Jet D2

Entertainment (p126)

12 El Monumental C2
13 La Glorieta C3

Shopping (p126)

14 Feria Plaza Belgrano B3

Sports & Activities (p126)

15 Parque Norte D2

Sleeping (p175)

16 Pampa Hostel A3

Key on p252

See map p249
Av del Libertador
Virrey Loreto
Zabala
11 de Septiembre
Villanueva
Migueletes
Soldado de la Independencia
Av Cabildo
Palpa
Teodoro García
Av Federico Lacroze
Olleros
Gorostiaga
3 de Febrero
Maure
Newberry
Matienzo
Arce
Av Báez
Ortega Y Gasset
Av I Chenaut
Arévalo
Arguibel
Hipódromo Argentino
LAS CAÑITAS
Olleros
Estación Colegiales
Zapata
Ciudad de la Paz
Av Luis María Campos
Huergo
Clay
Savio
COLEGIALES
Estación Ministro Carranza
Ministro Carranza
PALERMO
Dr Emilio Ravignani
Ángel Justiniano Carranza
Bonpland
Fitz Roy
Humboldt
Estación Palermo
Zapiola
Arenal
Av Dorrego
Costa Rica
Nicaragua
Soler
Guatemala
Godoy Cruz
Álvarez Thomas
El Salvador
PALERMO HOLLYWOOD
Av Juan B Justo
JSM de Oro
José Antonio Cabrera
Honduras
Gorriti
PALERMO VIEJO
Soler
Nicaragua
Uriarte
Niceto Vega
Av Córdoba
Plaza Serrano
El Salvador
See Enlargement
Serrano
Jufre
Castillo
Gurrachaga
VILLA CRESPO
Acevedo
Lerma
Malabia
José Antonio Cabrera
Av Scalabrini Ortiz
Aráoz
Loyola
Lavalleja
See map p254
Enlargement
Thames
Jorge Luis Borges
Costa Rica
Nicaragua
El Salvador
Plaza Serrano
Gurruchaga
Plaza Palermo Viejo
Honduras
Armenia
Gorriti
0 100 m
A
B
C
D
1
2
3
4
5
6
7

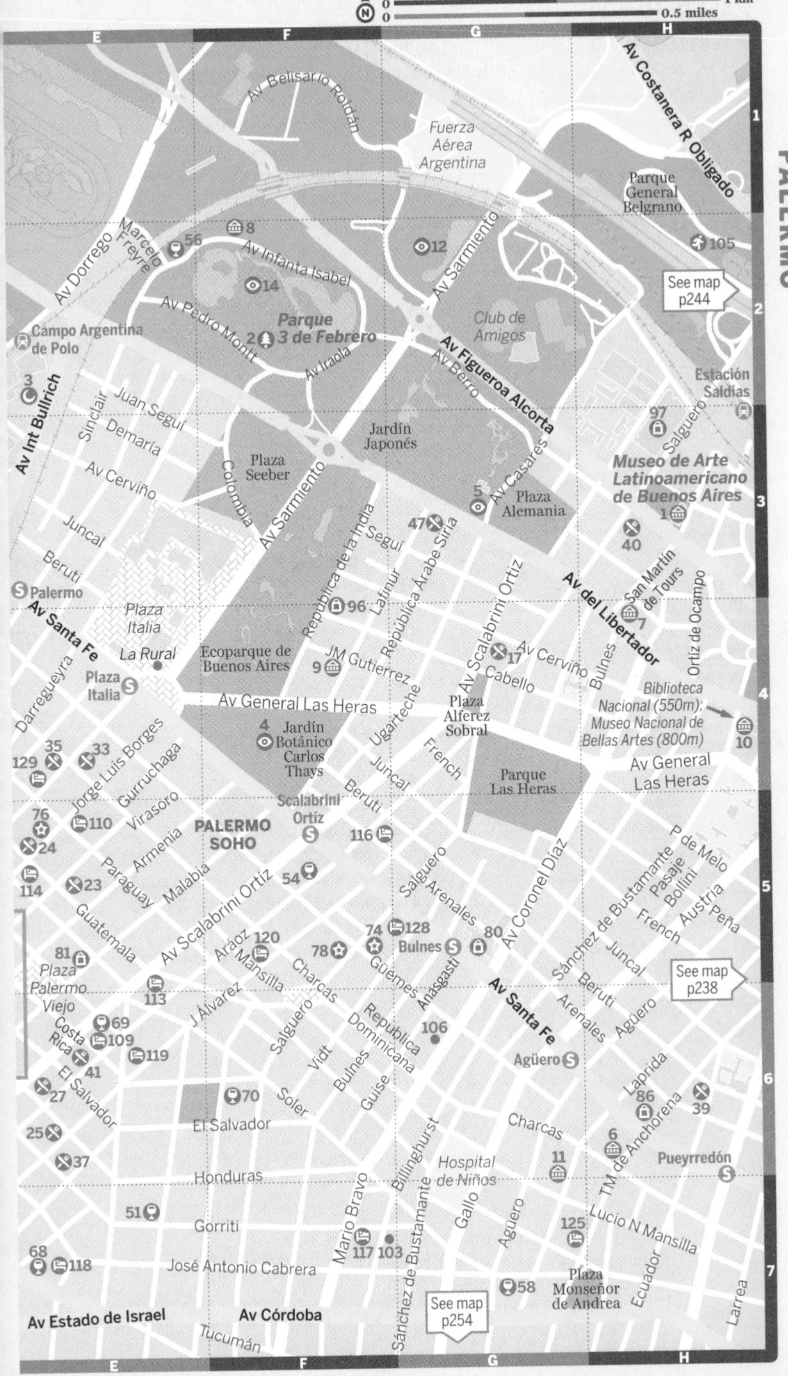

PALERMO
0 1 km
0 0.5 miles
Av Costanera R Obligado
Av Belisario Roldán
Fuerza Aérea Argentina
Parque General Belgrano
Av Infanta Isabel
Av Pedro Montt
Parque 3 de Febrero
Av Sarmiento
Club de Amigos
Av Figueroa Alcorta
Av Berro
Av Iraola
Av Dorrego
Marcelo Freyre
Campo Argentino de Polo
Av Int Bullrich
See map p244
Estación Saldías
Jardín Japonés
Plaza Seeber
Colombia
Museo de Arte Latinoamericano de Buenos Aires
Plaza Alemania
Av Casares
Salguero
Juan Seguí
Sinclair
Demaría
Av Cerviño
Juncal
Beruti
Palermo
Av Santa Fe
Plaza Italia
La Rural
Ecoparque de Buenos Aires
República de la India
Seguí
Lafinur
República Árabe Siria
Av Scalabrini Ortiz
Av del Libertador
San Martín de Tours
Ortiz de Ocampo
JM Gutierrez
Av Cerviño
Cabello
Bulnes
Biblioteca Nacional (550m); Museo Nacional de Bellas Artes (800m)
Av General Las Heras
Plaza Alferez Sobral
Ugarteche
French
Jardín Botánico Carlos Thays
Darregueyra
Jorge Luis Borges
Gurruchaga
Juncal
Beruti
Parque Las Heras
Scalabrini Ortiz
PALERMO SOHO
Virasoro
Armenia
Paraguay
Malabia
Av Scalabrini Ortiz
Guatemala
Salguero
Arenales
Av Coronel Díaz
Sánchez de Bustamante
Pasaje Bollini
P de Melo
French
Austria
Peña
Araóz
Mansilla
Charcas
Güemes
Bulnes
Anasgasti
Av Santa Fe
Juncal
Beruti
Arenales
Agüero
See map p238
Plaza Palermo Viejo
Costa Rica
El Salvador
J Álvarez
Salguero
Vidt
Bulnes
Guise
República Dominicana
Agüero
Laprida
Soler
El Salvador
Charcas
TM de Anchorena
Pueyrredón
Honduras
Billinghurst
Hospital de Niños
Gallo
Agüero
Lucio N Mansilla
Gorriti
Mario Bravo
Sánchez de Bustamante
José Antonio Cabrera
Plaza Monseñor de Andrea
Ecuador
Larrea
Av Estado de Israel
Av Córdoba
Tucumán
See map p254

PALERMO *Map on p250*

63 Mundo Bizarro........C6
64 Niceto Club........B5
65 On Tap........C4
66 Post Street Bar........D5
67 Shanghai Dragon........D7
68 Sitges........E7
69 Suspiria Resplendoris........E6
70 Verne........F6
71 Victoria Brown........A5
72 Vive Café........C4

Entertainment (p141)

73 Campo Argentino de Polo........D2
74 La Peña del Colorado........F5
75 La Viruta........D6
76 Los Cardones........E5
77 Salon Canning........D6
78 Thelonious Bar........F5

Shopping (p142)

79 28 Sport........A7
80 Alto Palermo........G5
81 Blackmamba........E5
82 Bolivia........A7
83 Bosque........B3
84 Calma Chicha........A6
85 Elementos Argentinos........B6
Feria Plaza Serrano........(see 13)
86 Galeria Patio del Liceo........H6
87 Harapos Patagonia........D5
88 Hermanos Estebecorena........B4
89 Humawaca........B7
90 Juana de Arco........B6
91 Libros del Pasaje........D5
92 Lo de Joaquín Alberdi........A6
93 Mercado de las Pulgas........B4
94 Mishka........B7
95 Monte Arte Étnico Argentino........B7
96 Panorama........F4
97 Paseo Alcorta........H3
98 Rapsodia........A7

Sports & Activities (p145)

99 Argentine Experience........D4
100 Bar du Marché........C4
101 Buena Onda Yoga........D5
102 Buenos Aires Fútbol Amigos........C5
103 DWS........F7
104 Pain et Vin........C5
105 Parque Manuel Belgrano........H2
106 Vamos........G6

Sleeping (p175)

107 248 Finisterra........D2
108 Abode........D5
109 Art Factory Palermo........E6
110 BA Sohotel........E5
111 Cabrera Garden........B4
112 CasaSur........B4
113 Duque Hotel........E5
114 Eco Pampa Hostel........E5
115 Hotel Clasico........C4
116 Infinito Hotel........F5
117 Le Petit Palais........F7
118 Livian Guesthouse........E7
119 Magnolia Hotel........E6
120 Mansilla 3935 B&B........F5
121 Mine Hotel........A7
122 Miravida Soho........D5
123 Palermitano........D5
124 Palermo Viejo B&B........D6
125 Reina Madre Hostel........G7
126 Rendezvous Hotel........B5
127 Rugantino Hotel........D5
128 The 5th Floor........G5
129 Vain Boutique Hotel........E4

A
B
C
D
1
2
3
4
5
Dorrego
See map p250
15
16
3
Av Córdoba
Thames
13
Gurrachaga
Castillo
Jufré
Av Corrientes
32
Av Juan B Justo
36
Malabia
Av Scalabrini Ortiz
Av Warnes
Camargo
VILLA CRESPO
9
Juan Ramírez de Velasco
Loyola
Lavalleja
Padilla
Murillo
12
Acevedo
Malabia
Aguirre
Angel Gallardo
Av Lambaré
Av Warnes
Aráoz
2
Av Ángel Gallardo
Trollo
Av San Martín
Mahatma Gandhi
Ferrari
Machado
7
Franklin
Bogado
5
Parque Centenario
Estivao
Av Acoyte
CABALLITO
Av Gaona
Río de Janeiro
Neuquén
Neuquén
Av Donato Alvarez
Parque Rivadavia
23
Av Acoyte
Av Boyacá
Primera Junta
Av Rivadavia

22 Ciudad Cultural Konex F3
23 Club Ferro Carril Oeste C4
24 Club Gricel G5
25 Complejo Tango G4
26 El Camarín de las Musas F2
27 El Cubo G2
28 Espacio Callejón F2
29 Esquina Carlos Gardel G2
30 Esquina Homero Manzi F5
La Bomba de Tiempo .... (see 22)
31 La Catedral E3

Shopping (p154)

32 Centrico D1

Sports & Activities (p154)

33 Acatraz F3
34 DNI Tango F2

Sleeping (p178)

35 Chill House F2
36 Pop Hotel C1
37 Racó de Buenos Aires E4

Our Story

A beat-up old car, a few dollars in the pocket and a sense of adventure. In 1972 that's all Tony and Maureen Wheeler needed for the trip of a lifetime – across Europe and Asia overland to Australia. It took several months, and at the end – broke but inspired – they sat at their kitchen table writing and stapling together their first travel guide, *Across Asia on the Cheap*. Within a week they'd sold 1500 copies. Lonely Planet was born.

Today, Lonely Planet has offices in Franklin, London, Melbourne, Oakland, Dublin, Beijing and Delhi, with more than 600 staff and writers. We share Tony's belief that 'a great guidebook should do three things: inform, educate and amuse'.

Our Writer

Isabel Albiston

After six years working for the *Daily Telegraph* in London, squeezing in as many trips as annual leave would allow, Isabel left to spend more time on the road. A job as a writer for a magazine in Sydney, Australia was followed by four years living and working in Buenos Aires, Argentina. Isabel started writing for Lonely Planet in 2014, having been back in the UK just long enough to pack a bag for a research trip to Malaysia. She has contributed to five LP guides.

Published by Lonely Planet Global Limited
CRN 554153
8th edition – Aug 2017
ISBN 978 1 78657 031 4

10 9 8 7 6 5 4 3 2 1
Printed in China